Questions of English

The impact and content of English as a subject on the curriculum is once more the subject of lively debate. *Questions of English* sets out to map the development of English as a subject and how it has come to encompass the diversity of ideas that currently characterise it.

Drawing on a combination of historical analysis and recent research findings **Robin Peel, Annette Patterson** and **Jeanne Gerlach** bring together and compare important new insights on curriculum development and teaching practice from England, Australia and the United States. They discuss the place of English in elementary schools and universities; the development of teacher training and the variety of ways in which teachers build their own beliefs and knowledge about English; the relationship between the teaching of English and the formation of the citizen and the international move towards outcomes based assessment.

Questions of English offers a lively and accessible guide through past and present debates about the English curriculum which will appeal to students and practising teachers.

Robin Peel is Principal Lecturer in English at the University of Plymouth, **Annette Patterson** is Senior Lecturer at James Cook University, Australia and **Jeanne Gerlach** is Dean of the Faculty of Teacher Education at the University of Texas at Arlington, United States.

Questions of English

Ethics, aesthetics, rhetoric and the
formation of the subject in England,
Australia and the United States

Robin Peel
Annette Patterson
and Jeanne Gerlach

London and New York

First published 2000
by RoutledgeFalmer
11 New Fetter Lane, London EC4P 4EE

Simultaneously published in the USA and Canada
by Routledge
29 West 35th Street, New York, NY 10001

RoutledgeFalmer is an imprint of the Taylor & Francis Group

© 2000 Robin Peel, Annette Patterson, and Jeanne Gerlach

Typeset in Goudy by
Steven Gardiner Ltd, Cambridge
Printed and bound in Great Britain by
St Edmundsbury Press, Bury St Edmunds, Suffolk

British Library Cataloguing in Publication Data
A catalogue record for this book is available from the British Library

Library of Congress Cataloging in Publication Data
Questions of English: ethics, aesthetics, rhetoric, and the formation of
the subject in England, Australia, and the United States / Robin Peel,
Annette Patterson, and Jeanne Gerlach.
  p. cm.
Includes bibliographical references and index.
1. English language – Study and teaching – English-speaking countries.
2. English language – Teacher training – English-speaking countries.
3. English language – Study and teaching – United States. 4. English
language – Study and teaching – Australia. 5. English language –
Rhetoric – Study and teaching. 6. English language – Study and
teaching – England. 7. Language and ethics. I. Peel, Robin. II.
Patterson, Annette Joyce. III. Gerlach, Jeanne Marcum, 1946– .
PE65.Q48 2000   99-36308
428'.007 – dc21   CIP

ISBN 0-415-19120-3 (pbk)
ISBN 0-415-19119-X (hbk)

Contents

Figures

Preface

In my first lecture before you, in January 1913, I quoted to you the artist in Don Quixote who, being asked what animal he was painting, answered diffidently 'That is as it may turn out'.

'On a School of English' in *On the Art of Reading*
by Sir Arthur Quiller Couch (1920)

This elusive figure, haunting the outskirts of Oxford for centuries, captures well the ambiguous stance which won Arnold himself a long-term influence: half Oxford academic, half romantic exile, he is not compromised by the fleshly institution (nor it by him) yet orbits around it as a necessary centre of gravity.

Baldick (1983: 48) describing *The Scholar Gypsy*

The questions

This is a book about English specialists, many of whom are troubled by notions of working within fixed frames or boundaries, and almost all of whom are operating within 'fleshly institutions'. In the following chapters we explore the relationship between the questions and beliefs that are currently being voiced in Australia, England and the United States and the material and historical factors which have helped shape them. We hope to demonstrate the historical antecedents of the views expressed not in order to 'explain' them but rather to consider the ways in which beliefs are formed and the questions which seem to dominate contemporary discussion. Through this process we are able to identify the kinds of questions which are exercising English specialists.

In so doing we are also and inevitably asking questions of English. It is important that such questions are asked by those who are 'inside' as we are living through a period when such questions have become very narrowly focussed by those who are outside. We are not, however, intending to devote any significant space to the familiar question 'What *is* English?'. This is the one question that those inside English, particularly in higher education, frequently *do* ask, and it is beginning to look increasingly narcissistic.

Moreover, there is a response to the question itself which we find attractive. It was given recently by Colin Bulman (1997) who was lamenting the attention given in *Cultural Studies* to the question 'What is Cultural Studies?'. For cultural studies we can read English:

> In fact, those who do need to ask 'what is cultural studies?' can get a succinct answer from Raymond Williams who argued that one cannot understand an artistic project or product without also understanding its formation and genesis within a society. The relation between a project and a formation is 'always decisive'.
>
> Bulman 1997, p. 13

Our own project is based on our own experience as specialists in English and as teacher educators, and on research carried out into the beliefs and perceptions of English specialists in schools, colleges and universities. The voices of students and teachers form a prominent part of our account of English in England, the United States and Australia, but we are keen to get behind those voices and to ask where they are coming from. So we have attempted to historicise them and to consider how they (and we) have been constructed by our histories. Furthermore, the gap between what we as teachers say we do and what actually happens in our classrooms has been noted by many researchers (Barnes and Barnes 1984). It is likely that what people profess to believe is less important for the way that they run their world than the pressures and influences that are exerted on them, and the social practices in which they have been inducted. But if, as we do, we believe in a dialectical world then ideas and beliefs can shape as well as be shaped, even though some ideas have to wait until the time when material and ideological circumstance allow their hour to come round.

In this book we propose a reading of some of the ideas and strategies which in our judgement should be available to a generation of students who will reach adulthood in the techno-cultural world of the twenty-first century. We explore the possibility that the practices of English and the specific strategies which English specialists employ are as much to do with the process of contributing to the formation of a particular kind of person as they are with the more obvious and more frequently articulated concerns with literacy, freedom, literature and the imagination. That person, our findings would suggest, is self-reflecting, self-regulating and more comfortable when enabling and supervising than when instructing and being didactic. Such strategies have been developed not because they produce more literate and knowledgeable students, but because they encourage aspects of the subject which prove valuable to society. The emphasis on the person, on affective response, on the experience and insights of the individual, help to validate and monitor qualities which are not given free play elsewhere. This may be a very desirable process: that it is normative is rarely acknowledged.

Inevitably, such a model of English has come into collision with the culture of the marketplace, which was the predominant ideology of the late twentieth century. It has not been well equipped theoretically to cope with this challenge. It seems in need of a new rhetoric, if it is to continue to enjoy the position to which it had become accustomed throughout much of the twentieth century. Several such rhetorics exist, as we show in the following chapters. In the United States the recommendation of the Gulbenkian Commission chaired by Imanuel Wallerstein has offered an interdisciplinary model and points out that the combination of cultural studies and post modern theory has occasioned the first revival of the humanities since they were eclipsed by the sciences in the nineteenth century. In England, where such an eclipse seemed to have been prevented, that rhetoric alone is not viewed so optimistically. In terms of curricular, pedagogical and theoretical developments in schools and universities, it is perhaps to Australia that we must look for signs of what the future can hold for English.

We feel that an international perspective is both timely and pertinent. Among other things, it can show that despite the globalisation of culture, specific cultural differences survive. If English can articulate those practices which form its 'cultural capital' in a technocratic society, it may be able to avoid the prospect which it is being offered in England, that of being an agency for literacy and nothing more.

If there is one irony above all others in recent developments, it is that the privatisation of culture masks the continuing centralisation of power. It is an irony identified by Regenia Gagnier (1996):

> The point is that despite pervasive market rhetoric, it appears that the government runs the universities in this country like planned economies under the old-fashioned bureaucracies, not really addressing how or whether we might produce better experts or intellectuals or technicians, or in what proportions we should produce them. Yet these are exactly the questions we should be asking. I think that this irony of market rhetoric over massive central planning should be pointed out, especially by those of us expert in the forms of irony. For English in the millennium, like so many things, will be determined by planning or markets.

What the set of practices that we associate with English are, why they have survived for so long, and whether they will adapt to ensure their survival in the future: these are three of the principal questions that have informed our analysis.

The arguments

The novelist Vikram Seth once described how during one of his daily walks along the edge of the Serpentine in Hyde Park he struck up a conversation with a man who was taking an early morning swim.[1] The man was so enthusiastic about the delights of bathing that he persuaded Seth to join the Serpentine Swimming Club, and although by nature the novelist was not a person who particularly enjoyed cold water or the vigorous exercise required by swimming, he was soon a complete convert. The Swimming Club turned out to be a remarkable community comprising people of all ages, ethnic groups and classes.

Sadly, Vikram Seth reported the club was now under threat: it has been forced to move out of its headquarters in The Pavilion, which for commercial reasons had been converted into a tea-room. This change could have been endured, but there was now a crushing weight of bureaucracy – all for apparently worthy reasons, because people could pick up infections from the lake, or suffer ill effects from diving into very cold water. Safe-guards have to be introduced – but these might have the effect of causing the club to close. This would be ironical, Seth pointed out: no member of the Serpentine Swimming Club has ever died as a result of swimming, and a good number have been much healthier citizens as a result of taking this regular exercise.

Questions of English is about the set of practices known as subject English, or to be more precise, a review of the beliefs and perceptions that inform those practices, in England, Australia and the United States. Although many of the long-time members of 'club' English take a view of recent changes in educational practice which chime with the wistful sentiments of Seth's story, there are many who do not. It would be easy to construct a picture of subject English as a romantic club whose extinction is threatened by the bureaucracy of accountability. As researchers, we were keen to avoid constructing this kind of binary, and we agreed that our work should not be predicated on a particular argument about English that our findings then became material to endorse.

Inevitably, however, the book contains its own argument. The evidence we present confirms that English is an important subject. It is a site for fierce debate and contestation, both at school and university level. That English has remained central to the secondary/high school curriculum is clear from documents which begin – or in the case of England complete – the move towards a national curriculum for English. That English's prime task is tied up with achievement of literacy is evident in the description 'language arts' in the United States and the 'literacy hour' in England. In Australia the term 'critical literacy' has emerged, and in all three countries there is a recognition by teachers that the kind of literacy appropriate in an age of Information and Communications Technology is different from that considered appropriate in the nineteenth century.

The focus of the book is on the way that the diversity of practice in

1 Vikram Seth, 'Today' Essay, BBC Radio 4, 3 April 1999.

English may conceal a commonality of pedagogy. That diversity is implicit in the range of rhetorical positions from which we report. Each of us has our 'roots' in subject English. The way that each of us has responded to our subject is a snapshot of the contrasting interests, experience and emphases that can be found among any group of English teachers. The early chapters that concentrate on England reflect my interest in the historicising process, in situating beliefs among the discourses and practices of the period from which they emerge. There is a danger in England – and Jeanne Gerlach reports that this is also true of the United States – that current concerns are discussed in a way that leads to the erasure of history, as if we are no longer living in a historical moment. I wish to challenge that notion, so there is a great deal of history in the early chapters of the book which map the subject's development in England. These chapters also reflect another of my interests in that they attempt to provide a cross phase commentary. I wish to discuss what has been and is happening in universities and primary schools in England as this complements English in secondary/high schools, the phase which is generally our focus.

Annette Patterson applies a reading of Michel Foucault and Ian Hunter to the development of English in England and Australia, picking up on some of the points I have made but questioning the category 'English' in a more systematic way, and challenging the usefulness of the Cox 'models' as a way of identifying pedagogical practice. In her analysis she argues that the pedagogical relationship is the crucial and central constant connecting early church and pastoral teaching traditions with contemporary critical reading practices in the English classroom. In providing space for the paradox of supervised freedom, English has served an important role in the managing of behaviour in a democratic society.

Jeanne Gerlach's account is a celebration of this relationship and the rich potential of subject English as a subject within the humanities, which still provides space for the personal, for discovery and for wonder in a world in which the call for evidence and accountability may seem to be marginalising these things.

The differences between us are apparent not only in the way we write, but what we write about and the way that we respond to current developments. Although the three of us are deeply interested in the questions that we pose, there is no consensus among us about how they should be answered. This is revealed in the way that we sometimes contradict and question one another.

This book is likely to be read by subject specialists, many of whom will be planning to teach in schools, and having discussed the issues and debates in university English departments in the opening chapters on England these are not repeated in the chapters on Australia and the United States, where differences in school practice become the focus. The opening section, therefore, is by far the longest.

For those subject specialists undertaking programmes leading to qualified teacher status, or for those already teaching in secondary/high school classrooms, some of the issues we address may seem rather remote from the twenty-first century world of increased state or government direction, where what an English teacher does is increasingly prescribed, inspected and assessed. The widespread emphasis on accountability and 'evidence' in England, Australia and the United States – an understandable response to concerns about literacy – poses a challenge to history, theory and experiment because it effectively offers closure on these issues. The busy practitioner is so preoccupied with preparing students for the requirements of assessment, providing the appropriate documentation, or getting ready for inspection that s/he is denied the 'luxury' of looking at English as a set of practices with a particular history. There is less time to think and reflect – and one strand of rhetoric coming out of government departments in England implies that there has been too much reflection, too much discussion, and not enough action. This is a seductive argument, especially when we see the literacy problems experienced by so many students, but the danger is that the 'action' required has not been thought through, and that it reduces teachers to the role of agents.

In fact, one of the arguments that emerges in this book is that English teachers *have* always been agents, though the model of agency which characterised the set of practices known as Subject English allowed for an autonomy and democratisation that has proved extremely useful. This is not to suggest a cynicism about change, but to emphasise how important it is that the new 'action' writes these qualities into its assessment and outcomes frameworks.

Whilst rejecting the old Romantic binary of 'free English teacher versus institutional bureaucracy', we would wish to challenge those over simplistic models of teaching which regard students as vessels waiting to be filled. The monitorial system, *Hard Times* and Payment by Results showed us the limitations of that pedagogical model, which is why it is important that we do not lose sight of our history. Over the past 400 years, some experiments have already been tried and found wanting.

Originally this book was going to be called 'Beliefs about English' and inevitably these chapters are informed by our own beliefs, and our own experience. What we all have in common is that we have all taught English at levels ranging from primary to postgraduate, and all three of us taught a number of years in secondary schools. We enjoy teaching, and we maintain strong links with our respective country's professional English associations. It is perhaps significant that we have all found ourselves at some distance from our starting points, however: Robin Peel is a Programme Director for the Masters' Programme in the University of Plymouth, Faculty of Arts and Education, Graduate School, Annette Patterson is a Senior Lecturer at James Cook University School of Education teaching sociology and literacy, while Jeanne Gerlach is Dean of the Faculty of Education at the University of Texas at Arlington. It is apparent from our research that it is extremely common for English specialists to start out their adult lives doing one thing, to then specialise in English and finally to end up moving into something a little different as their careers unfolded.

This is not a book about how to teach English, nor is it a book about the old battles between canon and culture, tradition and theory, literature and literacy, though we touch on all of these subjects. It *is* a book which discusses a range of beliefs that have been expressed by subject specialists and outside commentators during the past 150 or so years, and the beliefs and perceptions that have been expressed by those we have interviewed as part of our research. The project began with an examination of questionnaire responses in England and Australia, and Sandra Hargreaves and Robin Peel reported on this in *English in Education* (Peel and Hargreaves 1995). This book builds on those responses, but seeks to locate them in the context of what has gone before, and what may be coming after.

We hope that what follows will encourage all of those interested in subject English to question and evaluate the assumptions and beliefs that underscore what still remains one of the central subjects of compulsory secondary education, and an extremely popular subject in colleges and universities.

References

Baldick, C. (1983) *The Social Mission of English Criticism 1848–1932*, Oxford: Oxford University Press

Bulman, Colin 1997 Review of *A Cultural Studies Reader* in *The Lecturer*, April 1997, p. 13.

Gagnier, Regenia 1996 '"The Disturbance Overseas": A Comparative Report on the Future of English Studies', mimeograph.

CCUE Inaugural Conference: English in the Millennium, 10 September 1996.

Peel, R. and Hargreaves, S. (1995) 'Beliefs about English: Trends in Australia, England and the United States', *English in Education*, Volume 29 No. 3 Autumn 1995

Acknowledgements

Robin Peel

Robin Peel wishes to thank Rachel Canty, S.P (TUC), Fiona Davis (CBI), Fiona and Ingrid, Jessica, Kirsty, Barry Bryne, Karen Mansell, Ann Speirs, James and Paul, Sue Simmonds, Sian B, Felicity Carter, Amy Cope, Clare R, Natalie M (Bude Community College), Cherry Pearce, Kerry Gleen, John Hodgson, Jane Noon, Holly Cooper (Bideford), Malcolm Reed, Bronwyn D, Long Beach Community College students and staff, SUNY (Fredonia) students and staff, Cindy Thorn, students and staff (South Dartmoor School), Kate and Emily at Trinity College, Oxford, Estelle Morris MP, Jane Shaw (Chichester High School for Boys), Robert Gee, Gordon Taylor, Kevin Finnear (Chichester College of HE, Kelly Avis, Amelia Andrews, Paul Skelton (Woodroffe School) English lecturers at Bath College of Higher Education (as was), Liz Farr, Rachel Christofides, Mary Reeves, Georgina Cullen, Caroline Redhead, Max Saunders (Kings College) Ann Turvey (Institute of Education, University of London), Rachel Bowler, Jane, Rachel, Alice (King Edward VI School) Melanie Phillips, Kate Fullbrook, Sue Davis (University of the West of England) Michelle Newman and students at Easily High School, South Carolina, students and staff at Lander College, South Carolina, Bea Naff, Art Young and students at Clemson College, South Carolina, students and staff at Susquehanna College, Pennsylvania, staff and students at Canberra Church of England Grammar School, Canberra, the English Department and Head of English at Archbishop Lanfranc School, Croydon, members of the English Department at Croydon College of Further Education, members of the English Department at SDCAT, Bethan Marshall, Francis Curtis, Rosemary Brooke, the English Department at Smith College, Massachusetts, staff and students at Orange County High School, members of the English Department at two Birmingham Schools, Deborah Try and students at St Lukes School of Education, Exeter University, members of the English Department at the University of North London, and most of all Mary Bell for her support and encouragement – and not forgetting all of those who gave up their time but are not recorded here.

Annette Patterson

Many people have contributed to the Australian section of the book through conversations, commentary and, in the case of the students, through direct involvement in data generating processes. I thank all participants for their generous contribution of time, effort, ideas, humour, patience and commitment. To the Murdoch University English curriculum classes of 1995 and 1996 and to the James Cook University English class of 1997, a heartfelt thank-you for sharing your ideas about English in such a generous and open manner, and for all the good times we had together on the adventure that is English teaching. Many of you will recognise your comments in the following chapters, attributed or not as you saw fit. Thank-you also to the high school students at Perth and Townsville for the wonderful conversations we had, apart from the formal interview times as well as during them, and for the genuinely challenging questions of English that you posed. Many of my colleagues in the English education communities in schools and universities in Western Australia and Queensland also contributed in untold ways through comments and conversations over the five years of the project. Thank you, also, to Bronwyn Mellor for editorial assistance and for astute commentary as always, although, the mistakes that remain are my own.

Jeanne Gerlach

I would like to thank the West Virginia University Doctoral students who helped me explore *What is English?* in the US. I would also like to express my gratitude to University of Texas President Robert E. Witt and Provost George C. Wright who both encouraged me to finish this project even though my role is now primarily that of an administrator. Their constant support of my efforts to continue my research interests has been invaluable.

The four lines from 'Snow' by Louis MacNeice are quoted on p. 7 with the permission of David Higham Associates and are taken from *Selected Poems* published by Faber and Faber (1964).

Parts of Chapter 3 were originally published as separate articles in English in *Education and in Teaching* and *Learning in Higher Education*.

1 Introduction

Robin Peel

Rationale

From its earliest days as a school and university subject English has been concerned with attempts to define itself. To the sceptical, whether inside or outside the field, this preoccupation is seen as no more than mildly interesting navel gazing, revealing the field's deep anxieties and unresolved insecurities. It is true that English, despite being one of the younger school curriculum subjects, has within 100 years undergone a number of name changes, as if it cannot make up its mind what its function is. First criticism, then literary criticism, then English, English Literature and Language and finally literary studies, textual studies, culture and criticism and English studies. Each term suggest a differing emphasis, as do the debates about whether we should use the word language or languages, literature or literatures, and the questions that have formed the titles of conferences such as *What is English?* and *English, whose English?*

Ultimately it is the failure to reach agreed definitions of what we mean when we use the word 'English' that bedevils discussion and creates unnecessary misunderstandings. In *What is English Teaching?* (Davies 1996) Chris Davies, writing from a United Kingdom perspective, argues that the inability to make a clear distinction between literacy and the subject English, between the subject name and the language name resulted in a National Curriculum that 'fudges the distinction between specialist English and general literacy . . . [and that] renders hopeless all attempts at coherence in the subject's structure' (Davies 1996, p. 35).

In this book we aim to demonstrate that the ability to live with uncertainty, a plurality of voices and a tradition of questioning is one of English's great strengths. But we are talking about plurality within specialist English: we are not seeking to take on the great issues of initial literacy, of how we *initially* learn to speak, read and write, or how these cross-curricular abilities are developed in secondary school and college. In the sections which discuss the United States experience we shall be discussing the effects of separating a literacy from English, of having separate 'writing ' classes in a way that is not the case in England and Australia. If we argue for a separation, it does not necessarily have to be according to the American model.

One of the fundamental tenets of twentieth-century theory, which along with technology has been responsible for the most explosive reorientations of English in the past twenty years, is that thought, understanding and knowledge are grounded in difference, that experience begins when the I becomes separate from the you, the self from the other, and the way that the creation of binaries is often accompanied by the creation of hierarchy and anxiety. In the next chapter we begin our investigation by exploring the historical roots of some of these hierarchies and anxieties by taking a particular perspective on the history of English in England, and suggest that there is much to be learned from an exploration of the historiography and ideology of English studies.

In later chapters in which we report what specialists have said to us in England, Australia and the United States we hope to show that there is a great deal to be learned from an exploration of the beliefs which inform current debates about English across the world, and the relationship between present practice and historical precedent. Each of us has chosen to explore that relationship in our own particular way, because as writers we are not outside our culture, and the way that we report our research says something about the way we have been constructed and the assumptions that are specific to Australia, the United States or England. In the account of the emergence of English in England, for example the charge of navel-gazing proves difficult to substantiate, because in many ways the history of English in England reveals a reluctance to look at anything too long and with an analytical eye. Those such as Matthew Arnold, Churston Collins, Walter Raleigh and F. R. Leavis – the early crusaders of English as a field which incorporated all the disparate elements hitherto separately known as reading, writing, composing, reciting, and spelling and assembled them all under the umbrella of literary studies – such men favoured appreciation above abstract thinking, evangelism above science. Questions were asked more readily than a willingness to answer them. English was seen to be about something that was ultimately undefinable. Synthesis was valued above analysis. There was something reductive about defining, and a suspicion of the boundaries that definitions can create. This concern with borders, boundaries, territories is evidenced in the titles of English conferences such as 'Claiming the Territory' (Australia). It is reflected in the title and content of articles: Kathryn Southworth (Southworth 1995), for example, expresses in 'Falling Towers': the fate of the English Empire, an 'anxiety' about attempting to define English:

> There is . . . a danger in defining English . . . Those who have any stake in the education of teachers will be aware of how the notion of academic subject knowledge has been devalued in the DfE Circular 14/93 (in England). The recently published criteria for assessing primary teacher education have reduced it to very little more than knowledge of the primary school curriculum, whatever its virtues, and subject

competencies have become merely the ability to stay one step ahead of the children. We may shortly be contesting not so much one definition of English, but a definition of subject which is inimical to most ideas of education, let alone higher education.

Yet in her final sentence Southworth provides us with a reason why matters of definition and belief are important, for in England discussion of 'education for life' is encouraging acceptance of a unified system of education in English from infant to postgraduate level. The emphasis on learning outcomes and competencies, which is the language of contemporary pedagogy, forces educators to make decisions about what a module, a field, or a subject considers itself to be 'about'. This practice of self-reflection and self-regulation has always been a feature of the set of practices known as 'English'.

Origins and intention

Our investigations have drawn on our experience as teacher educators who have worked as English teachers in classrooms and are English 'specialists' ourselves. The present study has its precise origins in a presentation given by Andrew Goodwyn and Dana Fox at the International Conference of Literacy and Language at the University of East Anglia in April 1993. Entitled 'Whose Model of English?' the presentation reported on the findings of a piece of research which had interviewed teachers in England and the United States about the model of English they most valued, asking them to rank the five models of English described in the 1988 Cox Report. These were listed in a questionnaire we originally used, and it may be useful to list them here. We offered the Cox Committee's definition of each, but as these definitions themselves proved to be problematic and ambiguous, we shall leave them undefined, simply listing them for the purposes of discussion.

> Cultural Heritage
> Personal Growth
> Adult Needs
> Cross Curricular
> Cultural Criticism

The results of the Fox–Goodwyn survey were interesting, revealing as they did differences between England and the United States (in England teachers placed the cultural criticism model of English much higher than did their colleagues in the USA). It also set us thinking: how did teachers acquire these beliefs, and to what extent did they undergo modification as they progressed from being students who had specialised in English, to newly qualified English teachers, and then to more experienced teachers, sometimes Heads of English. And how did the views of English teachers in schools compare with the views of English teachers in universities and colleges, both those in English Departments and those in Education Departments (a separation which exists in some institutions and not in others)? Finally we wanted to see to what extent institutional structures facilitated or acted as a brake on curriculum development in English, and the extent to which beliefs were reflected in classroom practice, though this took us beyond our initial questionnaire. Our chosen methodology reveals our reservations about the questionnaire method as the main source of information.

Methodology

In *Versions of English*, a study of the varieties of English that were offered to 15–17-year olds in English schools and colleges, Douglas and Dorothy Barnes (1984) identify seven possible modes in educational research, each one borrowing its methodology from social science disciplines.

These modes are:

1. Assessment of learning outcomes
2. Surveys (such as the studies of teachers' attitudes)
3. Historical accounts
4. Studies of innovation
5. Classroom studies
6. Content analysis (of examination papers, syllabuses or other learning materials)
7. Sociological studies (studies showing curriculum as it operates in classroom practice – what teachers and students actually do)

As will become clear, *Questions of English* incorporates elements from 2, and 7 in particular, through a combination of interviews, questionnaires and observation. We have prefaced our discussion of the observed practice in each of the three countries with a historical account (3 above) and the discussion is further informed by elements taken from 4, 5 and 6. For example, the section which discusses some of the 'Voices' of students in Higher Education English in England includes an account of an innovative practice. Yet we are mindful of Foucault's observation that changes in public opinion precede changes in individuals.

Yet we would not claim that this book gives an insight into classroom practice: as the original title indicated, our aim was to explore English specialists' *beliefs*. As Barnes and Barnes remind us, 'Teachers' reports on their own teaching are notoriously unreliable' (Barnes and Barnes 1984, p. 11) and the gap between what we think we are doing and what the students actually experience in the classroom is well known by any of us who have been either at the receiving or giving end of teaching practice observation. Others, however, have argued that beliefs or 'personal constructs' (Kelly

1970) are the crucial elements determining classroom practice. This is Nancy Martin, writing in 1983, following an investigation in Western Australia:

> The term 'personal construct' has been used to refer to the system of beliefs and attitudes which underlie behaviour, and are the unseen prompters – perhaps 'determiners' is not too strong a term – of action. And these same 'prompters' are the major influence on each teacher's classroom climate for learning, rather than those surface features of the curriculum – books, resources, programmes etc; they are beliefs about children and how they learn; about authority and the teacher's role in the learning process; about himself or herself as a person as well as a teacher, and how both roles can be maintained within the structure of the institution which school is. In addition, there are the teacher's beliefs about Subject English: his, or her views about what English is, what the terms 'language' and 'literature' represent in classroom events; how the children learn to progress in reading, writing and understanding books. These, together with his or her over-riding beliefs about education and his place in it, are likely to be the most powerful elements in the contexts of the lessons.
>
> Martin (1983, p. 66)

A decade or so later we feel less confident about the autonomy of the individual, and Martin's perception of the power of beliefs and personal constructs is itself a belief which we shall want to consider in the light of our own comments made in the Preface.

Our method of research has been qualitative, though, as we have indicated, the starting point was a wider survey based on a questionnaire. We reported on that survey in *English in Education* (Peel and Hargreaves 1995) and indicated at the time the limitations of the questionnaire method. We then began a series of taped interviews with a number of secondary school teachers (ten from each country), twelfth-grade students who were planning to specialise in English at college or university (ten from each country), undergraduates (ten from each country), university or higher education lecturers (ten from each country). Where possible we supplemented these voices with the views of student teachers and non-specialists from the world of publishing, writing, commerce and industry.

Initial questions

Although it may be difficult to generalise about what goes on in English in one school, let alone one county or one country, we thought it might be profitable to consider the range of different practices currently under discussion in England, and to compare them with the issues and beliefs being discussed in countries such as Australia and the United States. At the centre of these discussions sit the sets of beliefs to which teachers subscribe, sets of beliefs which may be in the ascendant in one country, dominant in another, and fading in a third. So we started with a couple of questions. What do students who specialise in English, student teachers and teachers in schools, colleges and universities believe they should be doing in the curriculum time appropriated by the English Department? Are there any discernible patterns in the differences in belief that come under the umbrella of English/Language Arts, such as the anticipated differences of belief across the phases?

We decided it was a good time to find out by asking a small cross-section of specialists in England, Australia, and the United States. We wanted to know what kinds of beliefs about English they held, and what kind of model of English they were going to carry with them into the next century, and beyond. How did they acquire their beliefs, and to what extent did they modify them as they progressed through their careers?

Questions of English

Whatever ideological, pedagogical, theoretical and cultural assumptions may divide those who have chosen to work in the field called English there is one thing that is likely to unite specialists in England, Australia and the United States. Whether they are students, researchers or teachers, whether in London, Washington or Sydney, whether in the school, college or university phase, specialists are likely to agree that their work is largely concerned with the practice of asking questions. This is true of all disciplines: what English particularly encourages is the practice of asking questions of the self. The impulse to interrogate and challenge may well be characteristic of all Western epistemology since classical times, but whereas it could be argued that the sciences have seen questions as a stage in the process of finding answers, in the arts in general, and in English in its late twentieth-century manifestation in particular, to a large extent the questions *are* the answers. They have been directed inwards, eschewing empiricism in favour of an open-ended process of self-reflection.

Entering the field called English with a view to seeing if anything can be pinned down, or answered to anyone's satisfaction, is a confusing business. Whirling around are views and opinions, verdicts and complaints. Is any pattern discernible? The world at large may be forgiven for thinking that everything in education, everything in English can be sorted out into two straightforward piles – the subversives and the traditionalists, those who care about standards and those who care about having fun: the polarities beloved by the popular press. To judge from the way English is discussed by the media, everything can be reduced in this shorthand way to black and white, an either/or. But it is not just the media that divides the world into two: education, epistemology and Western thought as a whole, are constructed around binaries. Whether it is I/You or Self/Other, experience, according to Lacan, starts with difference. We know cold through heat, we know dryness through wetness. Yet we know that any 'pattern' is far more complex than that, with shades of difference, as Louis MacNeice observed:

> World is crazier and more of it than we think
> Incorrigibly plural. I peel and portion
> A tangerine and spit the pips and feel
> The drunkenness of things being various.
> 'Snow' from *Selected Poems* (1964: 96)

People involved in English have always challenged simplistic divisions and the creation of boundaries. Even if we acknowledge that for many in the public arena the priority is basic literacy, while for those within English the field primarily offers opportunities for questioning and imagining, there are questionable elements in these distinctions. On the other hand, it is not helpful to insist that difference does not exist. The priorities of the elementary language arts teacher – the language co-ordinator in the primary school – are different from those of the English teacher in the secondary school, whose concerns are different again from those of the university or college English specialist. Our concern is with the practices of English, and although we will be arguing there are commonalties, these operate at a philosophical and pedagogical level: the specific methodology will often characterise a particular phase. Initial literacy is the primary concern in the first years of schooling and, despite what is often represented to the public English specialists never abandon this concern for effective literacy, partly because they tend to be quite literate people themselves. Yet the problem of the public perception of English is an important one.

Equally important is the professional perception of English, the view professionals have of their own subject. For some in universities great it is to be alive in this blissful hour: English has never been more dynamic, more alive and more controversial. The repeated debates are testimony to the self-questioning nature of subject English, for the subject has legitimised itself by encouraging the self-questioning and exploration of the 'self' in the subject. If it is about anything, subject English is about the subject 'self'.

For others in higher education, the opposite is true. English is stuck (or it was in 1979): 'Let us admit that English Studies are in the doldrums' (Heilbrun 1979: 21). Students are voting with their feet: in England, Australia and the United States the numbers of students applying for 'English' courses at best remains steady, and in some cases is declining. Media and Communications courses seem more relevant, and sometimes require lower grades.

This study proceeds on the basis that English is not an entirely uninterpretable, shapeless mass, nor is it moribund. There are clearly some specific issues that can be isolated and historicised. 'English' is a core compulsory subject in the state curriculums of Australia and in the National Curriculum in England. For secondary school students it remains a key and significant part of their weekly timetables. It has official, institutionalised status in the way that Media Studies, for example does not. A representative of the Confederation of British Industry spoke to us of Media Studies as a 'soft' subject. Many employers, she reported, would ask of someone with a Media Studies qualification, 'of what use is that to me?'

English has been the subject of debate and discussion for over a century now, and the way that such a history is being written, with certain landmarks and roots being either agreed or contested, gives us a hold on some important issues. And there is perhaps one issue that the recent history, interpretation and experience of English encourages us to confront, and it is the one which gives the present study its focus: what are the goals of English teaching?

What is English for?

To ask what English is for, is to ask an inappropriate question as far as some people are concerned. In response to this question one of our respondents wrote: 'I don't think English is for anything: English just *is*.' One of the great legacies of progressive English teaching, a legacy which endures even though the term progressive is now largely moribund, was the belief that the practice of good English teaching, with its emphasis on the child's talking, writing and performance – its emphasis on hearing the student *voice* – was a liberating process that would allow children to escape the norms of society. There is something hugely attractive and exciting about seeing an anthology of student poems in print, about watching a performance of a scene that students have improvised, about reading a moving account of a moment of joy or a personal trauma. That is the stuff of English teaching for many English specialists in schools in England, Australia and the United States. Yet, through the work of commentators such as Ian Hunter, we have been encouraged to question the more unproblematic view of English as a purely subversive force, as a force which stands outside ideologies and allows students to question them. We are asked to revise this view in favour of one which is more consistent with Foucault's ideas on power and *complicity*. In *Culture and Government* (Hunter 1988) Hunter shows how both Arnold and the Scottish Sunday School reformer David Stow rejected the monitorial system not because they objected to the hierarchical and rigidly classified system on ideological grounds. Far from it: their objection was that it worked as a system of teaching, but it did not work as a system of training. For children to be effectively trained, there must be freedom to play *under supervised conditions*. Only that freedom, which will allow the kind of contact with peers that is so character forming on the streets, Stow argues, will children be able to grow in ways that are desirable and enduring. We would not teach a bird to fly by keeping it in a cage, we would not train a racehorse in a stable: therefore the school must be more than a room. It must replicate society, be an alternative, morally ordered society. The teacher–student partnership is central to this 'new' pedagogical model. So far from being an argument for the growth of the self for its own sake, the process is seen to be no less normative than that advocated by Joseph Lancaster with its system of monitors all overseen by the master from a high dais.

Any reappraisal of the role of English – and this reappraisal has been acted out most publicly in the universities – takes on an added importance because a case can be made for the belief that curriculum is about to take on the biggest seismic shift since popular education was established in the nineteenth century. The shift is the result of the new technologies, and the way that this gives students in schools opportunities to work in multimedia forms, across nations, and in collaborative ways. The rhetoric is of social justice (everyone's entitlement to access to the new media forms), of classroom without walls, of an information explosion and of student ownership of this information, whether it is through the internet or through taking laptops and sensors to conduct scientific experiments in the field. The manager of the School of the Future in 1995 was John Warren, an ex-English and Drama teacher, who argued powerfully that we should always ask the question: how are these new tools going to enhance the curriculum and enhance learning? Yet if the equipment changes, it is possible that the pedagogical relationship does not. In England Sally Tweddle has argued forcefully that the new technologies must be used by English teachers in certain ways, in ways that represent traditional good practice. So we need to ask ourself what normative purpose – if we now accept that all education is normative – a modified form of English, compatible with a curriculum in which the old subject barriers become redundant (because multimedia is largely cross-curricular) will be serving.

What of the more pressing and immediate issues?

We have spoken on the grand scale, going as far back as the 1830s and imagining as best we can the curriculum of the 2030s – a period of over 200 years. But it would be foolish to ignore the more immediate questions that arise from the here and now, questions and pressures which form the context for any perception of an English curriculum for the future. Quite specific agendas form the preoccupations of our three chosen countries. In England the 1980s and the 1990s have been preoccupied with the issue of assessment in schools, and the place of theory and the canon in universities. In Australia the issue of genre theory, arising out of systemic functional linguistics, has exercised, and in some cases divided the educational community in schools and university education departments. In the United States the issue of the canon, long debated, is revived by books such as *The Closing of the American Mind* (Allan Bloom 1987) and *The Western Canon* (Harold Bloom 1995), both of which argue that there should be a centre, a core to humanities in general and to literary studies in particular, and that that core should consist of the books which are the indispensable tools to thinking profoundly and intelligently.

Arguments about a core are central to any understanding of the current state of English. Those, like the two Blooms, who argue that the core should be the Western literary canon, are in the minority. Yet the need for some kind of core is likely to achieve widespread support. For many in higher education, English is an infinitely expandable field, and although there are likely to be disputes over whether that field is pyramidal, spherical or cuboid, or indeed has any shape at all, the majority seem to accept that as a space its form and boundaries may be debatable, but it is a useful site for enquiry.

Having said that, English at the end of the twentieth century is beset with problems of a practical kind. These exercise those in higher education, where 'an army of gypsy professors' on part-time contracts is roaming the United States, according to a report in *The Times Higher Education Supplement* (24 February 1995). Insecurity, larger and larger classes, under-resourcing of libraries and a decline in self-esteem – problems that university teachers in England, Australia and the United States used to be sheltered from, now haunt lecturers and professors too.

But this is as nothing compared to the practical problems that confront primary and secondary teachers. There is a hint of these in this comment from a researcher at Berkeley:

> Teachers don't talk about theory very much at all. But they do talk a lot about survival and, especially in inner cities, about all the traumas they have to deal with. They also talk a lot about how schools are administered – generally in ways that make it hard for them to do their jobs. Much of the talk takes the form of complaints.
>
> Freedman e-mail, 6 February 1996

English teachers, like most teachers, feel overworked and undervalued. Historically this has always been the case. The Roman pedagogue was a slave who accompanied the pupil to school, and as Juvenal points out in his tenth satire, earns as much in a year as the popular entertainer does in a day. But there are specific late twentieth-century pressures, linked to insecurity and the public baiting of teachers, which suggest that we have not advanced that far from Greek and Roman practices. The shifting sands of change mean that it is impossible to pitch tents and say 'this is the promised land', even for a year, let alone a decade or a career. Though many find the prospect of perpetual revolution disorientating, just as many find it stimulating. But just when such change agents, the pioneers and the experimenters in the field, are most needed and should be cherished, career prospects are suddenly reduced. A Head of English in England who has transformed her department, and is at a stage where her influence should be spreading, wonders what she is going to do next. There are no advisory teacher posts (a kind of roving consultant who would run courses and support fellow teachers), university teacher-education departments are shrinking, and she does not want to move out of English into the Senior Management Team of a school. The very best kind of teacher is frustrated and thwarted, and it is not surprising that this frustration can in other cases breed disenchantment.

We can all recognise this negative picture, but it is a partial one, because it does not take account of the ways in which teachers continue to ask questions about their practice, questions that move beyond the pragmatic to the theoretical. In England, Australia and the United States the healthy existence of professional organisations such as NATE, AATE and NCTE suggests a core of dedicated people whose roots are in the classroom and who continue to refine the relationship between theory and practice. In England the issue of the National Curriculum has been in some ways a distraction for teachers, inhibiting curriculum development, but in other ways it has united English teachers. The corollary of saying what they do not want, is a clearer focus on what they *do* want. In Australia the issue of systemic functional linguistics and genre has also encouraged debate and reflection, though in ways that are sometimes seen as not wholly productive. In the United States the portfolio issue, and the National Writing project, has facilitated discussion and the sharing of ideas. In England the Arvon Foundation has recently embarked on its own exciting writing workshop pilot.

Earlier we said very confidently that English as a field is not about to disappear. It has institutionalised status. But perhaps we should not be so confident. There are many reasons for undertaking this survey now, but one stands out. It is being claimed increasingly that the arrival of the new technologies has profound implications for the organisation of the curriculum. Old distinctions between arts and sciences, practical and theoretical, no longer hold as teams work together on computers. In developing car prototypes, designers work with engineers on computerised models. Previously the design team produced a model which they then passed on to the engineers. Now a suggested design feature will be adjusted in the light of comments from an engineer who will say what can be actually made, and the computer model suitably modified. The increasingly dynamic relationship between art, technology and science, and the changing nature of the professions combine to form a powerful argument for the reassessment of the traditional epistemological divisions and the way that we partition culture in our curriculum. When students produce their own multimedia packages in the classroom they combine words, pictures and sounds. All of these developments are at odds with one central feature of subject English, the emphasis on the individual. English, especially in the second half of the twentieth century, has encouraged the expression of the individual voice, and values the individual's experience. It is an individualistic practice, and collaborative reading and writing does not disguise this.

It is ironical that the claims made for information technology – that it is a unifying and inclusive force – are the same ones made for literary studies in the nineteenth century in England. For a brief period at the beginning of the twentieth century, between 1906 and 1921, English went through a period of rhetorical inclusiveness, starting with the founding of the English

Association and ending with the publication of the Newbolt Report. For a time those specialising in English in schools and universities were drawn into dialogue, and were united by a sense of common purpose. That cross phase unity was brief and inspired by political expedience as much as common interest. It did not last for very long. Say we pose the following question. To what extent do an elementary school language co-ordinator, a high school English teacher, a city college lecturer and a university English professor constitute a team? As the researcher quoted above says: 'I'd say that there's a fairly major communication gap in the States between what folks are thinking in universities and what is happening in schools.' This perceived gap is paralleled by the relative lack of dialogue between elementary and high schools – that is primary and secondary schools in England. The priorities and agendas of a particular phase are framed by the history of the curriculum which operates within a phase, and more obviously the needs and abilities of the students within that phase. Second-grade children are still coming to terms with the act of reading, and although it is never too early to address the issue of different readings, this will be given less attention than the process of 'learning to read' itself. One hopes that the opposite is true in a university English department. There is a very real sense in which the differences in perception that we shall be reporting are as much to do with age phase as cultural difference. Aware of this it may be asked why we have not separated our research into perceptions of secondary teachers, perceptions of college teachers, perceptions of undergraduates and so on. We could have done so, but that has been done before, as we discuss in the next chapter. We were interested in seeing if we could explore connections between history and practice, so that the questions are as much *of* English as a set of practices, as they are questions *by* English.

The questions about English that interest us are fundamental ones about theory and practice in the United States, in Australia and in England. They have all been asked, at different times, in different places, over the past twenty-five years: sometimes they have all been asked at one time, at one place by one group of people from across an English speaking nation. But usually they are asked by special groups of people with specific concerns, in different places, and in relation to their own needs. They have not been asked collectively, nor, as far as we are aware, with the use of voices which are as revealing of the nature of belief as they are of the beliefs themselves (many of which are unsurprising and could be predicted with the minimum of research).

In bringing together accounts of the catechisms of subject English in three national areas, accounts that embrace not only different phases but different countries, we may look as if we are trying to introduce at the end of the twentieth century a nineteenth-century practice: the construction of the grand narrative. Any such tendency towards universalism would be at odds with current beliefs about the value of difference and dissent, as explored by Lyotard (1979), and this is not our aim. We do not wish to deny plurality, where it exists. Instead, we want to ask a range of questions of English and to discover if there are features that are common to all three. If there are it may suggest support for a reading of subject English that makes connections between its origins and its practices. We wish to carry out an investigation into the beliefs that underpin current practice, because we seem to have reached a point in history where English could be about to undergo radical transformation as a discipline. What is not clear is whether such a transformation would involve a narrowing of the subject to include only those skills associated with literacy, with a very small minority going on to complete an advanced study and reading of the most demanding literature in English from the past 600 years. This is the conclusion proposed by writers coming from very different directions as we shall see when we refer to J. L. Wilson and Ian Hunter. Alternatively, English may continue to expand, as it has in England in both secondary schools and universities, becoming in the end a *metadiscipline*, a means of approaching and thinking about not just all texts, but all knowledge. It would be too simplistic to call this a left-wing agenda, as contemporary theory interweaves elements that appear both radical and reactionary, but it is the more radical, ambitious development, in line with the expansionist tendency in English. In one extrapolation from that tendency English continues to undergo a metamorphosis, loses its autonomy and its name, and transforms itself into part of a broader field of study called Cultural History, as proposed by Catherine Belsey

> Is there a place for English in a postmodern world? Does an academy where twentieth-century textual practice breaks down the nineteenth-century boundaries between disciplines offer English departments any worthwhile job to do? . . .
>
> I start from the assumption that English as it has traditionally been understood, as the study of great literary works by great authors, has no useful part to play in a pedagogy committed to a politics of change. In the course of the 1980s the institution of English has been firmly stripped of its mask of neutrality by Peter Widdowson, Chris Baldick, Terry Eagleton and Terence Hawkes, among others. As their analyses reveal, the conservatism of traditional English lies primarily in two areas: first, its promotion of the author-subject as the individual origin of meaning, insight and truth; and second, its claim that this truth is universal, trans-cultural and ahistorical. In this way, English affirms as natural and inevitable both the individualism and the world picture of specific western culture, and within that culture the perspective of a specific class and a specific sex. In other words, a discipline that purports to be outside politics in practice reproduces a very specific political position.
>
> Belsey 1989, p. 159

Catherine Belsey then goes on to propose a transformation of English into something called cultural history, a much broader interdisciplinary approach and quite in contrast to the narrowing of English proposed by the right.

These two alternatives immediately raise a host of other questions: are there not other models, is there not a version of English somewhere between the two, and most important of all, is there any sense of an enduring strand in English pedagogy that is likely to survive all changes to the content and methodology? Some of these basic questions come out of theory, questions about epistemology. 'What body of knowledge does English teach? How is that body of knowledge authorised, taught and examined?' (Guy and Small 1993). 'We argue in favour of no epistemological position – indeed we fight for all positions' (Elbow 1990). Other questions arise from anxieties about the future, as we tumble into the twenty-first century. *Are we leaving what is essential in English behind?* is a concern recently voiced by Harold Bloom in *The Western Canon* (Bloom 1994). Arguments about the canon have occupied English specialists for the last thirty years, and are often arguments about other things altogether. But debates about knowledge and the precise practices of English are being redefined from a more *post*-post-structuralist position, as in Guy and Small's *Politics and Value in English Studies* (1993).

Then there are questions about pedagogy. Until recently these questions about classroom practice, about teaching methods and approaches to learning, have in England been confined largely to primary and secondary schools. These have been the site of fierce ideological debates about methods – methods of teaching, methods of assessment, methods of classroom organisation. Group learning, coursework assessment, interactive learning – these have been the preoccupations of secondary school English teachers over the past twenty-five years. But these debates have started to spill over into higher education, as Guy and Small's book shows. The same is true of the United States, where Kathleen McCormick, in her 1994 book *The Culture of Reading and the Teaching of English* (McCormick 1994) has a chapter entitled 'Critical literacy in practice: response statements, collaborative projects, formal essays'. If we ignore the use of a phrase such as 'critical literacy', which has a meaning quite different from that operating in Australia, the attention to teaching methods suggest something of a change in higher education practice.

Even so, university English still seems most comfortable with debates about theory, and the need for more history, more specificity, more culturally informed commentaries and readings. As Steven Connor says in *Postmodernist Culture* (Connor 1989), English has adapted to include the Noah's Ark of theory, and a vessel designed as a ship has become a floating zoo. By rights it ought to sink, by rights the animals should be roaming freely on dry land or flying in the air like larks, but for the moment the vessel is keeping afloat. Higher education either loves to debate why this is, or gets on with looking after the animals, which predictably soon started to interbreed. But the ark is serving a utilitarian purpose, for English is continuing to serve as a training ground for the public services, and if the emphasis is now more on the intellectual and less on the affective, those attracted by the affective and the personal still find English is a relatively comfortable environment.

Then there are another set of questions, arising from the situation described above, questions about the history of the subject, and its precise origins. We shall consider those in a minute, but it is interesting that different readings of the history of English reveal different sets of beliefs about the nature of the subject, about whether it is conceived to have been imposed from above or established from below – whether it came from the government or whether it came from the people.

Which reminds us that the debate is seen to be of greatest interest to the people at large is one we have not even hinted at. It concerns the question of literacy, and the methods by which we may be more literate and articulate nations. Immediately we have slipped into using 'English' as the category meaning 'the language of English-speaking peoples'. This is how for many people who are not specialists English is defined. It is not literature, not a set of practices, but the system by which the majority of people in England, Australia and the United States communicate. What is English for? Reading, writing, and talking. That is what the National Curriculum in England says, and the politician, speaking for the man and woman in the street, will say that this is about standards, accuracy and correctness. No one needs to be reminded about this debate, though some readers will think they are distant from it. And as three members of the Centre for Literacy Studies at Bristol University remind us (Reed, Webster and Beveridge 1994) there is a great deal of misinformation about the supposed decline in literary standards in the UK – and this is (almost certainly replicated in) true of the United States, Canada and Australia also.

Finally we want to explore the implications of the differences in institutional practice, differences within countries but also differences between countries. A simple example will illustrate this.

In the United States university undergraduate courses are more broadly based than in England, and single subject specialisation comes at a much later stage than it does in the UK. Literary Studies are usually taught as part of a humanities or liberal arts course, and as Guy and Small point out, 'questions about the autonomy of English studies (its status, that is, as a specialist discipline) are neither as visible nor as pressing in the United States as they are in Britain. Neither are the institutional consequences at all comparable' (Guy and Small 1993, p. 57). So the question to be asked in the United States, and one that we did ask frequently in California, is whether it is time for literary studies to cope with the problem of breadth by becoming a metadiscipline informing others, as recommended by Christopher Norris (1988). Or do the demands of modularity create a cafeteria of choices which represents genuine plurality, giving freedom to the student to make up his or her own menu? In that sense the range of practices debated in English are reflected in the range of options. There is English, there is Literary Studies, there is Language, there is Literacy, and there is Media or Communication Studies.

Asking awkward questions

We are also keen to face some provocative questions about English in schools and universities, questions which are an extension of the popular concerns about literacy outlined above. They are characterised by a concern about standards, rigour, excellence, scholarship, and they can be found in any age. That these questions originate from specific groups and have their own agenda is clear, but they are none the less challenging ones. They represent a strand of belief that it would be foolish to ignore.

One United Kingdom example, an article whose title and context (the highly conservative journal *The Salisbury Review*) immediately give notice of the ideological position likely to be advanced, is 'Lice in the Locks of Literature' (Wilson 1988), to which Guy and Small refer in their closing chapter. Arguing that English has replaced Classics as the home of the general reader, J. L. Wilson bemoans the fact that English has no equivalent of classical translation, study of difficult texts or mental training that constitute rigorous training. (Ironically the study of theory in undergraduate Core Modules such as 'Culture and Criticism', if done properly would satisfy this need, but the content of such modules would be likely to appal her because it provides further evidence of the English specialist as critic rather than the English specialist as creative writer.) Students of English are largely 'vocationless', she says:

> Most of those who choose to read English do so because they have no alternative, they enjoy reading, English is their best subject at school, and they want to go to University. Often they have not read extensively – sometimes no more than their set texts. They have no picture of the broad sweep of English literature, no sympathy for cultures other than their own, and no intellectual equipment with which to deal with them.
>
> (Wilson 1988: 26–27)

Whilst the argument is flawed in that Wilson attributes these short-comings to a mismatch between what is taught in schools and university courses which have come out of the classical tradition (university courses may sound the same but actually their content and approach has changed radically since the arrival of theory), the broad principle holds good – there is indeed a mismatch. Wilson's solution is to make English Departments small and demanding so that those who read only for pleasure are excluded. Others would argue that the expansion of higher education means that the courses have to change in quite different ways, ways which are accommodating rather than excluding.

Nothing that has been said so far is novel. All of these questions have been raised, and discussed, in journals ranging from English in Australia to *Reading*, from *Junior Education* to *Textual Practice*. But in *Reading*, the journal of the United Kingdom Reading Association, there will be arguments about literacy largely with a primary school focus, whereas in *Textual Practice* debates about the theorising of Literary Studies in higher education find a forum. In the United States there are separate journals for every phase and interest, from *Language Arts*, through the *English Journal*, to *College Education* and *English International*. This reflects the huge empire of English, its fragmentation and specialisation. It has been the inevitable response to the growth of English. But how many English specialists will say that they feel actively engaged with all these debates, and all of these questions? Is it not more likely, that for reasons of phase, self-perception, membership of a particular generation, experience that some of these issues will seem much more relevant than others? How many secondary and further education teachers have felt engaged by literary theory? How many university teachers have really been interested in pedagogy and assessment arrangements? This is the one set of fundamental questions that have not been addressed, because in seeking connections rather than difference they invite a practice that is at odds with much cultural theory. What we would like to do is to find out to what extent teachers feel that they have thought through and been able to articulate this difference. Is it enough to say, as we all do, that a plurality of beliefs is a good thing? In the first part of Paul Auster's *New York Trilogy* Peter Stillman goes on walks around parts of Manhattan, and maps out the letters of T-O-W-E-R O-F B-A-B-E-L as he journeys the streets. His search for a universal language seems a rather futile, mad exercise. It is just that, but in so doing at least he reminds us of our own historical situation, and the need for alternative, thought-through and theorised strategies for the twenty-first century.

Assumptions about English: views from the page

Let us now elaborate on some of the key issues/assumptions/perceptions that appear to inform current discussion surrounding 'English', as revealed by recent articles and books. Before we do that we need to clarify what we mean by 'English'. Do we mean literacy, do we mean literary study, do we mean anything to do with the language identified as English, for which the phrase Language Arts serves as an identifier? For the purposes of discussion I think we mean the last, but the fact that the word means so many specific things in so many specific contexts, reminds us once again of one immediate problem: we may not all be talking about the same thing. Some wish to abandon it, because it suggests too narrow a concept. Yet in the majority of institutions in England the name survives, it becomes a kind of nest, even though like skylarks the members of the department may be flying far away from it. In identifying some of the assumptions that seem to inform current thinking about 'English', we shall use English in its historical sense, in the sense that saw the foundation of the National Council for the Teaching of English in the United States, and the English Association in England. English in this sense is not so much an identifiable field of study but a range of practices which contribute

to the formation of a particular kind of person that societies have found they
need, and which English is able to help produce. We shall consider what kind
of person this is in our final chapter, but wish to make it clear now that to
describe English as a technology which produces a certain kind of person is
not to decry it, as that kind of person may by exactly what we would wish for
in a dynamic, democratic society.

Let us now consider a range of beliefs that are informing current debates
about subject English.

1. English was not born in England

Instead, it was a means of ensuring homogeneity in the colonies.

> I have argued throughout that the teaching of English in Ontario schools
> was from its inception in 1871 a set of practices which enacted cultural
> politics at the level of theories of language and of the literary. This was
> hardly a situation unique to Ontario, however, since the founding of
> English studies generally can be located within the expansion of a global
> English empire. More specifically, in a colonial situation it arose out of
> the perceived need of an English elite attempting to secure their cultural
> hegemony by extending and revitalising a normalising language cur-
> riculum in the unstable circumstances of the late nineteenth century
> immigration, growing nationalism, and the shifting class relation of early
> industrialisation.
>
> Morgan (1990: 229)

2. We need to reassess the histories of 'English'

> Part of a more self-conscious recovery of English studies, therefore,
> would mean recognising the importance of curricular history. In an
> important sense, 'subjects are their histories' (Inglis) . . .
>
> Morgan (1990: 230)

For example, the first cross-phase report on English in England, the
Newbolt Report of 1921, written in the aftermath of the First World War
but informed by debates conducted in the pages of the bulletins and leaflets
of the English Association, deliberately set out to offer the study of English
as a unifying force which would heal class divisions and unite the nation with
the sense of a shared language/literature. The vision of English recommended
by the Board of Education subcommittee shone over the birth of many
English departments in England and shaped their crusading philosophy.
According to several of the contributors to a special edition of the Western
Australian journal *Interpretations* (subtitled 'Beyond Poststructuralism'
(1994)) English teachers would find it liberating to set themselves more
modest goals and to draw back from the 'grand projects of cultural develop-

ment or personal growth', projects which the authors see as the legacy of a particular historical role assumed by English.

3. There is a need to make students aware of contesting theories about the practice of reading and writing

The preferred option is not teaching theory as a body of knowledge, but 'through teaching ways of theorising our various reading practices [in a way that] assumes a 'dialogic classroom situation, in which different ways of reading – and their implications – are foregrounded and contested' (McCormick 1994).

4. The need for theory is in direct contrast (and in some ways a reaction) to the position taken up by F. R. Leavis and those involved in Scrutiny

> (W)hereas Humanism is a doctrine and Irving Babbitt's aim is to state and establish it in general theoretical terms, my own aim is to deal in doctrine, theory and general terms as little as possible. The main concern of these pages is with methods and tactics; these are what, keeping as close as possible to the practical, they offer.
>
> Leavis Education and the University, 1943

This echoes the Newbolt Report's description of the English as an essentially *practical* people. The impatience with theory, the origins of which form part of the discussion in the next chapter, had many long-term consequences, but one effect of an evangelical emphasis on method and principles – the goal of turning students into critically intelligent readers with a developed sensibility – however hopelessly ambiguous and problematic these terms may be – was to bring schools and universities under the same roof, to develop a sense of shared purpose, an aim which can be traced to the Romantic belief in unity and inclusiveness. An emphasis on the need for adequate theories of 'English' has had the opposite effect, and many of the specialists we came to interview believed the gulf between secondary and higher to be even greater than the gulf between primary and secondary.

5. In discussing 'English' we need to distinguish between a variety of experiences as well as of a variety of practices

For example, although the model of the reflective practitioner is a model that holds good for English teaching as much as any other, not all English specialists become teachers. If we separate out the experiences that 'English' offers, then the reasons for this become obvious.

Many are attracted to English for cerebral reasons – the love of ideas, the entry into other worlds it may appear to give, the opportunities for reflection that it provides. Although we understand these processes to be dialogic, the product of social interaction, they may appear to be private and solitary, and give space to those who enjoy privacy and solitude. Writers themselves may enjoy the social life, but they also have the capacity for solitude, alone with their pens, typewriters or word-processors. Readers too may be most fulfilled when alone with a text. This is one of the strong attractions of literary studies.

This capacity for one's own company is characteristic of only one kind of reader and producer. There are others who appreciate English precisely because it provides space to interact, whether through discussion, debate, performance, or production. This enjoyment is most manifest in drama, but it is not confined to drama. It is characteristic of media studies, or what in Australia is called Communication Studies.

Those specialists who are most fulfilled when engaged in the rough and tumble of verbal and non verbal interaction may be those likely to go on to become teachers. This is the model which the media likes to present: the English teacher in *Kes*, Keating in *Dead Poet's Society*, the young English teacher in *Heartbreak High*. All of these are represented as being more at home with people than with texts: we rarely seem them reading or writing in the conventional sense. Yet we see them performing, creating a text that they have fashioned, we presume, from their own reading.

Ideas/People: this is clearly not a dichotomy, an either/or, but a continuum. And the kinds of ideas, the kinds of people (academics? bar cronies? fellow performers?) are important in fixing an appropriate context. That said, it might be worth asking 'What kind of English specialist are you?' to see if specialists identify more with one than with another, more with people than with texts (assuming that we can separate the two).

6. There is a widening gap between the public perception of English and the specialists' perception

There is considerable evidence that a large number of men and women in the street view English as an activity designed primarily to improve practical skills in reading, spelling, handwriting, punctuation and, possibly, speaking. To such a view English is largely a matter of literacy, and people feel confident to assert this, when perhaps they would not feel so confident to say what science should confine itself to. Specialists, who tend not to have great difficulties in matters of basic literacy themselves (there are notable exceptions) tend either to take literacy as a given thing, or as a reductive, less interesting matter. In contrast to what we might called the 'monologic' view of English that we hear voiced by newspaper editors, MPs, and many parents, is the 'polyphonic' view of English specialists, who are interested in the variety of activities and practices for which English provides space. Can these two positions be reconciled? In the United States, where 'writing courses' continue right into university, there is less of a division. But in England, until recently, even primary teachers were inclined to give emphasis to the more imaginative potential of language, in the belief that the best way to achieve competence in language was to be motivated to use it in original and fulfilling ways. The UK and Australia have not been keen on service 'writing courses'. In England, however, the combined impact of the National Curriculum revisions, and the attention given to the public perception of English, has, it would appear, diminished the force and the certainty with which this rejection used to be expressed.

7. For a number of reasons, there is now a reassessment of the concept of literary value

Matters have not quite come full circle. But whereas the dominant set of theoretical positions that informed discussion of texts in universities once took it as given that values were cultural and historically situated and produced, and therefore understandable only in relation to their context rather than in relation to any idea of an absolute, the rejection of absolute conclusions is now being questioned. Evidence of this can be found in issues of *Textual Practice* from the early 1990s, where, for example, Antony Easthope (1990) and Steven Connor (1991) engaged in a literary and philosophical dialogue, and it is a theme taken up by Terry Eagleton. The issue concerns the difference between a discourse *on* value and a discourse *of* value, Shakespeare being an example of a site for such a discourse.

The key question Connor asks is: what values have encouraged us to be suspicious of essentialism and categorical imperatives signifying absolute value?

8. Methodology and Theory in English may appear to be pulling in opposite directions

If we take England as an example, over the past thirty years a number of examples of good practice have percolated up from the primary school, first into the secondary school, then into the sixth form or further education college, and finally into the university. Collaborative learning, active learning, group work, a recognition of the power of the visual: all of these are elements which reflective teachers wish to incorporate in their teaching and make available to students, *both because these practices yield good results and because they have been properly theorised*. The social nature of learning, and of language production, is the foundation upon which the theory of desirable current classroom practice is built. Concerns about coherence, progression and integration reflect another theoretical perspective with teaching implications: the wholeness of language.

In contrast, theory – theory applied to the construction and reading of texts – seems to take us in the opposite direction, away from coherence and integration to specificity and fragmentation. It is more usual to talk about specific practices rather than a totalising world view signified by the word 'English'. As Lyotard (1979) says:

> The grand narrative has lost its credibility, regardless of what mode of unification it uses, regardless of whether it is a speculative narrative or a narrative of emancipation . . . The social subject itself seems to dissolve in this dissemination of language games. The social bond is linguistic but it is not woven with a single thread.

The post-modern is thus a centreless universe, and so our readings of 'centred' texts – whether they are colonial, patriarchal, liberal humanist or religious – is unalterably different from what it was before. How best we can embrace the opportunities this decentredness offers, whilst retaining a centred 'frame' which gives our students some useful reference points, is a key question in the late twentieth century.

9. However problematic the term may be, we need to acknowledge the role of 'pleasure' in motivating learning in English

There is a problem here. One of the things most likely to motivate primary-age children is the delight that we can obtain from the world of books and the imagination. Secondary English teachers, too, are keen to set up stimulating, motivating tasks which promote active learning. So the message is: reading, writing, talking are enjoyable activities. Which they are. This is not only a special attribute of English, fun maths and science notwithstanding, but it creates an expectation which higher education English does not necessarily feel the need to satisfy. There is a different belief about what English is for.

10. 'The most universal quality is diversity' (Montaigne)

This is a belief commonly held among English specialists: the quotation above was actually used as the epigraph for an English Conference in California in January 1995. Pluralism is something to be celebrated. But is there no limit to what English can contain? Some have expressed a concern that it will collapse under its own weight, that it will become so baggy that it is impossible to lift, that it will cease to have an identity of its own. Will English survive deep into the twenty-first century, or should we anticipate a breaking up of the subject into specialisms, the Balkanisation of English? This is the belief of Guy and Small (1994) who argue that English is doomed unless it can agree on a single theory or body of knowledge treated in a properly theorised way. For these two writers there is something extra-ordinary about the unproblematic acceptance of a multiplicity of reading practices: '*Why* does English enjoy a unique position where adjudication between different theoretical positions, and therefore by implication the authority of particular explanations of texts, may only be "resolved" at the level of ideology?' (Guy and Small 1993, p. 16). Their gloomy prediction (gloomy if you think English is worth saving) is that such an open-house policy is disastrous, and will ultimately lead to the extinction of English. On the other hand the outcomes of English, the qualities which are assessed and institutionalised, remain so intrinsic to society that it could be argued that it does not matter that English cannot state what it is about. If English quite legitimately creates a particular kind of person, the self-correcting critical and reflective reader, then its survival in schools is assured. This does not necessarily ensure that it has a significant place in the college or university curriculum, however, as we can see with 'minority' higher education subjects such as music and physical education.

11. How do we live?

At the beginning of this century English was very much concerned with the issue of helping us to learn how to live in more civilised and sophisticated ways. Claims for the study of literature ranged from the belief that it could morally improve the reader to the idea that it sharpened the critical faculties and gave us insights into the sublime. At a practical level that belief inspires many English teachers in schools and universities. Yet in university arts faculties (and social science faculties too) there has been a radical revision of the way experience and knowledge is viewed, and claims for the *absoluteness* of anything are seen as problematic. This is certainly true of literary studies, and it raises important questions about the relationship between English and life. And the question will not go away, even when someone like Adam Phillips trades in a career in literary criticism for one in psycho-analysis. A reviewer neatly summed up the problem that faces Phillips and faces us all:

> In Phillips's books, the moral question at issue seems to be 'how to live' at the end of the twentieth century – without a belief in objective science, the unitary self or the march of progress. Instead of searching for the 'ultimate truth' about ourselves, Phillips argues, we should accept the infinite re-interpretability of our lives. We should stop thinking of our 'ego' as something solid and unitary, the 'owner' of its body; subjectivity is many layered and contradictory. Instead of imposing a developmental 'progressive narrative' on our lives, we must recognise the role of *contingency* . . .
>
> Ingleby 1994

But what does this mean for the English specialist teaching in the junior high, high or secondary school?

What are our aims and assumptions?

1. We live in an age when mission statements, goals, quality objectives and corporate aims provide us with enough textual rhetoric to inflate a fleet of dirigibles. Yet there is an important and valuable side to quantifying and articulating one's aims, for they make implicit assumptions become defensible (or sometimes indefensible) beliefs, and they foreground difference and commonality. Here, for example, are NCTE's beliefs, as set down in their pamphlet *Assumptions and Practices* (NCTE 1990):

ASSUMPTIONS ABOUT LEARNERS AND TEACHERS
Every person is a learner.
Teachers and students are a community of learners
Learners are aware of the uniqueness of each other's backgrounds, and value this uniqueness
The community of learners values experience as the stimulus for growth and change.
Language is the primary medium for growth and change.
Teachers and learners assume many roles, often shared, often overlapping, always interdependent and interactive. They respect each other in these roles.
Learning entails making mistakes in a climate of trust.
The classroom is an extended community.
The classroom setting contributes to the climate of the learning.

ASSUMPTIONS ABOUT KNOWLEDGE
Knowing is active and ongoing, a process of interactive learning.
Knowledge is not information, yet it requires information.
Knowledge is more than a mastery of facts and processes.

ASSUMPTIONS ABOUT LANGUAGE
Language is a vital medium for creating individual and social identities.
Students' language is valued and used as a means of learning, change, and growth within the classroom.
The power of language and the rules that it follows are discovered, not invoked.
Literacy has a wide range of genres and functions, which are important to teachers and learners.

Our most likely response to these statements is that they are a set of uncontroversial, worthy aims. Yet they represent a culture talking to itself at a particular time in history. In England a teacher who shares these aims nevertheless identified the fondness for rhetoric as specifically American. And there is a model of the self – the unique individual, with his or her own rights, that is very Western, and very American. The community is defined as a collection of individuals, using language – it does not specify English – as a medium for growth and change. So there are notions of organic, living growth inscribed here,

Yet what they perhaps most strikingly reveal is a powerful belief in the social nature of language, and the way that learning is inescapably an inter-active process. This is not a denial that some kind of learning takes place in a transmission model of learning, simply a belief that a better quality of learning takes place when there are opportunities to respond, question, share, collaborate. This is cultural, of course, and based on principles and philo-sophical beliefs as much as hard evidence. The collaborative classroom is the busy, active classroom, and it is the kind of classroom from which the students can emerge having enjoyed the session as much as the teacher. And this notion of enjoyment, of pleasure as motivation, is an integral part of the philosophy embedded in the NCTE beliefs.

2. Next, we shall consider a set of beliefs about education in general, viewing education as a whole, a seamless process, rather than something that is divided up into subjects. Here are some aims for education, as identified by a group of educators at Stanford (Stanford 1995).

What should children know?

Myra Strober
Interim Dean,
School of Education

If I were graduating from high school today, what would I most want to know? At the very core of my being, I would want to know that I respect myself. l would want a clear picture of my skills and strengths – perhaps cognitive, perhaps in other domains – and to be confident that with further training I could earn my livelihood. At the same time, l would want to know that I had the skills to build rich relationships with friends and family and to be an active member of my community. I would want to know a great deal about the intellectual, cultural and spiritual heritages that span the world and to feel a kinship with those whose heritages are different from my own.

Rafael Diaz
Associate Professor of Education,
School of Education

In my opinion, the two most important things a child should learn in school are the love of, or motivation for, learning, and the ability to learn on their own. We call this latter ability 'self-regulated learning'. The term includes children's capacity to formulate good questions, the ability to formulate a plan of study to answer those questions, effective learning and self-monitoring strategies to enact the study plan successfully, and the capacity for self-praise and self-reward. If we can teach children how to self-regulate their learning and how to collaborate with others in their pursuit of relevant answers to their most important questions, then we've done a major part of our job as educators.

Carina Wong
Staff Associate,
Workforce Skills Program,
National Centre on Education and the Economy

A growing number of states have legislated a Certificate of Initial Mastery (CIM). A CIM is one way of defining what children should know by about the tenth grade. First recommended by the Commission on the Skills of the American Workforce, the CIM guarantees that all young people meet rigorous, internationally competitive standards in both core academic and applied learning skills. It is a measure not only of what students know, but also what they can do with what they know. The key is that it is not a time-based standard, but a performance standard worked on over time.

Melanie Sperling
Assistant Professor of Education,
School of Education

After K-12 schooling, children should have writing skills that can serve them in a range of personal and academic situations. If, as they practice and use writing in school, children learn to communicate with both peers and adults, inside and outside the classroom; reflect on and puzzle over them-selves and the world around them; develop interests, discover opinions, and shape ideas that can enlighten others and lead to new learning; set down stories and memories that they and others can enjoy; reach by computer the growing number of individuals who meet on the technical super highway — then K-12 schooling has served them well. We can't forget, either, that it is primarily through their writing that children's knowledge is measured by teachers and administrators — whether it's knowledge of history, science, literature, or math. Writing, in that sense, is a critical gatekeeper as children move through the academic system, past K-12 schooling and on to college or the workplace.

Steve Rowley
Assistant Superintendent,
Bellingham School District

K-12 students in the twenty-first century are better served having the ability to acquire and analyse information than they are knowing vast bodies of organised knowledge through conventionally structured curricula. The ability to work intelligently and critically with information will require skills in the use and application of technology. Students must also be able to demonstrate problem-solving skills in meaningful learning experiences which integrate essential curricular concepts and disciplines. Unlike today's students, the graduates of the future must be able to see the relevance of school work in their lives, now and in the future.

Amy Jo Reinhold
Education Research Specialist,
Save the Children

A child should know how to learn, and that he/she will never stop doing it! He/she should have the knowledge and confidence to formulate questions about a subject and the creativity in using resources to find the answers and/or know where to ask for support. This entails knowing how to access information in a school, family, community, library, database, etc. Communication skills enable a child to use information obtained, so a child needs to know how to coherently express and summarise an idea in writ ten and spoken forms. Every child should know how to combine family and work, and how to blend independence with co-operation in work and play throughout life.

Amado Padilla
Professor of Education,
School of Education

Students should possess effective communication skills in English, foundational knowledge in math and science, and an appreciation of their own and other cultures, including art forms, history, and lifestyles. Students must also be able to use technologies as learning tools efficiently and creatively as well as possess the ability to problem-solve independently and creatively. In addition, students need to be able to participate meaningfully in both a democratic society and an interdependent global community, which means respecting others and having proficiency in a second language. The student should also value learning as a life-long activity, and recognise that knowledge and skill acquisition occurs in many different contexts throughout life.

There is a great deal to unpack in these statements, and we decided to present them to a group of English specialists at the Global Conversations on Language and Literacy conference in Heidelberg in 1996. Working in small groups, we asked the participants to select the three statements, which commanded the most widespread support. The unattributed statements were given the following numbers: Steve Rowley 1; Melanie Sperling 2; Myra Strober 3; Rafael Diaz 4; Amy Jo Reinhold 5; Carina Wong 6; Amado Padilla 7.

Following discussion the group leaders reported their preferences and the outcomes were recorded on the board. The results were as follows:

No groups included number 6 in their preferred three.
All groups included number 3 in their preferred three.

Number 6 concentrates on concepts such as core skills and applied learning. As an instrumental model of education, with a vocational, workplace emphasis, it was not attractive to the participants. It is the one that we might imagine employers wishing to endorse (we discuss whether this is the case in chapter 3) and we might speculate that parents too might respond favourably to the rhetoric of 'rigorous, competitive standards'. We discuss this in chapter 5). It did not match the aspirations of the international group of English specialists in Heidelberg.

If we turn to number 3, which did command widespread support, what is interesting about it is the focus on self, on the 'very core of [my] being', in advance of the references to cognitive and other skills. The focus is not just on the individual, but the innermost part of the individual. Although this statement was not made by an English specialist, we shall be considering the possible explanations for the popularity of this kind of statement among English specialists. For as the broad range of these quotations show, although our concern in this book is with the special subject called English, we shall not be considering it separately from the broad pedagogical and curricular framework in which it is located. In a subject which may be centreless (this issue is one we shall address in our final chapter) the *how* is just as important – perhaps more important – than the *what*. In primary and secondary schools, English specialists have concerned themselves increasingly with the *how*, and in many ways the pedagogy has outstripped the theory of content.

Finally, here are some extracts from a paper entitled *Shaping the Long-Term Strategic Vision* circulated by the Vice Chancellor of a new university in England in an attempt to identify the kind of learning that would take place in university in the twenty-first century. Towards the end of the paper the Vice Chancellor lists some of the elements which a three- or four-page vision statement might contain, and we have selected two which have obvious implications for English:

i. The student population will have become more international and will also reflect a commitment to equal opportunities.
viii. Appropriate technology will support our students on our campuses and in distance learning.

Here, in essence. are two reasons why the pattern of learning, and our beliefs about the role of English in learning, is about to change, and why we have decided to undertake this international investigation now.

Theoretical underpinnings

Although we readily acknowledge that each of us comes to the subject of this book framed by her/his own culture and experiences, we have tried as much as possible to interrogate those framings. We are each a member of our country's national association for the teaching of English, but our own varied histories and specialisms reflect the diversification and tensions that there have always been in subject English. None of us has the simple track record of a literature degree followed by postgraduate research in literature. We have all taken English courses as part of an interdisciplinary project usually at the interface of English and Education, and we are each interested in the part that history and the historicising process has to play in any under-standing of curriculum development and pedagogy as a whole. Yet English as a specific set of practices continues to fascinate us, however chimera like these practices may be.

If our approach to our subject is initially historical, it is also grounded in an awareness of the sociological and ethnographic approaches to the curriculum taken by Ivor Goodson and Stephen J. Ball in the 1980s and 1990s. In a series of books (Goodson and Ball 1984; Ball and Goodson 1985; Goodson 1985; Ball 1987) these two writers drew attention to the political frameworks in which education is shaped, and through ethnographic studies of schools and teachers emphasised the hidden curriculum as well as the formation and construction of curriculum subjects.

The model that underpins the early chapters is Weberian: a belief that the tensions in society between contesting forces, whether economic or political, are endemic and do not represent a phase in modern capitalist society but the necessary condition of it. They also draw on the discussion of education offered by Pierre Bourdieu and Michel Foucault, with an emphasis on subject formation through the agencies of habit and power respectively. Of particular interest is Bourdieu and Passeron's 'involved analysis of the extremely sophisticated mechanisms by which the school system *contributes* to reproducing the structure of the distribution of cultural capital, and, through it, the social structure' (Bourdieu and Passeron 1996, p. vii). This is taken further in the Australian chapters, where the reading of culture and power offered by Foucault, and reinterpreted and applied by Hunter leads to an ultimate belief in the power of bureaucracy and regulation as the shaper of practice. In as far as it is possible to generalise Subject English, as we discuss in chapter 2, has preferred a different, more utopian reading of culture, one which is predicated on the belief that the exercise of the imagination and the fostering of the expressive the individual can by-pass institutionalisation. The later chapters, from the United States, offer this more dynamic and utopian view through a greater emphasis on theories of learning, from Piaget through Dewey to Bruner. All are influenced by the work of sociolinguistics such as Vygotsky and Labov: no model of learning which treats the individual apart from the cultural and social discourses and expectations into which s/he is born can be considered adequate, nor one which uncritically sees the non-standard form as inferior to the standard.

It would be easy to create a binary in which the Weberian–Dewey axis is read as a pessimistic–optimistic world view. That would be a mistake. To emphasise social constructivism and the role of controlling bureaucracy in market economics is not to say that individuals or small groups of human beings are helpless in the face of the forces of expediency and management. Just because a river flows past your front door does not mean that you have to submit to flooding every winter. The river can be managed in such a way that there is space between the floods to exercise some choices about what to do in the summer. But it is clear from this metaphor that collective attempts to build up the river banks are likely to be more effective than individual initiatives.

Yet Subject English has always been a project predicated on individualism. It has its roots in Romantic theory, and its rhetoric throughout the twentieth century has emphasised the personal. The necessity for and beneficial effects of even a limited amount of progressivism are clear to see in our schools in Australia, the United States and England. Work displayed on classroom walls announce the presence of students as well as the wisdom of the ages. Their active participation in learning is encouraged and in English classes the student's own experience is often the source of the most successful work s/he produces. Yet in England and America, such developments have done nothing to change the inequalities in society.

The most significant shift in England at the turn of the century is the final step from a debate about English which is dominated by a discussion about the production and reading of imaginative literature, to a government directed programme which identifies the major problem as one of literacy. The programme is prescriptive, highly centralised and rigorously directed through specific targets and practices – for schools in their literacy hours, for teacher training institutions in their Initial Teacher Training programmes. A more striking illustration of the Weberian and Foucauldian analysis of power it would be difficult to imagine, unless one returns to nineteenth-century payment by results. As John Gray observed in a review of a recent study of Weber:

> For Weber, the spread of rational calculation throughout society is an undoubted good, in that it enables human wants to be satisfied more effectively; but it is also a cultural and moral hazard, since it drains social life of significance and subjects human beings to the meaningless demands of efficient administration.
>
> Gray 1997

If we emphasise the government department over the classroom, it is because we believe that is where attention is increasingly being focused, and where the arguments of Hunter (1994) and Donald (1992) lead us, as we shall later discuss.

Defining a subject: English and learning across the phases

At the beginning of the next chapter we shall draw attention to the difficulty in pinning down a stable, single meaning to the words 'Subject English'. But as if this is not enough, there is a further complication. For even if it is made clear that we are using the term to mean set of pedagogical practices associated with a subject in the curriculum, and are not concerned with other meanings of 'English' such as a cultural group living in Great Britain, or, less obviously, the language that had its origins in this group, that still leaves us in a sea of variables. For example, in England Bethan Marshall's work has shown very clearly that 'English' means something very different in primary schools from what it means in secondary schools and further education (Marshall, personal interview), and our own research shows that the models of English tacitly identified by universities differs markedly from those identified by specialists in schools.

So, for example, primary specialists may have a quite different model of learning from that of their secondary/high school colleagues, being more concerned with specific literacy skills and their measurement. In England the introduction of the literacy hour to primary schools formalises this model. The pedagogy is whole class for forty of the sixty minutes, and although the model is interactive it is teacher- rather than child-centred. Independent and group learning, the pedagogical model favoured in many secondary English lessons in England, is restricted to twenty minutes. At the third level, that of higher education, the 1997 CCUE survey provides a good insight into the state of English in universities and colleges of higher education in England at the end of the century. Although the report (CCUE 1997) records that the majority of the 71 per cent replies accepted that certain key skills are embedded in the English curriculum, it also identified a recurrent concern:

> A worry expressed by many respondents is that English should not be reduced to narrow, or vocationally-oriented perspectives which could stifle the imagination, creativity, originality and empathy which are seen as essential outcomes of current curricular models.
>
> CCUE 1997, p. 7

If that variation in emphasis according to the age-phase is true now, it was also true in the past. One of the reasons that we have acknowledged our debt to Foucault is that much of what we discuss in this book is an analysis of the tracing of *discourses*. One tentative reading of nineteenth-century debates about literacy, education and literature might examine the phase-specific differences in the discourses of education in this way:

Discourse	Text and Ideology	Context
Romantic	Stow/Child-centredness	Schools
	ENGLISH	ASSESSMENT PRACTICES ('silent', dominant discourse?)
Anti-revolution	Burke/State-nation-centred	Universities

There are many problems with this binary: these include the obvious exceptions, and the gap between rhetoric and actual practice. Schools did not become child-centred in the nineteenth century, and the dominant discourse may well have been the 'silent' discourse of assessment and inspection practices. And although it may be useful to see the conservatism of universities as reflections of Burkean warnings against the (French) revolution, and the institutionalisation of a national literature as an extension of these, there are of course discordant voices, such as that of Walter Raleigh. But an awareness of the contribution that an analysis of the dominant discourses can make to our understanding of a subject informs our approach. This is not a new insight: as we see in the collection of essays edited by Stephen J. Ball under the heading of *Foucault and Education: Disciplines and Knowledge*, historical material can be used very effectively 'to explore aspects of the constitution of modern education' through an examination of discursive practice (Ball 1990).

Although our discussion concentrates on secondary and tertiary English, the fact that there are very specific, and sometimes very prescribed, models of English teaching in primary schools should not be forgotten. Secondary and university teachers may not have much recent experience of these schools, but the students they teach not only have, but have had that experience in their formative years.

English, aesthetics and pluralism

One of the implicit accompaniments to any debate about the genesis and development of Subject English, is the genesis and development of the Aesthetic. Debates about aesthetics, whereby the rules of art are formulated and institutionalised, offer to any reader of Subject English an earlier, parallel and similarly paradoxical example of a set of ideas and practices with a rhetoric of autonomy realised through a system of material and commercial practices. In *The Rules of Art*, for example, Bourdieu (1996) traces the way in which Flaubert articulated a set of principles emerging from a belief in the pure gaze and the pure aesthetic, at just the moment when there was a market for symbolic goods. Flaubert both defines, and is defined by, an aesthetic which is demanded by publishers, salons and institutions. In part English, through its early identification with literary studies, joins with that project, and paradoxically makes similar claims for autonomy, as if uncompromised or unmediated by the walls of the fleshly institutions referred to in the preface.

In this book we are addressing a wide audience, and those whose work is rooted in the classroom may already be wondering if we have left the practices of English a long way behind as we consider the wider discourses that surround English. That practice and discourse are inextricably linked we take as given. And we are in good company. When a project of this kind was last undertaken in 1990, James Britton wrote an Introduction to *Teaching and Learning English Worldwide* (Britton, Shaffer and Watson 1990) a book which surveyed the beliefs about teaching English in a much wider variety of countries than is included in our own study. In his 'Introduction' Britton identified a specific tension as in the late 1980s individual specialists and institutional practice seemed to be moving in different directions:

> [G]enerally speaking 'professionalism' and high morale and efficient operating are seen as representing existing gains and pointing the way ahead; authoritarian control, top-down administration – central control of the curriculum in particular – are seen as reactionary, a brake on progress – and a state of affairs we have worked to leave behind. Essentially the contrast is between an educational regime of trust and one of surveillance.
>
> Britton *et al*. 1990, p. 1

That process of centralised control has proceeded apace at a much faster rate than was imagined in 1990. Part of our argument will be that the obvious surveillance which is now common practice in an age of accountability, inspection, published outcomes-based assessment and the rhetoric of the marketplace may be more overtly panopticon like than before, but that surveillance of one kind or another – even if the benevolent, minimalist kind – is a continuous feature of English throughout its history, and that the kind of binary opposition perceived by many of those who have lived through the second half of the twentieth century and summarised by Britton above, does not do justice to the complexities involved in the histories of English. Nor does it represent the kind of adjustments that have had to be made by those who have entered the profession during the last five years.

We began this chapter by identifying the pluralistic approach that has always been characteristic of English, and suggested that living with a certain kind of difference is one of its great strengths. Yet there is a danger too, and that is the belief that if all agendas are possible, then no agenda matters. In our final chapter we shall be arguing that certain democratic practices and frameworks are usefully provided by English teachers. But it is now generally accepted that English is not loosely about allowing children and students to find out things for themselves. Teachers are not gardeners, simply encouraging growth, regarding students as plants. They are more like topiarists, teaching apprentice gardeners how they can shape their own hedges. And they prefer certain patterns to others, and will convey these implicitly to others. These normative practices are not always acknowledged by English teachers and subject specialists.

We discuss our conclusions in the final section of this book. For now let us begin with an account of the position in England. Of the three countries surveyed it is not the first alphabetically, nor is it the biggest or most influential. But English did spread outwards to North America and Australia from England, and so there is a logical reason for starting there.

References

Ball, Stephen J. (1987) *The Micro-politics of the School: Towards a Theory of School Organization*, London: Methuen

Ball, Stephen J. (ed.) (1990) *Foucault and Education: Disciplines and Knowledge*, London: Routledge

Ball, Stephen J. and Goodson, Ivor (eds.) (1985) *Teachers' Lives and Careers*, London: The Falmer Press

Barnes, Douglas and Barnes, Dorothy (1984) *Versions of English*, London: Heinemann Educational

Belsey, C. (1989) 'Towards Cultural History – in Theory and Practice' in *Textual Practice*, Vol. 3, No. 2, Summer 1989, pp. 159–172

Bloom, A. (1987) *The Closing of the American Mind*, New York: Simon and Schuster

Bloom, Harold (1994) *The Western Canon*, London: Macmillan

Bourdieu, Pierre (1996) *The Rules of Art*, trans. by Susan Emanuel, Oxford: Polity Press

Bourdieu, Pierre and Passeron, Jean-Claude (1996) *Reproduction in Education, Society and Culture*, London: Sage Publications

Britton, James, Shaffer, Robert E., Watson, Ken (1990) *Teaching and Learning English Worldwide*, Clevedon, England: Multilingual Matters

Connor, Steve (1989) *Postmodernist Culture*, Oxford: Blackwell

Council for College and University English (CCUE) (1997) *The English Curriculum: Diversity and Standards*, Cambridge: CCUE

Davies, C. (1996) *What is English Teaching?* Buckingham: Open University Press

Donald, James (1992) *Sentimental Education: Schooling, Popular Culture and the Regulation of Liberty*, London: Verso

Elbow, Peter (1983) *What is English?* Urbana, Illinois: Modern Languages Association and NCTE

Easthope, Anthony (1990) *Literacy into Cultural Studies*, London: Routledge

Goodson, Ivor (1985) *Social Histories of the Secondary Curriculum*, London: Falmer Press

Goodson, Ivor and Ball, Stephen J. (eds.) (1984) *Defining the Curriculum: Histories and Ethnographies*, London: The Falmer Press

Gray, J. (1997) Review of 'Max Weber' by J. Diggins, *Times Literary Supplement*, 26 September 1997

Guy, J. and Small, I. (1993) *Politics and Value in English Studies: A Discipline in Crisis*, Cambridge: Cambridge University Press

Heilbrun, Carolyn G. (1986) 'Bringing the Spirit Back to English Studies', in E. Showalter (ed.) (1986) *The New Feminist Criticism*, London, Virago (1993: 23)

Hunter, Ian (1988) *Culture and Government: The Emergence of Literary Education*, London: Macmillan

Hunter, Ian (1994) *Rethinking the School*, Sydney: Allen and Unwin

Ingleby, David (1994) *Times Literary Supplement*, 23 December 1994

Inglis, F. (1985) *The Management of Ignorance: A Political Theory of the Curriculum*, Oxford: Basil Blackwell

Leavis, F. R. (1943) *Education and the University: A Sketch for an English School*, London: Chatto and Windus

Lyotard, J. F. (1979) *The Postmodern Condition: A Report on Knowledge*, trans. G. Mennington, Manchester: Manchester University Press, 1986

McCormick, Kathleen (1994) *The Culture of Reading and the Teaching of English*, Manchester: Manchester University Press

MacNeice, Louis (1964) *Selected Poems of Louis MacNeice*, Selected and Introduced by W. H. Auden, London: Faber and Faber

Martin, Nancy (1983) 'Contexts are more important than we know', in Roslyn Arnold (1983) *Timely Voices: English Teaching in the 1980s*, Melbourne: Oxford University Press

Morgan, Robert (1990) 'The Englishness of English Teaching' in Ivor Goodson and Peter Medway (1990) *Bringing English to Order*, London: The Falmer Press

NCTE (1990) *NCTE's Position on the Teaching of English: Assumptions and Practices*, Working Paper Developed by the Elementary, Secondary and College Sections 1988–89, Urbana, Illinois: NCTE

Norris, Christopher (1988) *Deconstruction: Theory and Practice*, London: Methuen

Peel, R. and Hargreaves, S. (1995) 'Beliefs about English: Trends in Australia, England and the United States', *English in Education*, Volume 29 No. 3 Autumn 1995

Reed, Webster and Beveridge (1994)

Southworth, Kathryn (1995) ' "Falling Towers": The Fate of the English Empire', *CCUE News*, July 1995, Issue 5

Stanford (1995) *What Should Children Know?* Stanford University School of Education Information Bulletin: Stanford, California

Webster, A., Beveridge, M., and Reed, M. (1996) *Managing the Literacy Curriculum*, London: Routledge

Wilson, J. L. (1988) 'Lice in the Locks of Literature' in *Salisbury Review*, 7 December 1988, pp. 26–28

Wimsat, W. K. and Beardsley, M. C. (1954) *The Verbal Icon: Studies in the Meaning of Poetry*, Lexington, Kentucky: University of Kentucky Press.

Part I

England: questions of history, theory and curriculum

2 English in England: its history and transformations

Robin Peel

'When *I* use a word', Humpty Dumpty said in a rather scornful tone, 'it means just what I choose it to mean – neither more nor less.'
'The question is', said Alice, 'whether you *can* make words mean different things.'
'The question is', said Humpty Dumpty, 'which is to be master – that's all.'

Lewis Carroll, *Through the Looking Glass* (1871)

ISSUES FRAMING A READING OF THE HISTORY OF ENGLISH

- Pinning down 'English'
- English as literacy: learning to read and write
- State education and the emergence of Subject English
- Mapping the history: before and after Subject English
- Assessment and history
- Where we came from: the historiography of Subject English

Pinning down 'English'

Any attempt to clarify the meaning of the word 'English' will tend to support Humpty Dumpty's observation that the meaning of a word is governed by whoever is in control. 'English' is a wriggling, elusive kind of term, one which refuses to be pinned down. Rob Pope opens his substantial survey of English Studies by confronting this slipperiness. He summarises the transformations that have taken place across the centuries about what the word 'English' is meant to signify (Pope 1998), but the more we try to be precise the more we are likely to end up quarrelling over definitions. By 'English', do we mean the language, literatures or Literature, a subject with a set of practices, literacy, or all of the above? The term resists and defies any such simple glossing.

Reading histories of Subject English can be a similarly confusing experience. One critic, Franklin D. Court, begins his account of the institutialisation of

English by informing the reader that 'the first serious efforts to introduce English literary study into the university curriculum in Britain were made in eighteenth century Scotland' (Court 1992, 17). According to Stephen J. Ball, Subject English starts to make its appearance in official reports in the late nineteenth century (Ball 1985, p. 54). Later a Board of Education *Report* covering the period 1882–90 notes that there had been a 'continuance of the emphasis in English which had prevailed in the previous period' (Board of Education 1910). The disagreement about countries and centuries is puzzling if goes unnoticed that the writers are discussing quite different phases of education and are flexible about terminology. Alastair Fowler (1998), drawing on the thesis outlined in Robert Crawford's *Devolving English Literature* (Crawford 1992) and following the line proposed by Court, argues convincingly that the Scottish Enlightenment in general and the Edinburgh divine Hugh Blair (1718–1800) in particular were responsible for the foundation of English literary studies, though Blair's lectures at Edinburgh University announced their field as 'rhetoric and belles-lettres' or 'rhetoric and criticism' rather than 'English'.

For a reference to 'English' to take on any meaning, certain specificities must be provided, such as how English is being defined, whether the context is elementary or secondary schools or universities, and the historical moment when the remark in which the word appears was made. To reduce the opportunities for contradiction there is a need to historicise texts. Between the years 1905 and 1912, for example, when a particularly interesting series of reports on English in schools was published there were struggles between models of English based on grammar and models based on the reading of literature, there were developments in child-centred pedagogy that were affecting elementary schools much more than secondary, and as always there was a time lag between the rhetoric of official publications and widespread classroom practice. All of these have an impact on how the word 'English' is to be read.

It is also necessary to consider the relationship between English and other practices. Some of these, such as rhetoric, classics, theology and literacy precede the emergence of English as a subject, while others, such as film studies, cultural studies, communication and media studies, gender studies and critical theory are not only younger than English, they can threaten to engulf and replace it. A third set of practices – close, careful reading, literary criticism and the creation of crafted, original writing, whether creative, discursive or critical, are contemporaneous with the emergence of English, and are so central to the school curriculum that they are likely to guarantee its survival well into the twenty-first century and beyond.

English as literacy: learning to read and write

The language called English can be traced to its Middle and Old English forms, but the set of practices which came to be discussed in a category and a subject called 'English' is little more than 150 years old. In the Middle Ages any reference to the idea of English as a subject on the curriculum would have created puzzlement: English was simply the language spoken by ordinary people, and in England it simply did not have the status of either Latin or French. To be literate in one's own local language was a mere staging post in the journey made by the small percentage of the population that was 'educated' towards the goal of expertise in the 'universal' languages of Greek and Latin, or the administrative language of French. Literature meant Classical texts, and grammar meant Latin and Greek.

As David Cressy has shown in his study of illiteracy in England 1530–1730 (Cressy 1981), the majority remained illiterate. Using court depositions as his source, he is able to conclude that during this period over half the population was illiterate, that illiteracy was more widespread among women than it was among men, and that throughout this period it remained stubbornly tied to occupation and social structure, despite periods of educational advance. Even after 1750, when as Roger Schofield shows in his study of illiteracy in England 1750–1850 (Schofield 1981) and using marriage registers as his source, the figure began to move towards the 40 per cent literacy rate which appeared to have been reached by 1850, the rate of progress was uneven and subject to regional, local and gender factors. Female illiteracy, for example, was very high in areas of high female industrial employment; for example, it was still 84 per cent in Oldham in 1846.

If English is identified with the set of practices in place in schools to encourage literacy, then it possible to trace something we would recognise as English teaching right back to the sixteenth century, as Ian Michael does in his comprehensively researched account *The Teaching of English from the Sixteenth Century to 1870* (Michael 1987). It is unlikely those in the grammar schools, the ragged schools, the elementary schools and the public schools in England would have encountered a subject simply called 'English'. Rather, there would have been lessons in handwriting, in spelling, in reading and in memorising literature for later recital. In the grammar schools and the public (that is private, fee-paying schools) Latin occupied the domain later to be occupied by English, in that in Latin the pupil would encounter literature, essays, rhetoric and grammar – this was precisely why the schools were known as 'grammar' schools. There were few schools for the poor before the Sunday Schools took on the role of educating them, moral improvement being the aim of a basic literacy programme designed to encourage the reading of the Bible. Eventually the state was to take over this supervisory role, with the passing of the 1870 Forster Act, which required Boards of Education to be set up, and to provide elementary education on the rates for all children.

In one reading Michael's account of the teaching of reading and writing in schools in England is testimony to the educational establishment's response to the rising clamour for increased literacy in the vernacular that dates back to the introduction of the printing press. Despite licensing bodies and laws, print could not really be controlled, and so it became necessary to control the reader. This is a point brought out with a slightly different emphasis by John Willinsky in 'Lessons from the Literacy Before Schooling' (Willinsky 1993), which describes the vibrancy of working-class print culture in the half century before state education. Whether through the production of petitions, 'hawked papers in the name of universal suffrage, a ten-hour working day and fair prices' or the desire for engagement and activism expressed in placard and poetry, there was an exuberant, outspoken form of literacy which state schooling conveniently buried. From dame school to the Chartists' setting up of the Peoples College in Sheffield in 1842, from the Female Societies to the Mechanics Institutes, from literary societies to the working-class Sunday Schools, there was a powerful tradition of autodidacticism on which English was to draw. According to Willinsky little of it led to economic self advancement: people read out of 'an interest in the new sciences and the stories that literature had to tell' and because they wanted to advance social and political causes. English was to draw on this broader, dynamic understanding of the power of language, one that went well beyond notions of 'functional literacy'.

There are other genealogies of English to be examined. One reading of the roots of English would go even further back, emphasising the role of Henry VIII in encouraging the teaching of English in English, and the spread of schools during this period. Another reading might focus on methodology. Michael's account of the changing fashion for phonics-based methods, abandoned in the nineteenth century when they were discovered to be unsuccessful, is a remarkable commentary on some of the late twentieth-century debates about reading methods that have taken place in the United States, in Australia, and in the United Kingdom. Yet another reading would explore the relationship between literacy and economics: Schofield, in the essay mentioned above, challenges the assumption that the coincidence in the rise in literacy and the rise in economic growth reflects a cause and effect. Our particular interest is in the history and genealogy of the pedagogy of English in England, acknowledges these readings, and attempts to add to them, in the light of the work of Ian Hunter, Pierre Bourdieu and others. Our reading reflects an interest in the kind of question indicated by the title of an essay by Johan Galtung (1981): 'Literacy, education and schooling: for what?'

State education and the emergence of Subject English

One of the drawbacks of reading the history of a country's education from the *inside* is that once a dominant national reading emerges all future discussion takes place in relation to that dominant reading. This is illustrated by considering the way that state education evolved in England in the nineteenth century. In the Whig reading of history, the reading that dominated the nineteenth- and early twentieth-century interpretation of events in both England and the United States, the spread of popular education in England

and the introduction of state education under the 1870 Act was the response to the demands of the population for access to the literacy and knowledge which had hitherto been only the right of the privileged. What this skates over, as Andy Green (1990) has pointed out, is why England was so *late* in introducing a public system of education, compared to much of the rest of Europe and the United States. Finding that neither a classic marxist interpretation (state education is a response to changes in the economic modes of production) nor a Weberian analysis (the introduction of state education reflects changes in the social structure) Green, drawing on Gramsci's theory of hegemony, proposes an explanation in terms of state formation.

In essence this reading of history acknowledges the brilliant success of England in the first stage of the industrial revolution in the early part of the nineteenth century. The failure to consolidate this position – ironically many historians trace the beginning of the decline of Britain, which continues to this day, to 1870 when both Germany and the United States became significant and ultimately successful rivals – is linked to the late development of state apparatus involving an effective bureaucracy and a national education system. This in turn led to a declining culture of innovation and a failure to match the pace of rapid technological advance that characterised the first state of the industrial revolution.

Why should this be? There had been attempts to introduce state education into England in the early nineteenth century but these had always been defeated by the ideological preference for voluntaryism, the same liberal-aristocratic alliance that defeated public education moves in the southern states of the USA during the same period. The argument advanced was always the same liberal one, that freedom and state education are incompatible. Green argues that it is right to see this partly as evidence of the power of the landowner class, but ultimately the dominant – or 'hegemonic' – rhetoric came not from a single class but was evidence of an ideology that had been mediated *between* classes. For society as a whole this meant the triumph of immediate financial interest over rational argument, and the characteristic 'amateurishness' of the English state. For education, even after the 1870 Act, it meant a system of education in which the voluntary sector continued to be the most important in terms of influence, whether in terms of private schools outside the state system, or church schools within it. The absence of a National Curriculum until 1989, and the shift towards the local management of schools in the 1990s can be seen as further evidence of the legacy of history.

Yet Green's reading of the history of state education as a missed opportunity to create the Chartist dream of democratic, emancipatory schools, largely because middle-class reformers were ultimately serving a class sectional interest which required policing and control rather than freedom and creativity, is itself questioned in Hunter's *Rethinking the School* (Hunter 1994). For Hunter what was is what had to be, and more important than the deep principles which the rhetoric of the time might espouse are the 'contingent circumstances in which the school system came into being' (Hunter 1994, Introduction) which a genealogical analysis can foreground.

Mapping the history: before and after Subject English

- Grammar and rhetoric
- Before and after English

Rhetoric and grammar

Long before the subject category 'English' emerged in the nineteenth century there were antecedents in a pedagogical tradition that came from the oral cultures of Greece and Rome. In classical times the practice of oratory – public speaking – gave rise to the study of *rhetoric*, the means by which the orator constructed his speech (this was a masculine discourse) and persuaded his audience. This was a tradition adopted up by the mediaeval church, and practised through sermons every Sunday. With the emergence of a print culture in the early modern period, the rules of rhetoric were applied to writing, and became the rules governing the writing of the essay, the paper, the dissertation. Questions about how an essay should begin, how it should organise its argument, and how it should end would have been familiar to the seventeenth- and eighteenth-century scholars and public schoolboys, and represented the next stage in language and literary study after the acquisition of basic literacy.

An alternative way of approaching language, one which was considered quite distinct, was through the study of grammar. This study concentrated on the content of language rather than its meaning, and assumed that the two could be regarded as separate. Recently Frances Christie has described the significance of this split for the history of English. In her essay 'The "Received Tradition" of English Teaching' (Christie 1993), she takes the argument forward into the second half of the twentieth century. She suggests that this division was responsible for the rejection of language study in the 'Growth' model that emerged in England following the Dartmouth Conference. As we shall see, the pendulum has since swung the other way, so that the current preoccupation is very much with our old friends grammar (in schools) and rhetoric (in higher education). The systematic teaching of grammar is recommended in *The Grammar Papers*, a series of essays published by the Qualifications and Curriculum Authority in 1998 to support the increased emphasis on grammar teaching and assessment (QCA 1998). Contentless English is regularly filled with fresh material, much of it recycled, but some of it new. Ruth Merttens, Professor of Education at the College of St Mark and St John, quotes Vygotsky as a reason why we ought to teach pupils grammar: it allows children to reflect more explicitly on their own use of language, and provides them with a metalanguage with which they can discuss their own writing (Merttens 1998). Such a view, once regarded with great scepticism by a significant number of teachers in England, is increasingly becoming the turn-of-century orthodoxy.

Before and after English

Any attempt to recount the history of the set of practices known as English must necessarily be a reading of the past that is as provisional as its predecessor readings, of which a number have been published. To do so from the perspective of the turn of the century in England offers one advantage, however, which is that for the first time in over a century English, as a subject domain in schools has ceased – perhaps only temporarily – from spreading. In countries other than England it is actually shrinking as a field. In England, however, it has entered a period of retrenchment, and is defending its ground, rather than taking over the ground of others. But in higher education in particular, that territory is considerable.

As figure 1 shows, the development of English from its incarnation as literary studies has paralleled the birth and growth of state education in England. Though their development has not been in perfect tandem, both English and state education are children of the grand-narrative reading of culture, which is optimistic, forward looking and positivist. As the diagram indicates, both practices overlayed (and disguised) the already existing practices of literacy and numeracy, and the promoters of each employed a rhetoric which proposed that state education in general, and English in particular, could become the agents of change which would bring about a transformation in society. In England they both expanded and developed their fields throughout the twentieth century, but whereas state control of the curriculum reached unimagined levels of prescription and assessment in the 1990s, English (precisely because of the success and strength of its twin) struggled to hold on to its position in the nest, and for once the cuckoo bird is in danger of being expelled by the offspring of the nestbuilders.

The preoccupation of English with its own survival marks its decline as the most high profile of subjects, and as figure 2 suggests, the continuing fragmentation of English has made it vulnerable in the face of the triumph of a marketplace ideology. English departments in schools, and to a lesser extent in colleges and universities, are presented with the prospect of a future in which their role is defined simply in terms of their ability to guarantee literacy: that was the emphasis given by the Labour Party which went on to form the government following the 1997 General Election.

It may thus be premature to envisage a future called 'after English', as the diagram suggests, because its role as a core subject in the National Curriculum and its assessment at ages 7, 11, 14, 16 and 18 ensures that it continues to enjoy a central place in school curriculum. But the 'it' is not the set of practices which have until now given English in England a particular

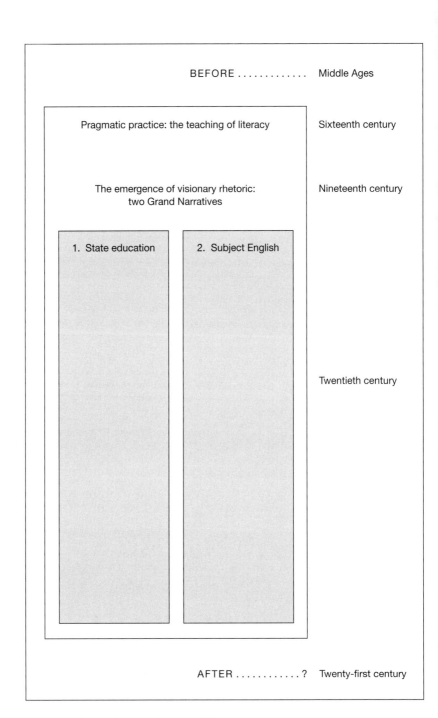

Figure 1 Before and after Subject English

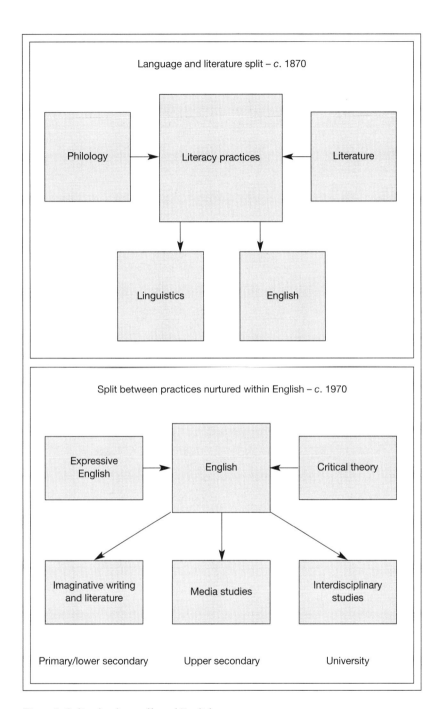

Figure 2 Splits that have affected English

character, and which we shall be describing and illustrating in this and the following chapter. Literacy and English are not the same thing. English includes literacy, but then so do all subjects which include reading and writing. English specialists in secondary schools, colleges and universities recognise the symbiotic relationship between literacy and English, but they have other ambitions for the subject. There are other configurations, including cultural studies, media studies, post-colonial studies and other interdisciplinary and multi-disciplinary combinations that may challenge the central place that English has won for itself in the twentieth-century school, college and university curriculum.

Assessment and history

In contrast to the widely shared belief that assessment should reflect practice, a belief we shall be reporting in the next chapter, there is much evidence to show that in most cases it is the other way round. The history of English in the twentieth century is the history of a battle to achieve recognition through assessment. In the nineteenth century that battleground had been the university, where after much opposition English had been grudgingly given the status of a degree subject. As Stephen Ball (1985) reminds us, schools had to wait for similar recognition until 1918, when English was included in the Modern Studies group of Advanced Courses that were the stepping stone to higher education. Again there had been opposition: initially, English had been omitted from the Advanced Courses altogether, and accorded the status of a subordinate subject, but intense lobbying from the members of the English Association, who were enjoying considerable influence at this time (given that they included Quiller Couch and Henry Newbolt we should not be surprised) successfully persuaded the Board of Education to include English as one of the two modern languages that could be taken.

At the other end of the century, after School Certificate, O level, CSE, 100 per cent coursework it is the National Curriculum Key Stage Assessments that are again determining practice. The dominance of the skills model of English, written into the tests at Key Stage 2 and Key Stage 3, prescribes the content and pedagogy of English in the middle school years. There is hardly anything more instantly revealing of the way in which the subject is constructed than the forms of assessment that are in use at the time. In the nineteenth century teaching in English involved rehearsal for tests involving the parsing of sentences and composition on an abstract subject. In practice this meant separate lessons in the principles of grammar and in imitative composition. The study of literature involved learning of lines of poetry by heart and an account of the lives of certain poets. Assessment is always governed by what it is possible to assess, and frequently by what it is easiest to assess. We may be amused by the narrowness and pedantry of early twentieth-century requirements such as the following:

Standard 4 (10 years)
Reading To read a passage from a reading book or history of England
Writing Eight lines of poetry or prose, slowly read once, then dictated.
'English' Parsing easy sentences, and showing by examples the use of
each of the parts of speech

Shayer 1972, pp. 4–5

But an examination of the grammar questions in Key Stage Two and Key
Stage Three English in England might give us pause to reflect.

Where we came from: the historiography of Subject English

History teaches us that once a community feels reasonably well established or
when it feels it is about to transform itself, it starts to write its own history. It
wants to know where it comes from, what its roots were, and what kind of
beliefs informed its early creation. There is a sense in which 'subjects are their
histories' (Inglis 1985). Over the past thirty years there have been several
studies of the origins of English, from D. J. Palmer's much-cited *The Rise of
English Studies* (1965) and Margaret Mathieson's equally influential *The
Preachers of Culture: A Study of English and its Teachers* (1975) to Chris
Baldick's *The Social Mission of English Criticism* (1983). Each of these understands 'English' to be a set of practices particularly associated with literature
and criticism, rather than the range of activities associated with literacy. In
'English for the English Since 1906' (Ball 1985) Stephen J. Ball begins by
emphasising the competing paradigms that accompanied the emergence of
English, as grammarian-led models influenced by the classics competed with
child-centred and literature-based models.

Frequently the more recent study offers a revision of the position taken by
a predecessor: Guy and Small (1993) challenge Brian Doyle's heavy emphasis
on the role of nationalism in the transformation of English in England
following the First World War and argue that Subject English has always been
weakened by having no clear object. Sometimes an overview is attempted, as
in Arthur N. Applebee's *Tradition and Reform in the Teaching of English: A
History* (1974) in the United States while sometimes the decision has been
made to concentrate on what are seen as key periods, as in John Dixon's *A
Schooling in English* (1991). A more recent American study than Applebee's,
and one offering a different ideological perspective, is Gerald Graff's
Professing Literacy (1987), while in *Culture and Government* Ian Hunter (1988),
drawing on Foucault's reading of culture, sees the emergence of popular
literary education as a product of, rather than resistance to, governance.

More recent discussion has included an emphasis on the emergence of
'English' outside England, as part of the colonial process of ensuring the
survival of the language and ideology of the dominant colonial culture. A
draft report from the Academic Standards Panel of the Australian Vice

Chancellors' Committee places the study of English in a specific historical perspective:

> The academic study of English was not, in the main, England's invention. With the partial exception of the University of London, English literature as a separate area of the syllabus became established in universities out-side England long before it found a place in its homeland. It made its debut in Scottish universities in the eighteenth century, and in the middle years of the nineteenth it began to emerge in such outposts of Empire as India . . . , New Zealand . . . , Canada – and of course Australia . . . as well as in the United States.
>
> ASP 1994

This kind of reading offers a contrasting perspective to the accounts of both Eagleton (1983) and Dixon, which emphasise the role of working class movements, whether the extension colleges, the mechanics' institutes or the societies of schoolmistresses, in the emergence of literary English as a subject in England in the nineteenth century. Elsewhere, in their collection of essays on ten pioneering women in NCTE, Jeanne Gerlach and Virginia Monseau (1991) emphasise the role of women in the development of English Education in the United States.

These contrasting versions of a history of English indicate how the origins of English have become the site for contesting readings of power, class and gender, all echoing current concerns about the role of English in the twentieth – and in the twenty-first – century. Some of these are explored in Goodson and Medway's *Bringing English to Order* (1990), many of the essays in which testify to the normative role always assigned to English. Let us now trace the roots of some of these beliefs and tendencies, by examining certain strands in the history of English in England. We shall concentrate on two, first by considering their origins in the intellectual frameworks of the seventeenth, eighteenth and nineteenth centuries, and then by focusing on the first quarter of the twentieth. Other studies have dealt thoroughly with the birth of English in the nineteenth-century universities, with the period of Cambridge English in the 1920s and 1930s, and with the post-Dartmouth period of the 1960s and 1970s. In the discussion of English in England, special attention will be given to the neglected pre-First World War period, and in chapter that follows the voices of those from the present will allow us to reflect on continuity and change.

ENGLISH AND SCIENCE IN NINETEENTH-CENTURY ENGLAND

- Teaching poor children to read and write
- Changes in schools and universities: looking beyond Matthew Arnold

- Writing Science and Literature
- English as Not-Science

Teaching poor children to read and write

In the early years of the nineteenth century, before state education was introduced in England, those schools for the poor which existed were run by Christian charities such as the British and Foreign School Society. Joseph Lancaster's school at Borough Road, founded in 1798, soon spawned a small associated training college, and from this the world came to learn of what was soon to become Lancaster's famous method. The pedagogical practice that was the monitorial system was regimented, cheap and self regulating, in that senior children (superintending monitors) were appointed to supervise middle management children (monitors) who in turn taught the workforce (the pupils). The teacher functioned as inspector.

The institutional base was the schoolroom (rather than the classroom) in which large numbers of children, subdivided into groups of fifty, who were in turn subdivided into groups of ten to fifteen pupils at 'draft stations', where the monitors instructed and questioned them. All of this is described in the British and Foreign Society's Manuals, which indicate exactly how the day is to be divided up, what is to be done minute by minute, and the precise cost of setting up a schoolroom of this kind (approximately £19. 8s. 0d.).

The teaching of literacy involved rote learning, dictation for writing on slates, and writing on paper. The 1837 manual indicates just how this was to be regulated by indicating the instructions to be called out by the superintending monitor (always the general monitor for arithmetic, for some reason). The following extract begins at a point when the pupils have been asked to show the condition of the textbooks from which they will be copying. A brief pause is understood to follow each instruction, as the command is carried out:

'Front'
'Lay-down – Books'
'Hands down'
Copyslips and papers are then distributed.
'Begin'
The writing commences: pupils are not allowed to exceed five lines.
At the close
'Writers'
'Clean pens'
'Show pens'
'Lay down pens'
'Hands down'
'Monitors – gather up pens'
Pens are collected by monitors.

'Gather up copies'
The monitors take up each boy's copyslip.
'Shew books'
The master inspects.
'Lay down books'
'Shut books'
Monitors gather the books, and put them away.

BFSS 1837

This procedure seems to be a very large, possibly whole school, exercise. Reading would take place at draft stations, using passages that had been previously written on the board, or books if available. One pupil would sound out letters, a more able pupil would repeat specific words, while a more able pupil still would read the whole sentence aloud.

To vary the teaching, the manual recommends the interrogative method, which involves the rapid firing of questions in exactly the manner of 'Bitzer – definition of a horse' in Dickens's novel *Hard Times*, which is no parody at all as the 1837 Manual has a section on The Elephant in exactly this style, and no humour is intended.

It is important to visualise this model of teaching, including the pedagogical relationship, that was in place when the elements of literacy – composition, reading, writing, grammar, literature and recitation, began to come together under the umbrella 'English' in the second half of the nineteenth century. By then the monitorial system had been found wanting. The 1856 *Handbook to the Borough Road Schools* (BFSS 1856) reports that collective teaching, led by the schoolmaster, had now taken over, with pupil-teachers serving as assistants, although the monitorial system had not been abandoned altogether, and used 'judiciously' still had a role to play. In the Index, under the heading 'Agency to be employed', Section 1 is Pupil Teachers and Section 2 is Monitors. An industrial model still pertained, and the pupils were still objects to be fashioned and engineered. Before we can discuss the journey made by Subject English away from this model, it is crucial that we have a clear picture of the way it functioned as part of the monitorial system. Its closest modern parallel is the method of drilling soldiers on the parade-ground: in 'Docile Bodies' Foucault (1991) pointed out the debt that nineteenth-century French education owed to the military, and the way that in England in particular the school became a 'machine for learning'.

Changes in schools and universities: looking beyond Matthew Arnold

If the monitorial school system allowed the teacher to be the inspector, the more expensive model of teacher and class meant that role passed to an outsider. The state inspection of schools began with the recruitment of the first two Her Majesty's Inspectors in 1839, following the payment of government grants for the education of the poor six years earlier. Inspection came with the grant. By 1850 there were twenty-three HMIs, usually recruited from the relatively comfortable graduates of Oxford and Cambridge, whose backgrounds and educational experiences were very different from those of the children they inspected. Their role become even more prominent following the Revised Code of 1862, which meant that payments to schools were dependent on the results of children in reading, writing and arithmetic: all three had to be passed if there was to be a grant for that particular child.

In earlier accounts of the emergence of English in the nineteenth century Matthew Arnold was often regarded as the dominant influence on the development of literary studies away from the mechanistic model that had developed in the monitorial schools and the early British schools.. As a poet, as an observer of contemporary culture, but most importantly as a School Inspector, he appeared unique in the way he brought together a variety of beliefs about aesthetics, education and literature which advanced the argument supporting the importance of Subject English as a unique practice in the school and university curriculum. His influence *was* significant, as the following discussion of the debates surrounding the rivalry of Science and English will seek to demonstrate, but several recent studies have challenged Arnold's centrality in debates about the pedagogy of English. Ian Hunter, for example, considers the way that the emergence of English coincides with a shift in the pedagogical relationship (Hunter 1988, 1994) and in this respect Kay-Shuttleworth and David Stow are the more important figures in the development of English in schools. Franklin Court (Court 1992) similarly argues that Arnold's influence on higher education has also been exaggerated, at the expense of early professors of English such as A. J. Scott (Professor of English at University College, London, 1848), F. D. Maurice, and David Masson:

> [T]he general, uncritical acceptance of the supposition that Arnold the literary critic, or Arnold the social critic, or even Arnold the School Inspector, was primarily responsible for the influence of the humanist myth out of which literary study evolved, really is the issue here, especially if the knowledge of Arnold is limited mainly to anthology pieces, as is so often the case.
>
> Court 1992, p. 6

Court takes a robust line on this subject, making a clear distinction between the creation of the belief in the humanising effect of literature and art (the 'humanist myth') and its impact on the curriculum and pedagogy of schools. As he points out, Arnold was not unequivocally in favour of the institutionalisation of literary study in either schools or universities:

> Arnold neither favoured autonomous English programs nor invented the direction that literary study actually took. He was the most

influential critic in England in the 1860s, but his influence on the teaching of English Literature never matched his success as a critic. That is the point that many current scholars who accuse Arnold of inventing English Studies seem unable to recognize.

Court 1992, p. 117

Court's argument is that although Arnold argued forcefully that literature should have a central place in the culture of 'high seriousness' that would act as an antidote to the perceived materialism of science, the utilitarianism of Bentham, and the economic man of the future as envisaged by Adam Smith, he had reservations about how this might be managed by those running the universities. Like many of his contemporaries, Arnold believed in the importance of identifying the essence of national style – the spirit of the nation – and that this was necessary to advance the race. 'He wanted to symbolically reinterpret history through the genealogical or evolutionary study of literature' (Court 1992, p. 109), but his belief in the value of disinterested inquiry – the 'modern spirit' – led him to a broad interpretation of culture, one which must of necessity draw on the best of the outside world. It must look beyond English Literature, not only into the past of the civilising Hellenic light, but into the best of the present European literature and thought. He was wary of the potential for the limiting, racial, nationalistic insularity that the study of English Literature as an autonomous element in the university curriculum could bring about. He admired the liberal German academies, and in his report to the Schools Inquiry Commission *Schools and Universities on the Continent* (1867) endorsed the view that state education could bring about the desired change, converting cultural authority into political authority through the process of state sponsorship. The model was not the promotion of English Literature but *Alterntums-wissenschaft*, a programme of comparative study in classical antiquity, which was quite different from the old pedagogical practice in England of treating Latin, Greek and philological study as ends in themselves.

On the subject of Arnold's influence Court concludes:

> What Arnold's discussion of Alterntumswissenschaft in the 1867 School report makes clear is that he did not direct the development of English literary studies in the last half of the nineteenth century . . . At mid-century, comparative philology, and not Arnold, was still the primary determining force shaping the development of English literary studies.

Court 1992, p. 116

The analysis of power put forward by Foucault and Bourdieu, and the specific arguments advanced by Hunter and Court have been influential, so that the simple 'top-down' models of the history of subject English are no longer tenable. If Hunter acknowledges the crucial role of Stow and Kay-

Shuttleworth in schools, Court points to the role of Brougham, the Whig peer, who was influential in promoting and realising the idea of a secular university for the educable masses (the middle classes), and in recommending literary study as part of the curriculum. London University was founded in 1828 as a result of this campaign, and the first Professor of English, Thomas Dale, who was appointed in 1828, had been supported by Brougham. The succession of professors of English at University College and King's College, London were clearly key players in determining the character of literary study in this and other universities. Especially influential were A. J. Scott, Professor of English at University College from 1848, and F. D. Maurice, who held the Chair of English Literature and History at King's College from 1840–1846, the complementary bringing together of the disciplines at King's being 'a key moment in the history of English studies' according to Court (Court 1992, p. 87). Finally, Court draws attention to the work of David Masson at University College.

In many ways Masson realised some of Arnold's fears about the consequence of institutionalising the study of English, as he was both caught up and contributed to debates about ethnography and racial identity, a discourse reflected in the examinations he set, and the course he instituted at University College. The interest in race led to an emphasis on language, and literature as part of national history.

> Masson should be remembered not only for his interest in using literature to promote the superiority of native English culture, but also for his support for history as a necessary complement to literary study.
>
> Court 1992, p. 131

By the 1870s, argues Court, his, rather than comparative philology, or the broader humanist horizons sketched in by Arnold, was the 'primary shaping force on language study'. English was to serve Empire:

> The spectacle of . . . five thousand students, with five thousand sets of circulating notes, setting out throughout the commonwealth [sic] to promote the bond between English literature and the English racial identity enables us to appreciate more clearly the tremendous impact that Masson and the English professors who succeeded him had on promoting and shaping the cultural and political character of the discipline.
>
> Court 1992, pp. 131–2

All of this is not to mention the part played by Mechanics Institutes, and Women's Associations, each of whom provided evidence of the democratic demand for literary study in the wider population, and the popularising role of Walter Raleigh, who in succession held Chairs at Liverpool, Glasgow and Oxford, being appointed to Oxford's first Professorship in English that did not include Anglo-Saxon in 1904. Each of these may have had a very significant, and sometimes unrecognised, influence on the way that English was actually taught and developed within institutions. But changes in practice take place in response to the success of one of a series of competing discourses, and in the following discussion of competing nineteenth-century discourses we shall see that Arnold had a significant part to play.

Writing, science and literature

Earlier I indicated the problematic nature of the term 'English': to use the word as a signifier itself begs a number of questions about the architecture and archaeology of knowledge. It is a term that is reluctant to be pinned down. There is, however, a discourse surrounding English, which is expressed in the titles of journals, conferences, professional associations and departments. In the survey of fifty UK university prospectuses carried out in 1995 (Peel 1995) it was revealed that forty-one advertised a section or department with 'English' in the title. Furthermore, the second of the two periods in which we shall be locating a discussion of our two key ideas – English as an alternative to science, and English as a self-regulating practice – is the period from 1906 to 1921, a period which coincides with the birth and growth of the body called the English Association. But let us start with one of the more interesting nineteenth-century debates, which feeds directly into the later period.

The well-documented anti-science stance taken in the nineteenth century by the advocates of literary studies was revived in the twentieth and informed thinking and discussion during the key period 1906–21, culminating in the definition of English as a school subject in the Newbolt Report of 1921. We shall summarise the ways in which English – which is how literary studies came to be known – has throughout its short history been conscious of its own vulnerability and imprecise identity and that it has sought to create that identity by establishing difference and by emphasising what it is *not*. As Margaret Mathieson pointed out in *The Preachers of Culture* (1975) the powerful mid nineteenth-century rhetoric about literature's power to humanise the subject and improve the moral condition of the mass of the population is rooted in anti-ness. It is initially anti-science, then it is successively anti-industrial and anti-modern, and we associate these *anti*-positions with Arnold, Lawrence and Leavis successively, writers whose definitions of culture involved experience and sensibility rather than pure abstraction. The persistence of debates about the 'two cultures' ignored the theoretical shift brought about by quantum theory in the first years of this century (at this point we considered making reference to Schrodinger's cat that is simultaneously dead and alive but decided we had sufficient animals in the title). Later on we shall be arguing that in becoming an increasingly broad field

English is reverting to the inclusiveness and breadth that was signified by the word *literature* in the sixteenth, seventeenth and eighteenth centuries, and that through this process fruitful links between scientific theory and literary studies may be reclaimed.

In this process, as English increasingly embraces the methodology of *discourse analysis*, it is incorporating a contemporary critical practice which transcends subject division, and which through the lens of genealogy is able to make links between apparently unconnected systems and fields such as – to borrow from an example from Stephen Heath – gynaecology, nineteenth-century opera librettos and Daphne Du Maurier's *Rebecca*. At the same time, English, at the end of the twentieth century, finds once again that it is attracted to a philosophical paradigm rooted in the anti-rationalism of Nietzsche and elaborated by Canguilhem and Foucault, a framework that will possibly reinforce the very science–arts binary that it would wish to challenge.

The origins of that particular binary are well known. In the battle to occupy the central place in a curriculum appropriate for a public school liberal education in the middle of the nineteenth century and in the battle to occupy the central place in the curriculum of the Board schools in the early part of the twentieth century English saw itself as having one great rival and that rival was Science, which despite the powerful sermons of John Henry Newman had begun to overturn the previously unchallenged dominance of theology in the universities. Science had a number of powerful, persuasive advocates such as Herbert Spencer, who in 1859 had published an essay entitled 'What Knowledge is of Most Worth?': 'To the question we set out with – what knowledge is of most worth – the uniform reply is – Science.' Arnold saw, in the growing power of the coming science, a moral and cultural impoverishment which was leading to the decline of belief and religion. Literary Studies, he had come to believe, was theology's natural successor. But unlike Science, which had no great difficulty in articulating its empirical methodology, its practical nature (one of the reasons it lost the debate in the public schools was the expense of new laboratories), English initially lacked a sufficiently precise manifesto to win public support (Arnold actually argued against the introduction of literary studies into the school curriculum), and compensated for this by advertising itself as a moral technology that was not only unlike science but was vastly superior to it. Arnold's contemporary, Edward Thring, Headmaster of Uppingham and like Arnold a believer in muscular Christianity but an opponent of brutish phil-athleticism, expressed the superiority of literature thus:

> The higher education must work in the region of the highest life. Now literature is the highest thought of the highest men in the most perfect shape. It is the life of the highest men transmitted. And this transmission of life takes place in any great degree through literature only.
>
> Thring, 1883, p. 140

As if these confident sentiments were not enough, one strand of the rhetoric sought to stifle any remaining doubts by claiming that poetry was *more* scientific than science.

Another strand attributed a particular, narrow meaning to the word Science, which Matthew Arnold and others sometimes caricatured as dry-as-dust fact-gathering of a kind associated with industrialism and materialism. Darwin, after all, had only been a collector of beetles. At the same time, by placing the Bible in a field – literature – which he placed outside science Arnold was inadvertently acknowledging the authority and power of science. The creation of the separate refuge of literary culture had long term consequences. The enthusiasm for science, the possibility that the excitement of science is primarily the fascination with systems and patterns that are just as symbolic and divorced from applications as metaphor was not acknowledged. Equally unacknowledged were the contradictions built into the promotion of literary study. In the mid nineteenth century, literary study in public schools and universities generally meant the study of classical literature, but this was now associated with a world whose understanding of the universe was believed to be extremely limited, having no inkling, for example, of a geological time scale, of electricity and evolution. Ultimately English was successful as a new subject at the beginning of the twentieth century because it occupied the logical ground of 'modern' literature, but this was not Arnold's intention, for he argued that in many ways the Hellenistic world was more modern than the moderns for the democratic, imperial qualities of Greece and Rome had parallels in mid Victorian Britain. Furthermore, Arnold's work as a cultural critic has to be distinguished from his work as a school inspector. The long argument of *Culture and Anarchy* was less useful in the educational propaganda war than the sustained attempt to belittle or reorientate science.

This reorientation and belittling occurred in other parts of late Victorian culture, and is suggested by the metonymic or syntagmatic part of the heading to this section, the part suggesting linear displacement. Helena Petrovna Blavatsky – Madame Blavatsky – was one of the joint founders of the Theosophical Society, a movement which attracted the interest of people as diverse as Annie Besant and W. B. Yeats and which once established soon had followers and branches all over the world. The Society was founded in the United States in 1875 – the same year in which the second edition of Arnold's *Culture and Anarchy* was published in England. Theosophy was an Eastern-inspired mixture of world religions and esoteric jargon which attached great importance to the hidden, the concealed and the symbolic – in contrast to what were perceived as Western modes of thought. It was mystical and spiritual and as its name indicated, claimed to be a universal, hidden science which was more true than what was commonly regarded as science. Science was materialistic, vulgar, and concerned with the surface appearance of things. In 1873, Madame Blavatsky had furnished her New York apartment with a number of stuffed animals, one of which was a stuffed baboon. This strategically positioned ape was labelled Professor Fiske, after an eminent Darwinian academic. Any visitor to the apartment would understand the message. Darwin had been ridiculed in a series of cartoons when *The Origin of Species* appeared in 1859. The scientific professor as stuffed baboon announced the folly of the belief that science was an end in itself. The alliance of science and religion in a secret doctrine was attractive to that wave of self-educated middle-class Victorians who attended séances or were attracted to the ideas of Edward Carpenter.

The other idea we intend to explore also involves making links between the opposite ends of this century. We hope to show that in England in the generation before F. R. Leavis, I. A. Richards and William Empson English was already conscious of its own protean ancestry and was anxious and embarrassed by this. In comparing the beliefs and reservations expressed in the early publications of the English Association, founded in 1906, with the comments and beliefs expressed in our own ethnographic research we hope to illustrate the historical antecedents of much of which we characterise as debates informing modernity and post-modernity. It is axiomatic, for example, that contemporary critical theory, much of which is grounded in the Saussurean separation of referent and language, and the belief that what we call the world is something we construct from language, has simultaneously offered the practices called English a death sentence and hormonal replacement therapy. On the one hand it leads to the belief that English is on death row – in chapter 1 we cited Catherine Belsey's response to her own question 'Is there a place for English in postmodern world?' as evidence of this. Furthermore, the opening comments in this chapter suggested that we might be entering an 'after English' phase.

Yet looked at another way contemporary developments in theory have provided English with a model by means of which its very decentredness, uncertainty and instability are qualities to be celebrated. The very plurality of English allows it to be considered not a meta-discipline, for that suggests an inside and an outside but as a kind of great basking shark drifting through the ocean with its mouth wide open. It has opened its great jaws to all the theories which threatened its demise, and ingested them. It is the natural home of theory. To use another metaphor, it has taken on the role of a tool with endless accessories for discussions of the paradigms and metaphors that inform our descriptions of the world. Hence the other part of the heading which, in contrast to the metonymic baboon uses the device of metaphoric substitution to illustrate the metaphoric axis itself, the site of condensation that is primary in Romanticism and Symbolism, according to Jacobson. A Swiss army knife has no one function, and is not a knife but knives, or rather knives, bottle openers, screwdrivers and at least twenty other things. It is difficult to say what a Swiss army knife is *for* exactly. It is for everything. It is for survival. It is for entertainment. Like English itself, its origins are concealed in its name. It is a penknife, which has become a collection of blades, none of which is intended to sharpen quills. It is divorced from the practice of writing. The pen no longer needs to be sharpened. None of this matters. All the various functions are held together by a recognisable red lozenge with a white Swiss cross on it. Everyone knows what these little red knives are: they are advertised in shops and magazines. Their enduring popularity and appeal are predicated on the belief that anything that possesses so many functions must be useful. English, which has as many blades as a Swiss army knife, has found that plurality of functions to be both a strength and a weakness, as we shall see.

Madame Blavatsky's baboon: English was not-science

Let me return to the first idea, namely that as university English sought to ensure a growing supply of recruits by establishing itself at the centre of the secondary school curriculum, it continued to play the anti-science card. The first twenty years of the twentieth century are a key period in the development of English in England, as it sought to consolidate its success in establishing for itself professorships in English at Oxford (1884) and then Cambridge in 1911. Schools of English had been established and it was now time to establish the centrality of English in the revised curriculum of the public schools and the newly created Board secondary schools. As Protherough and Atkinson (1991) remind us, English had been made compulsory in state schools under the 1904 regulations, and in 1910 a Board of Education report had endorsed its claim to have a definite (though not yet central) place in the curriculum of all secondary schools. The nine or so activities that in the 1890s had very often been taught by separate teachers (parsing, analysis, composition, reading, and literature, for example) were now more likely to be taught by a single teacher, though not necessarily a specialist. One way of defining that specialist, and stressing a need for him or her, was by creating difference, and by distinguishing English from science.

The rejection of what is perceived to be scientific method, which in the history of English could be said to date from the influence of Thomas Arnold's rejection of the teaching of science at Rugby on the grounds that physical science alone can never make a man educated or equip him with a moral sense, has its roots in late eighteenth-century Romanticism. The significance of Romanticism for the development of English is well understood. As Lionel Gossman discusses in 'Literature and Education' (Gossman 1982) in the seventeenth, eighteenth and early nineteenth century the term 'literature' is used in its broadest sense, and includes mathematics, history and science, Euclid's *Elements* as well as Newton's *Principia*. In the pre-industrial age the cultural binary was not along the science–arts axis, because there was no distinction made between the pure and the applied, or between any of the processes of learning. Instead, there was a distinction between the local and the universal, the seasonal and the timeless. Around the accumulated high culture into which only a minority was inducted were clustered notions of universality and the classicism that could be derived from an acquaintance with the texts of Greek and Roman antiquity. The classical culture which was available to the educated was contrasted with rural, oral culture which was local and unsophisticated. Reinforcing this particular binary was the belief that the ability to manage and exercise control over a symbolic system such as written language was the function which distinguished humankind from the beasts. The Protestant celebration of literacy as a means of gaining direct access to the Bible endorsed reading and writing in both the vernacular and Greek and Latin as an insurance against the regression into the bestiality of our fallen condition. In the Neoclassical age yet a third binary overlaid the other two and this was a binary along gendered lines. Opposed to the domestic, maternal world of oral culture were the manly activities (to use Gibbon's expression) of government, law, politics and literary culture, and these manly activities were all linked by the universal language codes characteristic of those engaged in public life.

The Romantic movement rearranged much of this intellectual furniture. In its attempts to unify culture, by seeking to valorise and rehabilitate the excluded – what Gossman calls the maternal, the infantile and the popular – Romantic ideology created a new binary, this time between the aesthetic and the utilitarian, between the literature of the imagination and the writings of the practical. In short, the world was divided into the changing world of practical knowledge and the enduring world of feeling, culture and wisdom. Experience, rather than the knowledge, was privileged. As Emerson says in his essay 'History': 'The true poem is the poet's mind' (Emerson 1841).

Matthew Arnold, who combined the roles of poet, school inspector and critic, inherited his father's reservations about science and though in his essays on literature he argued against modern poetry on the grounds that classical writers were more modern than the moderns, the decision to advance the cause of literary study through anti-science rhetoric found plenty of rhetorical ammunition in poetry and prose of the Romantics. Coleridge, who along with other Romantic poets is frequently recommended in the early twentieth-century model English syllabuses as a particularly *English* writer, provided the textual authority for nineteenth-century anti-scientism: 'I believe the souls of five hundred Sir Isaac Newtons would go to the making of a Shakespeare or a Milton' (Letter to Thomas Poole, 23 March 1801). Anti-science rhetoric informs Matthew Arnold's writing as both a school inspector and a literary critic. In his report on *Schools and Universities on the Continent* (1868) Matthew Arnold had carefully emphasised literary study's place in the *humanities* with the obvious corollary: 'The study of letters is the study of the operation of human force, of human freedom and activity; the study of nature is the study of non-human forces, of human limitation and passivity' (*CPW*, IV, p. 292).

Arnold then goes on to say that despite their prodigious ignorance of the universe those who have had humanistic training will continue to play a prominent part in human affairs because the 'human force' in them has been stimulated. Science cannot be placed at the centre of education because it is simply a collection of facts, passively acquired, and not, ultimately a human activity. This is a travesty of science, of course, but it was an enduring travesty. For Arnold the scientist takes apart, but the poet synthesises. If literary study involves the study of poetry, then that poetry can be appreciated but not subjected to scientific analysis. As he argues in 'Literature and Science', however impressive the scope of science may be, we are still stuck in the realm of information and knowledge:

> But still it will be *knowledge* only which they give us; knowledge not put for us into relation with our sense for conduct, our sense of beauty, and touched with emotion by being so put; not thus put for us, and therefore to the majority of mankind, after a certain while unsatisfying, wearying.
>
> CPW, X, p. 64

Sometimes Arnold takes another tack, arguing that literature can be more scientific than science. In 'The Study of Poetry' he argues:

> More and more mankind will discover that we have to turn to poetry to interpret life for us, to console us, to sustain us. Without poetry, our science will appear incomplete; and most of what now passes with us for religion and philosophy will be replaced by poetry. Science, I say, will appear incomplete without it. For finely and truly does Wordsworth call poetry 'the impassioned expression which is in the countenance of all science'.
>
> CPW, IX, p. 161

Sometimes the attack is personalised, and scientists are likened to cold ruthless French Revolutionaries, supervising the machinery of execution:

> The good of letters may be had without skill in arguing, or that formidable logical apparatus, not unlike a guillotine, which Professor Huxley speaks of somewhere as the young man's best companion.
>
> CPW, VI, p. 168

This is from 'Literature and Dogma' during the conclusion of which Arnold argues that the misapplication of science is responsible for many of the world's problems, including the decline of religion:

> [T]heologians have in themselves a faculty for science . . . [b]ut they do not employ it on its proper objects; so it invades the Bible, and tries to make the Bible what it is not, and to put into it what is not there.
>
> Bryson 1954

In much of this anti-science, anti-intellectual rhetoric, there was a sleight of hand. By 1860 it was clear that English education, whether in schools, Mechanics Institutes or Universities, would have to find a central place for science and technical education if Britain was to compete with its rival Germany, though successive governments were painfully slow in their attempts to do anything about this. So Arnold and his supporters effectively established literary study in the public mind as a corrective to science, a balancing force, so whenever science grew, English grew too. It was what Chris Baldick calls a process of 'shadowing'. But at the same time as chaperoning science, the practices known as liberal humanism and literary study were in Arnold's view *themselves* possessed of scientific attributes: '[A]ll learning is scientific which is systematically laid out and followed up to the original sources, and a genuine humanism is scientific' (Arnold 1954, p. 644).

In her analysis of the history of English in *The Preachers of Culture* Margaret Mathieson gives greater emphasis to the evangelizing strand in Arnold's essays and it is in relation to his celebration of literature in these public debates about the future of culture that Arnold is usually discussed as one of the founding fathers of subject English. Similar comments are to be found in his reports as a School Inspector, but they are not so prominent, and are accompanied by a diffidence which contrasts with the authoritative characters of inspectors' reports 150 years later. This is Arnold preparing his readers for what he is about to say in his 1852 Report:

> With the general state of education in my district . . . I cannot profess myself from personal observation familiar; and even with respect to the 104 institutions which I have seen, and my observations on which supply the material for this report, I feel that I am far from possessing that intimate acquaintance with them which I could desire; the great majority of them I have as yet visited but once: and I therefore wish to be understood in this report as calling the attention of managers and teachers to those facts connected with their schools which have principally struck me, and which I shall chiefly notice on future visits, rather than as confidently criticizing what I have seen in their schools.
>
> Arnold (1852) 1889, p. 3

It is in such a context, in this very same report, that he makes the following observation – not about the curriculum for elementary school children, but about the education of pupil teachers:

> I attach little importance to the study of languages, ancient or modern, by pupil-teachers, . . . but I am sure that the study of portions of the best English authors, and composition, might with advantage be made a part of their regular course of instruction to a much greater degree than it is at present.
>
> Arnold (1852) 1881, pp. 19–20

This is an argument Arnold was to take further in *Schools and Universities on the Continent* in 1868, following his investigation into the system of education practised in France, Switzerland, Germany and Italy. In France the teaching of rhetoric impressed him, as did the use of French literature:

> Even the selection of a body of English classics like this, excellent in themselves and excellently adapted for the purposes to which they are destined, is a progress which English public instruction has yet to make.
>
> Arnold (1868) 1964, p. 79

Arnold returns to this theme in his conclusion: 'We have still to make the mother tongue and its literature a part of the school course; foreign nations have done this, and we shall do it' (Arnold (1868) 1964, p. 299) and from there moves on to articulate his vision of a liberal education, one which breaks down the science–arts binary which elsewhere he had appeared to reinforce:

> To sum up, then, the conclusions to which these remarks lead. The ideal of a general, liberal training is, to carry us to a knowledge of ourselves and the world . . . The rejection of the humanities by the realists, the rejection of the study of nature by the humanists, are alike ignorant. He whose aptitudes carry him to the study of nature should have some notion of the humanities; he whose aptitudes carry him to the humanities should have some notion of the phenomena and laws of nature.
>
> Arnold (1868) 1964, p. 300

Such comments have contributed to the widespread view of Arnold contained in many earlier histories of English. There are three interesting remarks, however, which will be germane to our later discussion when we consider Ian Hunter's claim that David Stow and Kay-Shuttleworth were more influential in the furtherance of English and literary study in the elementary, and then the secondary classroom. In his General Report for 1860, Arnold ends by recommending an improvement in the quality of the anthologies given to children as they learn to read. In so doing he writes as follows:

> [Well-selected and interesting reading books] would also afford the best chance of inspiring quick scholars with a real love for reading and literature in the only way in which such a love is ever really inspired, by animating and moving them; and if they succeed in doing this, they would have this further advantage, that the literature for which they inspired a taste would be a good, a sound and truly refining literature.
>
> Marvin 1910, p. 83

We can extract two ideas from this passage, both quite familiar. Reading is associated with a pedagogy in which interest plays an important role, and reading is a practice which develops the cultivation of taste. Mathieson emphasizes the second, but it is important not to lose sight of the first. In 1867 Arnold argued not only for the need to address the interest of the child, but also for the freeing-up of the teacher and inspector: 'More free play for the Inspector, and more free play in consequence, for the teacher, is what is wanted' (Marvin 1910, p. 115).

In part this comment is part of Arnold's campaign against the stultifying effects (as he saw them) of the Revised Code, with its Payment by Results system. This was deadening teaching in the elementary schools which he inspected, and he railed against it in a number of his reports. It would be wrong to conclude from this that Arnold favoured what eventually became known in the twentieth century as 'progressive' pedagogical practices – he recommended recitation, memorising and grammar exercises after all – but he did identify a need to engage with a child's interests and notions of 'pleasure':

> Of such high importance, in relieving the strain of mental effort, is the sense of pleasurable activity and of creation. Of course a great deal of the work in elementary schools must necessarily be of a mechanical kind. But whatever introduces any sort of creative activity to relieve the passive reception of knowledge is valuable.

He ends his 1882 Report by quoting from a sermon given in 1745 by Joseph Butler, Bishop of Bristol: ' "Of Education", says Butler, "*information itself is really the least part*" ' (Marvin 1910, p. 230).

To place these remarks in perspective we need to look at the opening sentence of Arnold's General Report for the year 1880, which reveals his enthusiasm for English Literature, but a conventional view of what that practice involves:

> I find that of the specific subjects English literature, as it is too ambitiously called – in plain truth the learning by heart and reciting of a hundred lines or two of standard English poetry – continues to be by far the most popular. I rejoice to find it so; there is no fact coming under my observation in the working of our elementary schools which gives me so much satisfaction.
>
> Marvin 1910, p. 200

Even so, Arnold had been directly instrumental in prescribing 'real texts' (such as passages from *The Times*) for testing, rather than the meaningless blocks of text that led to recitations that were empty and divorced from the aesthetic life. We can trace this influence by comparing contemporary textbooks, such as *The Poetical Reader for Home and School Use* (Curtis 1871) which includes extracts from standard writers such as Shakespeare and Tennyson, and the *Revised Lesson Book for Standard VI of the Revised Code of the Committee of Council on Education* (BFSS n.d), which includes extracts from history, poems, pieces on architecture and India and has less of a moral purpose, being more clearly governed by the precise form of the assessment which it lists on the opening page:

Requirement of the Revised Code for Standard VI

A short ordinary paragraph in a newspaper or other modern narrative
Another short ordinary paragraph in a newspaper, or other modern narrative, slowly dictated by a few words at a time
A sum in practice or bill of parcels

Not long after his death in 1888 Arnold's place in the development of English became the subject for debate. Although his published ideas about the need for Literature to be at the centre of our culture were slow to filter through into practice in the school curriculum in his lifetime, he was regarded as a pioneer. An enthusiastic view of Arnold was recorded in 1912, twenty-four years after his death and ten years after the 1902 Education Act had established state secondary schools. M. E. Sadler, Vice Chancellor of Leeds University, spoke to the Yorkshire Branch of the English Association on November 8th on the theme of 'The Need for a National Ideal'. The official Bulletin reports him as having said that:

[T]he movement which, especially during the last ten years, had studded England with new secondary schools drew a great part of its stimulus from Matthew Arnold's writing published a quarter of a century before . . . Like Ruskin, he saw the necessity of the highest kind of public education for the well-being of the state . . . Matthew Arnold conceived the central power of national education to lie not in administrative machinery nor in statutory compulsion (though both of these things were necessary) but in a national ideal, deeply felt, universally diffused and intellectually formulated.

Bulletin No. 18, November 1912, p. 20

The irony is that Arnoldian liberal ethical impulse had already been eclipsed by the bureaucratic collectivism that sprang from the Fabians, and more immediately from Sir Robert Morant, who in 1902 had become Permanent Secretary at the Board of Education. By 1912 the central power of national education lay in 'administrative machinery [and] statutory compulsion'. Stow and Kay-Shuttleworth had realised this, and in his educational writings and actions Arnold would seem to have agreed.

Eight years and a devastating world war later, Arnold's reputation had undergone a revision. The Warden of Wadham College, Mr J. Wells delivered a paper to the English Association at University College on 19 March 1920. The paper was titled 'Matthew Arnold as critic of English Literature' and in it Wells carefully identified Arnold's limitations. Compared to Sainte-Beuve, the French author and critic who had produced significant reviews of Victor Hugo's work and a series of articles on the Romantic poets, Arnold had produced very little critical work. More seriously his nationalism and *manliness* were found wanting:

> Arnold, too, was alien to the whole imperial movement in England during the last half-century: connected with this was his absolute indifference to the love of fighting and the exultation of courage and strength which was a very real part of the nature of a complete man.
>
> Bulletin No. 40, May 1920

As we indicated earlier, Arnold is now inclined to be seen less as a preacher of culture and more as an agent of the state apparatus which ensures the efficient transmission of power. In Ian Hunter's reading Stow, Kay-Shuttleworth and Arnold are critics of the monitorial method of education – the system by which great numbers of children were taught not by teachers but by the monitors they appointed in the class – not out of principle but because as a system it was not working. Drawing on Foucault, Hunter illustrates how first of all David Stow's *The Training System, the Moral Training School and the Normal Seminary* (1834) encourages the idea that the playground *under supervision* is the ideal place for children to reveal the real life that is revealed in the street, but under the guidance of a teacher in whom they have confidence and who ensures that the playground is an effective moral training ground. Hunter argues that this belief was transferred into the classroom and as a pedagogical practice became supported by the claim that literature was morally educative. Literary studies, whose rhetoric celebrated the supposed freedom to respond and express one's opinion, a freedom that has been the hallmark of progressive English teaching from Dover Wilson to John Dixon, became an apt vehicle for this pedagogy. In Hunter's argument, therefore, English is primarily a moral technology and the normative apparatus (controlled by the machinery of examinations) by which power was exercised more effectively. Hunter develops this argument at length in *Culture and Government* (1987) and we shall return to this idea later. At this stage we should simply note that this argument has not gone unchallenged: in his biography of Kay-Shuttleworth, Selleck (1994) argues that although Stow's and Kay-Shuttleworth's ideas influenced the architecture of schools ('the playground, the gallery and the classroom were the outward and visible signs of the new vision of education which Kay saw in Glasgow in 1837' (Selleck 1994, p. 135) their pedagogies cannot 'be explained simply as an effort to impose a particular set of values on the working classes'.

Whether or not Arnold's role in arguing for a broad definition of elementary education in general should be subsumed by Kay-Shuttleworth's Stow-inspired campaign on behalf of pauper children and state education, whether his contribution to the drive to secure a foothold for English in the university curriculum has been overestimated, is itself a matter for debate, but his work as a critic and school inspector coincided with a period in which there was an increasing demand for English in schools and at university, and that his writing contributed to the way in which this demand could be represented and discussed.

The demand in schools is reflected in the statistics recorded in the Report of the Board of Education for the year 1910–11 (Board of Education 1912) which plots the development of the subject in the late nineteenth century. It is a useful complement to the rhetoric of the period. It is brief and pragmatic:

> Though the state began to concern itself with public elementary education in 1833, direct control of the school curriculum was not estab-lished until the issue of the famous 'Revised Code' of 1862 . . . From (1862) until 1895 the system of individual examination and 'payment by results' was a force . . . During the whole of this period . . . the curriculum of the Public Elementary School was shaped and determined very largely in view of grant-earning considerations.
>
> Board of Education 1912, pp. 3–6

The 1862 Code had tested children in the three r's of reading, writing (dictation and copying) and arithmetic, but because this was causing schools to neglect other subjects, schools were eventually rewarded if one other special subject was tested, the special subjects being geography, grammar and history. In 1871 the Special Subjects were expanded to include, among others, Languages, of which English Literature was a part. Thus in 1872:

> 59,774 children were examined in Geography (the most popular subject)
> 18,426 children were examined in Grammar (second most popular)
> 16,464 children were examined in English Literature (the fourth most popular, History being the third)

In describing development in the following years the Report notes: '[W]hat seems at first the most remarkable rise of all is that in English Literature. In 1876 the number of children examined in this subject was 34,931, in 1882 it was 140,772' (Board of Education 1912, p. 12). In that year (1882) a seventh standard was introduced as children were now staying on longer at schools. The assessment in English Literature for this standard gives the reader some sense of the teaching methods: 'To read a passage from Shakespeare or Milton or some other standard author, or from a History of England. To write a theme or letter; composition, spelling and handwriting to be considered' (Board of Education 1912, p. 13). In 1880 the class, or standard subjects had been expanded to include 'any others which can be reasonably accepted as special branches of elementary instruction and properly treated in reading books' (p. 12), and in 1882 again a further rearrangement of the class subjects allowed for the introduction of English (Literature and

Grammar). For a brief period English became a compulsory class subject, so that by 1890 English appeared triumphant. In a survey of 22,515 departments for older children, English was taught in 20,304, Geography in 12,367, History in 414 and Elementary Science in only 32. That year saw a relaxation of the rule regarding compulsory English, so that in 1890 the number of schools taking English went down from 20,304 to 16,280 while the numbers in all the above subjects went up. Yet this decline was only temporary: English was strengthened by the Education Act of 1902 and the Code of 1904.

That English at university showed signs of similar growth was due partly to the subject's popularity with those who had been denied a public school education. Terry Eagleton is wrong in attributing the revealing remark about the second-rate character of English Studies to a Royal Commission witness in 1877 – it was actually made by Professor Sanday at the Oxford Congregation meeting of 5 December 1893 – but Eagleton and Gossman (1983) are right to see the comment as an insight into the presumed groups at whom the new subject was going to be beamed. Drawing strength from the 1867 essays by J. W. Hales and Henry Sidgwick (*Essays in Liberal Education*), it had been argued that English should be studied in schools by those not going on to university, an idea which picked up on the Newcastle Commission's recommendation (1861) that pupil teachers should study English in the same way that public schoolboys study Latin and Greek. It is worth looking at *The Times* report of the 1893 meeting, which voted 110 to 70 to set up a Final Honours School of English at Oxford, to see what a shabby affair the institutionalising of English was. The much-quoted comment is that if an English School at Oxford is to be set up: 'The women should be considered, and the second and third rate men who were to become schoolmasters' (handout), and this is followed by Professor Sanday's observation that '[t]he reproach would be removed that five sixths of the work done in English Literature was done abroad', a remark which reveals the important role that the study of English was playing in the control of Empire. The needs of the Empire had been recognised when the rules for entry into the Indian Civil Service were changed following the 1855 report which had recommended public examinations as the route into the Civil Service of the East India Company. The Mr Raleigh who speaks rather dismissively of English Literature as 'a miserably inadequate training, however well taught' is presumably the Walter Raleigh who went on to become Professor of English in 1904.

ENGLISH IN THE EARLY TWENTIETH CENTURY

- The two EAs: Edwardian anxieties and the English Association
- Growing confidence: English and the nation
- Teacher, writer and text: the cases of Lawrence and Barrie

The two EAs: Edwardian anxieties and the English Association

In the years immediately following Raleigh's appointment, English made an attempt to define the purpose of English study in terms other than the social mission, the civilising mission that had been argued by Arnold and Pater. The education of women was not a cause to be taken up during a period of highly unpopular suffragette activities, whilst the training of the Civil Service for their work in the colonies was a factor which university professors sought to present more subtly through a celebration of the way that literature reinforced notions of 'Englishness'. So playing the anti-science card remained a powerful strategy in the battle to define what should sit at the centre of a liberal education.

As the novels and short stories of the late Victorian and Edwardian decades reveal, this period is characterised by considerable anxieties about the impact of science and technology and its more sinister potential to dehumanise and destroy. *News from Nowhere*, *The Time Machine*, *The Machine Stops*, *The Wind in the Willows* and *Tono Bungay*: all confirm worries about the world that advances in science were creating. Wells, whose own education had been scientific, was immensely troubled by the interpretation of Darwin that Herbert Spencer offered, with the prediction that evolution could result in mankind being replaced by some other dominant species. Wells disseminated these worries through his fictions, in which ants, reptiles or cephalopods have come to rule the world. Such worries were reinforced by theories of entropy, and degeneration. They provide us with some sense of the desperate intellectual climate in which the English Association was founded by London and Scottish academics in 1906, the same year as the Liberal landslide in the general election. Yet this period is much neglected in English historiography. In *A Schooling in English* John Dixon discusses 'three critical episodes in the struggle to shape literary and cultural studies'. These periods are the University Extension movement of the late nineteenth century, Cambridge English in the 1920s and the widening of literary and cultural studies in the 1960s and 1970s. Chris Baldick, in *The Social Mission of English Criticism 1848–1932* jumps from the 1890s to the First World War with only a passing reference to some of the discussion that went on in between.

Yet in many ways these years at the beginning of the twentieth century witness a transformation in the agenda that is set by English. In 1905 the Board of Education published a rather plodding document, *Suggestions for the Consideration of Teachers and Others Concerned in the Work of Public Elementary Schools* (Board of Education 1905), and although chapter 6 is entitled 'The Teaching of English' and speaks of the importance of English as it is both the mother tongue and the national literature, it sets very modest targets for the teacher of English:

The problem of teaching English in the Elementary School is most profitably approached by remembering that for the majority of the children the English course can aim only at securing the ability to speak, read and write in plain English with moderate fluency, intelligence and accuracy . . .

> Board of Education 1905, p. 29

Yet five years later the Board issued a circular with a very much more assertive, not to say imperious, ring:

In issuing a Circular on the teaching of English in Secondary Schools the Board do not think it necessary to dwell upon the importance of the subject. The claim of English to a definite place in the curriculum over every Secondary School is admitted.

> Board of Education 1910, p. 3

The Circular states that there is therefore no need to refute the view that a knowledge of English will be 'picked up' naturally. It is something that must be studied, and the teachers responsible for the subject should have studied it before they begin teaching:

They need not . . . be specialists in the strict sense of that word, but they should have something like adequate knowledge of the best English authors, and a real interest in some brand of English studies, whether the history of literature, or the art of criticism, or the science of literature.

> Board of Education 1910:3

The tripartite division, colonising history, art and science, is revealing, and is consistent with rhetoric that follows: 'Pure English is not merely an accomplishment, but an index to and a formative influence over character' (Board of Education 1910, p. 3). In the Circular English is discussed under only two subheadings, Literature and Composition, and under the former it deliberately refrains from offering a list of books. English is a subject which defies prescription, and the Circular announces that it will suggest principles, but not rules:

English is the last subject in which a teacher should be bound by hard and fast rules. No subject gives more scope for individuality of treatment or for varied experiment; in none is the personal quality of the teacher more important.

> Board of Education 1910, p. 3

It concludes with a rhetoric that seems remarkably modern:

The child's life in school is being brought into closer relation with his life out of school . . . [In English and almost every subject in the curriculum] the teacher of today uses the materials and experiences with which the children are familiar in everyday life.

Board of Education 1910, p. 40

Again, we must put this in perspective, in case this encourages the belief that we have stepped into the practices of the 1960s. The Circular recommends repetition from memory of both poetry and prose, and warns of the dangers of discussion:

[I]nstruction in literature must be more discursive than is usual in other subjects, but this fact has a corresponding danger . . . The variety of points at which literature touches life, the allusions and the suggestiveness of a great writer, may easily seduce a teacher into using a book as a peg on which to hang disquisitions or some historical, or political, or scientific subject. Such disquisitions . . . must be kept strictly in control, for whatever they teach it is not literature.

Board of Education 1910, pp. 9–10

Even so, the document is remarkable in its confidence and ambition, and contrasts strikingly with the tone of the 1905 document quoted earlier. How can we explain this difference? The fact that it is addressing secondary school English teachers is clearly significant. Although changes in elementary education, influenced initially by new child-centred ideas about infant teaching, were about to start moving up through the elementary school and eventually change the pedagogical practice in (English classes in) higher elementary schools and secondary schools, the rhetoric of this 1910 document is more revealing of the influence of the growing presence of English as a subject in universities, and the way that universities wished to recruit specialists who had studied English in state secondary schools. The subject's professionalisation is reflected in the founding of the English Association in 1906. Stephen J. Ball, in 'English for the English Since 1906' (Ball 1985) identifies the founding of the English Association as a crucial stage in the development of Subject English, not least because it is the beginning of the extensive documentation of English. Through a stream of leaflets and bulletins, conferences and branch meetings, from some of which I have already quoted, the English Association provided a forum for a discussion of the ways in which English should proceed.

The threat from science is a constant theme running through these publications. The British Association for the Advancement of Science had been established over seventy years earlier in 1831 and had long argued for more science teaching. The Science Association drew its members from the dissenting Liberal tradition, a group which had been largely excluded from the liberal humanist education. Since scientists in particular identified Germany's centralised education system as the key factor in its success and England's relative economic decline, throughout the late nineteenth century and early twentieth they had a powerful rhetorical weapon which could appeal to the national interest. Ironically, scientists too felt that they were being ignored. As Peter Alter (1998) points out, English scientists looked enviously to Germany, where research and professorships were valued (most English scientists in the second half of the nineteenth and the first part of the twentieth century went to Germany to complete their doctorates), and bemoaned the lack of serious interest in science in England. At Oxford there was an almost complete absence of research and theoretical chemistry and physics until well after the First World War and Robert Bellamy Clifton (1836–1921), Chair of Experimental Philosophy at the Clarendon Physical Laboratory, summed up the Oxford attitude in his remark that '[t]he wish to do research betrays a certain restlessness of mind'. This kind of gentlemanly amateurism, so typical of the *laissez-faire* approach, enraged such scientists as Sir Norman Lockyer, President of the British Association for the Advancement of Science. In a well-publicised speech delivered at the AGM in Southport in 1903, he deplored the neglect of science by successive British governments, and in calling his speech 'The Influence of Brain-Power on History' he deliberately alluded to the title of an important work published by the American naval historian Alfred Thayer Mahan in 1890: *The Influence of Sea Power upon History*. That had been taken seriously, and had led to financial investment of the kind for which science was crying out.

Despite the frustration expressed by those who wished to advance the cause of science, English perceived the potential dominance of science at the beginning of the century as a real threat to its own place in the curriculum, and the newly founded English Association began its life already on the defensive. Edmund Gosse, a founder member, expressed the Association's anxieties in Leaflet No. 25 using language not unreminiscent of Madame Blavatsky's *Theosophy*:

> The highest poetry is a mysterious thing, like the practices of the Society of Rosicrucians . . . If I am sure of any thing, it is that the Poets of the Future will look upon schemes of universal technical education and such democratic reforms as those which are now occupying the enthusiasm and energy of our friend the Lord Chancellor as peculiarly hateful expositions of the godlessness of a godless world.
>
> Leaflet No. 25, 'The Future of English Poetry' (June 1913)

The sense of alarm and invasion had been more evident in the address given to the 1910 AGM by Dr Gregory Foster, Provost of University College:

> If we can make English, English Literature and English history, so to speak, the centre of gravity to the work of the preparatory schools and of every other kind of school there will be no danger that the literary culture of this country will suffer. That danger is clearly before

us at the present time; you have only got to read today's newspapers and you will see that at the meeting of the Association of Science Masters a member is reported to have said that the day would soon come *when a literary headmaster would be an anachronism.* It is clear that, if that is the aim of our scientific friends, the English Association will have to join hands . . . with the Classical Association and every other good friend of literature.

Foster 1910, emphasis added

The italicised phrase indicates the power of the practices that characterised English to be identified as the qualities needed by the headmaster of a public school, and the contrast between this and later romantic rhetoric about English as a force monitoring society from the outside. But it would be wrong to suggest that English Association contributors were unaware of the contradictory nature of their own position. In the same year, 1910, C. H. Herford published a paper entitled 'The Bearing of English upon the National Life':

It may be laid down, I think, that the study of literature wants something if it be wholly out of touch with or wholly absorbed into any one of the three great provinces of human endeavour, three modes of the human spirit, which we may roughly denote by the names science, art and conduct. Literary history can never be fully reducible to a perfectly ordered body of knowledge, fulfilling the ideal of science . . . [b]ut even if the reduction of literature to scientific laws admitted of being carried out far further than it does, we should have to take account of facts for which our continuous and orderly growth is a less obviously apt analogy than that of the wind blowing where it listeth . . . [To] critics of the Symbolist school the quality of literature only begins when it becomes thus inexplicable, mysterious.

Herford 1910, p. 1

Even where the rhetoric of the English Association appears to be conciliatory, it is usually a disguised form of attack. Here is Sir Henry Newbolt, who was to become the Association's President and the chairman of the committee whose 1921 report bears his name. At the summer meeting of the Association held at Kings College on 21 June 1912 he delivered an address called 'Poetry and Politics'. This is how it was reported:

Mr Newbolt referred to the results of the common opinion that poetry is divided off from other activities. 'Science must steer and work the ship while Poetry decorates the saloon or plays in the band'. Huxley thought that common belief was wrong. The aesthetic and logical activities of the human spirit expressed themselves in Poetry and Science which are dependent on each other. Poetry alone could be invoked to awaken, stimulate and change human feeling, and the poet had more beneficent power than the legislator. Mr Newbolt quoted from Addison, Wordsworth, Coleridge, Swinburne and Rossetti in proof of this.

Bulletin No. 18, November 1912

In 1917 a special conference was called to defend the provision for Humanities Studies in all stages of the curriculum and to call for a comprehensive revision of national education from the point of view of present needs. A number of resolutions were passed, the first of which read thus: 'It is essential that any reorganisation of our educational system should make adequate provision for both humanistic and scientific studies' (Bulletin No. 30, January 1917). But the very next bulletin carried a report of Mr St Loe Strachey's paper on 'The Vital Element in Poetry' in which he:

> began by drawing an analogy between the failure of scientists to discover by analysis the nature of the ultimate principles that determine food value and the failure of critics to distinguish the vital element in poetry.

Bulletin No. 31, May 1917

In ways that were quite unpredicted the war saw a remarkable rise in the sales of 'serious' literature – Conrad and Henry James are cited in one report – and a decline in the sale of popular fiction. Booksellers and publishers had predicted a complete crash in book sales but this did not happen. The reaction against science that came with a full awareness of the dreadful destructiveness of mustard gas, machine guns, heavy artillery and constant military bombardment did not come until later, but the loss of the 'Titanic' and the failure of Scott's caterpillar tractor vehicles had continued the erosion of the belief in scientific achievement that nineteenth-century humanist rhetoric had begun.

Growing confidence: English and the nation

If the image of Madame Blavatsky's baboon is a useful metonymic trope to suggest the oppositional relationship of the new subject to science, then the metaphor of the Swiss army knife may suggest something of the ambitious multi-functional role that English began to promote in the twentieth century. But these two positions were not without internal contradictions, two of which stand out. One is the way that the belief in the socially unifying function of literary study was reconstituted by English teachers as a subversive strand which permitted teachers to take up a Kantian Romantic position *inside* the framework of the state institution. The paradox had been identified by Emerson who had praised the natural college in which the students gather round the natural teachers 'but the moment this is organised, difficulties begin'. (Emerson 197/83). The other problem concerned the chameleon like nature of English, which was always likely to lead to uncertainty and disputes, and seemed to make English vulnerable whenever it wished to present a unified front. But these were problems that Subject English was storing up for the future: they did not seem to dent the confidence of the rhetoric at the beginning of the twentieth century.

As we saw earlier, Thomas Arnold had refused to allow the teaching of science at Rugby, even though it was being strenuously advocated by Darwin, Huxley and Spencer on the grounds that science should sit at the centre of a modern liberal education precisely because it was a morally educative subject and that it would provide the modern 'man' with frameworks and methods appropriate for the new world. Advocates of literary study such as Matthew Arnold, Ruskin and Thring had successfully appropriated this rhetoric in arguing that English – which meant largely the rote learning of huge chunks of poems and plays – should occupy the centre ground because only English offered the morally educative influence that was needed at a time of moral crisis and uncertainty.

The problem with defining itself in opposition to science was that English was also defining itself as something that could not consistently be institutionalised and measured with all the machinery of assessment and regulations, even though it sought a place in the institutions it was the duty of Arnold the inspector to endorse to supervise. This paradox was a problem that Arnold passed to the next generation. In celebrating a belief in the superiority of the intuitive, the metaphoric and the symbolic over the analytic, the specific and the material those advancing the cause of English at the beginning of the twentieth century revealed not only a significant element of anti-intellectualism but also a deep anxiety about the vulnerability of English as it became part of the apparatus of state power. The warning from Arnold of the 'formidable logical apparatus, not unlike a guillotine' which I quoted earlier was extended to include a dread of the deadening effect of bureaucratic systems, which as we have seen, were to dominate state education from 1902 onwards. But within the Arnoldian legacy there was a curious paradox.

We need to remind ourselves that before 1850 there were no schools of English in English universities, and in schools there would have been sessions devoted to handwriting, spelling and reading, but these were not gathered into a frame called 'English'. This frame could not be formulated until the national debate about culture and identity had given an opportunity for Arnold and Kay-Shuttleworth to recommend English Literature as the apparatus by which the mass of the population could be socialised and aestheticised through a process which combined the appearance of direct free interaction with literature and a rigorous process of inspection. As I suggested earlier, both Kay-Shuttleworth and David Stow who a generation earlier in the 1820s had run the Glasgow Normal Seminary along innovative lines – shared the goal of seeking to establish the appropriate machinery to facilitate this moral training. Stow had rejected the nakedly hierarchical system of the monitorial method (teacher instructs monitors who instruct pupils) because it was *failing* in its goal of effecting the moral formation of children. His alternative approach involved a pedagogy which was reflected in early nineteenth-century reading primers:

> The true character and dispositions are best developed at play with companions similar in years and pursuits. A play-ground, however, may either be a moral training ground, or a mischief ground. It is the latter too generally when the children are left alone, without any authoritative superintending eye upon them . . .
>
> Teachers and parents, desirous of gaining the confidence of their children, must in fact, themselves as it were, become children, by bending to, and occasionally engaging in, their plays and amusements. Without such condescension, a perfect knowledge of real character and dispositions cannot be obtained.
>
> Stow 1850, pp. 143, 156

Michel Foucault, in *Discipline and Punish*, points to the ways in which the hierarchical method of training recommended in French military manuals of the sixteenth century was 'gradually imposed on pedagogical practice' (Foucault 1977, p. 159), and we have already hinted at the similarities between the monitorial system and the way in which soldiers of the second class would be exercised every morning by sergeants and lance corporals while these in turn would be exercised by their senior officers. In the first volume of *The History of Sexuality* Foucault argues that in the history of Western societies there has been a move towards the concealment of power, and that the public exhibition of power and control has been gradually replaced by the centralised apparatus of government which has extended freedoms but always under supervision. Hunter sees distinct parallels between this and the emphasis on personal expression *under the supervision of the enlightened teacher* that has characterised a very powerful strand in the pedagogy of English from the nineteenth century until the present day. Ostensibly a space in which the student can respond and interpret freely, the apparatus of assessment with all the hierarchical layers which are strikingly illustrated by the ten level National Curriculum system and the tiered papers for GCSE English, English is actually engaged in the reforming of its subjects, that is literally the re-forming of them. This pedagogical strand, which operates in a system which it claims to subvert, has been more noticeable in schools and colleges than it has in universities, but it is a powerful arm of the English movement, and has its antecedents not in the progressive 1960s as is often imagined, nor even in 1930s America, where John Dewey's influence had started to be felt, but in the first fifteen years of this century.

Teacher, writer and text: the cases of Lawrence and Barrie

We are given something of an insight into the way these elements – the belief in expression, the teacher of English performing as a romantic outsider yet all the while subject to the apparatus of inspection and reporting – through what we know of D. H. Lawrence as a teacher in Croydon. Lawrence took up an appointment at Davidson Road School in 1908. It was a new school, having been built a year before, the same year in which the English Association had its first meetings. On the Thursday of his first week at the school, he had attended a lecture at Whitgift School. The lecture, on 'Criticism' was given by W. P. Ker, Professor of English at London University, and had been arranged by the Croydon branch of the English Association. It was not Lawrence's only contact with the local branch, as we shall see.

As an assistant teacher in an elementary school Lawrence taught all subjects, but we have an account of his poetry and drama teaching from his headmaster, Philip Smith:

> He would have none of the 'We are seven, etc' category. Nor would he tolerate any with what he called a 'sniff of moral imposition'. I found entered into his records such as 'The Assyrian came down' (Byron), 'The bells of Shandon' (Mahony), 'Go fetch to me a pint of wine' (Burns). He considered that the best poetry for young people was through rhythm and the ring of words rather than the evasive appeal of an unreal and abstract morality.
>
> Nehls 1957, I, pp. 87–8

The juxtaposition of progressive active learning and the element of surveillance suggested by the phrase 'entered in his records' is even more noticeable in Smith's description of the occasion when a School Inspector walked unannounced into Lawrence's classroom:

> The intrusion was unexpected and resented. A curious wailing of distressed voices issued from a far corner. The sounds were muffled by a large covering black-board. The words of a familiar song arose from the depths:
>
> Full fathom five thy father lies;
> Of his bones are coral made.
>
> The class was reading *The Tempest*. The presentation expressed the usual thoroughness of Lawrence's attitude to the exercise in progress. It must not be spoiled by even official comment. Lawrence rushed with outstretched hands to the astounded visitor: 'Hush! Hush! Don't you hear? The sea chorus from *The Tempest*'.
>
> Nehls 1957, I, p. 86

Here we have an early illustration of that belief in the liberating experience of literature that refuses to acknowledge the existence of 'official comment' or the process of inspection itself. In promoting active learning Lawrence is building on the Arnoldian notion of morally improving literature and a perception of literature as something to be actively engaged with, but under supervision. So, Hunter argues, the role of the playground as a place which mimics the streets but allows children freedom under supervision is taken up by a progressive form of English pedagogy. It has its roots in John Dewey, Maria Montessori, Caldwell Cook, John Adams and Margaret Macmillan, who were recommending active learning methods for young children in schools. In this respect it is perhaps significant that Lawrence was teaching in an elementary school, for it was with the elementary schools that Arnold had been most concerned in his role as inspector, and his reports and essays had clearly helped prepare the way for new thinking about the pupil–teacher relation.

We see the case for this new relationship being argued most forcefully in Edward Holmes's *What is and What Might Be* (1911), a book which argued that in England elementary school children were over-trained, over-supervised and over-controlled with the consequence that when they left school they were helpless and unable to survive on their own:

> The excessive regard that has always been paid in our elementary schools to neat handwriting and correct spelling is characteristic of the whole Western attitude towards education. No 'results' are more easily and more accurately appraised than these, and it follows that no 'results' are more highly esteemed by the unenlightened teacher.
>
> Holmes 1911, p. 128

Holmes rails against the inspection system that had been dominant in England until relatively recently:

> Why is the teacher so ready to do everything (or nearly everything) for the children whom he professes to educate? One obvious answer to the question is that for a third of a century (1862–1895) the 'Education Department' did everything (or nearly everything) for him. For a third of a century 'My Lords' required their inspectors to examine every child in every elementary school in England in a syllabus which was binding in all schools alike. In doing this they put a bit in the mouth of the teacher and drove him at their pleasure, in this direction and that. And what they did to him they compelled him to do to the child.
>
> Holmes 1911, p. 7

The irony is that until 1910 Holmes had been Chief Inspector of Elementary Schools. Like Lawrence he worked both inside and outside the institutional structures, the scholar gypsy we described in our preface.

Holmes had also published a book called 'The Creed of Buddha' and ultimately it is the Bohemian and the Blavatskian in him that drive his belief in a new pedagogical relationship:

> My aim, in writing this book, is to show that the *externalism* of the West, the prevalent tendency to pay undue regard to outward and visible 'results' and to neglect what is inward and vital, is the source of most of the defects that vitiate Education in this country, and therefore that the only remedy for these defects is the drastic one of changing our standard of reality and our conception of the meaning and value of life.
>
> Holmes 1911, Preface, p. v

Holmes may have been ahead of the movement towards change in elementary schools, but what change there was, however modest by later standards, is indicated by the 1910–11 Report of the Board of Education, part of which Ball (1985) cites as evidence of the 'new English':

> Where a few years ago there would have been two lessons in dictation and one in composition, the proportion is now reversed . . . the subjects too on which they write are different. The formal essay on an abstract or general subject is more rarely set. Instead, the children write mainly from their own experiences. Formal grammar, instead of being treated as a more or less isolated subject, is soundly taught in connection with composition.

Ball makes the point that this is evidence of a bottom-up transformation of the practices of Subject English, and is quite different from the notion of a top-down influence from the universities. Ball argues that the model being developed in elementary schools came from teachers, inspectors and others who 'shared the "sense of mission" of English teaching in schools' (Ball 1985, p. 57), and that this development took place in the absence of 'any extant epistemic community available in the universities to further their cause'. The move towards encouraging children's expressiveness, in their own 'natural' language, not only in writing but also in talk, comes even earlier, in the 1905 Suggestions for the Consideration of Teachers and Others Concerned in the Work of the Public Elementary Schools, which stated that '(t)here should be no grammar teaching apart from the other English lessons, it should arise naturally out of the reading and composition lessons' (Board of Education 1905).

Lawrence stayed in teaching for little more than three years but his writings on education provide the reader with rhetoric not dissimilar to Holmes's. The combination of the Carlylean rejection of the mechanistic and the determination to overcome all obstacles reflects his reading and his missionary zeal. While in Croydon he delivered to a fund-raising session of the English Association a paper in November 1910 on the Scottish poet

Rachel Annand Taylor. The paper is written in a highly wrought aesthetic style, and there is an enormous contrast between the atmosphere of lush decadence that surrounds the discussion of the poet and her work, and the reality of school where he had 'tamed his wild beasts' by beating them into submission. That sense of detaching oneself from the difficulties of teaching in less than ideal conditions students whose main interest lies elsewhere is conveyed by the flight into romance that characterises Lawrence's reading and interest in music – Nietzsche and Wagner. The disjunction between rhetoric and practice is something that any account of a subject's development will do well to remember.

In 1911, the year in which *What is and What Might Be* appeared, Barrie published the prose version of *Peter Pan*, which had been hugely successful immediately following its first performance in 1904. What is particularly interesting about the prose *Peter and Wendy* is the way in which the text became a site for the decisions being made about the relationship between class and literary language. In 'Peter Pan, Language and the State', Jacqueline Rose examines the fate of *Peter and Wendy* when in 1915 it became accepted by the London County Council's Books and Apparatus Sub-Committee as a reader for use in schools. She shows how the Latinate literary language, and the reference to Hook's public school education (more precisely identified in the play by his dying words 'Floreat Etona') were carefully excised from the school version, and Rose reads this as evidence of the machinery of the state exerting a direct influence on the language frames into which children were to be inducted. In 1912 a Government circular (BoE 1912, p. 27) extended the separation through language and education announced in the second Education Act of 1902 which had made possible the establishment of schools for older elementary pupils whose language for learning would be English rather than the Latin of the public school child. In the 1912 circular English was distinguished from literary language, with the elementary school child being encouraged to use the language of experience and everyday life. This emphasis on expressiveness helps explain the LCC's decision to remove the Latinate expressions and literary tropes with which Barrie teases the child reader from time to time in *Peter and Wendy*: 'Ah, envy not Hook. There came to him a presentiment of his earlier dissolution'. In a key passage Rose identifies the processes at work here:

> For *Peter Pan* to become a *reader*, the overconscious signs of its status as *literature* must be erased . . . The language of the child – the language which it speaks, the language it reads, and the relationship between the two – was one of the central arenas within which this contradiction was played out. Here, the question of language becomes the question of *literacy*, and the question of literature hands over to that of *literary language* (how and what to speak, what to read and to what end?). By this almost imperceptible shift, both language and literature are released as objects of *policy* – policy by means of which the child's relationship to its

culture can be defined. Language is not there simply to be spoken, any more than literature waits to be read, like matter almost to be imbibed by the child. Both the language and the literature available to the child fall inside institutions which constitute them differentially, and with different values and meanings at different times. The point of examining *Peter Pan's* encounter with the schools is not, therefore, so much to demonstrate an outrage – the repressive educational machinery clamps down on the book for the child – as to show how both language and literature are constituted by just such 'machinery' in the first place. In this context, natural language or the idea of language as naturally expressive . . . appears not as something outside the range of these determinations, but as one pole of a fully structural opposition between natural and cultured language in the schools.

Rose 1984, p. 118

Quoting tellingly from both the 1912 Board of Education Circular cited earlier and the 1910 Circular on *The Teaching of English in Secondary Schools* (BoE 1910) Rose shows how official directives encouraged teachers to foster the 'natural' language of elementary school children. By 'natural' was meant a spoken vocabulary based on concrete objects and a written form based on speech. What was important about literature was the story, what was important about poetry was the content. The reverse was true in the newly constituted secondary schools, where style and structure are to be learned and narrative fiction to be excluded. Elementary schools, attended by those who would do mechanical and physical labour, were, as Arnold had intended, places in which literature was deployed to humanise and improve literacy, but in forms that were not classical or overtly literary. 'We do not want to carry our elementary schools into Virgil or Cicero' Arnold had argued (Marvin 1910). In those schools in 1911 a particular kind of natural language was being constructed, and *Peter and Wendy* with its Latin reference had to be edited to conform to this model of written expression. The example of *Peter and Wendy* illustrates the paradox that a literary text's ability to incorporate simultaneously many languages and discourses sometimes makes it problematic as part of the institutionalised moral technology – in this case schooling. Despite this it can be successfully appropriated, harnessed and utilised as part of the machinery of linguistic reproduction whose function is the formation of the subject. Modernist texts such as *The Portrait of the Artist* initially appeared to resist the process of institutionalisation, and had to appear initially in small circulation, coterie magazines, but they too have been appropriated and safely commodified as examination texts. The irony is that it is only in the making safe that they enter into the wider cultural domain at all. Barrie's text illustrates this process of appropriation and commodification in a condensed way: it was a set reader within four years of its publication.

Let me now turn to consider in what ways it was acknowledged at the beginning of the century that English was in possession of as many functions as a Swiss army knife, and that something needed to be done about this.

The difficulty English faced in seeking to define itself by means of what it was not (science) or by means of broad unfocused notions not specific to English (nationalism/modernity) is recognised in the early leaflets of the English Association: 'English is, whatever else may be said of it or against it, one of the most plastic, the most Protean of studies' (An Address delivered by C. H. Herford Litt D to the members of the Manchester Branch of the English Association reprinted as Leaflet No. 16, 1910). If we take the following year, 1911, the protean nature of English is demonstrated by the range of approaches and disciplines that form the subject of papers published in the two bulletins for the year. Ignoring the lectures on specific writers, these included papers on Berkeley and Hobbes, grammatical terminology, oral recitation, simplified spelling and the study of English place names. Generally, the bulletins and the leaflets vacate the ground occupied by the philologists, though maintaining the right to speak on matters of philology, discussing instead the central place of modern literature in the teaching of English. For some this raises a fundamental pedagogical problem, namely that 'Literature is the interpretation of life . . . The interpretation of life not only cannot be taught to anyone, but in a very peculiar eminent way it cannot be taught to children' (Professor J. W. Mackail, Meeting of the English Association, 11 January 1908, reported in Bulletin No. 3). It is a point made again and again over the next ten years. What is particularly interesting is the way that it is a view articulated by Henry Newbolt himself, who, like Matthew Arnold, was both a poet and a believer in the peculiarly indefinable nature of English. At the annual dinner held at the Holborn Restaurant on 10 January 1913 it was announced that Newbolt was to become a member of the Association, and part of his after dinner speech was reported in Bulletin No. 3:

> The one [principle] upon which he laid a great deal of stress was the principle of the indirect method, this method as applied to teaching, which he noticed was one of the main objects of the Association. Anything of the nature of poetry, of emotion, of feeling, of literature, could never be taught by any direct method whatever . . . Literature was not an animal, and did not have movements. Literature was just what people wrote.
>
> Bulletin No. 19, February 1913, p. 8

This is the essence of a pedagogical dilemma, which has been resolved by a specific set of practices which became part of the technology of English. 'To teach but yet not to teach' is the paradoxical goal that Subject English begins to set itself. In July 1918 the Association had held a conference on the teaching of English in schools. One of the speakers, a Mr Sharwood Smith, it was reported, was of the opinion 'that literature cannot be taught, and that is the business of the school simply to provide the right environment, the right soil and the right nutriment' (Leaflet No. 43 'The Teaching of English in Schools', May 1919). This is a view that refuses to go away: here is another poet who teaches, a more recent example than Newbolt:

> I think teaching literature in a school is an oxymoron. Great literature liberates the mind in an absolute way, frees it from concepts into vast expanse of primordial mind. Whatever the intention, by their very nature, schools are the opposite. They are built on hierarchies, on conservative thought, they are built on money values and people getting tenure or supporting themselves. The purpose of schools – or a common denominator of them – is to control people, not to enlighten them, in order to serve the functions of an often ignorant culture or government. Poetry frees the mind; therefore to teach it in schools is impossible.
>
> John Giorno, New York performance poet in Kravis (1995)

This view of literature has its roots in the Aesthetic theory of the eighteenth century, and the mystification of art and the symbol. In *Literary Theory* Eagleton gives this short shrift:

> The whole point of 'creative' writing was that it was gloriously useless, an end in itself loftily removed from any sordid social purpose. Having lost his patron, the writer discovered a substitute in the poetic.
>
> Eagleton 1983

This presented a difficulty for those seeking to identify a purpose for English. What is it *for*? If it was to engage with literature how could this be done when the dominant theory of literature objected to and resisted the dissection of the artifact, of the symbol which was to be appreciated as a whole, and could not be reduced to its constituent parts?

The domain was thus clear, but not what to do in or with it. Shakespeare and the Romantic poets were safe subjects. The English Association's 4th leaflet, published in 1908, is A. C. Bradley's 'Shelley's View of Poetry'. Eight of the first ten leaflets have a literary subject. And the very first Bulletin contained the following resolution, which was passed unanimously by the Teaching of English section of the Federal Conference on Education at Caxton Hall on 29 May 1907:

> That the object of the teaching of English should be to develop in pupils the power of thought and expression, and the power of appreciating the content of great literary works, rather than to inculcate a knowledge of grammatical, philological and literary detail.
>
> Bulletin No. 1, The English Association, 1907

On the other hand philologists had an enviably clear programme of work to attend to, and one of the strands of English continued to address issues relating to grammar, syntax and dialect. They may not have been the subject of the pamphlets published by the English Association, but they did form a significant strand of the work done in schools. Philology, however, was associated with research being carried out in Germany, and suffered a severe blow with the outbreak of the First World War. Yet I do not agree with Chris Baldick when he argues that the war is not only the turning point in English Literature but also in English literary criticism. Enough has been written about the pre-war developments in literary modernism for us to question the first part of the claim, but I think it is still the orthodoxy to attribute to Leavis and to *Scrutiny* a particular social mission for English that had been absent since Arnold. Yet what are we to make of these sentiments, expressed at University College, January 1912?

> Systematic training in English composition is more needed now than it used to be because we have now no help from the home. Every child used to have no end of stories told by nurse or mother, and they then told stories to each other; this is rare now. At a later stage parents used to read aloud to them, and there was very little trash printed; now no-one reads aloud, and there is hardly anything but trash. Moreover the children take their amusements passively, the gramophone is in the home: they come to school often never having used their faculties at all. A generation of town-bred cockneys, they have none of the training in observation and intelligence that comes from the country life. We have to do now what used to be done by nurse, mother, good books and the study of nature, and to bring out the latent faculties which would often have been vigorous in times gone by.
>
> Dr Rouse, 'English composition is the foundation of all other work'.
> Bulletin No. 16, February 1912

As an example of the manifold Swiss army knife functions of English, this not only anticipates *Mass Civilization and Minority Culture* (1930) and *Fiction and the Reading Public* (1932) by twenty years, it surpasses Leavis in the goals it sets the young subject.

CAMPAIGNING ENGLISH: ISSUES, PAPERS, PUBLICATIONS AND REPORTS IN THE MIDDLE OF THE TWENTIETH CENTURY

* The Newbolt Report and after: developments in the 1920s and 1930s
* Reformation and counter reformation in English: the Second World War and its aftermath
* Organisations, institutions and individuals: towards the 1960s
* Creativity and reaction: writing and the New English

The Newbolt Report and after: developments in the 1920s and 1930s

In the previous section we have paid close attention to the historiography of English in England, and to links between examples of mid nineteenth-century rhetoric on culture and the views expressed in the bulletins and leaflets of the English Association. Before ending our discussion of the first quarter of this century in 1921, the year of the Newbolt Report, we had indicated that we intended to consider the continuities and differences between those views expressed at the beginning of the century and those expressed at the end. Before doing this in the following chapter we need to summarise some of the developments in English in England in the past seventy-five years, in order to historicise the voices we shall be hearing in chapter 3.

The Newbolt Report of 1921, was the culmination and vindication of the work of the English Association, as it was written by a committee whose members were taken almost entirely from the officers of the Association. In its report the committee moved well beyond the initial concern that had caused it to be established, namely that pupils in England were not being provided with the necessary skills for the modern world. The report, officially called *The Teaching of English in England* (Board of Education 1921), together with George Sampson's *English for the English* was extremely influential in confirming the place of English as a central, humanising element in the school curriculum. Sampson made grand claims:

> English is by far the most important subject in elementary schools

and

> English [is] a means of access to formative life and beauty

and

> [English] is of all school activities the chief, the most important and the most practical, because it covers the whole of life of man from the cradle to the grave; it is the one school subject in which we have to fight, not for a clear gain of knowledge, but for a precarious margin of advantage over powerful influences of evil.

Underpinning all of this was an anti-testing, anti-science rhetoric:

> One danger of the present passion for science has already shown its head . . . Delight in measured results means a result for demands that can be measured . . . I want teachers to remember that they are first of all healers and not vivisectionists. I want them to see clearly that laboratory work in school is not education, and that to test a child's mind is not to

teach it. Dogs are not really improved by vivisection, even if the mind of the vivisector is.

In contrast:

English is not really a subject at all. It is a condition of existence rather than a subject of instruction.

Sampson (1970)

The Newbolt Report took a slightly different tack. English was a subject, and it had a unique role to play in the formation of national identity. English was not only humanizing, it provided space for a celebration of the nation *England*. In the immediate aftermath of the First World War there was a great desire that the nation's wounds be healed, and the nation's divisions (so obvious in the pre-war period, and scarcely masked in the conduct of the campaigns on the Western Front) were to be replaced by the unifying influence of a shared national literary heritage.

We believe that such an education based upon the English language and literature would have important social, as well as personal results; it would have a unifying tendency. Two causes, both accidental and conventional rather than national, at present distinguish and divide one class from another in England. The first of these is a marked difference in their modes of speech. If the teaching of the language were properly and universally provided for, the difference between educated and uneducated speech, which at present causes so much prejudice and difficulty of intercourse on both sides, would disappear.

The Teaching of English in England (Board of Education 1921)

Both the report and Sampson were ambivalent about whether the teacher of English had to be a specialist, however. On the one hand the rhetoric suggests that the English teacher is a very special kind of person, but the qualities necessary to teach English well could also be found in history or geography teachers, perhaps because English was and is perceived to be less about content and more about method.

Both content and method were being addressed, however. It is in this period that notions of a cultural heritage including a canon of works, and the specific Englishness of such writers as Shakespeare and the Romantic poets, were given greater legitimacy. Simultaneously, though much less influentially in England, there was a rethinking of the way in which English could be taught. We have seen how before the war a teacher such as Lawrence was already providing children with opportunities for drama and performance, and new approaches to teaching were proposed in books such as *The New Teaching* (Adams 1918) and Caldwell Cook's *The Play Way* (1917) with its emphasis on active learning and a refusal to make English imitate Latin by pretending that English has a straightforward grammar. In the United States John Dewey's liberal and pragmatic approach to education had become influential following the successful publication of *The School and Society* in 1899, *The Child and the Curriculum* in 1902 and *Democracy and Education* in 1916. But it is mainly in retrospect that we see these books as significant: the evidence suggests that English teachers in England, unsure of what constituted the *subject* of English, continued to rely on grammar and the rote learning of poems as the subject material and method, largely because this was the way the subject continued to be assessed. The same can be said for the Newbolt Report: in Brian Doyle's reading of the history of English, the autonomy of the new subject was more important for its development than the rhetoric of the report. Goodson and Marsh (1996) emphasise the solid, sombre professionalisation of English that took place during this period, exemplified by the foundation of the *Review of English Studies* in 1925. To rebut the charge of effeminacy, English was determined to publicise itself as a serious, academic subject.

The 1930s saw a consolidation of English in secondary schools and during the 1930s and 1940s was reinvigorated by the influence of F. R. Leavis and the Cambridge School of critics. With their emphasis on aesthetics the rhetoric shifted from literature as a nationalistic phenomenon (Leavis was a pacifist and in the First World War served at the Front in the ambulance service) to literature as a necessary element in the cultivation of taste. In practice, this taste continued to be defined along nationalistic lines. Leavis had little time for 'foreign' writers such as Proust. Eliot, Conrad and James were acceptable because they had the wisdom to come and live in England. They could become part of the Great Tradition, and the study of the works that formed this tradition would improve the minds of those who rigorously set about reading from it. Leavis shared Arnold's belief in the ability of literature to improve the discriminatory faculties, but did not share his liberal, democratic belief that the refinement of taste and judgement – a literary sensibility – could be acquired by the whole population. Nevertheless, his views, as outlined in articles in *Scrutiny* and in 'Mass Civilization and Minority Culture' (Leavis 1948) influenced a whole generation of secondary English teachers, and the book he co-authored with Denys Thompson, *Culture and Environment* (Leavis and Thompson 1933) provided a programme of work for upper secondary schools, with literature at the centre of that work. The ideology that underpins this book is made clear in the opening paragraphs:

> Many teachers of English who have become interested in the possibilities of training taste and sensibility must have been troubled by accompanying doubts. What effect can such training have against the multitudinous counter-influences – films, newspapers, advertising – indeed the whole world outside the class-room? Yet the very conditions that make literary education look so desperate are those which make it

more important than ever before; for in a world of this kind – and in a world that changes so rapidly – it is on literary tradition that the office of maintaining continuity must rest.

But literary education, we must not forget, is to a great extent a substitute. What we have lost is the organic community with the living culture it embodies. Folk-songs, folk-dances, Cotswold cottages and handicraft products are signs and expressions of something more: an art of life, a way of living, ordered and patterned, involving social arts, codes of intercourse and responsive adjustment growing out of immemorial experience, to the natural environment and the rhythm of the year.

Leavis and Thompson 1933 (1964, pp. 1–2)

Yet it would be wrong to see this, or any other period, as monolithic. There were other university schools of English, other approaches within Cambridge itself. Diagrams such as the one by Stephen J. Ball showing the complicated network of connections within 'The Cambridge School of English' (Ball 1985, p. 66) actually take us beyond Cambridge to Abbs and Marshall at the University of Sussex, Barnes and Holbrook at NATE, and Hoggart and Bantock at Birmingham and Leicester. In one sense, what is most striking about Leavis is his distancing himself from the academy and academic practices, so that his battles over his position and his eventual resignation signal elements of the 'Scholar Gypsy' romanticism which we signalled in our preface. Literature as an art and literature as an academic discipline has always lived with these tensions, and Frank Leavis embodied them in a particularly striking and influential way.

Culture and Environment was published in 1933. This was also the year in which the second part of the Hadow Report appeared, the first part, *Report of the Consultative Committee on the Education of the Adolescent* having been published in 1926. Before Hadow, most children in England were still educated in all-age elementary schools and Hadow, which was concerned in this first report primarily with the older children in those schools, proposed that elementary education should be divided into three stages: infant (five to seven year olds), junior (seven to eleven) and senior (eleven to fourteen). The school leaving age had been raised to fourteen in 1922 and the Hadow reorganisation was a significant restructuring. The main significance of this for English was that it made specialist teaching possible in the newly built senior schools for those over the age of eleven. The fee-paying secondary schools which had been established by the 1902 Act catered in 1938 for 470,003 children, over half of whom were fee paying. Although an increasing percentage of elementary school children qualified for free places (from 25 per cent to 46 per cent – an increase made possible by the two Labour Governments), they were mainly used by the lower middle class who could afford to pay (Simpson 1991, p. 28).

The 1920s and 1930s saw the birth of the modern English department in both schools and higher education. In a university this first saw the light of day at Cambridge and was as much the creation of I. A. Richards as Leavis. Leavis, Richards, Eliot and, a little later, William Empson, all helped define an occupation for English, and that occupation was literary criticism. Literary criticism in England had not hitherto achieved the status it had achieved in France, for example, where Sainte Beuve had established its authority. Literary criticism could be traced in England to some of the comments made by Dryden about his own poetry, and the argument that it is the poet's duty to undertake this examination and discussion of work. I. A. Richards in particular developed the version of this approach passed on by Matthew Arnold, who, as we have seen, believed that the study of poetry was mentally improving for everyone, if undertaken in a rigorous and organised way. In this respect he differed from both Eliot and Leavis, who felt that only a minority could appreciate literature. But collectively this group

> persuaded people inclined to doubt it that literature is a field of instruc-
> tion and enquiry that has its own integrity, its own boundaries, and its
> own intellectual diversity. They found a place within the university for
> something that was not the study of language, not the editing of texts,
> not the history of ideas, but the appreciation and analysis of what Eliot
> called 'literature as literature'.
>
> Menand 1995

It is in the 1930s that the figure of the specialist English teacher starts to make an appearance in contemporary fiction, though as Protherough and Atkinson (1991, p. 7) point out, he (and it is usually a 'he') is still something of a novelty. In schools it was the organisation and structure of education as a whole that was being debated, rather than the specific approaches to English which the Newbolt Report had successfully recommended in broad rhetorical terms. It was clear that secondary education would eventually be reorganised, and in the late 1930s evidence given to the Spens Committee suggested that there was a tide flowing in favour of multilateral schools. Following the first allied successes in 1942 that tide reached a flood as the advocates of reform – mainly from the Labour movement, the Workers Educational Association, the National Union of Teachers and the Trades Union Council – argued for a radical programme which Simon (1991) summarises as follows:

> 1. Abolition, or at least effective assimilation, of the public schools as a
> step towards the creation of a single national system of education
> 2. Secondary education for all over the age of eleven. Abolition of fees
> in all maintained secondary schools (including direct grant grammar
> schools). A common code of regulations for all secondary schools (and
> in a more advanced form, the establishment of the single, common or
> multilateral secondary school)
> 3. Raising of the school leaving age to the age of sixteen

4. Abolition of the dual system. All schools to be equally under public control.

It is worth considering how much of this agenda was actually implemented, because English had marked out its territory in an era of educational expansion and reform, and was guaranteed to be instrumental in, and to benefit from this change.

But the 1930s, partly in response to the spread of fascism and totalitarianism, saw another issue being debated, one in which English had a very vital role to play. Anxieties about the future of democracy in an age of mass culture led to the three different responses described by Donald in his chapter 'The Machinery of Democracy' (Donald 1992). As we have seen, Leavis argued for an educated elite as a counter to the influence of Hollywood, which he deplored. At the BBC Reith was also anti-Hollywood, but felt that the solution was to educate the masses through high-quality radio programmes. Grierson, the documentary film maker, took a different view, believing that popular culture and high culture could co-exist quite happily. In each case, the concern was for the formation of the citizen, and the supposition was the good individual was the good citizen. The role of the individual became central to discussion during this period, and people were to become good individuals through art, through drama, through literature, through *English*.

Reformation and counter reformation: the Second World War and its aftermath

Qualified visions in wartime: English, assessment and the public schools in the 1940s

The major piece of education legislation that emerged during the reforming period of the Second World War was the 1944 Education Act, which a liberal Conservative member of the wartime coalition government, R. A. Butler, steered through Parliament. The Bill was influenced less by the radical agenda indicated above, and more by the Norwood Report of July 1943 which recommended a tripartite model for secondary education, with separate, parallel grammar, technical and secondary modern schools, largely reflecting the Tory view outlined in the 1943 White Paper.

As for the Public Schools, it is important to remind ourselves of the unusual status of private, fee-paying education (because that is what Public School means in England – it is public in the sense that it is not a Church school) in England. In many countries parents send their children to fee-paying schools if they cannot get into the best state schools – they are, in this sense, second best. In England the public schools have long enjoyed a privileged status, particularly since the reform of the public school system (which in the eighteenth century had become notorious for its beatings, its debauchery and its low level of scholarship), a reform generally attributed to the influence of Thomas Arnold. It is not too simplistic to say that the Public Schools provided England with its governing class, who would not have an interest in improving the quality of state education until the public school system was swept aside.

The 1944 Act said little about the public schools. Butler, as he admitted in his autobiography, had shunted the 'Pullman carriage' of private education into a long siding by setting up a separate committee (the Fleming Committee) which did not report until three weeks after the 1944 Bill had completed its third reading. So far from being a radical measure, the 1944 Act confirmed a hierarchy of schools:

Public schools
Direct grant schools
Grammar schools
Technical schools
Secondary modern schools.

If this hierarchy reinforced class difference, with the secondary modern schools for the masses and the public schools with their imitators for the elite, then so did the examination system. Children sat an exam at the age of eleven, and on the strength of their performance in what amounted to a kind of IQ Test they were directed to the 'appropriate' kind of school. The established School Certificate and the Higher School Certificate (for those proceeding to university) were to be replaced in 1948 by the General Certificate of Education (Ordinary Levels) which did not involve groupings of subjects, but single subject qualifications. English was thus recognised as an examination subject in its own right, and became part of the machinery of assessment.

The reforming period of the war, culminating in the Labour Government of the immediate post-war period, did standardise secondary education, did make multilateral schools a legal possibility even if they had to wait another ten years before the true era of comprehensivation, and did lead to a programme of school building for the new secondary modern schools. The school leaving age had been raised in 1947 to fifteen. Yet this was not the social revolution that had been promised. The promised raising of the school leaving age to sixteen had to wait until 1972, with the first wave not reaching the age of sixteen until 1974. The macrocosm of education reflected the microcosm of English: such changes and modernising tendencies as there had been served simply to accommodate the rising demand of a lower middle or 'subaltern' class. In Gramscian terms, as Brian Simon points out, these groups were now successfully assimilated in the social complex. English had been recommended by Arnold as a means of stabilising the population, and the Newbolt Report had endorsed the unifying influence of the subject. And English was now a thoroughly established subject on the secondary timetable.

The counter reformation: the 1950s

The flirtation with radicalism was brief: at the end of the 1940s there was no marriage, let alone a honeymoon. The pattern for the next ten years was suggested by the publication of Eliot's *Notes Towards a Definition of Culture* (1949), with its concern with elites. The 1950s, which saw a return of a Conservative government, saw attention being focused on the grammar school end of the tripartite system. The new General Certificate of Education examination could only be taken at the age of sixteen, and thus excluded most secondary modern pupils who left at fifteen. There were some anxieties about the reliability of the 11+ as a predictor of performance: there was evidence that motivated 11+ 'failures' who stayed on until the age of sixteen were more successful at GCE than a number of children who had passed the test and gone to grammar school. Ten years after Eliot, C. P. Snow published his essay on the two cultures, in which he deprecated the 'crystallised pattern' of education. English teachers were among the earliest to perceive that class and poverty rather than intelligence were at the root of the problem. Local authorities such as Leicestershire began to pursue a policy of establishing comprehensive schools. Education was about to enter a decade of great optimism. The Robbins report of 1963 recommended ways of organising the massive expansion of higher education which the Crowther Report of 1959 had said was necessary with 'higher education for all' as the rallying cry. Also in 1963 the Prime Minister Harold Wilson had spoken of his dream of a 'university of the air', which was to become reality ten years later, thanks to the work of Jenny Lee, the Arts Minister, Arnold Kettle, a respected English university don who believed in the importance of social development, and Michael Young, who thought up the name 'Open University'. This period is identified by John Dixon as one of the three 'critical episodes in the struggle to shape literary and cultural studies' (Dixon 1991): in the same year as Wilson's speech the National Association for the Teaching of English was founded, and the Newsom Committee (Central Advisory Council for Education: 1963) published its report on pupils of 13–16 years of average or below average ability. English once again had an official publication emphasising the centrality and pervasiveness of the subject:

461 The use of language in thought and in communication must enter into every part of the curriculum

The report, however, followed this up with an observation emphasising how much there was to be done if English's contribution was to be effective. There was a readiness for a New English, it implies. The committee quickly identified the plurality of beliefs shared by the teachers they had met:

462 The teachers of English tend to think of their subject from three different but related points of view: as a medium of communication, as

a means of creative expression, and as a literature embodying the vision of greatness.

Grand aims for English were identified:

> 467 The overriding aim of English teaching must be the personal development and social competence of the pupil.

and the rhetoric remained recognisably Arnoldian:

> 473 All pupils, including those of very limited attainments, need the civilising experience of contact with great literature, and can respond to its universality, although they will depend heavily on the skill of the teacher as an interpreter. Sympathetically presented, literature can stretch the minds and imaginations of the pupils, and help to illumine for them, in wider human terms, their own problems of living.

But if sections such as this seemed to be echoes of an earlier age, the section that immediately followed was very forward looking:

> 474 Here we should wish to add a strong claim for the study of film and television in their own right, as powerful forces in our culture and significant sources of language and ideas.

The report, which in its entirety addresses the whole curriculum, the organisation of the school and the teachers who teach, expressed concern about the number of non-specialists teaching English. It also succinctly identified the paradox of English that simultaneously delights and troubles those we interviewed and whose voices we hear later in this chapter:

> 484 English is distinctive in the curriculum in that it is both all-pervasive and yet has relatively little subject matter of its own. In the greater part of the pupils' work concerned with communication, with the acquisition of information and with the recording and evaluation of experience, English performs a service function to other subjects: it is the other subjects which supply the content, and the occasion for strengthening the pupil's resources in language. English must not be a subject narrowly ensphered with its own specialist boundaries; neither must it disappear altogether . . . The English lesson . . . is most likely to offer those opportunities which allow adolescents to write out of themselves what they are not always prepared or able to talk about: in the writing, deeply personal thoughts and feelings may be disguised or transmuted.

The report reflects or anticipates the emergent interest in fresh ways of teaching:

481 The best way to study writing is to practise it. Children only learn writing by writing, and they are best prepared to write about their own experience.

English in schools was about to be influenced by a powerful belief in the importance of individual self-expression, a belief which, as we shall see later, had taken hold of a small but significant number of the primary schools visited by the Plowden Committee. We have seen that as a theory of education it had a long pedigree, and had been recommended in a succession of books and educational experiments (such as Homer Lane's 'Little Commonwealth' to A. S. Neill's Summerhill throughout the first fifty years of the century. In the United States it had received attention through the wave of progressive rhetoric during the 1930s. In England ideas took longer to filter through, but once they gained currency they were taken further and in more imaginative directions, as the delegation of American English teachers were to discover when they visited England in the 1960s.

Organisations, institutions and individuals: towards the 1960s

There are certain organisations, institutions and figures whose status and influence must be acknowledged in any summary of the period we are now entering. The period of the 1960s and early 1970s is seen as a radical, pro-gressive period by many and there is no doubt that a number of significant developments took place in English as a result of innovative and pioneering work undertaken by individuals and institutions. Local Education Auth-orities, especially when led by inspirational Directors of Education, were in a position to encourage change and experiment through the reorganisation of education in their area and the appointment of Advisors and the creation of Teachers' Centres to facilitate change in a climate and supportive environ-ment that sometimes makes this appear like a golden age. The Local Authority had played a key role in curriculum development ever since the 1902 Education Act set up LEAs, and at the same time gave greater autonomy to headmasters and teachers. The influence of the public schools, which until that point had been considerable, especially in providing a model for secondary pedagogical practice, was considerably reduced, and individual teachers, supported by a less oppressive inspection system, were able to conduct experiments in classroom learning. Many of these experiments were disseminated to a wider audience through the work of the National Association for the Teaching of English, which was founded in the early years of the 1960s by a group of people, many of whom were associated with the journal *English in Schools* founded by Denys Thompson. NATE was to become far more radical and innovative than the more sedate and conven-tional English Association, and the organisation became extremely influential on curriculum development and the apex of the triangle which had institutions and influential individuals at its other corners.

Often the two categories of institution and individual are inseparable: the work of Raymond Williams (*Culture and Society* (1958), for example) and Richard Hoggart (*The Uses of Literacy* (1957)) becomes bound up with the work of the Centre for Contemporary Cultural Studies, founded in Birmingham in 1964 and originally a research group within the English Department. As early as 1950 Williams had indicated what a post-Leavisite model of English might look like, and both his influence and that of E. P. Thompson is evident in the new readings of culture that English and Cultural Studies departments in universities were developing.

In schools the influence of another institution, the University of London Institution of Education, made itself felt as the work of individuals such as Harold Rosen, Nancy Martin, James Britton and John Dixon made a parallel leap away from the reading of canonical texts by celebrating and encouraging student writing and tapping into what was seen as the authentic voice of working-class children. Instead of reading an imposed body of someone else's 'great literature', it was argued, children should create their own.

Creativity and reaction: writing and the New English 1960–1980

The creative writing movement, which was enormously influential in shifting the focus of the practice of English from reading to writing, emphasised the importance of activity and production in the process of learning. As the titles of books by David Holbrook suggest – *English for the Rejected* (1964) and *English for Maturity* (1961) – the concern was with the majority of students who are not academically gifted and who were being failed by the approaches that were favoured by grammar – that is selective – schools. These academic approaches involved formal exercises such as *précis*, essay writing and 'literary appreciation'. New approaches – the New English – had been celebrated at Dartmouth, New Hampshire in the Anglo-American English conference that took place in 1966, a conference commemorated in H. J. Muller's account written for the wider public (Muller 1967), but most famously celebrated in *Growth through English* by John Dixon (Dixon 1967). In this influential book Dixon rejected what he identified as 'skills' and 'cultural heritage' models of English, favouring instead a process model which he called 'personal growth'. If, as he argued, English was contentless, it could be defined through the processes it encouraged, and these drew on the twin ideas of 'personal experience and an active use of language' (Sawyer 1998). Earlier, Dixon had collaborated with Simon Clements and Leslie Stratta in writing the influential *Reflections*, an illustrated anthology of prose and poetry intended to stimulate discussion and original writing in secondary schools (Clements *et al.* 1963). It signalled its rhetorical position by including Macneice's 'Prayer before Birth' in its Preface:

O fill me
With strength against those who would freeze my
humanity, would dragoon me into a lethal automaton
would make me a cog in a machine.

Echoes of Carlyle, the Romantic Poets and Arnold, mingled with a Leavisite view of culture (Hoggart's 'Spicy Magazines' from the *The Uses of Literacy*), a social realism (themes such as Family, Community and Work, Questions of our Time), photographs intended to stimulate thought in an empirical way ('Each photograph was chosen for its power to suggest new understandings of human experience') and, in the 'Questions of Our Time' section – which deals with topics such as racism and nuclear warfare – ideas for creative writing: 'when you really mean and feel what you write, then you write well' (Clements *et al.* 1963, p. 87).

In the 1970s continuing attention was paid to writing through the work of the London Writing Research Unit, whose most widely published members were James Britton, Nancy Martin and Harold Rosen. In a diagram labelled 'The London Connection' Stephen J. Ball places Britton at the centre of a complicated web of names which also includes Bernstein, Connie Rosen and Halliday (Ball 1985, p. 68). In some cases the links are through the Institute of Education, while in others it is through NATE or the University of London. Together with Douglas Barnes from the University of Leeds, who provides a link with Leavis, these researchers and practitioners proposed fresh approaches to language and learning, as outlined in *Language and Learning* (Britton 1970), *Language, the Learner and the School* (Barnes *et al.* 1971) and *The Development of Writing Abilities 11–18* (Britton *et al.* 1975). This fed through into schools, and the English classroom became a place in which students were encouraged to develop their skills in oracy, to write for real audiences, to write in a variety of forms, and to write freely and imaginatively. Nearly every English Department purchased its set of the 110 units of *Language in Use*, which provided a set of resource materials for teachers encouraging students to think, for example, about the way the world and its stereotypes was represented in the language of advertising (Doughty, Pearce and Thornton 1971).

There was simultaneously a reaction: in 1969 Brian Cox and A. C. Dyson edited a series of essays known as the *The Black Papers*, which called for a return to the rigour and standards that the authors felt to be disappearing as English teachers were charged with being less concerned with technical features such as spelling and handwriting than they were with effect and imagination. Cox is frank about the populist, anti-theory stance which they took:

The Black Papers liberated a repressed ideology which eventually was to play a part in making Mrs Thatcher Prime Minister in 1979. Their success in transforming the educational scene was a triumph for the

ordinary, the obvious, the instinctive and the natural over the theorists
and utopians of the 1960s.

Cox 1992, p. 4

Though their rhetoric tapped a continuing public anxiety, it went against
the grain of the general movement within English, which was reformist.
There was official recognition of this movement in the form of the Oracy
Project, and before that the School Curriculum Development Committee's
National Writing Project (quite different from the American model) which
ran for only three years, 1985–1988, but whose influence continued to be
felt through a series of publications such as *A Rich Resource: Writing and
Language Diversity* (Nelson/NWP 1990a) and *Partnerships for Writing: School,
the Community and the Workplace* (Nelson/NWP 1990b). These publications
sit on many School of Education Language Centre shelves as sad reminders
of the last government-funded research initiative in English that fed directly
through to teachers, the materials from the even more ambitious Language in
the National Curriculum project never officially being released.

Although among English teachers from this period it was a widely held that
such projects as Language in the National Curriculum, the Oracy Project and
the NWP itself were wound up much too soon, the first in highly controversial circumstances, there have been continuing voices arguing for the
centrality of imaginative writing in the English curriculum. These voices have
usually been those of practising writers themselves: Brian Cox, poet and
eventual Chair of the Arvon Foundation which runs courses for teachers to
practise writing alongside published writers, Ted Hughes, the Poet Laureate,
Peter Abbs and Michael Rosen. What they all have in common – Rosen
excepted – is a rejection of contemporary culture. Rosen and Hughes
approach life from very different philosophical perspectives but both share a
belief in the centrality of the practice of original student writing. Such a
belief has been articulated in essays by Abbs (1996), Cox (1995), Hughes
(1967), Dixon and Stratta (1986) and Harold Rosen (1973) and the work
of David Holbrook has been celebrated in a series of appreciative essays
edited by Edwin Webb (Webb 1996). All stress the role of language as a
culturally enriching resource for the present rather than a tool or a competency for the adult life of the future. Brian Cox was particularly active in
this campaign, writing in 1994 that he regretted very much the way that the
Black Papers had been used by right-wing groups to attack creative teachers
(Cox 1992, p. 6)

This fresh emphasis on original writing, which was revised and redirected
in essays by Andrew Wilkinson (1980) and Michael Benton (1978), found
expression in a very practical way through a series of imaginative suggestions
about 'Twenty-four things to do with a book' (Fox 1977) and 'Thirty-six
things to do with a poem' (Fox, Merrick *et al.* 1981), both of which emerged
from brainstorming sessions with teachers in conference workshops. It is
possible that these have had more immediate influence on practice than

the discussion from which they emerged, though they are themselves the commodification of that discussion.

The call for 'basics': schools, literacy and the single-bladed pen-knife

By the time the Plowden Committee delivered its report in 1967 a Labour Government had attempted to implement its educational policy of introducing comprehensive schools by issuing Circular 10/65 which required local authorities to submit proposals for the reorganisation of secondary education along comprehensive lines. Alongside this went a number of other reforms. Teachers were given more recognition through the setting up of Teachers' Centres, while the Schools Councils, the majority of whose members were teachers, were charged with looking at curriculum development. It was science, particularly through the Nuffield Science project, that was setting the pace in curriculum reform, but as we have seen new attitudes to writing were transforming English, and the Plowden Report (HMSO 1967) again spoke of the central place of language (para. 55). The report also expressed its hope that it would see less full-time class teaching, and in its rejection of streaming on the grounds that streaming ignored the needs of the individual it gave great psychological support to the move towards mixed ability teaching in the new comprehensive schools, a principle which English teachers at a NATE conference on the 'The Future of English' held in 1995, nearly thirty years later, were still identifying as the main belief to be defended in the continuing battle against centralised control.

By 1995 that battle had been virtually lost. A reaction to the progressive moves outlined above had not been long in coming. As we mentioned earlier, the first two Black Papers, edited by two lecturers from university English departments, had appeared in 1969, and in the early 1970s, as more comprehensive schools were set up, attacks on their size and indiscipline were delivered by journalists such as Jill Tweedie and television programmes such as the BBC's flagship current affairs programme *Panorama*. In 1975 a further series of Black Papers reappeared, this time proposing tests at ages 7, 11 and 14, while industrial leaders began to complain about the standards of school leavers. The much publicised case of the William Tyndale primary school in London, where teachers had taken the radical agenda implied by Plowden to a logical conclusion with a simultaneous collapse in confidence in the school from parents, symbolically marked the end of teacher autonomy. Teachers were beginning to be perceived as unreliable, and in the most sensationalised cases, irresponsible. The Schools Councils were wound up. Anxieties about literacy standards had led the Secretary of State for Education, Margaret Thatcher, to set up the Bullock Committee which reported in 1975 (DES 1975) and once again emphasised the role of 'language across the curriculum' in a phrase that provoked much discussion. English was everywhere: but then why should it have its own rooms?

The Bullock Report, as it came to be known, is an extremely interesting document, and has been read as both the high-water mark of progressive English and the roots of its decline. Despite its very specific brief – it has been set up as a Committee of Inquiry into Reading and the Use of English – it spread its net widely. Early on it identifies three views of English – personal growth, skills and social change – which the Cox Report was to expand on in its report some fifteen years later – and endorses the post-Dartmouth, growth-model belief that English is a subject without content:

> 1.6 It is a characteristic of English that it does not hold together as a body of knowledge which can be identified,quantified, then transmitted. Literary studies lead constantly outside themselves, as Leavis put it; so, for that matter, does every aspect of English. There are two possible responses for the teacher of English, at whatever level. One is to attempt to draw in the boundaries, to impose shape on what seems amorphous, rigour on what seems undisciplined. The other is to regard English as process, not content, and take the all-inclusiveness as an opportunity rather than a handicap.

It would be easy to see the hand of James Britton here, arguing for the expressiveness which the work of the London Group, and in particular Britton himself in *Language and Learning* (Britton 1970) had been actively promoting. To the dismay of one member of the Committee, a Headteacher from a Junior School in Surrey who wrote a Note of Dissent, the report claimed that there was little substance in the claim that 'schools are promoting creativity at the expense of Basic Skills' (DES 1975, p. 556). But although the rhetoric of the Bullock Report seems to favour the process model, *A Language for Life* is a subtle and complex document. It certainly rejected a return to the teaching of grammar in isolation, but it also rejects practices which privilege personal responses to social issues. Its concern with language almost inevitably led it gently to a skills model. Stephen J. Ball observes:

> The Bullock report effectively attempted to impose limits upon the range of activities that would legitimately pass as English teaching. Certain traditional practices were reinforced and some elements of innovation had received commendation, but the 'excesses' were clearly identified and censured. Probably most significantly the basic concern of English teaching with pupil skills is established in the report. It is this more than anything else which has probably made an impact on teachers' thinking and planning for work in English lessons.
>
> Ball 1985

It is significant that Britton, in a 'Note of Extension', argued for more expressive work. Yet, ironically, he was unwittingly instrumental in contributing to the role of Bullock in restraining English and redirecting it to language.

Following a change of government, the Labour Prime Minister, James Callaghan, made a well-publicised speech in 1976 calling for a raising of standards, a crusade, for teacher accountability and for control. The conditions were being created which would allow a major overhaul of education in England, and the election of a crusading, right-of-centre Conservative government under the leadership of Margaret Thatcher provided a political will to push these changes through.

Ironically, one of the first changes introduced by this administration was what is now generally regarded as a progressive one, namely the introduction in 1984 of a common exam for all children at the age of sixteen, the General Certificate of Secondary Education (GCSE), although there were to be tiered papers for children of different abilities. In 1987 Kenneth Baker, the Secretary of State for Education proposed a National Curriculum to bring the British system closer to the rest of Europe, and the Education Reform Act can now be regarded as the most significant piece of educational legislation since the 1944 Act. As well as preparing the ground for a national curriculum it introduced a number of other significant measures. It gave schools the opportunity to opt out of local authority control, it established a body to oversee curriculum and assessment, and it gave the green light for the application of market forces to education. So that while in one sense the state, through introducing a national curriculum, was finally getting round to doing what should perhaps have been done in 1870, it was simultaneously introducing measures which were in the long tradition of liberal autonomy and the local independence of schools.

The national curriculum was to be devised by subject committees, one for each of nine subjects. If Margaret Thatcher had not yielded to her Secretary of State for Education the national curriculum would have been a much narrower affair, with not nine but three committees. Kenneth Baker later revealed that 'She believed basically that all was needed in the national curriculum was English, Maths and Science. It was a sort of Gradgrind curriculum in my view, not a rounded one' (Kenneth Baker interview, *The Times Educational Supplement 2*, 2 May 1996, p. 3). Brian Cox was appointed Chair of the English Working Group, presumably on the strength of his Black Paper reputation, but the proposals included in the Committee's report *English for Ages 5–16* (DES 1989) were not at all reactionary and won the general support of the English profession, largely because Cox had been persuaded by the members of the committee who knew about schools that the report should be endorsement of good practice. Brian Cox, a poet and believer in children's writing, saw the tactical danger in presenting a right-of-centre party with what would easily be seen as a liberal and progressive framework for English, and famously put chapters 15, 16 and 17, the attainment target and assessment chapters, at the beginning of the report, in the hope of deflecting attention away from the actual substance of the proposals (although it can be argued that the assessment arrangements *are* the substance of any curriculum). The Government was not fooled, and in the late 1980s a series of working parties, not now under the chairmanship of Cox, revised the original document, slimming it down as it did so. Professor Cox later went on to describe these revisions as the 'Great Betrayal' (Cox 1992).

Annoyed as they were by the loss of what, with hindsight, teachers had affectionately begun to regard as 'their' curriculum there was in many eyes an even more naked act of government hegemony. This was refusal to publish and disseminate the findings of the Language in the National Curriculum project, which was effectively consigned to the dustbin. LINC had been set up following the recommendations of the Kingman Report in 1988. Millions of pounds were spent in seconding teachers and organising regional groups which investigated how knowledge about language could be taught to children in interesting and imaginative ways. The fruits of several years' work were reported to the government, which had hoped for a more simplistic recipe for a return to what was seen as traditional grammar work, and the report remained unpublished. The views and beliefs of teachers were now not considered acceptable, because they were not perceived to address the problems of literacy in ways that were acceptable in a climate that was distinctly right of centre. The expansionist, Swiss army knife model of English was seen to be discredited.

By 1996 the shift that had begun in 1969 had become a powerful public orthodoxy. Politically there appeared to be a complete consensus. Traditional methods were espoused by both Labour and Conservative parties. In a keynote speech delivered in Didcot Girls' School in June 1996 the leader of the Labour Party, who was to become the next Prime Minister, recommended the abandonment of mixed ability teaching in comprehensive schools, a principle which had united English teachers at a National Association for the Teaching of English forum in London a year before. A Skills Audit published in the same month seemed to show that Britain was lagging in literacy and numeracy, and the Secretary of State for Education announced proposals for a 'national curriculum' for teacher training and a special paper in 'grammar, spelling and punctuation' for all fourteen year olds, in addition to the two, prescribed Key Stage 3 English papers, the Shakespeare paper and the Comprehension and Essay paper. A *Panorama* programme broadcast on BBC television on 2 June 1995 examined the way that mathematics was taught in Taiwan, and implied that the reason that children from Pacific rim countries were two or more years ahead in their mathematics performance was because of whole class teaching. The Chief Inspector of Schools recommended that at least 60 per cent of teaching in primary schools should be whole class teaching. The Labour Shadow Secretary of State for Education agreed. The emphasis on individual differences, and on the individual child was to be replaced by an emphasis on what the whole class could do together. Having lost control of the curriculum, teachers were about to lose control of the style in which they chose to teach, though it could be argued that the emphasis on group work and tasks for three levels of ability within the class amounted to an equally normative orthodoxy. As we shall see, for those entering the profession who have not known a world other than the one in which they have grown up and been educated themselves, there is no sense of loss.

Furthermore, the process we have just described as an increase of government control of the curriculum with the marginalisation of teachers can and has been read quite differently. In 1996 Melanie Phillips published her account of these years in *All Must Have Prizes* (Phillips 1996). In Phillips's reading, a liberal orthodoxy in education has resisted all efforts to impose external control, and she had English specialists (alongside teacher training colleges) in mind when she wrote the following: 'The history of education in the last few years has illustrated the awesome capacity of a relativist establishment to frustrate and even deform a set of founding objectives'. Phillips has strong left-wing credentials, and so it would be wrong to dismiss her rage against teachers, and English teachers in particular, as the anger of a frustrated right-wing government. Her rhetoric simplifies the influence of a cultural orthodoxy, but as our research shows, there *is* strong evidence of an orthodoxy in England. The question that we were interested in was not 'How could so much survive a government onslaught' but in whose interests is it that certain practices survive all the legislation and rhetoric in the world.

OTHER IDENTITIES: ENGLISH AND THE RHETORIC OF SCIENCE IN UNIVERSITIES AND SCHOOLS, 1970 TO THE PRESENT

- Colonising science: reconceptualising English in higher education
- English in schools: completing the shift from literature to language
- Language, empowerment and the new literacies
- English in the marketplace

Colonising science: reconceptualising English in higher education

Earlier we touched on the science–arts divide, which has its roots in nineteenth-century definitions of English, carried over into the twentieth, and reached a climax in the passionate exchanges between Snow and Leavis on the subject of the 'two cultures' in the 1950s. Yet if we consider the critical methods proposed in the 1930s by two of Leavis's contemporaries, I. A. Richards and William Empson, and put this alongside the so called New Criticism of the United States, we see evidence of an approach that willingly adopts a quasi-scientific methodology. Here, for example, are Wimsatt and Beardsley, writing in the 1950s:

The Affective Fallacy is a confusion between the poem and its results (what it is and what it does) . . . It begins by trying to derive the standards of criticism from the psychological effects of the poem and ends in impressionism and relativism. The outcome is that the poem itself, as an object of specifically critical judgement, tends to disappear.

Wimsatt and Beardsley 1954, p. 21

The emphasis on the close observation of language – close reading – is analogous to the scrupulous observation of the transformations that take place in a laboratory experiment, and has remained a grounding practice in English Post-16. Another influence, as figure 2 showed, came from Continental Europe, where the application of scientific strategies, which had always characterised the practice of linguistics from which literary studies had set itself apart, had pioneered new approaches to texts in Prague and Russia as early as the 1930s. A strand is traceable from Russian Formalism, to structuralism and semiotics. Such a strand, which really started to have far-reaching consequences for English in England from the 1970s onwards, initially and mainly in universities, has more than the appearance of science. The economic reasons for this were as powerful as were the theoretical ones. Funding was streaming to science and social science projects. The Humanities were underfunded. There were strong economic arguments for adopting a more rigorously theoretical approach and the increased importation of concepts and analytical strategies taken from psychology, anthropology and linguistics began to transform literary studies in higher education in the 1960s. Although these approaches have since been overtaken by post-structuralism they were an essential staging post for contemporary cultural theory.

English in schools: completing the shift from literature to language

If one draws conclusions from the rhetoric of reports and other publications alone, then it seems reasonable to conclude that within the field of English there has been a significant shift from poetry to prose. English in universities is a less romantic subject. The New English's emphasis on experience and writing had led to a concentration on poetry and narrative. Suddenly all the curriculum development associated with these developments in the late 1960s and 1970s was put on hold. English teachers were faced with a set of changes which initially they thought they had control over. The stream of legislation and reforms introduced throughout the 1980s and the 1990s preoccupied English teachers, many of whom placed themselves in the vanguard of the battle against the test arrangements for fourteen year olds, the so-called Key Stage 3. The other great battle was to retain 50 or 100 per cent coursework for English. Concessions were won, but the overall fight was lost. It was tempting to represent English teachers as romantic Cavaliers in the face of the dour Roundheads.

With hindsight, the 100 per cent coursework, which had been seen by many specialists as an exciting feature of the new GCSE in English, was the last brilliant flaring of English teachers' autonomy in the second half of the twentieth century. A maximum of 30 per cent coursework was now permitted: students who had been able to choose their eight best pieces of work completed over two years, were now obliged to take exams once again, and these exams counted for the bulk of the assessment. The model of the inspired English teacher, free agent and arbiter of what was aesthetically successful – a model that has its roots in Leavis, however much the form of assessment may have changed since the 1930s – was to all intents and purposes overthrown by these developments which saw literacy replace literature as the defining term for debates about English in schools.

But as Bill Green points out in his Introduction to *The Insistence of the Letter* (Green 1993), the shift in England, Australia and the United States is complex, for there are several available discourses relating to literacy. Green identifies three in particular:

> [There] are those statements organized by the concept of '*functional* literacy'; those organized by the concept of '*cultural* literacy'; and those organized by the concept of '*critical* literacy' . . . Each constructs the category 'literacy' differently, and this means by extension not only different constructions of education and society, as well as the relation-ship between them, but also – more specifically – the category 'curriculum' itself.

In England the dominant discourse is the one relating to functional literacy, the one driven by 'human capital discourse' (Lankshear 1991) of the kind we shall touch on in our summary. The cultural literacy discourse, revived in the United States by figures such as Alan Bloom and E. D. Hirsch Jr, is to be found in England, often in the observations of those suffering from the ennui of post-structural exhaustion, mainly in higher education, or in the editorials of the tabloid press. Critical literacy is more marginalised, and is overshadowed by the dominance of the government driven mission to raise standards in the 'basics'.

Language, empowerment and the new literacies

Against this background of struggles and battles with centralising forces, curriculum discussion in English has become paralysed. Many English teachers have transferred their allegiance to media rather than literary studies, because media offered opportunities to discuss theoretical issues – matters germane to 'critical literacy' in a context which was familiar to the majority of students, utilising modes of assessment over which students had more control. This would not have been possible had not the students moved with them, and this would support Melanie Phillips's thesis that the progressive establishment can outmanoeuvre any legislation that the state seeks to throw at them. Such a reading tends to exaggerate the extent to which English teachers in the main have been able to preserve their autonomy, attributing to certain 'elites' (Phillips's word) more power than they actually have. There have been changes in English which sit outside this rather simplistic oppositional reading of the right-wing versus trendy teachers.

In a series of publications initiated by Richard Andrews attention has been focused on the relationship between narrative and argument, with an attempt to revisit the notion of rhetoric. In England argument and rhetoric had always been the Cinderella in English, unlike in Scotland and the United States where the development of English had been rooted in rhetoric. The importance of organising ideas, of selecting relevant information, of using aids such as writing frames and boxes, has taken English away from its former preoccupation with imaginative literature.

The other great area that should have been the focus for national projects was the new technology, and although Kenneth Baker did initially ensure that every school had a computer by offering matching funds, the pressures on school budgets and the local management of schools had meant that schools were about the only large organisations in England where you would not see computerised technology wherever you turned. The willingness is there – there is a National Council for Educational Technology and an important New Technologies Committee in NATE – but there are no new resources, and where the government has set up City Technology Colleges for school-age students these have been part-funded by business and the emphasis has been on the vocational. This has not helped the reputation of the computers among English teachers. Added to this is the generation gap – teachers themselves are not necessarily computer literate, and there is no longer any substantial local authority training to support them. Nevertheless schools are now coming on line, and there may even be advantages to entering at a later stage. The local primary school may have more up to date equipment than *The Financial Times*, which went electronic fifteen years before and was still using the same equipment.

It is in higher education that the greatest changes have taken place, with the English department becoming the natural home for theory, so that the gulf between cultural studies and literary studies is no longer as great as it was. But university English departments too have had to cope with a significant cut in funding, and a new management culture which no longer sees universities as places of research and scholarship, but as industrial units.

In schools a new orthodoxy is developing, partly fuelled by research into discourse analysis, partly driven by assessment and government regulation. The issue among English teachers has always been empowerment, and the debates have been about the best route to ensure that students are empowered. If power is the key issue, then access to power through the dominant discourse, which is Standard English, is seen as the key. The left and the right can unite on this, which is why a hybrid Labour government, ostensibly rooted in the left but budding with right-wing educational flowers, can insist on such things as the literacy hour and assessments which test Standard English. Grammar is back, but in an environment of a multimedia, techno-cultural world. History never repeats itself, but rhetoric does.

English in the marketplace: skills and the revived rhetoric of literacy

In this chapter we have looked at the way we have talked in England, and the way that we talk now, about English and about education. We have asked: how has the subject been conceptualised in the past, and what has been its relation to education as a whole? How is English seen now, by teachers and by politicians?

We have seen that English emerged as a subject in England in the nineteenth century amidst debates about the proper education for the populace at large, and the proper education of a gentleman. At the turn of the century it marked out a clear space for itself, and defined itself in relation to these two separate practices of education. It did so by creating an uneasy, but highly successful alliance, between the vocational and aspirational rhetoric of the time. That alliance has remained a source of tension throughout the history of English in England, where the term crisis was the Pollux to its Castor. As the century progressed, English became the most vociferous bird in the curriculum nest, if we judge it by the noise it made in its various campaigns.

Subject English is no longer the site of regulated play, as Hunter argues it was in the nineteenth century. That is not to say that the discourse and rhetoric of supervised play as a normative process has disappeared: it has reappeared with a vengeance through the concept of 'total schooling'. With primary schools beginning to offer breakfast clubs and after-school clubs it is possible for children to be at school from 8 am to 5.30 pm. The Headteacher of Legh Vale County School is happy to see this as the future, and his comment reflects the discourse of self-regulation and enlightened supervision: 'What happens before and after school is play, directed play, but play all the same' (*The Observer*, 24 May 1998). But what of Subject English? On the eve of the 1997 General Election in Britain, English in schools remained a big subject – one of the core subjects of the National Curriculum – but now, at the turn of another century, amidst educational debates which focus on concepts such as skills, competencies and 'zero tolerance of failure' it cannot hope to remain in the dominant bird unless it undergoes some kind of transformation. English's two powerful historical agendas – access to literary culture, and access to a culture which provided pupils with the opportunity to find their own voice, remain powerful shaping principles in schools. But they have defined English in ways which appear anachronistic when put alongside the hegemonic rhetoric of the marketplace. This is true even of the universities, where critical theory has in a sense already transformed English, but not in ways that fit easily with the new rhetoric of the university as a skills factory. As Regenia Gagnier has pointed out, this rhetoric is less positive in England where the massive expansion of higher education is described as the 'massification' of education. But it seems inevitable that Britain will follow the United States, where the same expansion is described as the 'democratisation' of education.

In *Cultural Capital* John Guillory argued that the 'cultural capital' that was represented by high culture is no longer of use in a technocultural and technocratic society. Society invests in education for a number of reasons, but it does so largely to ensure the formation of the kinds of subjects it needs. In the nineteenth century and the early twentieth there were workers who needed to achieve technical competence in basic literacy and the command of the expressive non-literary English of orality. There was also an officer class, whose mastery of high culture marked them out as the group entitled to give orders. Until the Great War that separation, with a middle group that could successfully separate itself from the working class but could never hope to make it into the officer class, determined much of the legislation and administration of education. Arnold did not want elementary school children to read Virgil – Latin was reserved for the Public Schools, which required the payment of fees.

But if English was to be the Latin of state schools, it was to be an expressive English, though it took fifty years for that to become obvious. The approaches to the curriculum that had been recommended in *What Is and What Might Be* (Holmes 1911), *The Play Way* (Cook 1917) and *The New Teaching* (Adams 1918) – active, child-centred, *expressive* – were particularly congenial to an English that was read to replace the high-culture model with something more egalitarian. For a certain generation of English teachers, as we shall see in the next chapter, the years in which this new model reaches its ascendancy – the 1970s and early 1980s – are seen as golden years. In England the rapid erasure of that model, can be seen most strikingly in one very simple event – the annual Easter conference of the National Association for the Teaching of English. At the end of the 1980s this was attracting over five hundred participants, with workshops celebrating imaginative and expressive ways of developing pupils' English through drama, writing and media. In 1997 attendance had shrunk to 150 with workshops on grammar and spelling being by far the most popular ones (*TES*, 11 April 1997). If teachers in schools and universities had been labouring under the misapprehension that they were the ones governing education, the 1990s, following the Education Reform Act, showed how little power they really had in determining the curriculum if the state should decide otherwise. The golden years were only possible with the permission of the state, and were not in spite of it at all.

Such a realisation can lead to demoralisation, and it is easy to see why the older generation of English specialists would have reason to be demoralised. The principles for which they fought so hard and which they thought they had won – the rejection of a mechanical, exam-driven model of English and the celebration of an expressive model that was attentive to the needs of the individual – are now viewed by society at large as ill conceived. One thing has not changed – the individual still sits at the centre of contemporary educational rhetoric, but it is the individual as consumer not the individual as conceived by Romantic theory. As consumer it is skills – transferable skills that are the cultural capital which society demands – and these skills are too specific and measurable in ways that can be easily assessed. This is the reification of English when judged by the grand visions of English in its heyday. Yet, as we shall see, a new generation, which has only known this world, remains as keen as ever to make a success of that world, and can see many positive things in that world – the inspiration given by the national curriculum, the sense of a clearly mapped out curricular area and the challenge of coping with change – this new generation is ready to look forward and not backwards. Many welcome prescription – the prescription of a literacy curriculum, the prescription of the National Curriculum – because they say that it removes the kinds of uncertainties of the kind that the real books versus phonics used to create. The rules are becoming harder and clearer by the day. Standards, targets, competencies – this is the current rhetoric, and the model of the primary curriculum with its emphasis on English, Maths and Rhetoric is the model that Margaret Thatcher had originally wanted. The market economy exists, and will not go away. The question is, to what extent does this new conceptualisation of education in particular and of English in particular, represent evidence of continuity or a final disruption with the past? As Chairman Mao suggested when asked to comment on the effect of the French Revolution, it is probably too early to tell.

Summary of some key strands in the history of English in England

Antecedents

- Tudor cultural nationalism that coincided with the English Reformation and the break with Rome under Henry VIII (Doyle 1989);
- Accession of James VI of Scotland to English throne: persuaded Scots that their economic interest was now tied to England (Court 1992);
- Study of rhetoric and *Belles Lettres* in Scotland and the Dissenting Academies in England in the eighteenth century, transferring to the curriculum of University College, London in the 1820s (Doyle 1989; Court 1992).

Transformative moments

- Establishment in 1830 of a Chair in English literature and history at Kings College, London, with English as part of the core curriculum (Court 1992);

- 1904 Board of Education directive establishing English as a subject in secondary schools (Ball 1985);
- Founding of English Association in 1906 (Ball 1985; Doyle 1989);
- Dartmouth seminar 1966: the textualisation of 'personal growth';
- 1975 Bullock Report and the rise of critical theory: the recentring of language;
- 1989 Education Act: establishing a National Curriculum.

Historical issues

- Relationship between Subject English, literacy and grammar;
- Relationship with the foundations of state education in the nineteenth century;
- Relationship with science (Arnold, the English Association);
- Relationship with Classics (Doyle 1989);
- Gender (Green 1993; Baron 1986) (see also chapter 4);
- National and Moral Identity (Arnold, Newbolt and Leavis) (Ball, Kenny and Gardiner 1990);
- Pedagogy (Stow, Kay-Shuttleworth: see Hunter 1988);
- Role of Mechanics Institutes and University Extension Movement (Dixon,1991; Eagleton 1900);
- Cambridge (the F. R. Leavis network and Literature) versus London (the James Britton network and Language);
- English as literary criticism;
- Influence of institutions (e.g. the Institute of Education, University of London), publications and organisations (eg NATE in the 1960s and 1970s);
- Relationship between English and creative writing;
- Relationship between media studies, cultural studies and English;
- Pedagogical implications of information technology;
- Current monitoring and directing of English through inspection, assessment at key stages and National Literacy Strategy.

References

Abbs, Peter (1996) *The Polemics of the Imagination: Selected Essays on Art, Culture and Society*, London: Skoob
Academic Standards Panel, English (1994) 'Report of the Academic Standards Panel, English', Australian Vice Chancellors' Committee (Draft)
Adams, John (ed.) (1918) *The New Teaching*, London: Hodder and Stoughton
Alter, Peter (1988) 'Science and the Anglo-German Antagonism', in T. R. Gourvish, and Alan O'Day (1988) *Later Victorian Britain 1867–1900*, London: Macmillan
Applebee, Arthur N. (1974) *Tradition and Reform in the Teaching of English: A History*, Urbana, Illinois: NCTE
Arnold, Matthew (1852) 1889 *Reports on Elementary Schools 1852–1882*, ed. Francis Sandford, London: Macmillan

Arnold, Matthew (1868) 1964 *Schools and Universities on the Continent: The Complete Prose Works of Matthew Arnold*, Volume IV ed. R. H. Super, Ann Arbor: The University of Michigan Press

Arnold, Matthew (1960–1967) *Complete Prose Works of Matthew Arnold* (ed. R. H. Super), 11 volumes

Atkinson, J. and Protherough, R. (1991) *The Making of English Teachers*, Buckingham: Open University Press

B and FSS (n.d.) *Revised Lesson Book for Standard VI of the Revised Code of the Committee of Council on Education*, London: Depository of the Society

B and FSS (1856) *Handbook to the Borough Road Schools*, London: Borough Road Depository

Baldick, C. (1983) *The Social Mission of English Criticism 1848–1932*, Oxford: Oxford University Press

Ball, S. J., Kenny, A. and Gardiner, D. (1990) 'Literacy, politics and the teaching of English', in I. F. Goods P. and Medway (eds.) *Bringing English to Order*, London: The Falmer Press

Ball, Stephen J. (1985) 'English for the English Since 1906', in I. Goodson (ed.) (1985) *Social Histories of the Secondary Curriculum: Subjects for Study*, London: The Falmer Press

Barnes, D., Britton, J. and Rosen, H. (1971) *Language, the Learner and the School*, Harmondsworth: Penguin

Bateson, F. W. (ed.) (1965) *Matthew Arnold: Essays on English Literature*, London: University of London Press

Benton, Michael (1982) 'How authors write . . . how children write: Towards a rationale for creative writing', in Adams (1982)

Board of Education (1905) *Suggestions for the Consideration of Teachers and Others Concerned in the Work of Public Elementary Schools*, London: HMSO

Board of Education (1910) *The Teaching of English in Secondary Schools (Circular 753)*, London: HMSO

Board of Education (1912) *Report of the Board of Education for the Year 1910–11*, London: HMSO

Board of Education (1921) *The Teaching of English in England*, London: HMSO

British and Foreign School Society (1837) *Manual of the System of Primary Instruction Pursued in the Model Schools of the British and Foreign School Society*, London: Borough Road Depository

Britton, J. et al. (1975) *The Development of Writing Abilities 11–18*, London: Macmillan

Britton, James (1970) *Language and Learning*, London: Heinemann

Bryson, John (ed.) (1954) *Matthew Arnold Poetry and Prose*, London: Rupert Hart-Davis

Bulletins of the English Association (1907–) London: The English Association

Christie, Frances (1993) 'The "Received Tradition" of English Teaching: the decline of Rhetoric and the Corruption of Grammar', in Bill Green (ed.) (1993) *The Insistence of the Letter: Literacy Studies and Curriculum Theorizing*, London: The Falmer Press

Clements, Simon, Dixon, John and Stratta, Leslie (1963) *Reflections: An English Course for Students Aged 14–18*, Oxford: Oxford University Press

Cook, Caldwell (1917) *The Play Way*, London: Heinemann

Cox, Brian (1992) *The Great Betrayal*, London: Chapmans

Cox, Brian (1995) Cox on the Battle for the English Curriculum, London: Hodder and Stoughton

Court, F. (1992) Institutionalizing English Literature: The Culture and Politics of Literary Study 1750–1990, Stanford: Stanford University Press

Crawford, Robert (1992) Devolving English Literature, Oxford: Clarendon

Cressy, David (1981) 'Levels of illiteracy in England 1530–1570', in Harvey J Graff (ed.) (1981) Literacy and Social Development in the West: a Reader, Cambridge: Cambridge University Press

Curtis, John Charles (1871) The Poetical Reader for Home and School Use, London: Simpkin Marshall and Company Ltd

DES (1975) A Language for Life: Report of the Committee of Inquiry Appointed by the Secretary of State for Education and Science under the Chairmanship of Sir Alan Bullock, London: HMSO

Dixon, J. and Stratta, L. (1986) Writing Narrative and Beyond, Ottawa: Canadian Council of Teachers of English

Dixon, John (1967) Growth through English: A Report Based on the Dartmouth Seminar, 1966, Oxford: Oxford University Press

Dixon, John (1991) A Schooling in 'English', Buckingham: Open University Press

Donald, James (1992) Sentimental Education: Schooling, Popular Culture and the Regulation of Liberty, London: Verso

Doughty, P., Pearce, J. and Thornton, J. (1971) Language in Use, London: Arnold

Doyle, Brian (1989) English and Englishness, London: Routledge

Eagleton, T. (1983) Literary Theory, Oxford: Blackwell

Emerson, R. W. (1841) 'History' in Selected Essays, Harmondsworth: Penguin, 1985

Evans, Colin (1993) English People: The Experience of Teaching and Learning English in British Universities, Buckingham: Open University Press

Foster, T. G. (1910) 'Address', Bulletins of the English Association, No. 10, Feb 1910, London: The English Association

Foucault, M. (1977) Discipline and Punish, trans. by Alan Sheridan, London: Penguin Books

Foucault, Michel (1991) 'Docile Bodies', in Discipline and Punish, London: Penguin Books

Fowler, Alistair (1998) 'Leavis of the North: the role of Hugh Blair in the foundation of English literary studies', The Times Literary Supplement, 14 August 1998

Fox, Dana and Goodwyn, Andrew (1993) 'Whose Model of English?', Presentation, International Convention on Language in Education, University of East Anglia, Norwich, England.

Fox, Geoff (1977) 'Twenty-four things to do with a book', Children's Literature in Education,Volume 8, No. 3

Fox, Geoff, Merrick, Brian, et al. (1982) 'Thirty-six things to do with a poem', in A. Adams (ed.) (1982) New Directions in English Teaching, Sussex: Falmer Press

Galtung, Johan (1981) 'Literacy, education and schooling: for what?' in Graff (ed.) (1981)

Gerlach, Jeanne and Monseau, Virginia (eds.) (1991) Missing Chapters: Ten Pioneering Women in NCTE and English Education, Urbana, Illinois: NCTE

Goodson, Ivor and Medway, Peter (eds.) (1990) Bringing English to Order, London: The Falmer Press

Gossman, Lionel (1982) 'Literature and education', *New Literary History*, Volume 23, No. 2 Winter, pp. 341–71
Graff, Gerald (1987) *Professing Literature: An Institutional Study*, Chicago: University of Chicago Press
Graff, Harvey J. (ed.) (1981) *Literacy and Social Development in the West: A Reader*, Cambridge: Cambridge University Press
Green, Andy (1990) *Education and State Formation*, London: Macmillan Press
Green, Bill (ed.) (1993) *The Insistence of the Letter*, London: The Falmer Press
Herford, C. H. (1910 'The Bearing of English Studies upon National Life', *Leaflets of the English Association*, No. 16, London: The English Association
Hoggart, Richard (1957) *The Uses of Literacy*, London: Chatto and Windus
Holbrook, David (1961) *English for Maturity*, Cambridge: Cambridge University Press
Holbrook, David (1964) *English for the Rejected*, Cambridge: Cambridge University Press
Holmes, Edmond (1911) *What Is and What Might Be*, London: Constable and Company
Hughes, Ted (1967) *Poetry in the Making*, London: Faber
Hunter, Ian (1988) *Culture and Government: The Emergence of Literary Education*, London: Macmillan
Hunter, Ian (1994) *Rethinking the School*, NSW, Australia: Allen and Unwin
Inglis, F. (1985) *The Management of Ignorance: A Political Theory of the Curriculum*, Oxford: Basil Blackwell
Interpretations (1994) Journal of the English Teachers' Association of Western Australia Volume 27, No. 3, 'Beyond Poststructuralism' Cottesloe, Western Australia
Langan, Mary and Schwarz, Bill (eds.) *Crises in the British State*, London: Hutchison
Lankshear, C. (1991) 'Getting it right is hard: Redressing the politics of literacy in the 1990s', in P. Cormack, (ed.) *Literacy: Making it Explicit, Making it Possible – Selected Papers from the 16th Australian Reading Association Conference, Adelaide, South Australia 7–11 July 1991*, Carlton South, Victoria: Australian Reading Association
Leaflets of the English Association (1907–) London: The English Association
Leavis, F. and Thompson, D. (1964) *Culture and Environment*, London: Chatto and Windus
Leavis, F. R. (1943) *Education and the University: A Sketch for an English School*, London: Chatto and Windus
Leinster-Mackay, Donald (1987) *The Educational World of Edward Thring*, London: The Falmer Press
McCormick, Kathleen (1994) *The Culture of Reading and the Teaching of English*, Manchester: Manchester University Press
Marvin, F. S. (1910) *Reports on Elementary Schools 1852–1882 by Matthew Arnold*, London: Board of Education/HMSO
Mathieson, Margaret (1975) *The Preachers of Culture: A Study of English and its Teachers*, London: Allen and Unwin
Menand, Louis (1995) 'Diversity', in F. Lentricchia and Thomas McLaughlin (eds.) (1995) *Critical Terms for Literary Study*, London: The University of Chicago Press
Merttens, Ruth (1998) Conversation with the authors, unpublished.

Michael, I. (1987) *The Teaching of English from the Sixteenth Century to 1870*, Cambridge: Cambridge University Press

Muller, H. J. (1967) *The Uses of English*, New York: Rinehart and WilsonMyhill, Debra (1994) Letter to the authors, n.p.

NCTE (1990) *NCTE's Position on the Teaching of English: Assumptions and Practices*, Working Paper Developed by the Elementary, Secondary and College Sections 1988–89, Urbana, Illinois: NCTE

Nehls, Edward (1957–9) *D. H. Lawrence: a Composite Biography*, 3 volumes, Madison: University of Winconsin Press

Nelson/National Writing Project (1990a) *A Rich Resource: Writing and Language Diversity*, Kingston: Nelson

Nelson/National Writing Project (1990b) *Partnerships for Writing: School, the Community and the Workplace*, Kingston: Nelson

Newman, John Henry (1929) *The Idea of a University*, London: Longmans

Newman, John Henry (1955) *On the Scope and Nature of University Education*, London: Dent

Palmer, D. J. (1965) *The Rise of English Studies*, Oxford: Oxford University Press

Peel, R. W. (1995) 'The Changing Pattern of English in Higher Education: Continuity and Difference', *CCUE News*, issue 5, July 1995, Exmouth: CCUE

Phillips, M. (1996) *All Must Have Prizes*, London: Little, Brown

Pope, Rob (1998) *The English Studies Book*, London: Routledge

Protherough, Robert and Atkinson, Judith (1991) *The Making of English Teachers*, Milton Keynes: The Open University Press

QCA (1998) *The Grammar Papers: Perspectives on the Teaching of Grammar in the National Curriculum*, London: QCA

Rose, J. (1984) *The Case of Peter Pan*, London: Macmillan

Rosen, Harold (1973) *Teaching London Kids*, London: LATE

Sampson, George (1921) *English for the English*, Cambridge University Press

Sawyer, Wayne (1998) 'Growth through English', in Wayne Sawyer, Ken Watson, and Eval Gold, *Re-viewing English*, Sydney: St Clair Press

Schofield, Roger S. (1981) 'Dimensions of illiteracy in England 1750–1850', in Graff (ed.) (1981)

Selleck, R. J. W. (1994) *James Kay-Shuttleworth: Journey of an Outsider*, Ilford, Essex: The Woburn Press

Shannon, Richard (1974) *The Crisis of Imperialism*, London: Hart-Davis MacGibbon

Simon, Brian (1991) *Education and the Social Order 1940–1990*, London: Lawrence and Wishart

Stow, D. (1850) *The Training System, The Moral Training School and the Normal Seminary*, London: Longman Brown Green

Thring, Edward (1883) 'The Theory and Practice of Teaching' in Leinster-Mackay (1987) *The Educational World of Edward Thring*, London: The Falmer Press (1987), p. 140

Tristram, Henry (ed.) (1952) *The Idea of a Liberal Education*, London: Harrap

Webb, Edwin (ed.) (1996) *Powers of Being: David Holbrook and his Work*, London: Associated University Press

Watson, Ken (1994) *English Teaching in Perspective*, revised and edited by Sawyer, Hargreaves and Durrant, Sydney: St Clair Press

Wilkinson, Andrew *et al.* (1980) 'The Development of Writing', *English in Education*, Volume 14, No. 2, Autumn 1980, Sheffield: NATE

Willinsky, John (1993) 'Lessons from the literacy before schooling 1800–1850', in Bill Green (ed.) (1993) *The Insistence of the Letter*, London: Falmer Press

Worthen, John (1991) *D. H. Lawrence: The Early Years 1885–1912*, Cambridge: Cambridge University Press

3   Beliefs about 'English' in England

Robin Peel

Context: Subject English in England in the year 2000
Population of England: 47,880 (2+)
Number of schools: 26,194 maintained and independent (containing 8
million pupils)
Stages of compulsory schooling: primary (usually 5–11), secondary (usu
11–16 or 11–18). Students may leave at 16. Many proceed to either terti
colleges (16–19). One third go on to university (higher education).
Significant private school system: yes. Only 7 per cent of total number
schools, but have disproportionate influence.
Number of universities: 73
National or District (State) Curriculum) National Curriculum
Standardised Assessments in English: at age 7 (Key Stage 1), 11 (Key Stage
14 (Key Stage 3)
Publication of results: individual results reported to parents. School's resu
published in newspapers.
Examinations leading to qualifications: General Certificate of Second
Education (Key Stage 4: usually taken at 16, Advanced Level English (usu
taken at age 18). Alternative vocational qualifications in communications n
be taken at 16 and 18.
Inspection of schools?: yes. Four-day inspections, leading to reports that
available to the general public.
Teaching qualifications: Qualified Teacher Status (required of all the
teaching in state schools) obtained either through successful completion o
one year post-graduate certificate in education course (PGCE: most second
school teachers and some primary school teachers) or a four-year Bachelor
Education (BEd) degree (most primary school teachers).
University of school based training: a partnership, but increasingly sch
based
A National Curriculum for Teacher Education?: yes; the Governm
requires institutions to teach in conformity with the published curriculu
which prescribes what must be covered during the year(s) or 'training'.
Probationary year?: yes – called an Induction Year
Statistical sources: DFEE Statistics of Education – *Schools in Engla*
1998 London: The Stationery Office, 1998 *Education Year Book* 1998/
London *Financial Times*/Pitman Publishing 19

First soundings: questionnaire responses

In chapter 1 I described the origins of this book in the contrasting responses of American and British teachers to the models of English described by the Cox Committee in their 1989 report. We wanted to know not simply what models of English specialists endorsed, but the means by which they arrived at those models, the extent to which they modified their views over the years, and their perceptions of some of the current issues that dominate discussion in the field. We initially devised a questionnaire (Appendix A) and in England this was distributed to over 200 specialists in schools, universities and colleges. These included secondary-school English teachers, university lecturers, student teachers (BEd Primary), English majors (BA undergraduates) and students who were contemplating taking an English course in Higher Education. What emerged from the initial findings was evidence of a widespread belief in the enduring nature of human behaviour, and of 'English' as a personal subject which provides space, pleasure and opportunities to reflect on moral and ethical issues. A high proportion of the respondents agreed, or strongly agreed, with the 'personal growth' model of English, being the one which emphasises the development of the individual as understood in traditional humanist terms. They also agreed with the suggestion that literature deals with issues which transcend time, and with the notion that what we read in an English course has a role to play in the way we conduct our lives.

There was general support for a broader interpretation of the term 'text', one that goes beyond books of the kind – Shakespeare's plays for example – that once provided the traditional fare of school and university syllabuses. Even the most conservative of groups – surprisingly these turned out to be the undergraduates on BEd or BA courses – who largely endorsed the traditional 'cultural heritage' model of English, were open to the idea that texts for study should also include examples of popular culture, including films and television programmes.

There are two striking features of the UK part of the survey. The first is predictable, but has implications for cross-phase liaison between universities and schools. This is the contrast between the support from students – both secondary and tertiary – and secondary school teachers for a model of English which nourishes individual self-development, provides pleasure and opportunities for creativity and personal growth, and the scepticism evident in about 50 per cent of the university lecturers sampled (mainly the younger generation of lecturers) about notions of pleasure and the idea that there is an authentic personal self in any of us at all. This is quite consistent with post-modern literary theory which views many of the beliefs and perceptions we assumed to be essential as phenomena which are in effect fabricated by the values of the society and culture in which we live.

The second major finding is less predictable. It is that teachers and other English specialists embrace a variety of views, some of which appear to be contradictory. Many of the respondents who endorsed the 'personal growth' model also agreed with the post-structuralist view that we have just referred to, namely that the meaning of texts is governed by historical and cultural factors, and although these beliefs are not mutually exclusive, they do represent very contrasting views of truth and authenticity. The holding of apparently contradictory views has implications for curriculum development. If teachers are torn and pulled in two separate directions by their beliefs, then they will want to share this debate with their students in the classrooms. Yet it may be that there is no contradiction at all, and that the term 'cultural analysis' was interpreted by respondents as meaning something other than engagement with post-structuralist reading practices. There are problems of definition in the five Cox models, as we found in Australia when we discussed them with teachers in Perth and Adelaide.

VOICES: INTERVIEWS, LETTERS AND CONVERSATIONS

Voices 1: 'You can talk about it over dinner'

Our questionnaire research had provided evidence of some broad areas of agreement which would support a tentative answer of 'yes' to the questions 'Is there a species of human beings known as English teachers, with shared characteristics and aspirations'/'Is there any sense in which certain practices or perceptions endure, despite the great differences between the way in which it is taught in the 1990s compared to the way it was taught 100 years ago?'. In the previous chapter I discussed the characteristics of the rhetoric of the newly formed English Association, and the way that it drew on Arnoldian notions of character formation with a preference for broad goals rather than the specific material competencies which were seen as the province of science. A shared, definable goal was identified in this rhetoric. This may reveal more about the rhetoric than the practice. In *What is English Teaching?* (Davies 1996) Chris Davies argues that English teachers in secondary schools tend to be good at writing 'recipes' – agendas for English that emphasised the philosophical aims rather than the action to be taken. The function of such recipes, he argues, is to create group identity. Viewed sympathetically they are illustrative of an open minded liberal humanist approach, which seeks to include as much as possible. He quotes from subject department Statements of Aims:

> Our general aims are . . . the development of the personality through greater self knowledge and through the extension of horizons by perception of the experiences, actual, or imaginative, of others . . .
>
> The responsibility of teachers is to the experience of children, their minds, emotions and spirits: it is a matter of knowing the right magic to lead one child from a closed alley of experience to an open one . . .
>
> Davies 1996, pp. 16 and 28

Viewed less sympathetically, Davies argues, these may be viewed as 'vacuous and pious pronouncements . . . that make English teachers feel good about themselves and their work'. The explanation for this romantic emphasis on broad aspirations of liberating children from prescription, rigidity and specificity is to be found in the history of English, and the influence of Arnold, Leavis, Dixon and Holbrook that we described earlier. It is interesting that Davies conducted this part of his investigation in 1986, two years before 'the National Curriculum began to close down the horizons' (Davies 1996, p. 25).

Much has happened since then, but the voices we heard showed strong traces of this romanticism. In the United Kingdom part of the investigation we carried out interviews with over 100 people in England, and what was striking about those we interviewed, all English specialists in some way or other, was their remarkable diversity of personal experience which they were willing to share with us. This may be true of any group of people working in any other curriculum field, but the richness of the lives outside the specialism bears a possible relationship to the pluralism and patchwork nature of the field itself. Here is Elizabeth, Head of English in a secondary school, telling her colourful story:

> It was very complicated. I was brought up in Bath, my father was a Civil Servant and had very old-fashioned ideas about what women should do and I was programmed really to meet and marry a man just like my father which I very successfully did at nineteen. I met a Naval architect, he was clean-cut, quite good looking, terribly reliable and I married him. We had two children and when I was thirty-three I ran away. So at thirty-five I had run away, great disgrace, and I hadn't been trained for anything before I married but I always loved reading and he was quite good at painting, my father, and I inherited a sort of facility for painting. So I painted as an amateur and I ran away with a man who was a potter and a painter and we went and lived in Yorkshire and I had my third child, Benedict, who was illegitimate and when he was about five I was cheerfully encouraged by his father to go and do something. So I thought, I'll go and do a degree. I'd got some A-levels while I was nursing him. So I went off to Leeds and you had to fill in an UCCA form and I didn't know what it was but it seemed to me there were five choices so I put down English and Fine Art, English and Philosophy, RE, I just had to build up the five. And then I went to be interviewed and they said, We're not quite sure what you want to do. And I said, I don't mind what I do. And why had I chosen them? Because they seemed to be handy, only 10 miles away. I was 40 then, 39. And then they asked me some questions I couldn't answer and in these awful gaps about what I felt about Lawrence, I didn't know what sort of answers I was supposed to give, I said, Well you should have me, shouldn't you? If I knew the answers I wouldn't need to come here. This was greeted with a poe-faced silence and then I left, and

I thought it didn't sound very hopeful. But two days later I got an offer for a degree in English and History of Art, no, History of Art and English. So I went off to read the degree. I met a miner's daughter and she was very canny, so she was 30 and I was 40. There were fifty or sixty students doing this particular option and one of the options in the English course was whether you did Early English, Anglo Saxon and Medieval English or whether you did Shakespeare and the rest, and she was very canny, she'd worked in the Co-op in the Midlands somewhere, and she said to me, Look, all of them have just come from school, they've done their A-levels, bet they all go for Shakespeare and stuff they know, let's go for the Anglo Saxon because they won't want to do that. And she was absolutely right. So six people went for the early option which meant we had a really nice time because we had these wonderful books from the library in Leeds University, the early books about linguistics studies, and the other fifty chased two copies of Shakespeare in the library! And this kind of set me into looking into early forms of English and then, because I was interested in Art anyway, I just got really hooked into Medieval Art. For my first dissertation I was quite lucky in one way because I got hooked into an American archaeological dig in South West France by another history too complicated to say, so I wrote my first dissertation on a very unusual area, Cave Churches in South West France, which nobody knew anything much about. That gives you a great advantage. In the meantime my husband-figure had fallen in love with a student, he was 50 and she was 25, so off he went leaving me with Benedict aged 5, no job, we didn't own the house, I had no profession and I was 42 then. So I finished that degree but I did quite a good dissertation and I got a scholarship or something to do a research degree in South West France, to do a BPhil so as I'd lost everything I thought I might as well do that. But I didn't really want to be a teacher at all, I wanted to be an artist. So I went off and did some research on Medieval alabasters which, again, was again a very minor area, and I was offered then further research by the Courtauld Institute but by then Ben and I had been on our own two years and really it was just so difficult to live on a grant and my older boys were themselves students, so I thought: Well I'd like to do teaching. And then, of course, you can't teach History of Art, so I became an English teacher.

Here is Michael, a Head of Department in a university:

I left school after taking a couple of undistinguished A-levels, having been much more involved with acting and things in the Sixth Forms and I decided to go out to work straight away. So I went into advertising which seemed quite a reasonable thing to go into for someone who's interested in words and language and so on. I worked in advertising for three or four years, then a couple of years in Harrods Department Store doing various kinds of menial tasks. I was doing the Christmas post one year in Chichester and got friendly with someone else doing the post there and he said, 'There's a good kind of wheeze around which is that you can get into teacher education and they give you a grant as you're mature', I was twenty-three or twenty-four, 'and you can get a fuller grant than most people and it's quite a good laugh'. So I said, 'Okay' so I applied to Bognor College of Education. This was a two-year fast-track mature student entry and I went and chatted with the Principal who was very much into mature students and it was very rewarding really. I did the two years there and enjoyed it enormously and specialised in English and Art, alongside junior/secondary training. I did teaching practice in junior and secondary schools.

If their backgrounds are diverse, the same thing cannot be said of the reasons that specialists give for their being attracted to English As our questionnaires revealed, as one might expect, a delight in reading is the main motivator. This is Michael:

I think it was the reading that made me want to specialise in English. I learnt to read early and have always enjoyed reading ever since. All the time I was working in London I always read as much as I could and I just thought it was a pleasant kind of luxury to be able to do this and play football and do all the other things you can do at college.

Michael gives the desire to do more reading as the reason for his decision to do an English degree, even though he had a teaching qualification and had been teaching English for some years:

I know this sounds pious but I just wanted to read some more and get back into it. Because, as you know, when you teach it is very difficult to read much. You talk about a novel a month if you're lucky at secondary level . . . I was thirsty again, differently I suppose, for that run through from Chaucer to Ted Hughes or whoever it might be.

These are taken from two of the transcripts from the fifty in-depth interviews which were informed by the fifteen questions listed in Appendix B. From these interviews we have identified ten themes and from these we have posed ten questions. We believe they represent important issues that will have an impact on the ways that English is taught.
These themes are:

Pedagogy and practice
The special nature of English
The machinery of assessment
Ethics and aesthetics

Intellectual practices
Key moments and influences
Writing genres
Media and the new technologies
Skills and the workplace
Views from non-specialists

We shall first report on what was said to us, and then relate the beliefs that were being articulated to the history that was discussed in chapter 2. In brackets after the name is the status of the speaker, using the following abbreviations, unless otherwise identified:

SST = secondary school teacher
ALS = A-level student: years 12/13
PGCE = Post Graduate Certificate of Education student
TT = teacher trainer
U = undergraduate
UL = university lecturer

Ten questions from England

Pedagogy and practice: how do we teach?

Let us begin with a comment from a student teacher, expressing a view that is not unusual in the culture of English:

> The trouble is when you've got 32 kids in the class you can't please every single child. There are a few things I've been pleased with – last Tuesday the bell went and they didn't realize and they carried on working – but it's quite disappointing that sometimes you aren't going to please every child and it's the old thing, do you please some of them all of the time or all of them some of the time?
>
> Ursula (PGCE)

Ursula is strongly motivated by the need to please, the need to construct situations in which the students become so immersed in what they are doing that they voluntarily carry on working. She goes on to explain where this belief has its roots:

> We've been taught on the course all these creative ways of teaching and got really excited about it and I'm actually apologizing to the children saying 'I'm really sorry, don't let that put you off'.
>
> Ursula

A similar sense of guilt is expressed by Fiona, an experienced secondary English teacher:

I often feel guilty in a way about trying to impose things upon them (the students) that, yes, I might value and the Government might value and incorporate as necessary to teach in its National Curriculum, but that actually don't touch the pupils' lives with a reality very much at all.

Fiona (SST)

What is interesting here is the separation of the desired pedagogical relation – one in which the teacher is not seen to be imposing the curriculum from which Fiona distances herself (*its* National Curriculum) from what the teacher feels herself obliged to practice or implement. She feels compromised and like Ursula feels uneasy about this. Ursula's sense of unease translates itself into action: the idea of apologising to children about the nature of the lesson, in the manner of a would be friend, gives us something of an insight into the desired pedagogical relationship that the practice of English strives to achieve. It is hard to imagine a chemistry or maths teacher in a secondary school adopting such a position, though in primary schools in England the need to motivate children through interest and investigative activities became a significant part of the pedagogical rhetoric of child-centred learning in the 1960s.

As a pedagogy it is seen as a way of drawing students into the desired areas of study through establishing a personal relationship. Kathy Smith, a lecturer at the Central College of Speech and Drama, recommends it for all students, and she has worked with children with very severe behaviour problems:

If I were advising new teachers about teaching in offsite education, and how to work with students with challenging behaviour, the most funda-mental key is the relationship you establish with the students. You have to remember that these students are students who've been failed by the system, who often have low self-esteem and low self-confidence, and you have to think why they are behaving in the way they are behaving. In some of the units where I worked, there was often a risk with volatile students, and I remember stepping in on occasion on fights between students who were very angry; but the relationship I had with the indi-vidual students prior to the incident usually meant that I did not become the object of their anger; although the possibility could not be totally ignored, I usually felt safe. Working with students in these situations, the very first thing you must do before you even try to teach anything is to establish a relationship of trust and respect, where the student feels listened to, and respected. The difficulty with learning for any student, but particularly for students who have 'failed', is that in order to learn, you have to admit that you don't know, and that's a difficult thing to do.

Perhaps because such a pedagogical view is so long established – we saw glimpses of it in Stow, who spoke of the need of the teacher to bring himself/herself into level relationship with the pupil – it does not always need to be articulated by those who nevertheless subscribe to it. Ursula's tutor, a teacher trainer, who has been visiting schools as part of a national investigation into the teaching of 13 and 14 year olds, identified not the pedagogy but the content and methodology of recent practice:

> If you asked me what developments I have been excited about over the past few years I would want to mention four things. The first is the improvement in the quality of planning and recording that is going on in English classrooms. The second is the teaching of pre-twentieth-century texts – having been obliged to do this by the National Curriculum teachers have taken this on in imaginative and inventive ways. The teaching of knowledge about language – grammar – has also been tackled in some very exciting new ways. The same is true of the teaching of Shakespeare at Key Stage 3 [Year 9 students]. Teachers have really risen to the challenge here. Not just through performance, because drama teachers recognise that what English teachers are doing with Shakespeare is not just about the performance, it is about the text.
>
> Jane (TT)

Even so, we can detect evidence of the personalist pedagogy that places high value on the imagination and the need for interest and excitement, particularly when tackling a topic such as knowledge about language. This personalist pedagogy, with its emphasis on the value of the individual's experience and potential for growth, is successful in cultivating a particular understanding of English as a subject which provides space for enjoyment, self-reflection and growth. This is a Year 12 student, Amy:

> English is something you can enjoy, and [you never finish English] because there's discovery all the time, plumbing the depths within yourself. And you keep surprising yourself all along the line about how much is coming to you. There is a growth within children and if English stopped at the age of eleven (assuming they all were reasonably literate by then) I think imaginations would be severely stunted. I think there must be time to dream and I think English is a wonderful medium for the imagination. I think it opens something so deep within, personally in my mind, that it is as though whatever poem we are reading at the time is rather like a technicolour film going on with my own characters taking part in whatever is being said. That's what I call 'dreaming', that wonderful stirring up of the imagination within somebody which actually can't happen, or very rarely happens, because I think that most of us need to be tutored to be able to get to that point.
>
> Amy (ALS)

Amy expresses here a faith and willingness to achieve the desired understanding, the desired leap of the imagination, through a process of trawling deep within herself. Here is Bernard, an experienced teacher from the same comprehensive school:

> I enjoyed literature for the same reason that I used to enjoy writing. It is because I am engaging my imagination and responding to someone else's. Linguistics sounds like science to me.
>
> Bernard (SST)

If this self-reflecting and self-adjusting goal, with an identity sometimes defined in opposition to science, is the dominant discourse – and our research in England suggests that it is evident in the majority voice of secondary specialists we interviewed – there are nonetheless other positions which view things from a slightly different perspective. Here is Elizabeth, the secondary Head of English, explaining why she rejects the arts–science difference:

> I don't think English is that special you see, I don't see the difference in teaching English and teaching Science and teaching Maths, although the moral dimension isn't perhaps there in Maths, though who am I to say? I wouldn't get anywhere with the boys in this school if I started teaching English in some kind of way that was linked direct to some kind of moral teaching and/or thinking about poetry as such. And I just say to them, look this is just like what you do in science. You just look at how it's made. See how it's made, just get to know it and then maybe you can make something a bit like that because we all learn from taking things apart. I don't think there's anything wrong with that, though those who denigrate literary criticism, call it tearing it apart, tearing it to shreds. I think that's absolutely ridiculous. I think it's like a jigsaw puzzle. You turn all the pieces over and you put some pieces here, some bits up there and then you build something, and I just think English is like that. When I am working with boys, if somebody gives me a quite nice piece then I'll say, Are you good at Maths, I can see that by the way you've thought it through. And you can, can't you? And I think it's a marvellous subject for hypothesising, for inspired guessing. Didn't Einstein say his theory for relativity came to him not in words but in a series of psychic grunts? It's the business of just thinking. I like the idea that what we think with is texts and what we think with in Science is, I don't know, Bunsen burners are part of it, and I think it's a real shame in a way to have Science faculties, Arts faculties, if one of them's emotive, one of them's cognitive, it seems to me just as much emotive stuff goes on over there, just as much cognitive stuff goes on over here. It's just a fascinating business isn't it?
>
> Elizabeth (SST)

Elizabeth became an English specialist very late: her resistance to the science–art binary reflects neither an encounter with literary theory nor an earlier scientific background, but is the product of an interest in art, history and language. She came into English with an interdisciplinary perspective, and her pedagogy and interests have been shaped by this earlier experience.

There is a case to be made for the cohering of science and English. I am using *cohere* in the sense in which it was used by Georges Canguilhem, one of the important influences on Foucault. Subjects or systems or thought *cohere* when they are perceived to be adjacent, sharing what Chomsky and Wittgenstein have encouraged us to regard as 'family resemblances'. Consider the following as a description of some of the more contemporary aims of English, for example:

Experimental and Investigative English
Students should be given opportunities to:
- ask questions e.g. How? Why? What will happen if . . . ?
- use both first-hand experience and . . . secondary sources to obtain information
- turn ideas suggested to them, and their own ideas, into a form that can be investigated
- make comparisons and to identify trends or patterns
- indicate whether the evidence collected supports any prediction made

As may be obvious, these are from the 1995 Curriculum for Years 2 and 6 (7 and 11 year olds) in England and Wales, although we have changed the heading for they are actually taken from the experimental and investigative *science* strand, thus reinforcing the points made earlier by Elizabeth. The one difference is apparently slight but actually decisive: in English the questions are turned in on the self, to encourage a problematisation of the self.

So we have a paradox. As studies of nineteenth-century texts have shown, science and literature can be seen as symbiotic discourses. English is perceived to be quite different from science, however, and it has had to battle hard against this perception, as Rachel, a PhD Medievalist in her last year of research, pointed out in a written response:

> English as an academic discipline is 'constructed' by other fields of academic study. It isn't 'scientific' in its approach because of its perceived recourse to 'subjective' methods of inquiry, which is the reason it is sometimes denigrated. I suppose that recent critical approaches to reading literature in aligning 'English' with philosophy and sociology are responses to these pressures.

The PGCE students that we surveyed came from a highly motivated group who had been inspired by their tutor. They spoke with enthusiasm of the ways in which they had learnt new teaching techniques:

I came from a 'drama' background, and anticipated my classroom practice being a long festival of performance. Media approaches revealed new opportunities, and the course, placement school and National Curriculum breathed new life into reading and writing for me – often beginning with enactive learning, then moving on.

Male (PGCE)

I knew that I wanted to be a practical and innovative teacher. I certainly don't agree with the notion of books out, heads down, no talking. I think if you do an activity which is memorable then the students will remember the information. I don't want to teach in the way I was taught at school. A teacher on my Teaching Practice has been most influential in my professional development, and I have the utmost respect for her methods of teaching and discipline. I guess she has moulded me into the teacher that I am.

Female (PGCE)

In complete contrast, many university English tutors still begin teaching without any training in pedagogy. Geoff, a Head of English in a higher education college, lamented the assumptions that lay behind this:

It's assumed if I have a PhD I can walk in, if I'm wacky enough, into any university or college of higher education and start lecturing from day one. Quite frankly there is no training that I'm aware of that takes up problems of pedagogy. I think culturally this country does not value pedagogy very highly, unlike some European countries. So it's not surprising that teaching practices can be stale, uninformative, unhelpful, alienating, as well as the opposite. I think it's very much a hit and miss affair. I don't know the answer to this other than a culture shift which takes education seriously, but at the moment it does not.

Geoff (UL)

At the end of the twentieth century, encouraging signs that this cultural shift is about to occur in England are hard to find. One university tutor spoke of the 1980s and 1990s as an educational 'Dark Age'. Yet the very fact that English specialists reflect on the pedagogical relationship, and the need for English students to be taught in appropriate ways is perhaps itself evidence of an implicit person-centred pedagogy which comes with the territory. Here is Patrick, a former Head of English, recalling why he and his colleagues seized the opportunity to rewrite their English courses when his college was absorbed into a polytechnic:

[The existing practices] made it very difficult for our student to progress through the mark system very effectively. It was partly because of that background up to the time we joined the Polytechnic and partly student dissatisfaction with the courses we were teaching. I remember teaching a very interesting, I thought, second-year nineteenth-century poetry course and we despaired about the non-attendance, the lack of reading ahead, the indifference, ironically something colleagues are talking about now in relation to current students. We felt that although we loved the material we just weren't delivering it right.

Patrick (UL)

Tom went on to describe the change in the pedagogy and the introduction of writing workshops and portfolios of work. So the pedagogical method adjustment favoured by Stow in the nineteenth century is re-enacted in an English department 150 years later. And for exactly the same reason – the existing practices are not working. And when, for a variety of reasons to do with overcrowding, greater emphasis on theory, and a consequent scepticism about what it means to be an individual, this preferred pedagogy is less obvious, a sense of disappointment and thwarted expectation rises to the surface:

> It's not your work any more, it's appreciating other people's work. I personally preferred to dig and delve into what I did and getting that analysed.

Natalie (ALS)

This is the remark of a student commenting on the transition from ten years of expressive writing to the kind of analysis demanded at Advanced Level, but it could equally be the comment of a first-year undergraduate writing of the challenge posed by theory. Several of the higher education specialists we interviewed were sensitive to these challenges, and once again a note of apology was discernible. This is Tim, an English lecturer from a higher education college that had received an 'Excellent' for English in the last inspection:

> I think a lot of students do experience shock in relation to theory and there's a sort of paradox which has often been observed, by which the content of theory may be extremely radical but the difficulty of it and the sense of it as a highly technical abstract discourse make teaching practices rather conservative, so one finds oneself reverting too much to a tutor-led (practice) . . . We are looking at ways of teaching theory and reviewing it, and have been for some time.

Tim (UL)

The special nature of English

When we quoted Elizabeth, the Head of English who argued that the way she approached English was not significantly different from the way she believed science would be approached, she began by stating that English was not special. Those who have been nurtured by English and nothing else (Elizabeth had started out as an art teacher), tend to disagree. There is considerable evidence that the late nineteenth-century belief in the special, holistic, nature of English continues to be held in the late twentieth century. This is the voice of Mark, a Year 13 student in the process of applying to do English at university:

> The thing about English is that it includes everything. It's got bits of psychology, history, politics, science in it. It's got everything.

And here is Paul, another Year 13 student:

> I think people have a very narrow-minded view of English. I say to people I'm studying A Level Literature for Advanced Level and they say, 'Oh, I hate reading, I couldn't do that'. But it's more than just reading. I mean you look at human nature on the whole. You really find out what life is about for other people and what life is actually about.

The bigness and scope of English is an important part of its appeal. Here is Jemma, a PGCE student:

> As far as I could see English was about people. Who they are – what makes them tick – what's going on in their lives – who is in their lives and why. This interested me – finding out about equations and weights etc. didn't. For me English was immediate, it was about me. It had a relevance that all other subjects didn't.

'It was about me' is a sentiment frequently expressed by those we interviewed. Here is Tom, explaining why he chose to become an English specialist:

> If I were to isolate why I pursued English I would say that in English in my use of language, and in the study of others' use of language I found a way of making sense of myself and the experiences I had.
>
> Tom (PGCE)

A student-teacher from the same group emphasised that for her English is special because everyone talks, everyone needs to communicate, so English provides something for everyone. When asked whether she didn't believe that science and maths could generate the same enthusiasm she agreed that for some people that was the case, but 'you can't talk about them over dinner'.

Another student-teacher was even more certain about her belief:

Of course English is special. That's why I chose it. Because there's no
boundaries with English. English is unique. Our tutor is always laughing
and saying 'Oh, that's typical English students'.

Ursula (PGCE)

I think English is so flexible compared to all the other subjects. They are
all so rigid.

Polly (PGCE)

The relaxed view of English as a field which allows those who enjoyed
lively dinner conversation to continue this practice in the classroom is the
attitude which those who opposed the setting up of schools of English in
universities deplored and used to justify their opposition. It survives in a way
that provides ammunition for those who feel that English is without rigour.
Georgina is a third-year undergraduate who started on a chemistry course but
was then asked to leave. So she took up English, because she enjoys talking
about books and reading:

I'd much rather read a book than see a film. You don't get many good
films.

She is a bright student, and has not found Subject English too taxing:

To me it's been light relief for three years, more like hobby . . . You can
get away with spending less time on English . . . I would carry on at post-
graduate level if you didn't have to study. It beats working!

Her friend Caroline had similarly chosen to major in English rather than
her stronger subject history because in history 'more work was involved'; but
Caroline wished she had been made to write more:

The university could have made things more demanding. We could have
done more essays – one a fortnight, say.

The sheer scale of the field frequently excited comment:

I feel that English (more than any other subject) prepares students for life
in the broadest sense. 'English' is such a huge subject area and deals with
emotions, creativity and human reaction to life in general.

(PGCE)

English is an all-embracing subject.

(PGCE)

Another student teacher used an almost identical phrase:

English is all-embracing both with reference to texts and to the skills needed in this field. I am also a Classicist and find the two subjects complement each other perfectly.

The belief in this large agenda is often conveyed to students by their teachers. Here is a Head of English rejecting the view of English we saw articulated in the Newsom Report of 1963, a view of English as communication:

> I have never looked upon English as a kind of service industry that enables people to use skills of spelling and punctuation and expression for other subjects. Nobody else does poetry, nobody else does novels, imaginative literature, nobody else really looks into plays in the way we do. We've had this debate with the teachers on the Personal, Social and Ethical programme, and I say that we contribute to this because we really do discuss the moral dimension of things and choices, life choices and that sort of stuff but we don't do it in quite the arid way they do it in PSE classes . . . I think it's subversive in the sense that it should make people think for themselves about things . . .
>
> (SST)

English teachers in England are often heard to speak of the subversive character of English, with a note of quiet pride. Yet that confidence has been undermined by the loss of autonomy and the growth in accountability, assessment and inspection. Here are two different responses to the changes – adjustment (some would say compromise) and defeat:

> I was young and visionary in my social idealism. I believed in the perfectability of man [sic] and I was much taken by the idea of education as a subversive activity.
>
> (Former SST)

> I am disillusioned that the profession [in England] has so meekly allowed the government to impose their massively unimaginative views on to us. I can never admire colleagues who are happy with the National Curriculum. For from looking at new and interesting literature, and at the influence of the media, we are constrained by tests and set texts to admire the past and ignore the present. There are many good practitioners about who fight this tide of mundanity – but I do not intend to remain alongside. It is a sad and lost cause. Education is in itself in need of major rethinking – the British system does not work.
>
> (SST)

Yet people change. The first speaker is Chris Woodhead, who is head of the school inspection 'service' in England, the Office for Standards in Education. As time has passed he moved closer to the view of the world advanced by his predecessor, Mathew Arnold. His beliefs have undergone a transformation now that he is no longer a classroom teacher, and the views he was reported to have expressed at a conference for Grant Maintained School Heads was positively Arnoldian:

> Mr Woodhead . . . sees his task much more in terms of initiating young people into the best that has been thought and said, equipping them with the knowledge and skills that they will need to find a reasonable job, and teaching them about morality and taste.
>
> (*Times Educational Supplement*, 24 March 1995)

English is special, but we would argue that its special character lies in its role as an agency for a particular kind of pedagogy rather than for its ability to subvert or tap into a unique kind of imaginative creativity. It may in the process stimulate certain students in highly significant ways, but what it offers *all* of its students is a training in the importance attached to self-reflection and self-regulation in a seemingly non-interventionist environment. More controversially our research in England would encourage us to argue that not only is English normative rather than subversive, it is at its most normative when it convinces its participants of their freedom, independence, individuality and power to question. And as our research seems to show, it is very successful in inculcating this belief in many of its specialists in schools, colleges and universities.

The machinery of the state: questions of assessment and the National Curriculum

Earlier we saw how Ursula – Ursula the student teacher rather than Ursula Brangwen, though similar remarks would apply – felt that there was a conflict between her desire to teach in a way that made English enjoyable for the students and the assessment arrangements made mandatory in English at each of the Key Stages. Her particular concern is the national tests for 14 year olds:

> [W]hat they're doing is very dry . . . Shakespeare, the SATs tests, all that's doing is actually putting them off.
>
> Ursula (ST)

On the other hand we began by noting a description of the way that English teachers in schools had turned the four strands in the National Curriculum itself from ugly ducklings into something resembling four swans. Here is a student teacher on a PGCE course in Exeter:

> I think that because I have been 'brought up' (to a certain extent) with the National Curriculum, assessment, GCSE and so on, I have always had a

clear idea about the way English is taught and how I wanted to teach it. I have developed within it.

Among older teachers, however, there is still a bitter resentment about what has been lost:

> We have been in tremendous turmoil, haven't we, for ten years or more, particularly in the National Curriculum. Not that I object to that in itself, because I think the first document defined very well the subject area of English, but it's the testing that really killed it. I mean the business of Shakespeare for everybody in Year 9, for example, which we're doing because we think we owe it to the kids and we think we're making a success of it but you find yourself, particularly in Year 9, pushed into ways of doing the subject and organising it in ways that I would really rather not do, you know, rather sterile and very backward looking.
>
> (SST)

Sometimes there is a glimpse of the deep anger that runs just beneath the surface:

> I get extremely irritated with the idiocy of some people who influence us, you know the nonsense of the Standard Assessment Tests, some of the nonsense of Key Stage 4 [examinations for Year 11 students] and the complete nonsense of cutting down course work at Advanced Level [Year 13].
>
> (SST)

Then there is the more reflective, but equally strong, questioning of the assumptions on which the machinery of an English National Curriculum is based. Here is someone from the University of London Institute of Education:

> I have had many conversations with my Department here about the value of literature and what it means to try and organise a National Curriculum around stages of literature. I am interested in what we are asking, what kind of notion of development in reading do we have that wouldn't allow us to say these are experiences that are appropriate or possible at this age, and so on.
>
> (TT)

Kathy Smith comments on the changes that she has witnessed:

> Much later, as a teacher, and comparing my early experiences of teaching Northern Examination Association English syllabus in the 1980s with

my later work with students within the constraints of the National Curriculum, I have found that the lack of flexibility of the National Curriculum made it much more difficult to relate to students in a constructive way, so much more difficult because I felt confined by the tick boxes of the National Curriculum . . . if you're working with students with wide social, emotional and educational needs, then to be held down by a National Curriculum which says 'this is what you've got to teach', no matter what you have in front of you in terms of student, and it dictates the texts and what you have to achieve, when perhaps the aims are not entirely appropriate to the groups you have in front of you, is actually very constraining.

She went on to express dismay about the amount of paperwork, the constant sense 'that someone is watching over your shoulder to see not so much that the learning is going on but that the teaching is going on':

You have to have evidence that you have taught something, whether the student has learned it or not.

Charlotte Raven, a columnist in *The Guardian* and former editor of *The Modern Review*, expressed the view that she would hope that it was possible to combine a controlling framework and opportunities to interest students, but she had some reservations:

[I have] the obvious reservations about assessment not conveying the whole picture. That it may result in the Dead Poets Society kind of teacher eliciting from the less able a significant response that may be unchartable. I worry about that being the pay-off, as all liberals do!

On the other hand, assessment regulations can be a force for change, can be transformative. Michael, a PGCE co-ordinator, recalled the intellectual adjustments he made at York University, due to the assessment requirements:

[York] had – and still does have – a far reaching assessment system. I think it was the assessment that changed [my thinking] and the number of choices you had within the degree that changed some of my notions and in particular the fact that we were required to do a degree in English and a related subject. It was also a requirement of the course that you had to do two modules in a second language, which for me was French. (TT)

Janet White is Subject Officer for English at QCA, and has considerable experience in the field of assessment. The Qualifications and Curriculum Authority differs from SCAA in the much larger scope of its responsibilities. In covering qualifications both academic and vocational, and in addressing learning from pre-school to 'the third age', the Authority is concerned not only with curriculum development and the evolution of assessment but also monitoring international developments, setting targets for schools, developing a coherent national framework of qualifications and 'carrying out research to support its policy proposals and to evaluate their effectiveness' (QCA 1997). England – and QCA's role centres on England – is unique in developing a systematic, regulated approach to the description, assessment and inspection of the curriculum, with national tests in core subjects such as English supported by extensive illustrative and innovative materials produced by people with a background in English teaching and innovation. In addition to the Key Stage tests, QCA is currently working on Baseline Assessment and the refinement of Desirable Outcomes for pre-school children, and has developed optional tests for Years 3, 4 and 5 (for children aged 8, 9 and 10) which for a number of reasons have proved hugely popular with schools. The huge apparatus that is QCA, a government-funded organisation that costs millions to maintain, is a key part of the Government's declared aim of raising standards, and a key element in this strategy is the monitoring of the curriculum through mandatory assessment. It is conceivable that there could be national tests at the end of every year of compulsory schooling.

QCA is aware that there is a danger that English could be subsumed in the much wider debate about literacy, and is keen to make sure that assessment does not become restricted to a repetition of a few, narrow 'basic skills'. Neither does it have any intention of telling teachers how to teach: the materials it produces, nevertheless, do have a curriculum development role. English teachers are not always very good at developing appropriate assessment methods (Janet White argues), perhaps because there has been a resistance to what have in the past been seen as narrow forms of assessment that do not reward achievement. Assessment can be innovative as (interviews at KS1 for example) and can ensure entitlement and good practice, as the Shakespeare assessment at Key Stage 3 has demonstrated across the country. The Key Stage 1 Reading test for 1998 supplied every child in the country with his/her own copy of *Miss Emily and the Bird of Make-Believe* by Charles Keeping, and there is evidence that children are excited by the ownership of these well-produced books and treat the test as an adventure in growing up. It would be wrong to imagine that they are anything like the comprehension tests in Ridout's *English Today* (1948).

Another important task which QCA has been set is the development of the idea of Key Skills. The move towards standardised, outcomes-based assessment is all part of a drive towards accountability. In England QCA intends that this will provide an opportunity to revisit the National Curriculum for English as revised by the Dearing Committee to identify where aims and objectives are being met, and where they are not. Again, with the potentially narrow focus on literacy in mind, there is a need to revisit those parts of English which address the wider skills developed drama, media and

ICT. At A Level the debate about 'cores' – what skills an advanced level in English Literature and/or Language should be testing – should be resolved in 2001.

The view of QCA is that, despite reports or research that seem to suggest the contrary, in England the past ten years have not been a period in which literacy standards in England have shown any significant decline. The whole declared purpose of QCA is to raise standards, and the test as to whether this whole apparatus of testing, inspection, publication of results and centralised control of the curriculum has been successful will be measured by (please insert a phrase here – I offered you the choice of a rise in standards of literacy, a more successful workforce, a set of citizens more attuned to the needs of the twenty-first century and I am not sure which – if any – of these outcomes you would wish QCA to be measured by!). It is a huge enterprise, and possibly only China and France have such a comprehensive centralised national system. As an apparatus for assessment affecting every aspect of institutional learning, it perhaps even surpasses its rivals.

The battles over assessment reflect an understanding of its importance as the key factor influencing curriculum and pedagogy. The dominant model – which in schools is a growth model modified but not transformed by social theories of language – can survive only if the assessment arrangements provide opportunities for students to feel they have some control over their own writing by being able to select those pieces of reflective and imaginative work which they have drafted and revised independently. This is why multiple choice and the exclusive use of one-, two- or three-hour written papers was rejected in favour of coursework, oral assessment and 'controlled conditions'. The older forms of assessment did not work because they were perceived to encourage 'teaching to the test' and English teachers were not able to practise their preferred role as facilitators, discrete supervisors who stressed the importance of the children's own experience and work. That is what the technology of English prefers to assess (if it must assess at all, and we have traced the rhetoric which argues that English is concerned with qualities that are unassessable). And, it can be argued, English will never completely lose the battle, even though it may lose some ground, because the society in which it carries out these normative practices needs subjects who are shaped in this way, as well as in the way that science shapes them.

Ethics and aesthetics: not whose but how?

Earlier we traced some of the ways in which English was rooted in Arnoldian aesthetics, and how the education of taste has been the preoccupation of early twentieth-century critics such as Sampson and Leavis. In *Culture and Environment* Leavis and Thompson pay tribute to Lawrence's anti-industrial rhetoric and his diatribes against ugliness. We noted how Lawrence had discovered Nietzsche whilst a schoolteacher in Croydon, and it is Nietzsche who defined the human being as an aesthetic rather than an ethical being.

That being the case, all that matters to Nietzsche are those individuals who have the capacity to promote 'the oligarchs of the spirit', the aristocratic artists. In England there are contemporary critics such as A. N. Wilson who continue to argue such a position, though even the public (i.e. private) schools adopt the rhetoric of a kind of liberal egalitarianism that Nietzsche loathed. A neo-Victorian underclass is being created in Britain, but its existence is not defended.

Yet Aesthetics does remain an issue, partly because Nietzsche's genealogical approach was taken up by Foucault, whose work informs so much contemporary critical thinking. In many ways it is *the* issue, but in schools still trying to resist simplistic notions of 'good' literature imposed on them by the Government the comments on 'taste' are likely to reflect that particular agenda.

On the other hand it is a significant element in the attractions of English:

The aesthetic value of literature and language that I find in English is what appeals to me. There is something so very special when, after sifting endlessly through books, one finds a piece of work that is special. Sifting through realms of rubbish, or 'good' literature until one encounters a poem or novel that sparkles and the words are so sweet to savour.

(PGCE)

Through my learning of English in language and literature, I discovered a world which seemed to be beyond the experience of my home and family life. I found English to be full of richness, humour, imagination, a way of glimpsing – and exploring – alternative pleasures and ways of living from those I saw around me in my working-class environment. Partly it was a romanticized view. Also I gradually realized the power of being able to use the language and to communicate and create myself through how I used the language.

(PGCE)

The significance of the remark that it was partly 'a romanticised view' is revealed by a later comment made by this student teacher:

I didn't previously conceive how classroom management would limit the methods and materials which could be used, and how lack of space in schools would reduce or remove opportunities for creative work.

As for ethics, this is sometimes confused with morality, and specialists are wary of entering this territory. Yet English encounters ethical issues all the time: a contemporary example concerns the text *Lolita* and the most recent film version. Should students have access to this text as part of their English studies, or in a society shocked by recent evidence of the abuse and exploitation of children should an ethical decision be made to censor this text? This is the classical challenge to the non-interventionist pedagogical role, and the issue is so difficult it is often side stepped. Professor Lisa Jardine stated publicly the classical liberal humanist position that these texts should not be censored, and although these issues are discussed on television, radio and in newspapers, they are now beginning to be subject of university conferences.

We did not ask direct questions on the subject of ethics and aesthetics, and as we have noted the reluctance to be seen as interventionist, a belief which springs from the rhetoric of freedom and growth (you don't get healthy chickens if you keep them in battery cages) meant that there was unease when addressing issues such as teaching the National Curriculum and canonical literature and an implicit belief that English should not be normative, and that in the ideal classroom it will not be normative. This remains, therefore, a question to be asked of English, rather than by English in schools. Nevertheless, it is an issue that teachers live with daily, and concerns such as the following sit just beneath the surface for many teachers:

> I do get very frustrated when I go in to teach a lesson and I have spent most of the lesson teaching them about good behaviour and what is right and what is wrong.
>
> Polly (PGCE)

And this is preoccupation that young teachers like Polly soon learn from other teachers, whether through informal discussion or professional research:

> I think obviously you want them [the students] to learn the subject knowledge, but when I was doing my research assignment I interviewed one teacher who said she felt the most important job was to make sure they understand and learn good behaviour and to have values and respect other people in society.
>
> Polly

What is significant about this is not that the teacher said it, but that it is a response that Polly has internalised and remembered, even though she was yet to begin her own teaching career.

From those who have immersed themselves in popular culture, as postgraduates and later in the world of work, there is something of a desire to return to questions about what is good and bad. This is Charlotte Raven:

> Everyone's talking about popular culture [which] is now less rich in a number of ways, Hollywood being one of them. People have thrown out everything that aspired to quality and significance. The ennui we are feeling under [Prime Minister] Blair is the ennui you feel after a critical

theory degree. There's a desire now to talk about meaning, truth, about why one thing is better than another, to move outside the parameters of the current debates . . .

Intellectual practices: learning from within or from without?

In a personal-growth pedagogy, the emphasis is on allowing a child to develop, with the teacher as gardener. The imagery is of nature, of what is natural, and we have seen how it is possible to identify a strand in English which since the nineteenth century – and possibly before – has sought to create a learning environment which is as close as possible to that which is perceived to be the most natural for children – the world of play, of natural enquiry and inquisitiveness, of delight in story and dreaming. English has always sought, we have been arguing, to import these qualities into the classroom, just as Stow sought to import them into the school playground, with the supervisory teacher in attendance.

Another model of learning would emphasise how much of what we learn comes from that which is outside us, but which we internalise. Culture, history and language itself. It would be foolish to suggest that either of these models is one which would deny elements taken from the other. The rejection of binary oppositions is now a *sine qua non*. And it is the plurality of English – the celebration of difference whilst holding on to some kind of practical connecting methodology that we have tried to convey through the model of the Swiss army knife – that is most likely to allow a link to be made between school and university perceptions of English. Here is Stephen Greenblatt, stressing the need to maintain some kind of balance and control over something that is fundamentally unstable by citing a bicycle riding analogy:

> I think that, even without Derrida, that I began in school to develop a sense both that meaning was not simply mine to make up and that meanings were multiple, unstable, complex, shifting. After all, riding a bike involves learning to do a fantastically complex series of adjustments and risking falling off.
>
> (email 15 February 1995)

And here is a young university lecturer from Kings College, London recalling his reasons for specialising in English:

> [The attraction of English] was to do with literary forms rather than other discourses like philosophical or symbolic logic, although I was interested in those as well. But I think it was not specific to a particular genre. Part of the excitement of the thing was that there were all these different branches . . . and they were all being opened up and also related to each other and it seemed really exciting.

A student teacher from Exeter spoke more tentatively. Her broad comment was representative of many of the responses we recorded:

> It is hard to provide a list of concrete reasons as to why I chose English and why it still inspires me everyday. This subject can be appreciated both at an emotional level and can also be approached logically and analytically.
>
> (PGCE)

So as we move from university towards school a different model of learning begins to emerge. Our first two speakers spoke of the practices of English involving an engagement with something outside the self, whether it was the metaphor of the bicycle or the example of discourse. The subject is formed by a relationship with the outside world. The model is not quite the *tabula rasa* of Locke, but there are similarities. The self is a site for processes and does not have a centre or an existence of its own. Barth has used the image of the onion – we have our layers, but there is no middle.

The student teacher quoted above introduces the affective and the influence of Kant and Coleridge and German Romanticism has been important in the construction of a model of identity with which English has worked over the past hundred years. There is something beyond reason, there is the combination of the affective and reason which we call understanding, or the imagination. The creative imagination lies at the core of human experience, and it is the job of the English teacher to release it in students. This is a very different model of learning, with a very different agenda. It is the one we have encountered in specialists in schools, whether students or teachers, student teachers or PGCE co-ordinators.

It has been argued that the very tensions which arise from the inability of English to define itself or agree on a single approach are paradoxically its greatest strength. The point is well made by Lionel Gossman:

> At the present moment a case might be made for the educational value of the study of literature precisely because, despite everything, it continues to resist routinization (the multitude of warring methodologies, theories and practices is striking illustration of this); precisely because it fails to provide positive doctrines and lessons, but, on the contrary, continually opens up abysses before us and confronts us with uncertainty; precisely because, in short, it is the place where we encounter not presence, as the Romantics hoped, but absence, not security but insecurity.
>
> Gossman ibid.

As an idea this is challenging and exciting. As a prospect for a student teacher, who suddenly finds his or her horizons broadened with the discovery that English can include so much, this can be daunting. Furthermore, as a rationale and curriculum vitae for English it can appear to the outside world as remarkably woolly. We noted how Chris Davies's study of departmental booklets confirms a breadth of vision bordering on the incorporeal. The strong belief in growth from within, and of development in English as being something that is almost impossible to measure on any linear scale made the broad rhetoric of Newbolt and Dartmouth vulnerable to searching questions when accountability became the watchword.

Key moments and influences: how do we appear to change?

From the oral and written evidence we gathered it is clear that the formative years for English specialists are those from the age of sixteen onwards. In a subject dominated in schools by a belief in a personal-growth model it is not surprising that a person – usually a charismatic English teacher – frequently played a crucial role in shaping specialists' beliefs. Some of our interviewees were drawn into English by their own experiences as school students:

> I liked my English teacher and wanted to be like him. That was what got me interested in English.
>
> (PGCE)

> I enjoyed English enormously at school, I would say for the subject's sake, but also because my favourite teachers were English teachers. My father was in the police, I went to eight different schools, but in every school it seemed that the English teacher was the one I liked, respected the most and just had the most in common with.
>
> (SST)

> I remember admiring one of the teachers at school because he just seemed to make everything so interesting and current, that's what I liked, he would bring in song lyrics and you would look at them rather than poems, the originality of it was so attractive, I suppose. I think that's what attracted me, seeing people being so original.
>
> (SST)

The desire to strike up a special relationship is well documented in films such as *Dead Poets Society* and *The Prime of Miss Jean Brodie*. Occasionally teachers who had taught in traditionalist schools would recall how it was the English teachers who had tried to break down barriers between pupils and teachers:

> I was in a very stuffy English department with John O'Connor . . . They were in many ways a little bit hidebound and I was prepared to experiment. I mean John and myself were the first people in that particular school to start calling pupils by their first names, for example.

When you think of English you can't imagine calling people by their surnames now! I am talking about 1968/9.

(SST)

It was not always the teacher–pupil relationship that was cited as being formative. Sometimes it was the intensity of the classroom situation:

> I was very lucky in Year 10, the 4th form, I got to do English Language a year early and then in the fifth form three of us did English Literature, while all the rest of our top A set did Maths, additional Maths, and so on from the age of 15 I was taught Literature in a group of three, sitting around reading books and things so that was quite a formative influence on me.

(Head of English)

There is evidence of the enduring influence of Leavis, if only as the source of an approach which is now challenged. Not unlike a Catholic upbringing, contact with Leavisite ideas was formative and influential in shaping perceptions and beliefs at school and university:

> I was taught English at school by fairly liberal humanist Leavis methods and I was taught at York which was in a sense the place that Leavis retired to so there was a continuity in English in that way.

(TT)

For another Head of English the key moments came much later. He taught for a number of years and then decided to take a Masters degree:

> The MEd was a blessed year in which I could recover my wits and take stock and then go back into schools, not exactly like Clark Kent turning into Superman but with a slightly different approach, and then able to learn. I also met another seminal figure. I met Peter Medway and he was on supply in the school I worked at in Newton Abbot and in a way he was quite an influential figure because he was a man who was quite prepared to have difficult classes, to have noisy classes but still believed so much in what he was doing that that was all right.

For those moving from university English back to school English as teachers, an enormous reorientation readjustment is necessary. This is Helen, who became a PGCE co-ordinator herself, recalling the impact of the PGCE at the University of London Institute of Education:

> The impact of that year was huge, inestimable. Coming into classrooms and seeing . . . I think that most of what I think about English has developed through my use of teaching and of being in classrooms, and

that really started with the PGCE years. Suddenly the content was less interesting than the processes and practices in classroom that made the content work or not work . . . So yes, I would say it was huge.

(TT)

Helen was also influenced by a number of teachers, both at school and then later when she was doing an MA:

I think there was a teacher of a kind of Miss Jean Brodie personal charisma that ought to be rejected. *Dead Poets Society* awfulness, that of course made an impact. Going to the Institute of Education [University of London] to do the MA was wonderful. Jane Miller influenced me through many things that were kind of there already, like girls and gender, teaching girls, reading girls. Jane was the perfect person to talk it through with. And Tony Burgess. But the other influential people are the kids in schools, they are what shake or confirm things you might think about Shakespeare!

These responses do not differ greatly from those recorded by Protherough and Atkinson (1991, p. 25) where the findings of a small survey revealed that other English teachers were the most cited influence, followed closely by academic subject study. As we noted earlier, the National Curriculum has become an important factor in shaping student-teachers' perceptions of English as they reorientate themselves from a subject centred definition to a people centred one. If there is one thread running through the revised National Curriculum (DfE 1995) it is the sense of writing and performing for a specific audience, the notion of others, whether readers, listeners or spectators. It reveals the influence of whole language approaches which emphasise process rather than product.

Apart from teachers and curriculum documents, initial teacher education, much maligned in England, can be very influential – certainly at the time, though it is not always seen that way in retrospect. Many of those we interviewed at Exeter University School of Education spoke highly of their PGCE experience:

The PGCE course has used a number of techniques in presenting methods of teaching English which have forced wider the issues involved as I perceive them. The experience of teaching itself has made me look at the way pupils themselves regard the subject and consequently affected the way I teach them. I find my attitudes to English itself are quite separated from the teaching of it – attitudes to personal writing and so on.

(PGCE)

This splitting is something that is forced on many specialists who enter school teaching, whereas those who go on to teach or research in universities survive the transition from student to lecturer with their views generally intact. These views may be modified in the light of reading and contact, but there is nothing as transformational as the experience of learning to teach, rather than study English:

> The approaches suggested in the PGCE course have challenged my attitudes toward the teaching of certain areas. Our tutor has stimulated our styles and techniques quite considerably.

The reorientation that takes place – and in England some PGCE courses have modules called 'Reorientation' and are quite explicit about this process – is strikingly effective in some instances:

> Through the course we were encouraged to teach English in a lively, expressive manner which has shaped and changed my whole attitude towards English lessons.
>
> (PGCE)

> Since starting the PGCE course my view of English teaching has expanded, and I feel that I have developed a much clearer picture of what is required, and of myself as a teacher of English.
>
> (PGCE)

These two comments bear witness to the normative power of English: what is significant is not so much their willingness to praise the course but their acknowledgement that there is a definite method which they have learnt to appreciate and with which they can now identify:

> The PGCE Course has turned my ideas about teaching English inside out. I may still believe some traditional aspects of the subject are important but I can see different methods of achieving that end.

On the other hand, several of these student teachers spoke of the way that experience in school and time and financial constraints had influenced them:

> I'm slightly less idealistic now.

Both Polly and Ursula revealed a different set of beliefs in the second half of their interviews, compared to the positive goals and aspirations they had described in the first. There were practical obstacles to the realisation of the things in which they believed:

> You can't make a child understand a certain way, think a certain way and then when it goes home it has the opposite told to it. You're constantly

banging your head against a brick wall. One boy in my class had no idea
of how to listen to other people talking. He was constantly interrupting
and his parents felt their role was just to clothe him and feed him.

Polly (PGCE)

Young people are changing dramatically, they're growing up far too
quickly for their own good and that's to do with the media and television
and all the rest of it. I'm quite shocked sometimes with what comes out.
My role is changing, you never purely go in and teach your subject, that
never happens, something else happens that you have to deal with and it's
getting more so.

Ursula (PGCE)

In encounters with real classrooms and real children these young specialists
(both in their twenties) seem to draw on a set of beliefs formed in their own
childhoods, perhaps by their parents and immediate families. It is not that
the experience of teaching in school or university causes a revision of the
idealism, it is that a former set of beliefs (about human behaviour) rush in to
fill the gap created by the failure to succeed in realising the more idealistic
goals. Human subjects may be shaped, but human subjects can also resist
overt shaping as Stow and Kay-Shuttleworth's proposals tried to accommodate in the nineteenth century.

Writing genres: where next with writing?

Elsewhere (Peel 1995) I have written of the historical reasons why English
specialists do not generally regard themselves as writers in quite the same way
as music and drama specialists regard themselves as performers. In schools
children are encouraged to be writers, and to practise and publish imaginative
writing. This was the great lesson of the New English, which emerged in
England and was readily taken up by the United States and Australia. The
varieties of writing children are encouraged to do – collaborative, for specific
audiences, on the word processor, to record, to argue, to reflect, to seek
information, to respond, to try out ideas, for assessment – means that
students spend a significant amount of their school, college and university
lives writing. Yet those specialists who decide to go into teaching soon find
that the one thing that they now do much less of (as teachers) is the very thing
that they are asking students to do a great deal of. Teachers continue to read
(if much of that reading is student writing rather than reading of their own
choice) but unless they are teaching in universities with a research culture
writing begins to be limited to assignment booklets and student feedback.
Some of those we interviewed had used their time at university to extend
their experience of writing:

I had some semi-mature and infantile and mature friends all of whom got together and used to do bits of writing and so on and giggle as we read our poems to each other . . . We submitted various things to the kinds of internal magazines which the kind of student body which has got any life will produce.

(UL)

Another English lecturer in a college of higher education had been attracted to English because of his interest in what he called creative writing:

When I was starting out as an undergraduate I suppose the thing that comes to mind would be that I was interested in creative writing quite strongly and [English] was the closest thing to that. I suppose what I thought about it impressionistically was that it gave me more freedom than anything else, imaginatively and intellectually.

Adrian (UL)

Freedom is an important part of the vocabulary of English teaching, but not all specialists felt that they experienced it as undergraduates. Emily, now a PGCE co-ordinator in London, had a very disorientating experience, which she nevertheless enjoyed. She is recalling her time as an undergraduate at Oxford:

The weekly essay sat so oddly with the tutorial where you took it along and you read it out and she hadn't read it before, so what was an essay in that context? Some kind of performance? In some cases it wasn't even given in for any kind of sustained comment. It was a sort of . . . how did we write essays then? A gathering together of critical texts, kind of cunning plagiarism that we all played where we knit together other people's views of Tennyson or Dickens, there was pleasure in the doing of that job. Not a lot of space for, it's corny, but what I might think, but that didn't bother me too much, it was quite an interesting exercise to do that weekly gymnastic. That was never an issue, what it might be to rethink your style or look at other ways of planning what you have to say. That was taken as read.

There were no obvious signs that in England fresh thinking about writing is about to lead to a revision in practice. In 1996 the United States National Writing project held a Summer Institute in England, and the focus there on writing across the curriculum and writing to learn suggested developments that have not taken root in England. This is understandable: whereas a great deal of innovative work on narrative, on writing poetry and more recently the writing of argument came out of a series of projects in the UK in the 1970s and 1980s, now discussion of literacy tends to dominate the agenda, and a period of retrenchment is evident. Some of those we spoke to were involved with projects involving the use of writing frames (arising from genre theory, which has been developed in Australia) while others were setting up writing workshops following attendance at a pilot course run by the Arvon Foundation, but it is significant that neither of these projects are funded by central or local government. It is very much left to teachers to pioneer developments themselves in small groups, and such developments as exist are likely to place writing in the context of hypertext, media and the new technology, which is where curriculum initiatives certainly are taking place. We wanted to look at the relationship between writing and reading in higher education in more detail, however, and carried out further research on which we report later in this chapter.

Media and the new technologies: beyond English?

The extent to which English should realign itself to the new technologies is a subject which tends to divide specialists, not always along generation lines. Some who are willing to embrace change in all other respects have a problem with the hyperbole. This is Emily again, describing the different perceptions of her students:

> The question comes up every day with PGCE students who arrive with degrees even as old as mine and those who have just come from universities and their understandings of English as a subject are as different as you would imagine, so the tensions about what do we mean by English come up every day, in my job and is it 'English' to do a series of things, what kinds of practices do we want to develop around the name of English – this is an issue, I think. And if it's not the literary text then where does it stop, what does it embrace? For example, why should my PGCE students be interested in spending a session on the English and Media Centre's new pack on *Advertising* with a brand new one on *Newspapers and Journalism*? Why should that be English? So I think my job throws up every day the tension you are talking about. And there's a lot of the kind of Luddites like myself with a nervousness and resistance about some of the things I think I could be going along with but I make excuses about not wanting to surf the Internet although I'm terribly interested in ethnographies of readers so why shouldn't I be interested in what people are up to in a different form?
>
> Emily (TT)

Martin, a Head of English in a medium-size comprehensive school, expresses similar ambivalence:

> I think I've got two reactions. One is always thinking that all these things are machinery, or recalling what Emerson is supposed to have said when he heard that New York could now talk to California: 'But have they got anything to say?'. That I think is the key thing. It's all very well to be able

to communicate on the Internet but what are we actually going to say to each other. So one bit of me has that almost Luddite kind of reaction, a certain scepticism really, and feeling, no what we're really talking about is *meaning* and when we talk about meaning, it doesn't really matter whether it's in books or on tape or on video or on the World Wide Web. Having said that, I'm actually on the WWW myself and I'm actually quite keen on computers and I word process a lot of stuff myself but them I'm a kind of wordy person anyway. I certainly communicate e-mail with several friends and several teachers. I'm in regular contact with a Head of English in Leeds. He's on the Associated Examining Board Subject Committee, and we exchange files over the Internet, schemes of work and letters and things like that. Students don't contact me yet but as it gets going I am sure it will happen.

The problems are practical ones: the cost of equipment, the fact that although there is occasional rhetoric from the political parties about the need to wire up our schools, the fact is that the only scheme to provide them with equipment other than what their small budgets can provide is one whereby industry passes on its out of date computers to schools! Emily's comments reflect this reality:

Alex McCleod persuades me with wonderful enthusiasm that this is the future. My experience in London – perhaps I am in the wrong schools – is that I see very little of this. Largely schools don't have the equipment and the message has not got through. I mean we're still working mainly with very limited software, literacy programmes supporting reading, yes I have seen some interesting programmes, but not much beyond that. I want to ask 'Where has Jimmy Britton gone?' I want to see those ideas about language and learning in literature taken forward as well.

Emily (TT)

Such comments seemed to be in marked contrast to the beliefs expressed in the publications we examined, publications such as *English in Education*, the English and Media Centre magazine, *NATE News* and *The Times Educational Supplement*, all of which featured articles celebrating the opportunities offered by the new technologies to create multimedia texts which were not only professional looking and relatively inexpensive, but encouraged questions about audience, agency, selection and language to be asked in ways that were immediately comprehensible. But if the materials are changing, and the name too – Media has started to challenge English's popularity as an A Level and university subject – then the pedagogy remains consistent, with the emphasis on student investigation, experiment and reflection, with the minimum of teacher intervention. Student familiarity with complex technology is likely to reinforce the minimalist intervention strategies, so that although it is quite possible that the name English may be superseded by the term Language Arts, Communications or Media and Language Arts, the set of practices associated with English are likely to survive.

But the division of opinion about the role and value of media study should not be underestimated, and our research suggests that the division is some-times traceable to the division in generations but not the generations one might think. If we take two people who work in the media – Phil Redmond, the producer of *Grange Hill*, *Brookside* and *Hollyoaks*, all very successful soaps, and Charlotte Raven, editor of the *Modern Review* we get a contrasting set of views. This is Phil Redmond:

> It's usually people from privileged, well-educated backgrounds (who suggest that soaps discourage reading). Television is life's greatest stimulator of discussion, and the ability to converse is part of literacy . . . Our education system is driven by a strong middle-class ethic, but the majority going through are working class with different cultural values. Kids have to read *To Kill a Mockingbird* for GCSE – a terrific book, but you don't need to teach them in the nineties about forty-year old values in southern America. *Brookside* and *Grange Hill* are better teaching aids for kids than most classics. They learn about plot, character development and irony, and you can explain this is what Shakespeare and Dickens do. We're all about the same thing – births, marriages and deaths.
>
> Redmond 1998

In contrast, Charlotte Raven said that she was bored by this kind of argument:

> I think that mainly when people say that they are [reading popular culture] they are not. There's a lot of popular culture which is immune to analysis. The thing that we should be teaching people to do is to discriminate between what is significant and what is not. I can't really understand what media studies does . . . an advert (or a soap) is fairly interesting but in order to interpret it you don't need analytical tools of the same kind of quality that you need to apply to something harder.

Charlotte Raven is of a younger generation than Phil Redmond, and there is some evidence from our research that media studies, like feminism, reveals a reaction against the reaction: those who fought to broaden the English curriculum are now regarded as the status quo itself to be subverted.

Skills and the workplace: why does instrumentalism have a bad name?

The answer to this question may appear obvious. There is widely held belief among English specialists – and this is one belief that unites secondary and higher education, unites believers in personal growth, believers in canonical literature and believers in critical theory – that schools are not training grounds for industry. Education should be about leading out and not leading in to employment.

> I have never looked upon English as a kind of service industry that enables people to use skills of spelling, punctuation and expression for other subjects.
>
> (SST)

Vocational English is a concept that seems to trouble many English specialists. Although students and the public at large accept the central place of English in the curriculum precisely because the ability to talk and write and read are even more essential in a post industrial society than they were in the nineteenth century or first eighty years of the twentieth, English specialists have tended to be uncomfortable with notions of communication skills for life and work. Dickens's plea for 'fancy' in *Hard Times* (1854) is echoed in John Freeman's question 'Where is the Wonder?' (Freeman 1998). As Protherough and Atkinson point out (1991, p. 9), in 1921 in *English for the English* George Sampson had argued that the purpose of education is 'not to prepare children for their occupations, but to prepare children *against* their occupations'.

Since the First World War mass unemployment has modified the image of school as a place conditioning children for the world of work. The nature of work has itself changed, with short-term contracts replacing long-term careers. Recent studies, particularly those undertaken by genre theorists in Australia and Peter Medway, first in England and then in Canada, have focused attention on the place of language in the workplace: for a variety of reasons the movement from research into 'literary practices' (poetry, narrative, personal writing) to research into knowledge about language has been one of the most noticeable and significant shifts in English in the last decade of the twentieth century. There are still anxieties about instrumental English, English as a service industry, English as a standard language which ignores the richness of variety. Some of these are discussed by Mark Reid:

> GNVQ [a new vocational qualification for 16–18 year olds] core skill criteria . . . have no recognition of the generative possibilities of language, of the relationship the personal and the expressive have with the 'adult needs' of the workplace. What GNVQ needs is a model of language use – rather than functionalist communication skills – that is rich and generative, that posits workplace language as an object of study, that recognises and uses all of the strengths of English teaching and teachers and which supplants the tick list of (oxymoronic) transferable skills.
>
> Reid 1996

English teachers have begun to discover that 'language', far from being the dry stuff that comes a poor second to literature, actually interests students a great deal. The Language in the National Curriculum project did a great deal to stimulate thought and to encourage fresh approaches to knowledge about language, even though its resource materials never achieved official publication. Thousands of teachers had been on LINC courses, and 'cascaded' their findings to thousands more. Work done by Peter Medway (1994), Rachel Ward (1996), and Malcolm Reed (1996) have built on this foundation, and in Mark Reid's words, have undermined 'the instrumental model of language use prevalent in the workplace . . . and [show] the enabling possibilities of language [teaching]'.

There are other interesting reasons why the world of work is beginning to be regarded with less suspicion by English teachers. Thinking people are needed to operate the new technology, so that the image of the workplace is not quite what it was in the industrial age in which Arnold was writing. Furthermore, the technologies are blurring distinctions between learning which takes place at school, home and work. And the aims of organisations such as the Confederation of British Industry are not narrowly focused at all. Here is a list of the Core Skills identified in *A Vision for our Future* (CBI 1995):

Core Skills

Core skills are central to all work and learning. They are valued by employers and essential for individuals because they help us become more flexible in learning and work and better able to take change in our stride. They are:

Communication	The ability to write and talk appropriately for a particular purpose and audience, and to understand and interpret information through reading and listening
Working with others	The ability to work both independently and co-operatively with others
Application of number	The ability to use arithmetic and statistics in practical situations
Improving own learning	The ability to analyse one's own skills and abilities, to plan and evaluate learning
Problem solving	The ability to identify and evaluate problems and devise appropriate solutions
Information Technology and performance	The ability to use computers to handle and distribute information

Most of these bear some relation to the work that is undertaken in and the goals that are set by English. Here is a comment from a PGCE student who has almost certainly never encountered the CBI document but whose perception of English is remarkably in accord with it:

I don't think that English is something that is only used in the four walls of the classroom. It is a subject which is alive everywhere. It helps to develop your interpersonal skills, confidence, and opinions and enables you to communicate effectively with others.

As a recent research project at the University of Northumbria at Newcastle discovered, students are beginning to respond to the drive to make them more reflective about their own learning:

At first I hated Progress and Modernism so much. I thought, what on earth is the point of doing this? If I'd wanted to do a History degree I'd have done one ! Now I can see it is relevant.

The author of the Report notes this about student perceptions of English:

Many of their comments suggested that they were very conscious of the need not only to redefine notions of the subject, but themselves as students in relation to it.

Johnson 1998

She cites as an example of this the students' understanding of the importance of independent learning in higher education, as the following student comment implies:

[M]y idea, of a university was very Bamber Gascoigne [the erudite Chair of a television general knowledge quiz show called 'University Challenge'] – everyone walking around in gowns and that – and I thought you'd just come and absorb all these facts. But it isn't like that at all . . . It is about developing your thoughts: you get to see how things relate to your own life . . .

The changing, goal-orientated nature of higher education English is one of the key perceptions that emerges from this study:

Lectures, seminars, tutorials, ongoing critical and learning journals all offer students opportunities to develop the high-level intellectual abilities (including critical evaluation, independent judgement etc.) and skills on which they are formally assessed . . . In conclusion, these Northumbria students' perceptions of the changing English curriculum serves as a useful reminder that 'English is orientated towards informed, intelligent participation in, and response to . . . creative and cultural life' and that 'reading, interpretative and communication skills are integral to the training it gives' (CCUE)

Johnson 1998

But what of individuals outside institutionalised education, what of those directly involved with the world of work: what do they think?

Views from non-specialists. Don't you want these things too?

In the previous chapter we noted the way in which the Newbolt Committee, first committee set up to address the subject of the teaching of English was made up almost entirely of members of the English Association. This sense of ownership, of specialist knowledge and expertise being acknowledged by the Government of the day, was very satisfying to the young subject in 1921. It is not surprising, therefore, that there is a defensiveness about English which has, in England, seen this position of authority gradually eroded, so that decisions are seen to be made by 'outsiders' brought in to tell English teachers how to teach (as in the case of the Director of BP who was brought in to revise the Cox version of the National Curriculum) or even worse, former English teachers who subsequently distanced themselves from all that they formerly believed in.

Yet, as Peter Griffiths points out, there is a certain irony in all this, because the Newbolt Committee did not find that its proposal to place great stress on the importance of a nationalising 'literature' met with the opposition from industry that might have been expected:

It might have seemed that this form of education would have been dysfunctional in terms of certain of the stated aims of the previous generation; after all, time spent on the study of literature, whether within a liberal-nationalist framework or otherwise, is time not spent on the acquisition of reading and writing as decontextualised skills. However, the investigations of the Newbolt Committee led it to the conclusion that this was not in fact the case . . .

. . . *what the leading firms of the country desired most of all in their employees were just those qualities which a liberal education rightly understood, should develop in young people. Indeed their chief count against the schools was that present-day education was not liberal enough, and in particular, that it was conventional and divorced from reality (p. 129)* . . .

. . . It would appear that what is being alleged here, by people who had a clear stake in the outcomes of the educational process, is that the so-called mechanical exercises of spelling and punctuation were not as effective a means of generating the skills and attitudes which were required by employers as were the reading and guided study of approved literary works. But since it is self-evident that these skills and attitudes do not transfer in any mechanical and obvious sense to the activities conducted on shop-floors and in offices, I would suggest that what is being discussed, and in fairly obvious fashion, is the transmission of a dominant ideology that has certain specifiable and unequally distributed benefits.

Griffith 1992, p. 10

Earlier we saw how potentially broad and ambitious were the core skills set by the CBI, and we can see this also in the sets of skills identified by the Association of Graduate Recruiters (see Appendix C), which are:

Self-awareness, Self-promotion, Exploring/creating opportunities/Action planning/Networking/Matching and decision making/Negotiation/ Political Awareness/Coping with uncertainty/Development focus/Self-confidence/Transfer skills.

Despite the fact that nearly all of these are desired outcomes of what we have described as the normative pedagogy dominant in English, there is still huge suspicion of the demands made by employers and others who are not familiar with schools and colleges.

Outsiders (a term which assumes that there is an inside) can be perceived in two quite different ways. There is the image of the ruthless employer, the utilitarian Gradgrind who employs a McChokumchild and wants nothing but facts, nothing but that which is useful. There is the ignorant philistine, and again Dickens provides the model in Squeers. Finally there is the ambitious careerist, the managerial nineties man or woman who are perceived to be more interested in style than substance. All of these are the demons of those who work in either schools or universities. Yet if we actually listen to actual 'outsiders' their language is often quite layered and the messages they are communicating are more complex than they initially appear. Here is Estelle Morris, on the eve of becoming a Minister of Education in the Labour Government of 1997 arguing for a distinction between what politically it is necessary – and right – to argue, and a larger agenda, one which can remain part of the practice, if not of the rhetoric of politics:

An education system must produce young people who are literate and numerate and can communicate I think people will judge it by that . . . It is important that we value accurate writing, careful listening and good communication. This is really important and I don't think people will look much beyond that. Teaching styles will be judged by whether they help achieve these things.

Earlier Estelle Morris had argued that there was a tacit contract between society at large and the public institutions that service it, and that as long as the agreed outcomes are being met then the methods used in schools by teachers (for example) do not particularly interest that public. In the language of market economics, if the product is delivered then generally the methods do not come under close scrutiny. The broad aims which Chris Davies argues are characteristic of English are not of any real interest to the world outside, nor is its methodology, as long as English delivers acceptable standards of literacy.

There are non-specialists who do believe that the methodology and pedagogy *are* important. One journalist who worked for *The Times Educational Supplement*, argued for a series of broad aims for English, such as a love of reading and the development of the growth of the individual, but then it emerged (perhaps unsurprisingly) that she had been an English undergraduate and had also trained to be an English teacher.

So what seems to be sought by non-specialists is not broad rhetorical aims but a variety – and the range needs to be noted – of very specific outcomes. Here is Fiona Davies, Policy Adviser for the Education Policy Group of the Confederation of British Industry:

> When we talk about communication it is more to do with knowing your audience, how to communicate with them, how to tailor the information you have and process it specifically for your audience, knowing the situation, not just the grammar . . . Yes you do have employers complaining about the levels of literacy, it is true, but good employers are not hidebound by the idea of what I call basic literacy in terms of harping back to the Golden Age. A factsheet from the Better English campaign [puts it into perspective]. It said that British Industry lost, I think, several millions of pounds a year through poor literacy, people having to retype things, having to have them redone, and the lack of understanding that can lead to a lost order. So it is a problem, and there is a two way pull on employers to plough money back in to retrain their employees as well as the loss of business that comes when someone couldn't read an order so it doesn't get processed.
>
> But I want to go back to the six core skills I was talking about earlier. They are communication involving reading, writing and speaking, IT, Number application, team working, problem solving and evaluation . . . If you take the last three – problem solving, self evaluation of your own learning technique and team working, all of these can be facilitated by a study of English that allows the use of the imagination to stretch beyond things, to be able to see round subjects.

In many ways this is the answer to Melanie Phillips's puzzlement that the cry for good standards of basic literacy, a cry that she says comes from everyone except English specialists themselves, goes unheeded despite the power of legislation and curriculum reform. Her analysis is flawed because it assumes that society really wants these things more than anything else, whereas Fiona Davies's comments seem to confirm that industry (and therefore government) needs subjects who have the self-reflective, and self-regulating skills that English is seen to foster, and that it is therefore in the nation's interest to have the set of practices that Melanie Phillips mistakenly sees as examples of irresponsible betrayal by an intellectually bankrupt elite. It does not matter that English accommodates a relativism which Phillips castigates as a totalitarian ideology: the CBI appointed Fiona Davies as their spokesperson, and she admits that

> I am a relativist and the rest of my office are absolutist.

but she would have the 'classics' because they represent an unfamiliar reading experience for children.

> Reading is not necessarily the text itself but the philosophical things that come through it, the ways to approach it, analyse it, process it – all of this is very important.

Fiona read English at Oxford, encountered theory, and all those influences that appear to be the bane of both the left in England (as represented by Melanie Phillips) and the right (as represented by Sheila Lawlor from the Centre for Policy Studies, the Conservative Party think-tank). Fiona reflects on this irony:

> The indications would seem to be that if an arts student like me can get into a company like this then it must be that arts subjects are producing [certain desirable] qualities in their students [such as] problem solving, team work, self-evaluation of your learning processes and communication.

Hearing this, it is very difficult not to come to the conclusion that Ian Hunter was correct in identifying the set of practices that English fosters as practices that the society as a whole needs and values, and that these practices can be fostered only in the pedagogical relationship which English would abandon if it became the content-driven practice that the left and the right would seem to be arguing for. Here is Estelle Morris again arguing for a shift away from, although not an abandonment of, the emphasis on 'creativity and the development of the whole individual' that, she argues, characterised an earlier decade:

> In the seventies, English teachers perhaps put too much emphasis on expression at the expense of the technical side. Children's English has to be a balance and the technical side should be done in the primary school.

The politician's argument here is similar to that of Melanie Phillips in that both are identifying English with literacy. They wish to focus on the acquisition of technical literacy because working-class children are competing with middle-class children in the wider world and that is how they will be judged. Yet Estelle Morris was not arguing for an either/or for later in the interview she returned to a celebration of the kind of pedagogical relationship which English specialists seem to favour:

I think that compared to the type of commerce in Japan we're much better [in England] at self expression. The whole area of English teaching which covers communication and expression – about working outside the various curriculum boundaries as well as inside them – is done well in this country. I also sense that we are good at developing positive and supportive relationships between teachers and pupils. It is a more individual relationship, whilst at the same time being a teacher–learner relationship. Some kids' whole education is made successful because of the success of this relationship between them and the teacher. If you are lucky you find a teacher whom you can relate to and who supports you. I think we're so much better at this because we are not so rigid.

Earlier in the interview she had made a very similar point. In recommending drama she had praised its ability to provide 'an avenue for expression' for children who did not succeed elsewhere and the way that it 'affected their behaviour and their attitude and their self-esteem'. In *Culture and Government* Ian Hunter places the following quotation from John Dixon alongside the quotation from David Stow that we cited in chapter 2:

Drama, like talk, is learning through interaction. The actor may and must find within himself what it is to be angered, hurt, intimidated, ashamed vindictive . . . but he finds this partly in response to another person. Together they learn to support and confirm each other's discoveries. Because each of us in acting makes public what he knows and can say, others can join in our learning. And the teacher too has the work before him, in progress, open to his sympathetical inspection. Thus he too is positioned to help the work along, to suggest changes of perspective, to focus attention, as the man who observes can.

Dixon 1967, pp. 38–9

At Congress House, a Trades Union Congress Policy Officer who similarly identified creative and student centred elements in what she saw as examples of good current practice in communications:

There is The Better English Campaign, and one of the most successful features is what they have done with, poetry, actually getting some sort of creativity and imagination going through holding a poetry day in London. The TUC is quite marginally involved with the campaign so we weren't actually much involved with that activity, but I hope that it really did get out to children who haven't really had too much experience or been exposed to poetry before because I think that the target is not to get to those that have already got the skills and are successful, but to others. It seems from what I hear to be very good in generating enthusiasm and getting young people excited about poetry.

Trevor McDonald, the ITN newscaster who is the Chairman of the Better English Campaign, has written about his own fascination with poetry dating from the recitation of poems in a hot Caribbean playground. He thoroughly endorsed the London Poetry Day, and would have attended if the Moscow elections had not intervened:

> It seemed to me that poets and other writers – those who worked with and appreciated the power of language every day – were natural partners in the Campaign's task of helping young people to use that power for themselves.
>
> Mcdonald 1996

The Better English Campaign was an open-ended government-funded response to the many claims that literacy standards had fallen. With its slogan of 'Language is Power' it had the support of the Confederation of British Industry, the British Chambers of Commerce, the Institute of Personnel and Development and the TEC National Council. Trevor McDonald, like Brian Cox, Matthew Arnold and David Stow before him, had been persuaded that these ends were more likely to be achieved by indirect rather than direct methods.

The belief that 'language is power' is shared by other non-specialist organisations. The Policy Officer for Education and Training at the TUC identified a second encouraging trend in England, the recognition that we should think in terms of life-long learning:

> Another exciting development is the UNISON Return to Learn scheme which I think for people who have left school with very little education and training and few of the necessary skills for employment or recog- nised qualifications, is actually very successful in introducing adult workers to learning. It's important in terms of improving employment prospects but it also makes a tremendous difference to people's partici- pation in the work-force and people's participation in union structures. We see that from a number of people who have been through the courses of the last few years and have since become active in union structures.

When asked to look into the future, and to envisage the kinds of changes in the employment patterns we would see in the twenty-first century, this is what she said:

> I think we'll see the trends that we have seen in the last few years, becoming more defined in the 21st century, so you'll see a shrinking of the big old industries. You'll see a decline of jobs which could be done by unskilled, manual workers and what we'll see is what we see at the moment which is a reliance on more professional, managerial jobs and qualifications which are needed for those. There will be more skilled jobs

across the board and obviously information technology will be increasingly used across the board which has an impact on the skills that are needed there.

I think regrettably that the pool of available jobs is shrinking and will continue to shrink. Although unemployment is going down the actual number of people in work has declined over the last few years. Job insecurity will continue to be a problem with all short-term contracts and other forms of flexible work and more and more temporary workers and in that situation the ability to communicate to work out what your rights are and how to get around the labour market from A to B is needed.

In such a world, the practices of English, which support self-orientation in a disorientating world, are unlikely to become redundant. English, we would argue, was developed in England as a set of practices appropriate for a time of industrial change, and if the physical technology is different in the present post-industrial revolution, the requirement for a moral technology is not.

Summary

The evidence of these interviews suggests that there are sets of beliefs that are shared by a significant number of specialists and non-specialists and that this amounts to what we might call a dominant discourse and pedagogy. The majority of people we have interviewed have been more interested in asking questions and encouraging their students to ask questions than in perpetuating the cultural heritage model of English that the Chief Inspector of schools seemed to endorse in his 1995 speech. English now shares common ground with science – not nineteenth-century science, for the clockwork model of Newtonian mechanics has been overturned by quantum theory, the uncertainty principle and chaos theory. Physics now asks such questions as "What happens to an atom when it is being observed?' and for about sixty years or more has been asking the kinds of questions that English has only started to address relatively recently. Both fields – English and science – have undergone a transformation which in one respect is remarkably similar. In both schools and universities in the nineteenth century the purpose of classes in science and literature was to pass on the discoveries and insights of the past. It was not to add to the sum of human knowledge through investigation. Oxford, for example, did not include a research element in its chemistry school until well into the twentieth century. Likewise, English emphasised the achievements of the past, often at the expense of the literary potentiality of the present. It was partly due to the powerful reformulations and reformations that occurred in the pedagogical practices in schools in the twentieth century, with the emphasis on investigation, practice, and discovery that English in universities has started to embrace the *atelier* or workshop approach.

Yet, as we noted earlier it is the plurality of English – the celebration of difference whilst holding on to some kind of practical connecting methodology that I have tried to convey through the model of the Swiss army knife – it is this that seems to offer most relevance for the future. And although we have been suggesting that science and literature now share common ground, as for example, scientists emphasise 'the simultaneity of science and myth as system for containing and constraining possibility' we should take note of the warning from Gillian Beer (from whose recent study of science in cultural encounters that was a quotation) (Beer 1996) that 'new alliances between scientists and humanists should not make us too sanguine – they may themselves be a symptom of the danger we face which obliges the sinking of real differences'. For those differences exist. Unlike science, English does not feel obliged to strive for closure. It does not refer to something that is out there, it does not feel the need to reach conclusions about how things are in what science by its very nature assumes to be a real world that exists *somewhere*. English can ask questions about how things *might be*. John Henry Newman said something very similar when he wrote in *The Idea of a University* in 1858: 'Literature expresses not objective truth, as it is called, but subjective; not things but thoughts.' Those who currently work within the field of English or Cultural Theory see this engagement with ideas as an activity that is given sanctuary in English in universities, colleges and schools.

Yet for others this willingness to tolerate a broad, unfocused pluralism is a betrayal by English teachers of their mission. This is Brian, a former English specialist, now Dean of a university faculty. He begins by reflecting on the science–arts debate:

When I was reading A level English in the early 1960s, we were indeed absorbed by the Snow/Leavis scrap about two cultures, and we were led – there's no question about it – by several charismatic English teachers into feeling frightfully superior about not being scientists. Science, after all, needed Maths (so we were told) and Maths was hugely dull and difficult. So we got tremendously serious about literature instead (especially Lawrence, because he was 'morally serious'). We erected extraordinary calibrations to sort the 'good' from the 'great'. We never bothered to read 'bad' books . . .

But now, more than thirty years later, all that seems so arid and silly. Do you think we are still inviting young people today to adopt similar habits of demarcation? I'd have thought much has been achieved since then in breaking down the barriers – from English through the study of linguistics (a science) and from science in the publication and avid readership of popular science books . . .

[I am] concerned, though, that English specialists may be building their case too strongly on adamant refusal to define their territory (having the courage of the lack of their convictions, as you might say) . . .

What's wrong with a prospectus for, 'English' which says that it is a complex of related studies embracing (at least):
the serious and critical reading of literature past and present
the creation of a literate society through the schools (with its own curriculum and pedagogical processes)
the examination of a body of critical theory, and its application to texts
the study of the cultural significance of literary texts (and so of culture itself)
the study of the English language
the history of that language and its expression (particularly in print) across the English speaking world
the systematic encouragement to write literature and criticism from its students
Something like that. It may borrow from other disciplines in fulfilling this prospectus (and rightly does). But these definitions mark its boundaries, its distinctiveness from other subjects. Unless it can do this, it will find its position within the educational curriculum very vulnerable.

This would go some way to satisfying Guy and Small's belief that English needs to have a clear object if it is to survive into the twentieth century. And the culture of the market economy which informs primary, secondary and tertiary education makes it increasingly likely that English will be forced to articulate what it does well, or disappear.

Past, present and future

In this study our goal has been to explore not simply the perceptions of English specialists, but the ways in which those perceptions have been formed, and the way that both the subjects (the people) and the subject (English as an institutionalised practice) has been shaped and formulated. In this first section we have paid particular attention to the Fred Inglis quotation cited in chapter 1: 'In an important sense "subjects" are their histories'. Let us compare what we have heard in these interviews with one of the histories in particular, that history of English which sees it a subject given curriculum prominence because it is able to help young people become self-regulating and reflective. In other words, let us relate it to the work of Ian Hunter.

One of the features of Subject English pedagogy that we identified was the desire to develop practices that allowed the free development of the individual, and this set up the dilemma of how to 'teach and yet not to teach'. This belief in the ineffability of what lies in the heart of English was clearly evident in the kinds of comments we noted in the sections on pedagogy and the special nature of English. The anxiety expressed about direct intervention, about an overtly didactic approach, about being seen to direct and control – this, together with a sense of satisfaction and ease in a discrete facilitative role, in which students seem to be self-motivating, self-correcting and self directing, with the teacher as presence, supervising indirectly – there was clear evidence of this belief. Even where specialists have engaged with a wide range of contemporary theories about the construction of self and the formation of subjectivity, there is a reluctance to take on the role of the controller, a reluctance to question the supremacy of the individual. Here is the editor of a recent series of literary texts designed for school students. You can almost hear the internal wrestling with a set of heterodoxical beliefs:

> You will interpret the stories in an individual way that is governed by such things as your personality your experience of life, and what you have read, your views and attitudes to issues, events and relationships – and much else besides.
>
> Judith Baxter 1996: 241

We also quoted in our study of the early years of the English Association statements from members who claimed that literature could not be taught. The belief in the special nature of English, which taps elements deep with the self, was reflected in the many comments which emphasised the private, personal, sometimes therapeutic nature of reading and writing. Two graduates who were awarded firsts on a degree course which encouraged original or creative writing, spoke to us of the private nature of much of the writing they have continued to do after university, of their reluctance to submit to public scrutiny or even to the eye of a sympathetic reader. They argued strongly for writing which is an end in itself, which does not seek to communicate, to say anything to anyone. Caroline, who had gone on to take an MA in creative writing at the University of East Anglia, argued strongly for a search for the universals in writing, for finding out what we share and have in common as human beings:

> When people ask me where I live, I say 'Inside my body'. I am not interested in saying I come from Cornwall or Norwich or wherever. I think that identification with a particular place can be dangerous. I believe that we should get rid of all our cultural baggage when we travel – that we should understand and immerse ourselves in another culture. That's what I always do.

In short, a specific category literature having been created in the early nineteenth century and taken up as the material for English at the turn of the century, Subject English gladly inherited an accompanying set of beliefs in the importance of personal experience, in the role of the individual creator, and in the commonality of humankind which shares universal experiences such as loss, bereavement, love and so on. This set of beliefs, into which students are inducted in school indirectly, not by being told that this is the case but being asked to look for these universals through a series of assignments and questions informed by a belief in personal response, has survived the questions that are frequently asked about English, and which have seen a realignment *vis-à-vis* media, knowledge about language and the new technologies. This, we would argue, is not the triumph of literature, but the triumph of the pedagogical method which initiatives in the methodology higher education English of the kind that we shall now illustrate continue to favour.

We need, however, to make a distinction between the pedagogical practices that are still dominant in English in secondary schools, and the pedagogic relationship that has emerged in universities. There is an important difference, and it is one which Ian Hunter does not fully acknowledge. For although the preceding comments included evidence taken from under-graduates and post graduates, suggesting that there is a strand within college and university English that shares the pedagogy and the aesthetic that is dominant in secondary schools and further education colleges, higher education in England is a somewhat different world. Those who are now coming to teach in universities have not been re-orientated towards the dominant pedagogy in the way that would be secondary school teachers on PGCE courses have. Those who encountered and enjoyed theory at univer-sity in the 1980s, and are now teaching it in the 1990s, are more likely to be concerned with issues of race, gender and ideology, together with the various reading practices available to students, than a pedagogical practice of the kind Hunter identifies. The preoccupation of those who we have interviewed and heard presenting papers at conferences lies in their own reading and publication, and in the individual lives of students who knock on their doors rather than with the issues of 'to teach and yet not to teach'. When presented with a statement from the departmental handbook which referred to the 'collaborative and group work approaches favoured by the English Team', Alison, a member of that team, said curtly 'Not favoured by all of us!'. So in England there is evidence that during their three years at university under-graduates will experience a different kind of pedagogical relationship to the one they experience at A Level, where the teacher is often supportive friend, and there is an intimacy whose absence many students initially miss.

As we have seen, in schools beliefs about English are revised through human contact. An influential teacher will instill a belief in an approach, in a method of reading, in a method of teaching, a belief that endures and influences that individual through memory when he or she wishes to become a teacher. Teachers in turn are influenced by other teachers; English teaching in schools is informed by a Romantic aesthetic which privileges the affective over the intellectual, and the method over the outcomes. There is little point in arguing, as Tony Bennett does in *Outside Literature* (Bennett 1990), that English should not be a moral technology. If it was not successful at being what it is, then it would not have been born in the way that it was, and it would not have survived. It is a bit like arguing that sharks should be vegetarians, or that dogs would be more attractive if they did not bite. In universities dogs can be silent, and sharks can be vegetarians and dogs and sharks can mate. It is the *hybrid* that offers itself as model in higher education, the hybrid culture, the hybrid identity, the hybrid form and ultimately the hybrid subject. There is no monolithic African-American identity, no monolithic 'woman', even no monolithic author function; even Barthes, Foucault and Hunter would seem to fall into the trap of creating generic typologies. English has already become a hybrid, so hybridity and interdisciplinarity has become the norm.

So we have confirmed that there is evidence of one set of practices that dominates secondary English, with a personal growth pedagogy and reader-response reading practice being favoured by the majority of those we questioned. In university we have found evidence of hybridity, with students being offered a range of reading practices, and a diversity of pedagogies, some of which share similarities with a pedagogy of science. The intellectual is given precedence over the affective, the analytical over the imaginative. So why do students continue to apply to read English (in whatever hybrid form it is offered) and how do they effect the transition from a practice at which they appeared to sit at the centre to a set of practices which question the idea of the centre without replacing it with any clear end of its own? This seemed an important enough question in England to warrant a section of its own.

Voices 2: Reading English at college and university in England

Despite our need for engineers, scientists, computer experts and multi-linguists, English remains an oversubscribed subject at university in England. English departments may not have the well-fitted rooms, the resources and equipment of other subjects, but they certainly have the students.

What is it that is so attractive about English? Why is it that so many people want to specialise in it, and are prepared to spend a large proportion of their lives engaged in activities that in the early nineteenth century were considered the prerogative of leisure time, or the coffee club aesthetes? As we have seen, the answers are various: a love of reading, the attractive image of English as a degree subject, the fact that the self and reflections on personal experience are seen as central with very little specialised knowledge seeming to be necessary. When we asked specialists in schools, colleges and universities what drew them to English, they invariably referred to the satisfaction and fulfilment provided by reading. In England relatively few specialists will say that what drew them to English was writing, performance, media analysis or the possibilities opened up by the new technologies, though these are – or soon will be – significant elements or organising principles in the practice of English. A good number of students will refer to the opportunities for discussion provided by English, though it does not seem to be essential that this discussion is centred on what is traditionally known as imaginative literature.

What seems to be important is the notion of English as a *personal* subject, whether this is articulated loosely as 'how the things we discuss relate to *me*', or more theoretically as 'how things we engage with position us as subjects: the making of subjectivity'. English is seen to provide space for such experiences, and this accounts both for its popularity as a subject and its vulnerability as a discipline.

It accounts for its popularity in that it is seen as an accessible subject, one in which previous knowledge and experience – a previous history of reading either at home or at school – is perceived to be relevant. Students do not feel that they start from a deficit: it is imagined that there is no, or at worst very little, specialist knowledge.

But because it is seen by the world at large as a subject which engages with the affective, which is less concerned with skills and knowledge and less demanding on the intellect than other subjects, it is often perceived to be less rigorous.

We decided to do two things: to ask a colleague to report on the ways in which he had approached this problem of rigour and difficulty through an experiment with journals and to comment on his case study. Following the case study we decided to carry out further detailed interviews with higher education specialists, both student and teachers to see if we could detect patterns in the responses of those whose base was higher education rather than schools. First, then, here is Francis Curtis's report on a classroom experiment in his higher education college.

Case study 1: the role of subject specialists' logs in student self-reflection

> I have discovered the aspect of myself which could be called the 'Jig-saw' reader. I read 'Jane Eyre' originally because I had already read 'Rebecca'. I then read 'Wide Sargasso Sea' by Jean Rhys.
>
> Sarah Newall

Sarah then goes on to explain in her reading log that this 'Jig-saw' aspect of herself has been referred to in the *Ways of Reading* seminar as 'intertextuality'. She grasps the idea that intertextuality is predicated as much upon the relationships which exist between particular texts and particular readers as upon text alone. The format of the reading log both invites and encourages her to use her own, authentic voice in expressing her self-reflections on what kinds of reader she is: to use a distinction current today (Entwistle and Entwistle 1991), her comment shows a 'deep' rather than 'surface' approach to her own learning as she grapples with making this 'intertextuality' concept her own.

We need to know, in the different institutional contexts of higher education English Literature study, what kinds of readers our students are in order to support, guide and develop the nature of the reading demands we place upon them and which they place upon themselves. This recognition is generally

absent in the higher education, because by a curious sleight of hand a
student's readerly role is often assumed to be comparable to having passed
some sort of L-test by virtue of entering higher education. He or she can now
begin to set about the *real* business of HE English: interpretation. A National
Curriculum discourse of 'levels' and 'targets' does not help matters, of
course. An environment in which learning is discussed, documented and
'delivered' through a metaphorical domain of hierarchy, a contemporary
Great Chain of Being, is not exactly conducive to regarding the student
reader, like all readers, as perpetually mobile – intellectually and emotionally.
It is revealing to apply, in the domain of higher education English student
reading, those post-structuralist insights which suggest that the individual is
socially and institutionally constructed. The production of meaning in the
act of reading rather than writing (Barthes 1977) on the part of the individual
student reader, then, becomes a worthwhile focus of attention.

The intention here is to make more explicit the productive and socially
interactive reading practices of higher education English student readers
by looking at the learning, unlearning and relearning of some fifty student
readers, in two groups, who took a first-year module called *Ways of Reading*
in the Autumn Term 1994 and Spring Term 1995. We worked together each
week in a three-hour session with a reading log as the form of assessment.
The aim was to encourage them to reflect critically upon themselves as
readers, as active producers of meanings whose own sense of reader identity
would emerge productively in post-structuralist terms of fragmentation
and contradiction as well as coherence and consistency. All participants,
including the tutor, kept a reading log, and logs were shared in discussion
between tutor and students. Our students are comfortable with the public
sharing of personal writing, particularly in the Creative Writing modules,
where reading and writing journals are kept. Half the students quoted in this
part of the study readily gave their permission, after reading the draft, for
their comments to be published under their own names. The names of all
others have been changed. The students' reading histories and archaeologies,
identities and motives as readers, together with the language used to record
and discuss their reading, form the substance of what follows. We consider
also what seem to us to be some significant issues of teaching method and
learning process which are relevant to developing readerly self-reflection in
the context of higher education English Literature studies.

The *Ways of Reading* module aims to define some characteristics of readerly
competence, to provide an opportunity for students to explain their own
reading histories and to distinguish between some major 'extrinsic'
approaches to texts. We start off in the first session by posing the question to
all of us 'What kinds of reader am I?' and by introducing some theories of
reader psychology, purpose and text–reader relationships. This session also
introduces the group to the idea of keeping a Reading Log as the assessment
mode for the module. The assessment notes for the students include the
sentence 'Keeping a reading log will involve skills in critical self-monitoring

which may be unfamiliar to some at the beginning'. This recognises that for almost every student the Reading Log will present a challenge. Many will never have kept a reading log in their secondary schooling, or they do not associate it with Higher Education at all. At the end of this class and in the logs themselves anxieties are voiced, as individuals realise that a new, not a 'building on what I already know from A-level', demand is placed on them. Voices from the Spring Term asked 'How many books do we have to write about?' 'Can we discuss any book we like?' 'What about *Jane Eyre* [a set text for this module]?' 'Do we record our emotional responses?' Suzanne recorded this on 9 January: 'We were informed today that we must keep a "reading log". This has left me in a state of confusion. What is a reading log? How should it be set out? Am I to write about the content of the books or our own responses? I do not consider myself to be a well motivated reader, or any sort of reader. By next week I have to read *Jane Eyre*.'

The set texts for *Ways of Reading* are *Jane Eyre*, Brian Friel's *Translations* and Daphne du Maurier's *Rebecca*. The choice of *Jane Eyre* and *Rebecca* is designed to raise issues of *genre*, the canon and intertextuality, while *Translations* is there to promote discussion about self-identity through language and cultural readings. The whole student group is organised into smaller working groups who keep a *Group Reporting Sheet* and pool their notes on activities and tasks. We give part of each week's session to a discussion of student experiences in keeping their log and individuals read out entries to each in their working groups. So it is pleasing to read in Suzanne's log, a week later, 'I'm feeling more confident about this log after today's lesson' (16 January 1995)

The archaeology of individual reading histories, identities and attitudes revealed by log entries and reporting sheets shows how explicitly students can recover and revisit the traces of their readerly lives. The dimension of confidence, intellectual and emotional, figures largely in responses and is often tracked back to childhood experiences and the physicality of text-tokens. Maria's early, 18 January entry reads:

> As a young girl I acquired an enormous, red hardback edition [*Jane Eyre*], impressively imposing and impossible to hold. Although abridged it housed melodramatic illustrations of a wonderfully deranged Bertha Mason and all the horrors of Lowood School in full, glossy colour. These powerful and somewhat sensationalised images of brutality towards children paralleled other contemporary TV images; the roasting scene of *Tom Brown's Schooldays*, remains a vivid recollection . . . Now I possess a cheap paperback produced during the *Wordsworth Classics/ Penguin Classics* price war . . . I feel closer to this edition, and my present preference for reading paperbacks is indicative of my own release from the tyrannical and misconceived notion of the inaccessibility of books. My changing attitude towards the book's physicality has had a profound effect on my reading confidence.

The demise of the NBA and competition pricing policies, which have increased accessibility dramatically, give the canon debate an ironic twist. The 'classics' are now more available to a wider readership than ever before, so what price the 'classic', 'popular' distinction? Here, Jemma's comment on the link between how reading confidence and the classics yields another perspective. She has been required to read Virginia Woolf's *A Haunted House* for another module. Late in January her log records:

> Before I even turned over the front cover, I was faced with two problems, (a) that I was feeling awful with the 'flu and (b) the prejudices I had already formed. These being, that Woolf was a very elitist writer and that my intellect as a reader would prove inferior in the understanding of her texts. These fears had been established from various sources, from fellow students who had already had a taste of Woolf, to the lady in the college bookshop who offered her opinions whilst I was purchasing the book. After trying to unload my inferiority complex, I began.

This combination of peer group pressure and bookshop Charon-figure which mediate the rite of passage into Virginia Woolf mitigate the opportunities offered by cheaper classics available in, e.g. Tesco's. The stereotype of intrinsic difficulty with 'classics' is alive and well. It is noticeable in many log entries that reading confidence is associated with a blanket notion that the classics are 'difficult' but worthwhile.

Mark writes, early in October 1994: 'The thought of plodding through three hundred or more pages of what has been pre-defined by Penguin Publishers for me as a "classic", fills me with dread.'

The fundamental issue here is of ownership ('pre-defined'), not difficulty. In class, students frequently characterised themselves as 'conscript readers'. Our purpose, gradually, was to plan sessions so that students would acquire the analytical tools to deconstruct their own reader profiles in a more sophisticated way, to see themselves as part of an empowering, as well as disempowering reader–text relationship, from a more post-structuralist perspective. During the second session in the Autumn Term we offered a reader typology e.g., 'Paperback Reader', 'Plain Reader', 'Tabloid Reader' etc. and asked the group to extend this list. The additions, discussed below, were perhaps less revealing than the attitude shown by several students at the end of the class. In a review session the question 'Why are you trying to categorise us as readers?' was put forcefully by one, an attitude which was voiced by others in subsequent weeks.

A sense of alienation occasioned by a sense of being shut out from other cultural worlds, is often evident in the logs. Access to these worlds is often perceived by these students as possible via knowledge acquired in specific formal educational settings. They see themselves, in this respect, dispossessed.

Isobel writes: 'The frequent Greek and Latin references alienated me as a reader. It annoyed me that I couldn't understand the language.' This discomfort with literal translation is echoed in comments which, interestingly, equate the process of reading with translating text, word by word. Partly, but not entirely, a throwback to 'A'-level experiences working with Chaucer – one of these students was mature, non-standard entry – 'reading as translation' persists into higher education. Mark's experience of re-reading Carol Shield's *The Stone Diaries* is keyed back to his recent 'A'-level: 'Suddenly I was translating Chaucer again, stopping at every work, analysing it and finding out what it meant.' The motives which students have for reading were articulated partly through working groups creating their own typologies of reader and partly through comments in the logs. The group responses ranged far more widely than the personal log. We asked 'What kind(s) of reader are you?' after sketching out a brief typology: 'Serious', 'Paperback', 'Hardback'. Groups then produced their own lists. Here is a selection of what emerged: 'Enchanted', 'Elitist', 'Snob', 'Plain', 'Tabloid', 'Fashion', 'Skim', 'Conscript', 'Beginning'.

An enchanted reader was motivated by a desire to enjoy, relax, lose themselves effortlessly in a book. The elitist reader was identified as a 'snob'; the group reporting sheet records: ' "SNOB READER": orientation – anything Russian or Greek or sounds clever'. The 'plain' reader, it turned out, read paperbacks rather than hardbacks and the 'tabloid' reader read predominantly magazines and illustrated non-book text. The 'fashion' reader tended to be allied with the 'snob' reader whose motive for choosing particular texts was purely to impress their peer group. An alternative term was 'coffee-table reader'. The 'skim' and 'conscript' readers were motivated by boredom and educational duress respectively, but 'institutional' readers were defined rather seriously as Foucauldian prisoners in hospitals and prisons. The 'phobic' readers had a fascination, usually morbid, for sci-fi and horror themes or characters and would read obsessively in these areas. The 'collector' tended to read by author, collecting all their books. The 'generic' reader read by genre and the 'beginning' reader was assumed to have a limited vocabulary – no one actually owned up to this suggestion in the class!

What figures prominently in this list of motivations for reading is the social motivation for reading, reading as an activity beyond the self to accommodate pressures from one's peer group, still a significant factor for adults and certainly not confined to the received stereotype of early adolescence. Yet endorsing a considerably complex profile of reading motives in higher education, the reading logs also presented motives characterised by a concern with self. Reading has a dual function both as a process of emotional intensity and as a source of insight into the self in several log jottings. Penny records her responses within the space of a few days to A. S. Byatt's *Possession*:

Wednesday 1 February, 8.00 pm
I live within this book. I know I am an onlooker but I empathise and anticipate what might happen next.

Sunday 5 February, 2.30 pm
I enjoyed it tremendously, but now I have finished my 'Possession', I feel almost a bereavement.

Maria is quite explicit in recognising the dimensions of self which inform the experience of reading at the same time as recognising a problem and dialectical dynamic in reader–text relationship:

> My motivation for reading is increasingly fuelled by a desire to uncover psychological dimensions in the text. The pattern is influenced by my growing interest in psychology, coupled with an intrinsic need to construct a framework of meaning whereby my own understanding of self and text is enriched. The danger inherent in this manner of reading is the case with which personal meaning can be projected onto the piece, perhaps obscuring an enduring message stranded outside my own, potentially limited, interpretation.

Also, Maria, commenting on her response to *Jane Eyre*, noted that a gender perspective might be relevant to her: 'To a certain extent I believe that I often search for a shared feminine experience.' What evidence there is points to an uneasiness, occurring before embarking on a higher education course, of 'committed' reasons for reading. Mark records waking up early one morning and starting to read Daphne du Maurier's *Rebecca*. This text reminds him of his 'A'-level experience when obliged to study *Jane Eyre*: 'I now realised that although in the sixth form we were "all lads together let's burn our copies of Jane Eyre, eh?" ' At the beginning of the module we had asked my students to note down any aspects of the physical conditions for reading which they thought worthy of comment. Here, some intriguing insights were forthcoming.

Familiar circumstances as Mark points out above, of reading early in the morning or, late at night, are frequent. Also reading with the television on is not uncommon in the logs. However, Maria formulates a distinctive connection between some aspects of narrative and the physicality of motion:

> I have taken to reading whilst travelling. The train might be viewed as an appropriate environment for reading, both containing a parallel of movement and destination. This inactive experience of reading in this situation suits the nature of this particular novel [E. Waugh's *Decline and Fall*]. Waugh writes with a perceptive but uncomplicated style, which stands up to the inevitable interruptions and allows re-entry without loss of narrative. In contrast, *Jane Eyre* required a greater involvement, and was consequently best approached in a private, silent place. This suggests that the tools of interpretation required affects my physical relationship with the text.

Maria's ability to represent her thinking clearly and expressively by inventing a novel illustrative metaphor is valuable. It reveals something telling, a capacity to express in concrete and empirically revealing terms the dimensions of her reading experience. The linguistic features of students' own discourses provide an enlightening keyhole view of how, in higher education, reading is perceived and understood. Robert Hull, drawing on Merleau-Ponty's distinction between 'sedimental' and 'constitutive' language (Hull 1985) has demonstrated how important it is for teachers to value and interpret the actualities of what pupils say. 'Constitutive' language, the individual self-formulation of readers' own log jottings, is a different stratum of information in contrast to the often 'sedimented' language also found in the logs. While both yield worthy material for different purposes, the 'constitutive' features present in the logs give direct access to the student understanding of their reading experience and of the critical terminology introduced in formal teaching sessions. Their own discourse signifiers project a range of fresh meaning which deconstructs their reading in illuminating ways.

Maria, in the entry quoted above, has made the critical term 'enactive' her own by developing a 'narrative equals travelling metaphor'. In similar fashion, Sarah reveals the quality of her understanding and application of the concept 'intertextuality' in her reading experience as follows:

8 January 1995
Five days since I last wrote in this log. Well I finished *Jane Eyre* on the 13th, only because I made a conscious effort to do so, and in the wake of this I have discovered the aspect of myself which could be called the 'jig-saw' reader. I read *Jane Eyre* originally because I had already read *Rebecca*. I then read *Wide Sargasso Sea* by Jean Rhys, because I was told it gave another history to the *Jane Eyre* story; I found myself making comparisons between the novels, and recording facts about character histories etc. I have decided that these novels are the larger pieces of the jigsaw puzzle, and I am slowly filling in the smaller central parts, which began with Carol Shields' *The Stone Diaries*, I am now hunting for further novels which have been inspired by, or contain elements, of Charlotte Bronte's novel – is this 'intertextuality'? I think it is.

Sarah's language shows her experience of reading through notions of coherence, conceptual boundaries and steady exploration of a disciplined kind. Couched in the metaphor of a game or puzzle, her encounters with narrative forms are rendered in terms of enigma but also a type of conquest, 'filling in the smaller central parts'.

Several log entries recorded figurative language which emphasised forms of physical pressure in the experience of reading. The cognitive and emotional processes in reading get felt as physical realities. Mark looks back on his own reading history and writes, 'Like so much I have been force-fed over the years', brightening up later to say 'I no longer plod wearily through a novel'. Jeremy, weaving in to his notes physiological metaphors comparable to Mark's 'force-fed' adds in a technological dimension:

> My need for popular (pulp) fiction is substituted in most cases by the televised versions. I cannot be bothered with scanning graphemes, preferring pixels as an easier and more attractive form of vegetation.

Finally, Penny's's heartfelt image, quoted above, that on finishing A. S. Byatt's novel *Possession* she felt 'almost a bereavement' again conveys considerable force in expressing the empathy of relationship between text and reader. All these examples of students' own language used to represent their own experiences of reading are vivid, concretely imagined and evocative. They uncover seams of understanding and insight which, in the formal settings of essay or seminar paper, would more likely remain hidden.

Some indications in the logs suggested that explicit teaching of theoretical concepts has value in promoting effective learning. Jeremy, for instance, describes himself as 'a plurality of texts' and Sarah coins the phrase 'jigsaw reader' for herself. Both students, probing beneath the surface of their reading experiences to more profound self-awareness, formulate and adapt the concept of 'intertextuality'. This introduction of theory led a week later to a clutch of entries linking 'intertextuality' to intellectual, higher education challenge. Sarah again, recollecting her recent reading of *Rebecca*, finds a parallel in *King Lear* 'which I studied for "A"-Level. This shows how I, as a reader, bring an active knowledge to a text.'

The Reading Log was clearly perceived by most students as an unanticipated yet valuable learning experience. It is heartening to cite the balance which runs throughout the sample in the context of all too familiar claims for divisiveness in new and old orthodoxies for higher education English Studies. While Emily's reading of *Jane Eyre* 'has increased my desire for an understanding and deeper knowledge of classical texts', Lesley concludes her log by recognising 'Much of English culture, and therefore English literature, was based on male experience and used male imagery and language. Our culture now is largely multi-racial and this affects both authorship and readership.' Running through many of the entries is an acknowledgement that the device of the Reading Log has functioned to empower them by rendering visible and public the role of readership in the construction of significance.The reading Odysseys in this group of English students recognise, in a positive sense of mobile, intellectual challenge, the equal claims of Scylla and Charybdis.

Observations on the case study

Francis Curtis's case study demonstrates how English teachers are constantly striving to revise and improve their teaching in an attempt to make the material more relevant. As the history of English in England has shown this has frequently led to transformation in methodology, changes in assessment and broader definitions of text. In this example the keeping of journals – a practice which commanded support through developments in the teaching of writing in the 1970s and 1980s – is introduced to the methodology of higher education. On one level, English in England is consistently re-inventing itself, and every decade sees a new emphasis or development.

But what is equally notable about this case study – and we would argue that this is true of English as a social practice as a whole – is the operation of certain constants. The aim of the experiment was to promote student self-reflection, and implicit in this is the notion of self-correction. The pedagogical relation, too, is consistent with that observed in Stow and Arnold – the teacher is a discrete supervisory presence with the desired learning/transformation in reading practices taking place within the student with the minimum of intervention. Intervention comes at the level of the where and the how – the fact that this is a compulsory module, and that journals were to be kept. It is the student voice we hear, and not Francis Curtis's, although it could be argued that we do hear his voice, or the voice of English as an institutional practice which rewards self-reflection and personal adjustment. Near the beginning it is claimed that the Reading Log 'both invites and encourages [Sarah] to use her own authentic voice', a description which is consistent with a growth model of English. Similarly the favourable comments on the state of empathy which existed for Penny in her reading of *Possession* assumes that this is a core rather than a learned experience. Both of these beliefs may be accurate: to identify them as beliefs is not to invalidate them. They are characteristic of much of the thinking and pedagogy of schools, as we have seen.

In concentrating on *reading* the case study had, ironically, conformed to a long established emphasis in subject English. In the nineteenth century, the reading (and, initially, the memorising) of literary texts is what constituted the practice which came to be known as 'English'. It subsumed and co-ordinated all the other activities which formed part of school instruction – spelling, handwriting, composition and recitation – and as is well documented (e.g. Mathieson 1975) the privileging of reading occurred for reasons associated with claims made for its moral and 'civilising' effects. During and since its transformation in England from a nineteenth-century university subject principally concerned with philology or history, to an early twentieth-century practice primarily concerned with literary analysis, English has successfully managed to disguise this original normative, moralising role. Instead, as Hunter (1988) points out, much twentieth-century rhetoric has chosen to emphasise the subversive, liberalising and sensitising potential of a subject which considers itself resistant to dominant cultural tendencies. There has always been a strong crusading element in English.

As a crusading force, it has been able to assemble a large army in higher education, because it has generally has been a popular subject among students at school. This is partly because undergraduates do not feel that they start from a deficit: they believe that they are already familiar with the world that they are reading about, and they have already mastered the skill of reading. Furthermore, as our research has shown, students are invariably drawn to English because of something they describe as the pleasure of reading. In theoretical terms that 'pleasure' can be understood as the paradox of Desire, which seeks endlessly to achieve possession of the Other, the object of desire, whilst at the same time publicly repudiating it. In higher education English courses, in which students are frequently asked to grapple with *writerly*, texts that interrupt and disrupt familiar narrative expectations, our Reading Log study showed how some students articulated an initial resistance and discomfort at having this desire frustrated. In her recent essay on Desire (Butler 1995) Judith Butler refers to Thomas Mann's *Death in Venice*, in which Ashenbach, futilely seeks to suppress and overcome his desire for Tadzio by returning to the discipline of the aescetic commitment to art. Both possession and displacement are impossible in the same way that, in Lacanian terms, the subject's quest for a return to its prelinguistic origins is impossible. The Other can never be obtained, because its existence is necessary for the existence of the subject. Understandably, our students are not always eager to embrace this prospect if it is presented, as a bleakly confrontational challenge.

The Reading Log module had been designed to give students ownership so that they could themselves be the agents of this challenge. Among other things it had confirmed the extent to which higher education students are already formed and positioned as readers before they embark on their undergraduate courses. It is not productive if tutors conclude that these new readers are rigid or inflexible: more useful to regard, this perceived immobility as something that higher education seeks to unlock. It was precisely to unpack fixed notions of a *completed* reader now ready to 'interpret' texts that the logs focused attention on the act of reading itself. But this study had raised broader issues relating to higher education students' history as readers, including the driving forces that brought them to 'read' English, and their perceptions of the range of practices, including performance, interpretation and the production of original writing, that constitute the subject. We then wished to address some of these issues and to relate them to our brief comments on the case study.

Case study 2: the voices of students in the Midlands and the South-west

We were keen to increase our awareness of the predominant frames within which students such as those described by Curtis had developed as readers. One way of approaching this was to see if we could identify the models of English with which a cross section of English specialists from secondary, further and higher education most readily identified. As we were including phases that precede higher education we looked to the National Curriculum document for English, not the current slimline version but the 1989 recommendations of the committee chaired by Brian Cox, which had identified five such models. The report (DES 1989) labelled these as Personal Growth, Adult Needs, Language across the Curriculum, Cultural Heritage and Cultural Analysis. As the report acknowledged, specialists in English are likely to endorse a variety of models: the question is, which models are given most favoured status in schools and colleges? For hinging on this were the attitudes to reading (and writing, analysis and hermeneutics) into which students are being acculturated.

We carried out a small qualitative survey through tape-recorded interviews with specialists from throughout the Midlands and the South-west of England. As before, all of interviewees, who had been fully informed of the purpose of the research and had given their permission to be quoted, were asked a standard set of questions about the way they had been drawn to English, and the way that they perceived, practised and revised their approach to the subject.

We were aware that what we were recording was no more than a snapshot of beliefs that are constantly undergoing rearrangement and revision. We noted earlier the way in which Chris Woodhead, the Chief Inspector of schools had once seen English as part of a wider, subversive crusade but now, with the benefit of maturity:

> Mr Woodhead . . . sees his task much more in terms of initiating young people into the best that has been thought and said, equipping them with the knowledge and skills that they will need to find a reasonable job, and teaching them about morality and taste.
>
> *Times Education Supplement*, 25 March 1995

These sentiments, with their echoes of the crusading rhetoric of Matthew Arnold and F. R. Leavis, conform to the Cultural Heritage model of English identified by the Cox Committee in their 1989 report, combined with the skills element that informs the model which the Cox Committee named 'Adult Needs'. Research (Peel and Hargreaves 1995) has shown that among secondary school teachers in England, the United States and Australia these are the least popular of the five models identified by Cox, and this was confirmed by the voices recorded in, our own survey. There was an almost universal rejection of the vocational model of English, and however implicit notions of cultural heritage may have been in what was said to us, there was no explicit recommendation of it as a model.

Beyond personal growth

If there was one constant that ran through the responses of those we interviewed, it was one that could have been predicted. Irrespective of age and position, our interviewees invariably cited the private enjoyment of reading as the main factor which encouraged them to choose English as a specialist subject. We must be precise here, to the point of seeming pedantic. The love of reading referred not to the activity of reading itself, nor to the reading of all the material that had been set before them. It referred very specifically to the reading of imaginative fiction, or narratives with a strong emphasis on character, plot and satisfactory closure. The love of reading actually meant a readiness to engage in a specific reading practice with a specific kind of material.

Very rarely was this fond recollection of reading linked to a memory of a pleasure derived from writing:

> I have always enjoyed reading and especially when I was younger, writing my own stories . . . I love thinking about and discussing the ideas behind texts and find writing good essay very rewarding.

For most, it was the reading alone that singled out:

> The reading of books, is what initially attracted me to English. I have always loved reading – particularly . . . novels . . . I'm not so keen on doing actual creative writing, as I feel unsure about it . . .

Some were unequivocal:

> I have always loved the written word and have read continuously. My efforts at writing have always been failures.

For certain students, reading offers escape:

> Being a shy person I prefer to listen and to take notes . . . Reading a book allows me to escape into a different world which helps me alter my outlook on society.

For others the world of books provide the stimulation of company:

> I am interested in English because I like the feelings and emotions which certain texts evoke, especially if they engage your imagination and stir you to think.

One American student commented:

> I enjoy being able to totally escape into someone else's thoughts and feelings.

These perceptions, typical of so many others, have implications for the way in which we induct students into higher education English. The pleasure of escape, can be identified with the escape from self, the state of existing away from, self that is the *ex-stasis*, of ecstasy. In the study of English this is the pleasure of being transported by *readerly* texts, and the voices we have just heard are consistent with those of the 'enchanted' readers that were described in the first part of this paper. The strong belief that English offers a legitimation of this experience of enchantment goes some way towards explaining its popularity among school and college students. This belief is evidence of the success of the Personal Growth model. With its emphasis on the individual's response and development the concept of Personal Growth has obtained enormous currency in English teaching in schools for the past thirty years, though its organic metaphors of inner growth can be traced to the beginning of the century. Of the five models identified by Cox this was the most frequently endorsed by secondary English teachers in England, the United States and Australia (Peel and Hargreaves 1995), and it is not difficult to see why. Yet for a generation of student readers whose dance culture seems to emphasise a desire to expunge the self, obliterate it through a revealingly named drug and an incredibly fast, exaggeratedly repetitive music, notions of personal growth, rooted as they are in organic models of culture, leading to future fulfilment and fruition, may well be redundant.

What is important in such a culture is the now, and many of those we interviewed seem to have seized on the one strand in Personal Growth which they perceive as an endorsement of the pleasurable gratification reading can supply. Yet there is a significant gulf between the 'uncomplicated' pleasures described by the students above and the kinds of experiences described by a former undergraduate who is himself now a higher education tutor.

> [The attraction of English] was to do with literary forms rather than other discourses like philosophical or symbolic logic, although I was interested in those as well. But I think it was not specific to a particular genre. Part of the excitement of the thing was that there were all these different branches . . . and they were all being opened up and also related to each other and it seemed really exciting. The English Department of my school was also interested in literary theory, not in the way that one would understand it today, for the teachers had been very interested by people like Empson and Richards and they were actually teaching some of that material . . . In my own experience it was Empson who, was more influential than Richards and I think that without perhaps having been able to articulate it theoretically at the time I and my contemporaries had assimilated the poetry reading of Empson, where it had become possible to talk about ambiguity as simply a self-serving concept or a justification in itself of literary form, so that in simply unearthing the ambiguities one was as it were doing one's job as a critic while failing to address the difficulties of that very act of pleasure. My current undergraduates don't seem terribly bothered by the idea of unitary meaning; they are perfectly

at home with the notion of complete relativity in a way that certainly my teachers would have been appalled by, I think, and I don't know if I would have welcomed so explicitly myself as an undergraduate, though I think unconsciously I was beginning to adopt it.

There is a great deal to unpack here, but most importantly, these comments alert us to the challenges posed by the reader who has come to believe that any reading is legitimate, a reader who is no less frozen than the reader who demands closure and explanation.

Reading through writing

In the English courses at the University of Plymouth and Chichester Institute of Higher Education, as elsewhere, reading and writing are seen as a continuum, a manifestation of the dialogic process described by Bakhtin. Until its reduction in 1994, the significant coursework element in some GCSE and A Level English syllabuses allowed space for original writing to be included as a significant part of assessment. Coursework assessment of 50 per cent and 100 per cent was a short-lived experiment and in practice, as we have seen, the celebration of original student writing is, sadly, one strand of Personal Growth not endorsed by the majority of students who embark on higher education English courses.

We say sadly because we believe that Reading Logs and workshop pieces supported by commentaries extend the higher education student as a reader as well as a writer. The late Ted Hughes, who had long supported the idea of the English specialist as writer, responded to our questions with a long letter, part of which refers to a survey carried out by *Varsity* when he started reading English at Cambridge in the 1950s:

> In 1951, when I went up to Cambridge University to read English *Varsity* [the University Student Newspaper] sent a questionnaire to all new English students: main question, why are you reading English?
>   Like me, nearly all of them (over 400, as I recall) had shown precocious talent at school – for poetry, fiction, drama, etc. and like me all were hoping that reading English at University would somehow help them to inherit the full possibilities of their gift. In the replies (as I recall) over 400 said as much – they were reading English because they wanted to go on to write poetry, fiction, drama, as mature artists. I noticed this because I didn't reply to the questionnaire.

Ted Hughes then goes on to comment on how not one emerged as a writer. As Sawyer and Watson (1995) say:

> At some time in its history 'subject English' chose literary criticism as a curriculum paradigm that has continued to influence the study of

literature in the senior high school years especially, but also in Years 7–10. Imagine the different kind of subject we would have today if a production – based, rather than a consumption-based, paradigm had been adopted – so that senior students particularly were producing poems, plays and films rather than largely reading, and reading about, other people's texts.

(Sawyer and Watson 1995)

If the emphasis on creative writing that Personal Growth encouraged in schools has not translated itself into a generation of practising writers, then what of the two remaining models identified in the DES document? Few of those we interviewed in schools and colleges emphasised a 'Language Across the Curriculum' model, either in the original form described by the Cox Committee as a model which sees English as something which permeates every other subject, or in a form which developments in higher education have encouraged, a model which sees English as a metadiscipline which provides strategies for exploring the construction of knowledge in all subjects and practices, from history to science, from CD Roms to Milton. But what of the final model, the one that, Cox calls 'Cultural Analysis'?

The marriage of practice and theory

English is rooted in print publication, and the specialists we interviewed, however much they expressed an interest in dramatic performance, media and IT, continued to see English largely as Literary Studies rather than cultural or textual studies. The split between English and Media has reinforced this traditional definition. We have seen how the historical emphasis on reading continues to find support among specialists at different phases, either because they like to read, or because, as higher education tutors we see reading as the site for fruitful post-structuralist exploration.

In practice, the decision to specialise in English is often a pragmatic rather than a literary one. Sometimes the reasons given for choosing English given by students were disarmingly frank: the following remarks from average students at one of the newer universities contrast with the idealism remembered by Ted Hughes from his Cambridge days:

The reason I'm doing English is because it is the only subject I could have done from my A Level grades.

I chose English because it was the subject I found easiest at school, and the one I liked best.

Contemporary Oxbridge students are no less pragmatic. This was Emma's reason for taking English:

[It] was because I was good at it really, and had always done much better at English than at other things, and from when I was in middle school I had a perception of myself as being talented at it. (It disappeared when I got to Oxford!)

For Clare it was the opportunity to read and talk about literature, but not to spend a life in English:

It's always about talking about books. [There is] obviously a lot of reading at the moment. But you can get a lot of extra pleasure on top from talking about books to somebody who knows how to talk about books. It is not exactly social because most people aren't very good at talking about books. There are very few people you can ever get a good conversation with. And seeing a book you like in a new light or whatever . . . [English is] less utilitarian isn't it? I didn't do English to go on to do something else like you might do Law, or Biochemistry or whatever. I did it because I wanted to read books for three years.

Both students paid tribute to the influence of good teachers, whether at A level or university:

I had some good teachers. I had a really nice bloke at A Level who I really got on with, I just really clicked with him.

I had a very good teacher at A Level who really expanded so that there was a lot more to a book than met the eye so that's what I particularly liked about it. He was perhaps the second best teacher I've ever had in my life, the best being the one I've got now. He was really inspiring, he really cared about books and he was very good at talking about them.

Clare's reasons for admiring and recognising the influence of one of her present tutors were very similar:

Basically I think it's because he loves books. He's a real Dickens expert and I'm studying Dickens with him, he loves Dickens and I think that's the main thing. Also he's extremely intelligent and extremely well-read and because he's intellectually very formidable he does inspire people. I'm sure my I.Q. rises about 20 points when I go in there just because it would be too embarrassing if it didn't. You want to work well for him and that goes for all the students. But basically it's because he really loves books.

The Cox Committee called the fifth model of English 'Cultural Analysis', and though there is a problem with their definition we have taken this to be a model of English informed by the kind of critical theory that characterises cultural studies and the post-structuralist reading practices with which our reading log course sought to engage.

These two Oxbridge students both from state schools, were totally divided in their response to literary theory. Clare, given the opportunity to avoid courses in theory, had done so. She was uncompromising about her reasons:

> I don't like theory. I can't stand approaching a book from some high-falutin point of view. I like to approach a book from the book. Start there and see what's interesting about the author and how they write and what they're interested in. I hate starting looking at a book and getting angry because it's not feminist or because it's not Marxist or whatever. And that stuff just irritates me. I'm not really a theoretically minded person, I just don't understand that kind of thing . . . I mean I see English Literature as the books, not the individual theories of Marxism, or whoever. And if you start from the point of the books you can actually find a lot of the theory is quite irrelevant. I've never seen them as being particularly relevant to me . . . and we've had to do a very skimpy course, and some of them I don't find particularly enthralling. I seem to have got on perfectly happily without them!

Emma was far more circumspect, saying that she could not really understand how you could feel you had really done a degree course if you had not encountered theory, since that is where all the interesting debates were being carried out at the moment. Emma felt herself to be a little at odds with the other students, perhaps because she had been to a state school, had not done Latin and grammar, had taken a coursework A Level. She was not prepared for the 'history of literature' approach, as she called it. She felt she had been forced to adapt:

> [There you see] the difference between looking at the history of literature and . . . personal response . . . Before I came here I thought of English as something being intimately tied up with yourself, and about yourself really. It's just my perception has really changed. I realise now that there's stuff you have to learn and there's stuff which is interesting which you might not like. Before, I don't think I could have got my head round that, that something you don't instinctively warm to is actually valuable.

There, it appears, we touch the heart of it. Most students who come from state schools – and the majority of English undergraduates are from state schools – have had experiences similar to Emma's, and have expectations that are similar to Emma's. There is considerable evidence that most students who apply to major in English think that English is 'intimately tied up with yourself', and is rooted in the pleasure of reading and/or writing. They are unprepared for the fact that English in higher education does not make those assumptions. And it comes as a shock. Here is Lyn, a mature student at the end of her first semester at the University of the West of England, one of the new universities, speaking of her encounter with theory:

> Well luckily I had talked to someone about it because if I hadn't I'd have had a nasty shock, I think. So yes, I was primed as you say for this literary theory and people, I had spoken to a couple of second years, and they said: 'Oh, literary theory, it's horrible, it's awful, it's really difficult and you won't like it, but you'll have to do it.' And then you get to the second year and they did say that they saw the relevance of it in their second year and they were able to use it but it wasn't a pleasant experience! You know, learning about the different theories: I don't know what I think of it. At first I didn't like it because it smacked of sociology to me: not that I'm anti-sociology, but I thought that this isn't what I wanted to be doing. I want to be doing English, why am I doing all these theories, and we're talking about how it could be psychology as well, talking about a psychoanalytical approach and all the rest of it. What's all this got to do with me? . . . I had an idea of what English is but it doesn't seem to be it now, but I think, well, is this the latest fashion that I've come into? I've been out of it for a long time and in the meantime it's changed.

There are many Lyns in our universities, not simply the increasing number of mature students who have had to store up enough treasure in the world before they can afford a university course, but students who arrive straight from A Level who have not imagined that university English might expect them to read difficult texts which they found alien. The challenge faced by those involved in teaching English is to carry students forward from the unsettlingly solipsistic position that comes from a misreading of reader-response theory, to the more reflective and interrogative position contained in the idea of the making of subjectivity or subjectivities.

The Reading Log was one method by which students could become more sophisticated and more critical readers within the dominant pedagogic frame. Clearly it is not the only one. There are other strategies which could and should be practised alongside those described here, strategies which question the dominant discourse and which allow for a consideration of the normative character of the dominant pedagogical practice. These other strategies would include an emphasis on production, of text making and text reflecting through commentaries, and on interventionist strategies that insist on new readings. Perhaps most exciting of all is a reconsideration of the nature of language in the context of the new technology, where print, picture and sound intermingle, and where language use becomes collaborative, resists closure, and blurs boundaries. This is the new environment our students are beginning to inhabit, and unless we want English to become a minority subject like Latin, we need to respond to the changing intellectual frameworks being established by a techno-cultural world. The web and the internet illustrate through a strange conjunction of the personal and the interpersonal (through e-mail you can talk to people throughout the world, without the distracting (and sometimes disempowering) badge of gender, class, or nationality, yet precisely for this reason there is no face nor body language with which to communicate) a practical demonstration of many of the demanding concepts of post-age theory that the voices we heard earlier in this article found so formidable. Through foregrounding what might be called the *lens* through which we read and through which we write, the lens that is variously the IT screen or the censored, edited version of Marlowe's *Dr Faustus*, that we work with as a text, we may discover strategies that make the transition from A Level English to university less of a trauma and brick wall for many of our students.

In the end then, it is not a question of a new orthodoxy – critical literacy/ cultural analysis – replacing the old – the now not-so-new English. Rather it is – and Peter Medway's reading of Britton (Medway 1995) and Bill Green's reading of Moffett (Green 1995) show how this can be done – the incorporation of the best of the past in a conscious and frank assessment of the pedagogical implications of the present. Our research seems to suggest that in higher education there is a need for this eclectic weaving of new tapestries, new webs, so that we and our students can engage with fresh ways of teaching and learning during a period of tremendous instability, questioning, government pressure and theoretical ferment. What is encouraging is that the supply of thread seems infinite, and every time a web is damaged a new one will be made.

Dominant discourses

If we subject all the voices we have recorded, to even the most cursory kind of discourse analysis elements of a dominant discourse are readily noticeable. This discourse is characterised by notions of escape, resistance, pleasure and creativity. It is frequently a discourse of anxiety and self-regulation. This characteristic of liberal humanism is observable even in those who have rejected the ideology of liberal humanism in favour of a cultural materialist, view, for example. There is a willingness to revisit and recognise the value of former readings: there is a recognition of the provisionality and tentative nature of the discipline. As we have noted this perhaps reflects a reading (or misreading) of the practices of science. In the nineteenth century, envying science's certainty literary studies was happier to make final, categorical statements about value and worth. As science was revealed to be a much more provisional and diverse discipline than had at once been thought – relativity, quantum physics and changing models of evolution emphasised the unfolding nature of human knowledge – so English embraced and celebrated diversity. That diversity is written into the rhetoric of the subject and the discourse which emerges when specialists speak about the subject.

Summary: English in England – diversity and uniformity

In these two chapters we have explored some of the historical and ideological factors which have helped shape English over the past 150 years. We have also traced how these have contributed to a recognisable and characteristic discourse which many English specialists reproduce when they are invited to reflect on and speak about their perceptions and practice.

Education as a whole, and English in particular, has been driven largely by an empirical approach: what has been favoured is that which observation has appeared to recommend. The transformation in the approach to writing that sat at the heart of the New English, the most influential development in English brought about by teachers in the past fifty years, was an approach which emphasised the centrality of the child's experience. Science and theory have not greatly influenced the approaches to English adopted in primary and secondary schools. In England both inside and outside the profession the term 'expert' is a term of mild abuse, implying a remoteness from the field of common sense on which it is safer to rely. Allied to this is a positivist approach – one which is more interested in 'facts' than causes. Middle-class children read less than they did in the 1950s. Therefore, English teachers are failing. This may or may not be true, but the position is clearly more complex than that. At government level there has been a consistent unwillingness to address these complexities as the 'back to basics' rhetoric indicates.

In higher education English has embraced theory. This creates problems of its own. English continues to attract undergraduates who think that English is easier than science. At school English lessons have given students a space to think for themselves, to offer their own views, to have some control over what they read and how they respond. Those children who enjoy talking, reading and writing about their experience do not feel that they start from a deficit, a body of knowledge which they have to grasp before they can be said to have achieved anything. It is important that English provides this space. But it is also important that there is more of a continuity between school and university English, especially now that one in three are going on to higher education.

As we considered in chapter 2, it is arguable that the presence of the debates and forces outside education, in the economic and political world at large, are more influential in shaping developments in education than debates within the profession itself. If that was implicit in the nineteenth century, it has become explicit in England at the end of the twentieth. Industrialists speak of the need for more manufacturing awareness in young people, and the need for better language skills. In June 1995 the Secretary of State for Education Gillian Sheppard announced a reform of teacher training, with a national curriculum for the training colleges and schools of education. In the light of statistical evidence that a number of other countries, both in Europe and on the Pacific rim, are outperforming English children in the 'basic skills', teachers are to be taught how to teach these. Phonics, whole class teaching and classroom discipline are to be 'covered' so that Newly Qualified Teachers feel more prepared. English teachers have always resisted this 'instrumentalist' model of English, because of their belief in the empower-ment potential of language. Yet, as Julian Sefton-Green argues, if the next model of English (whether it is one proposed by Gunter Kress or the ones we discuss at the end of this book), does not deliver jobs, why is it better than the traditional one? 'Reconceptualising literacy in a non-instrumental fashion ignores the fact that it appears to be market forces determining children's futures, not what education can offer them' (Sefton-Green 1996).

There are some skills which are clearly transmittable. Reading is one of them. It is almost impossible to learn how to read without being taught. The same remains true of writing in longhand. As for speaking, children learn to do this for themselves and with greater access to computers the same may be true of reading. This growing autonomy, which in an increasingly techno-cultural world means that children can often do things which their parents cannot, suggests that there is a sense in which teachers English teachers cannot be 'prepared'. They do not know more than the people they teach. Or if they do, they know more about things which the children do not necess-arily value. What should English teachers do about this? The consensus seems to be that English should concentrate on doing what it does best. Two recent studies offer different understandings of what this actually is. In *Valuing English* (Knight 1995), Roger Knight argues the case for the centrality of literature, a case that continues to be made by the English Association to whose Newsletter he is a contributor. In *What is English Teaching?* (Davies 1995) Chris Davies argues that English should address three areas: literature, certainly, but also media studies and knowledge about language. All can become areas of shared knowledge, where the role of the teacher is to assist students in the recognition of what they have already seen but may not have noticed. English is a field for thinking. It is a dialectic, and without what to overload English there is also a place for discussing about how we reason, how we argue, and practising these elements of English as well as the imaginative and technical ones.

This is perhaps the greatest shift discernible in England at the end of the century. Literature is no longer at the centre. It may be argued that English no longer has a centre. More productively it can be argued that English has moved from what Mark Reid (Reid 1996) calls the 'fictive' English classroom to the 'real world'. This is a shift from literature to the languages of communication, communication through literary texts, certainly, but also through technology, in the workplace, in the media and through consider-ation of the implications of literary theory, genre theory, knowledge about language (see figure 1 above). Students are interested in examining and experimenting with the ways we speak. English language, along with media studies, has become an increasingly popular subject at Advanced Level. But if English as a framework offers opportunities for integration particularly in the primary and lower secondary schools, departmental and examination structures fragment English. In Colleges of Further Education, media is often taught by Drama and Performing Arts departments, which are quite divorced from English. It is possible that modularity in 16–19, following the Dearing Commission's recommendations concerning a unified curriculum 16–19, will help solve this problem, but in universities modularity has not led to greater integration: if anything there is is a shift towards greater specialisation.

The new digital technologies, the globalisation of cultures, the effects of literary theory – these all have a significance on the way students and specialists in English experience and apprehend the world. In such a climate it is difficult to look forward, and this is the reason why in England people look back. Uncertainty makes people want to cling on to what they know. But we cannot cling on for ever to old logs, however buoyant they were when we first grabbed hold of them. They too will sink. How can we get out of the water, and back to the living trees? We are being forced to rethink our practices, and are less in control of events than we thought we were. There will be no grand agendas for English any more, of the kind envisaged by Arnold and the Newbolt Committee. The literary text is no longer the island we once thought it. It is an event through which stream a host of influences, and it is those influences, and the way that they shape our reading, that have become the focus for English, which is why some specialists prefer to rename it Semiotics or Cultural Studies. But in the middle of the blizzard of National Curriculum testing, prescribed syllabuses, management culture and market forces it is difficult to look into the future. Yet English, like England, needs to look outwards to effect the transition from world power to important but small democracy. In England many people seem to find that difficult. Being an island with an imperial past is a positive disadvantage, and the transition in England seems likely to be more painful than it is elsewhere.

References

Abbs, Peter (1996) *The Polemics of the Imagination: Selected Essays on Art, Culture and Society*, London: Skoob

Adams, John (ed.) (1918),*The New Teaching*, London: Hodder and Stoughton

Arnold, Roslyn (ed.) (1983),*Timely Voices: English Teaching in the 1980s*, Melbourne: Oxford University Press

Barthes, Roland (1977) *Image-Music-Text*, Glasgow: Fontana

Baxter, Judith (ed.) (1996) *Kate Chopin's The Awakening and other Stories*, Cambridge: Cambridge University Press

Beer, Gillian (1996) *Open Fields: Science in Cultural Encounters*, Oxford: Oxford University Press

Benton, Michael (1982) 'How authors write . . . how children write: Towards a rationale for creative writing', in Adams (1982)

Bennett, T. (1990) *Outside Literature*, London: Routledge

Board of Education (1921) *The Teaching of English in England*, London: HMSO

Britton, James *et al.* (1976) *The Development of Writing Abilities (11–18)*, London: Macmillan Education for the Schools Council

Butler, Judith (1995) 'Desire', in F. Lentricchia and T. McLaughlin (eds.) (1995) *Critical Terms for Literary Study*, London: University of Chicago Press

Canguillhem, Georges (1978) *On the Normal and Pathological*

CBI (1995) *A Vision for our Future: A Skills Passport*, London: CBI

Central Advisory Council for Education (1963) *Half our Future* (Newsom Report), London: HMSO

Clegg, Alec (1964) *The Excitement of Writing*, London: Chatto and Windus

Cook, Caldwell (1917) *The Play Way*, London: Heinemann

Crichton, Alexander (1798) *An Inquiry into the Nature and Origin of Mental Derangement*, London

Davies, C. (1996) *What is English Teaching?* Buckingham: Open University Press

Davies, Chris (1996) *What is English Teaching?* Milton Keynes: Open University Press

DES (1989) *English for Ages 5–16*, London: HMSO

DfE (1995) *Key Stages One and Two of the National Curriculum*, London: HMSO

Dixon, J. (1967) *Growth Through English*, Oxford: Oxford University Press

Dixon, John (1969) *Growth Through English*, London: Oxford University Press

Dixon, John (1991) *A Schooling in English*, Milton Keynes: Open University Press

Entwistle, Noel and Entwistle, A. C. (1991), *Developing, Revising, and Examining Conceptual Understanding: The Student Experience and its Implications*, Edinburgh: University of Edinburgh

Fox, Geoff (1977) 'Twenty-four things to do with a book', *Children's Literature in Education*, Volume 8, No. 3

Fox, Geoff, Merrick, Brian, *et al.* (1982) 'Thirty-six things to do with a poem', in A. Adams (ed.) (1982) *New Directions in English Teaching*, Sussex: Falmer Press

Freeman, John (1998) Unpublished comments on a piece of student work that had been externally examined. In possession of the authors.

Green, Bill (1995) 'On compos(IT)ing: writing differently in the post-age', Paper presented at the Annual National Conference of the Australian Association for the Teaching of English, Sydney, 13–16 January 1995

Green, K. and LeBihan, J. (1996) *Critical Theory and Practice*, London: Routledge

Holbrook, David (1964) *English for Maturity*, Cambridge: Cambridge University Press

Hughes, Ted (1967) *Poetry in the Making*, London: Faber

Hull, R. (1985) *The Language Gap*, London: Methuen, pp. 30–1

Hunter, Ian (1988) *Culture and Government: Emergence of Literary Education*, London: Macmillan

Johnson, Rebecca (1998) *Update: Assessment and the Expanded Text Consortium*, Issue 1, Spring, Newcastle: The University of Northumbria at Newcastle

Knight, Roger (1996) *Valuing English: Reflections on the National Curriculum*, London: David Fulton

A Language for Life (Bullock Report) (1976), London: HMSO

Leavis, F. R. (1962) *Two Cultures? The Significance of C. P. Snow*, London: Chatto

Leavis, F. and Thompson, D. (1964) *Culture and Environment*, London: Chatto and Windus

McDonald, T. (1996) 'The Better English Campaign', *Poetry News*, London: The Arts Council

Mathieson, Margaret (1975) *The Preachers of Culture: A Study of English and its Teachers*, London: Allen and Unwin

Medway, Peter (1995), ' "Coming to Terms with Experience": Britton's English in UK Schools', in *English International*, Volume 3, No 1, June

Menand, Louis (1995) 'Diversity', in F. Lentricchia and Thomas McLaughlin (eds.) (1995) *Critical Terms for Literary Study*, London: The University of Chicago Press

Ministry of Education (1963) *Half our Future*, London: HMSO

Nelson/National Writing Project (1990a) *A Rich Resource: Writing and Language Diversity*, Kingston: Nelson

Nelson/National Writing Project (1990b) *Partnerships for Writing: School, the Community and the Workplace*, Kingston: Nelson

Peel, R. (1995) 'Primary Teachers as Writers: preliminary survey of BEd English students' perceptions of writing', in *Reading*, Volume 29, No. 2, July

Peel, R. (1995) 'Primary Teachers as Writers', *Reading*, Volume 29, No. 2, July

Peel, R. and Bell, M. (1994), *The Primary Language Leader's Book*, London: David Fulton

Peel, Robin and Hargreaves, Sandra (1995) 'Beliefs about English: trends in Australia, England and the United States', *English in Education*, Autumn 1995

QCA (1997) *Qualifications and Curriculum Authority: An Introduction*, London: QCA publications

Reid, Mark (1996) 'Editorial', *English in Education*, Volume 30, No. 2, Summer

Ridout, Ronald (1948) *English Today 5*, London: Ginn and Company

Sampson, George (1921) *English for the English*, Cambridge: Cambridge University Press

Sawyer, Wayne and Watson, Ken (1995), 'New models: Personal Growth for the 21st century', Paper presented in the Metaphors and Models strand at the IFTE Conference, New York City, July

Sefton-Green, Julian (1996) 'English in the Futures Market', *The English and Media Magazine*, No. 34, Summer

Simon, Brian (1974) *The Politics of Educational Reform, 1920–1940*, London: Lawrence and Wishart

Simon, Brian (1991) *Education and the Social Order 1940–1990*, London: Lawrence and Wishart

Webb, Edwin (ed.) (1996) *Powers of Being: David Holbrook and his Work*, London: Associated University Press

Whitehead, Frank (1966) *The Disappearing Dais*, London: Chatto and Windus

Wilkinson, Andrew *et al.* (1980) 'The Development of Writing', *English in Education*, Volume 14, No. 2, Autumn 1980, Sheffield: NATE

4 Shaping the English specialist: initial teacher training for English teachers in England

Robin Peel

We had a wonderful (English) teacher. There was something creative about his teaching and he brought the texts to life.

Kathy Smith (1997)

[I]f I had to choose between a so-called University, which dispensed with residence and tutorial superintendence, and gave its degrees to any person who passed an examination in a wide range of subjects, and University which had no professors or examinations at all, but merely brought a number of young men together for three or four years, and then sent them away . . . If I were asked which of these two methods was the better discipline of the intellect . . . if I must determine which of the two courses was the more successful in training, moulding, enlarging its mind, which sent out men the more fitted for their secular duties, which produced better public men, men of the world, men whose name would descend to posterity, I have no hesitation in giving the preference to that University which did nothing, over that which exacted of its members an acquaintance with every science under the sun . . .

How is this to be explained? I suppose as follows: when a multitude of young men, keen, open-hearted, sympathetic and observant, as young men are, come together and freely mix with each other, they are sure to learn one from another, even if there is no-one to teach them; the conversation of all is a series of lectures to each, and they gain for themselves new ideas and views, fresh matter of thought, and distinct principles for judging and acting, day by day.

It is seeing the world on a small field with little trouble; for the . . . students come from very different places, and with widely different notions, and there is much to generalise, much to adjust, much to eliminate, there are inter-relations to be defined, and conventional rules to be established in the process, by which the whole assemblage is moulded together and gains one tone and one character.

Newman 1852

Having traced the history and histories of Subject English, and having heard from those whose lives are bound up in the subject, whether as students, teachers or employers, I wish now to look more closely at the influences brought to bear on the second of these groups. By examining the way that teachers – and by teachers we principally mean teachers of English in secondary schools and colleges, but also include those who teach English in primary schools and in universities – are simultaneously influential and influenced, I hope to provide some observations that throw light on current practices.

Shaping and being shaped

Carrying out the functions of an English teacher is not necessarily synonymous with being a specialist in English. Government reports throughout the twentieth century testify to the number of people teaching English in schools who have trained as teachers, but not necessarily with English as their main subject. If, as those within the subject have often argued, it is difficult to pin down its content then it has been easy to assume that there is no expertise. There is a long and honourable tradition that has argued that the expertise comes from the pedagogy, rather than from the possession of deep knowledge.

Enthusiasmos – the quality of enthusiasm for one's specialist subject – is the quality that is often described as the hallmark of the memorable, *inspirational* teacher. To convey the delight that can be derived from reading, from writing, from expressing thoughts, feelings and interpretations in language to others, so that they discover it for themselves – that is a very pervasive and powerful pedagogic model. For some it is a model to be emulated, for others one to be avoided.

It is clear from the earlier interviews with student teachers how high a priority they gave to the need to form the right relationship with their students. It was also noticeable in the chapter on the history of the subject – and it will be noticeable again in this chapter – how long-established a precedent there is for this, one which goes back as far as the model proposed by David Stow in the early nineteenth century. If the centrality of the teacher–pupil relationship was masked in the majority of the nineteenth century by conflicting models of the child, the need to train children to pass certain tests and for them to submit to a dull curriculum, the centrality of the teacher's role and the relationship he or she established with pupils was given renewed emphasis at the beginning of the twentieth century as statements on teacher-training began to be influenced by child-centred theories of pedagogy. These statements are found not just in Holmes, Montessori, Steiner, Homer Lane or John Dewey, but in statements from the thoroughly official *Handbook of Suggestions for the Consideration of Teachers and Others Concerned in the Work of Public Elementary Schools* (1905), as will be demonstrated later.

English teachers were perhaps in the best position to shape themselves according to this new model of supportive, enthusiastic humane facilitator. They were more likely to see themselves as missionaries, as evangelists whose goal was to spread a love of literature and language to all. In school stories it is often the English teacher who is the kindly one, the inspiring one: from *Jennings* to *Zen and the Art of Motorcycle Maintenance*. In television and films the same is true: *Kes*, *Dead Poets' Society*, the Australian soap *Heartbreak High* even the Tom Hanks character in *Saving Private Ryan*. And it is not just that the writers of many of these stories are ex-English teachers: the practices of English allow an enthusiasm and sensibility that can be inspirational for the majority, whereas the practices of science seem to permit only an enthusiasm that can be valued only by a minority. In the rhetoric of the subject, English, as it moved towards literary study and expressive personal writing, sought to be inclusive and pleasurable, whereas grammar study tended to be *exclusive*.

Many writers have drawn attention to the significance of gender in the practices of English. The relation between masculinised grammar and feminised English, and the construction of English as a gendered discipline are topics that inevitably emerge from a subject which in its beginning form (literacy) is taught predominantly by women, and which at Years 11 and 12 and university level is taken by many more women than men. Bill Green (1993) refers to the 'return of the repressed, in culture and schooling' and the way that 'the assertion of the interpersonal over the ideational aspect of schooling . . . can be mapped readily onto the ideological category "woman"', while Goodson and Marsch (1996) consider claims that institutionalisation of English as a serious university subject contributed to the development of the women's movement in the second half of the twentieth century.

The English teacher in the movies: teaching, gender and desire

In her study of the representation of English teachers in films, Dale Bauer (1998) discusses the changes in cinema treatment of classroom desire, with the move from the desire for knowledge in *Dead Poets' Society* to the relationship between sexual desire and teaching in *The Mirror has Two Faces*. The shift from the 'ostensibly anti-authoritarian' Robin Williams English teacher in *Dead Poets' Society* and the 'idealistic' Michael Caine English lecturer in *Educating Rita* of the 1980s to the seductive 1990s English teachers such as the Michelle Pfeiffer character in *Dangerous Minds* and the Sally Kellerman character in *Back to School* is not only a shift in gender, but it encourages us to ask the question that Teresa Ebert asks in another context: why this 'libidinisation' and 'eroticisation' of pedagogy? Bauer acknowledges the role played here by theories, including feminist theories, which contain an advocacy of pleasure, but argues that the message of the Bush/Reagan era films is that corporate authoritarianism always wins (the Robin Williams character Keating is sacked, his moment of subversion is presented as a brief moment of carnivalesque, a brief interruption before the conventional pre-school values are restored) whereas the Clinton era films show English teachers channelling 'sexual energy into erotic discipline' (Bauer 1998, p. 307), a theme taken to remarkable lengths in *The Mirror has Two Faces*. The Barbara Streisand English Professor is a brilliant, inspirational teacher in the Keating mould, but in the course of the film she has to complete herself by coming to terms with her own image and body. Not satisfied with her pedagogical success because she cannot bring the Jeff Bridges maths professor she has married to bed, she subjects herself to a make-over. Needless to say, it works.

The world of the film studio – even when it is more Pinewood than it is Hollywood – may seem a long way from the politics of the actual classroom, and as Bauer points out, most of the action in these films takes place outside the classroom. But her point about the sublimisation of desire into a desire to 'transform either the classroom or the self', and the anxieties about such a process that these films register, does have a resonance when we return to the testimony of actual teachers in England.

The role of the teacher in encouraging inclusivity and pleasure in primary and secondary schools is considered very important by Kathy Smith from the Central School of Speech and Drama:

> I was very influenced by the staffing in all my subjects. In one subject, for example, I gave up completely because I loathed the teacher – I know that sounds terrible, because you can't loathe someone you don't know. But there are some teachers who are more engaging than others: I remember in my sixth form, we had a wonderful teacher who was on an American exchange – he came over from America for a year and replaced a rather weak English teacher (who went to America for a year) and he taught *Macbeth* and the poetry of Shelley, and Golding's *The Spire*. There was something really creative about his teaching and he brought the texts to life. I think the role of the teacher in teaching English is incredibly important because at school level – although not necessarily so much at university level because by that point you've decided that you like the subject, you're interested in the subject, you're good at it, there is a sense of competence – at school level, there's a sense of having to 'sell' the subject to the student in a particular way because students don't really know what they're good at, and they might surprise themselves, given the right kind of support in teaching at that level . . . As a student at school, the most important thing for me was to be able to relate to the teacher, either through respect for a teacher with a great amount of knowledge or, on a more personal level, to relate to a teacher who was interested in what I was doing and with whom I could discuss the small amounts of knowledge I was gaining at the time, and who would encourage me in the right direction. I think the worst combination was a teacher who rambled at length about things that seemed irrelevant, and was also someone to whom I could not relate as a person.

This is a view which would still have widespread support from within the profession. It is worth considering how that view has itself been shaped, and the extent to which forces within teacher training, within schools, and within the politics and rhetoric of education have encouraged or discouraged such a view.

Voice of a teacher trainer

Bethan Marshall is a lecturer in the School of Education at King's College, London. She has been an English teacher in schools, an English advisor and a member of various government consultative committees at the Department for Education and Employment. She writes for the *Guardian* newspaper, is an active member of NATE and appears regularly on the radio. Her experience and evaluation of current developments in English in England locate her at the boundaries of contesting traditions and discourses: like so many specialist, she is positioned both inside and outside the agencies of the 'fleshly institution(s)' to which we drew attention in the preface.

Her own experience of English at a formal, direct-grant girls' grammar school influenced her decision to apply for either English with American Studies or English with History at university: she did not want to take Single Honours because that involved linguistics, which she equated with the dry parsing that passed for grammar teaching in her school. English was her first choice of subject because it was something she was good at, and although she had an 'appallingly bad English teacher' her mother, who was also an English teacher, had contributed to an environment in which a love of books became natural. This is what English meant: an escape into literature, not meaning into Mills and Boon, but into the swooning Romanticism of Keats and Jane Austen. 'I just liked words. I liked what words could do.'

When she started the English course at Nottingham University, the biggest adjustment was not the encounter with structuralism and critical theory, much of which she just found dull (she was to rediscover its usefulness as pedagogical tool when she came to work with children in schools), but the discovery that she was no longer to be spoon-fed, and now had to find out things for herself. Yet there were points of contact that meant she was not entirely on her own. She was inspired by Tom Paulin, then in the English department at Nottingham, impressed by the way he politicised and historicised the texts they studied, whilst all the time demonstrating a marvellously keen eye for the nuances of language.

Bethan Marshall took a PGCE course principally as a safety net, as she had planned to be a journalist. But she found she liked teaching. She thinks she was an awkward PGCE student, however: in the early and mid 1980s the radical teacher – and she identified with the concept of the radical English teacher – promoted authenticity in writing. Chris Searle was the model, and though part of her was deeply sympathetic to the practice of encouraging children to find their own voice, the distinct emphasis on social realism ran counter to her own delight in literature as escape. Creative writing, in this orthodoxy, seemed to be privileged over reading as a learning tool. But since then the orthodoxy has shifted, she said, as a reassessment of Standard English has led to a new pragmatism: discourse analysis has led to new under-standings of the discourses of power, and Standard English is one of those discourses, whereas non-standard forms are not. She is a pragmatist: she was sceptical about Mixed Ability teaching, but then found that it worked. She discovered and demonstrated to herself and others that the class that contained both a pupil who had problems with literacy and one who could read Dostoevsky could and did operate successfully.

She had a similarly pragmatic reaction to the National Curriculum. At first she, like many other English teachers, had feared that it signalled the end of child-centred education. But the Cox curriculum that emerged was some-thing that she and others found they could live with, and it was actually a very useful tool when she became an advisory teacher. The Cox model was broad – but when it was passed over to Pascall and others to be rewritten it became narrow. She believes in entitlement, but not in prescription. In her view, the current curriculum model, tied as it is to narrow assessments, is not an entitlement curriculum.

In the meantime she had begun studies and research of her own. She was particularly interested in the models of English that informed teachers' practice. Her own research showed that whereas secondary teachers subscribed to a literary model, primary teachers divided down the middle with 50 per cent of her sample describing a skills model and 50 per cent a creativity model (no secondary teachers identified with the skills model). In her view, primary teachers did not teach in a way that reproduced what English specialists would have recognised as an English lesson. English was taught through creativity, through Humanities, or through spelling, but not through 'books', using reading as a learning strategy. So she has welcomed the literacy hour, because it ensures that primary children have some experience of a well-structured English lesson, which is what it has the potential to be. But she does not welcome the current way that teachers were being required to acquaint themselves with the vocabulary of grammar: this was more about rules and behaviour than it is about knowledge about language and linguistics. The shift in terminology was revealing. In official curriculum statements, what had been known as 'Knowledge about Language' was now known as 'Standard English and Language Study' – a significant change. But she also became interested in the issue of assessment, and the way that English specialists are able to demonstrate the skill of 'con-struct referencing' when it came to assessing students' work, so that even if they valued different things in writing they would reach a consensus on what constituted a certain grade, based on a shared aesthetic judgement, confirming that there existed a community of interpreters. So it did not really matter what your philosophy was – it would not radically alter assessment judgements.

But Bethan Marshall was interested in the philosophical and ideological assumptions that underpinned specialists' perceptions of English. She has identified her own five models. Firstly, there were the Old Grammarians, with an Arts background, who subscribed to an inspirational model. They were elitist and gloomy, and they included people like Cox and Hoggart. Next there were the pragmatists, who believed in critical theory, were pragmatic about current developments and generally optimistic, not unlike New Labour. Thirdly, there were the Liberals, who believed in personal growth and the authentic voice. Fourthly, there were the technicians, who believed in teaching skills and subscribed to a passive model of learning. Finally there was the group that Bethan categorised as the Critical Dissenters 'which is where I would place myself'.

From present to past: a brief history of teacher training

The English subject specialist in the secondary school in England continues to be the most numerous of the species. Every primary school will have its own English specialists, but that is one person for up to 400 children. Almost every university has its own English department, but in England and Wales there are only just over 100 universities, compared to the 10,000 or so (?) secondary schools. Since every student has an English lesson with a person who should be an identified specialist (though many are not – there is still evidence of the belief that 'anyone can teach English') nearly every day, there is a big demand. It is a core subject in the National Curriculum: it is central to the timetable.

At the time of writing a healthy number of people in England still want to be English teachers. Though the numbers applying for PGCE courses in certain subjects have shown a dramatic decline – between 1995 and 1996 there was a decrease of 8.24 per cent in Chemistry, 12.86 per cent in Maths and 24.82 per cent in Physics (UCET 1997) in English the numbers have not shown similar signs of drying up: in 1996 there was an increase of 12.8 per cent in the number of acceptances from the previous year and there was no talk of a shortage. Undergraduates continue to be attracted to English teaching in schools and colleges even at a time when an upturn in the economy provides greater opportunities for other kinds of work. The evidence gleaned from our interviews suggest that the contemporary student teacher is motivated by an enthusiasm for the subject, an enthusiasm which is inextricably linked to an enthusiasm for the development of the students they will be teaching.

Those students who will reach adulthood in the new century inhabit worlds that are markedly different from the world that their nineteenth century predecessors inhabited: student teachers in English are eager to engage with that world, having grown up in it themselves. The patina of materialism and ephemeral hedonism available outside school, even to those for whom the world offers no promise for the future – perhaps especially for this group – permits a lifestyle that would be unrecognisable to an early twentieth-century teacher of English whose charges jumped straight from childhood into work. The construction of the young adult, the erstwhile teenager and adolescent, is, superficially, returning to what it was in the nineteenth century before sentimental notions of childhood had been invented. The early encounter with the world of drugs, sex and sexuality, and parental absence may seem not unlike the features of the urban streets of nineteenth-century England. But the social belief in the innocence of childhood has not disappeared, and the pervasiveness of technology, street fashion and compulsory education means that the two worlds are not equivalent, and the construction of the Leeds twelve-year old in 2000 is very different from the Leeds twelve-year old of 1900.

Yet the construction of teaching itself, the frames and assumptions within which the end of century English teacher works, these would not be so alien to the English teacher of 1906. In fact, much would be remarkably familiar to the early twentieth-century educator struggling to escape the limitations of the model that had evolved in the nineteenth century.

The nineteenth century and before

[The university], at least, found it quite impossible to imagine what the contents, structure or purpose of any organised study of English Literature might be, and the only safe place it could find for English in the hierarchy of examinations was in the guise of a paper on 'the Grammatical Structure of the English Language' in the matriculation which was the test for admission to the degree courses. The subject rested in this lowly, but honourable estate until 1859.

Thompson 1990

Why is the teacher so ready to do everything (or nearly everything) for the children whom he professes to educate? One obvious answer to the question is that for a third of a century (1862–95) the 'Education Department' did everything (or nearly everything) for him. For a third of a century 'My Lords' required their inspectors to examine every child in every elementary school in England in a syllabus which was binding in all schools alike. In doing this they put a bit in the mouth of the teacher and drove him at their pleasure, in this direction and that. And what they did to him they compelled him to do to the child.

Holmes 1911

Before the nineteenth century, the category 'English' teacher did not exist, but there were teachers of reading, writing, grammar and rhetoric. As it was the Church that had a monopoly of education provision in England it is unsurprising that the first English organisation to call for all teachers to have some kind of qualification was the Society for the Propagation of Christian

Knowledge in 1699. The requirements were relatively modest and imprecise: evidence of a good education, a reasonable ability in handwriting and arithmetic, a command of English and membership of the Anglican Church.

Another hundred years were to pass before the training of teachers was to be institutionalised by two different religious societies, the National Society and the British and Foreign School Society. The former, associated with Bell and the 'Madras System' took on the responsibility for training teachers in 1811, three years before the British and Foreign School Society, an organisation associated with Lancaster and the Monitorial System, though Lancaster had by then resigned from the movement. Together these societies laid down many of the characteristics of teacher training that have survived in England until this day: the professional certification of teachers, a period of probationary teaching and the recommendation that training should be residential. This last requirement was expensive and although Lancaster had built a hostel for the Borough Road students in Southwark in the first decade of the nineteenth century residential training colleges did not really begin to mushroom until the late 1830s and early 1840s, and only then as part of the Church's bid to outmanoeuvre the State in the battle for the control of elementary education. The Home and Colonial Infant School Society's Training Institution opened in 1837 and in the succeeding years college after college was founded: ten years later there were over twenty such colleges. The Diocesan College in Chester had students in residence from 1840, as did the National Society's college for women (Whitelands) and for men (St Mark's): these, like all the other colleges with the exception of Borough Road, were Anglican, and even Kay-Shuttleworth's influential and experimental training college which operated under his direction from 1840–1843 and sought to professionalise teaching, saw elementary teachers primarily as 'Christian missionaries' (Dent 1977, p. 13).

Even at this early stage we see the differences in emphasis that continue to characterise the debate about teacher education. The first Principal of St Mark's College, Chelsea was the Reverend Derwent Coleridge (the son of S. T. Coleridge), who as Dent describes, shared Kay-Shuttleworth's belief that teacher training 'should be conducted in a closely knit residential community', and thus anticipated by more than ten years the argument advanced by Newman in the quotation that appeared at the head of this chapter. In one crucial respect, however, the Rev. Coleridge differed from Kay-Shuttleworth: 'Kay-Shuttleworth held that the primary purpose of a training college was to produce effective teachers; Coleridge that it was to nurture educated and cultured persons' (Dent 1977, p. 14). Today many would regard this as a false binary, but it is a binary that has proved hard to dislodge and it is one that informs much of the rhetoric in contemporary debates about the kind of teachers needed in England.

If the Church set the agenda for the provision of education and the training of teachers in the first half of the century, it was, as we have seen, a combination of fears of economic rivals and the fear that religion was in decline that gave the arguments for state educational provision an impetus in the second half of the nineteenth century and the first quarter of the twentieth. Although material factors may have been the decisive ones, the argument for economic stability was often couched inside a moral rhetoric. Hence, from 1850 onwards, 'the great campaign for better instruction, education at all levels; unreliable habit is the only remaining dyke before the now rising flood of unrestrained instinct' (O'Hanlon 1984, p. 48).

The pupil-teacher system

At this point we need to stress the centrality of the pupil-teacher system in England which, when it was finally abolished in 1927, had been in place for nearly 100 years. It was this system, rather than the system of colleges, that provided the majority of bodies charged with running nineteenth-century English elementary school classrooms.

The pupil-teacher was a thirteen year old who was paid to stay on in the elementary school and undertake teaching. It was the logical extension of the monitorial system – paid monitors worked much better than unpaid ones – and had been the practice in Holland since 1816. Kay-Shuttleworth had been to see it in operation there and in 1838 introduced the system to a Poor Law School in Norwood where zealous pupils were paid a small salary, provided with a uniform and a room to sleep, and given extra education in the evenings. Eight years later a national system devised by Kay-Shuttleworth was launched with grants being paid to schools to pay for their pupil teachers, who began their five years' training at the age of thirteen under the auspices of the Elementary School headteacher.

But Kay-Shuttleworth had also been influenced by the Scottish educator David Stow, who attached great importance to the status of the teacher and the role of the teacher exercised in moral formation of the pupil. This was not simply an ideological shift – it mattered greatly who was in front of the class – it was a spatial one as it involved a shift from the idea of the school-room to the idea of the *classroom.*

The pupil-teacher system proved highly successful, although it never realised Kay-Shuttleworth's ambition for it to be the first stage in teacher training, partly because the majority of pupil-teachers never proceeded to Normal Schools and partly because a teaching certificate could be achieved without any attendance at a training college. As a system, however, it won praise from all the HMI's who at first hand saw it in operation and examined the pupil teachers. There was a renewed attempt to encourage pupil-teachers to proceed to training colleges when the Queen's Scholar system was introduced in 1852, offering awards to the best pupil-teachers. The training colleges benefited from both the increase in numbers and, in theory, the quality of the intake.

It proved a costly system, however, and Robert Lowe's Revised Code regulations of 1862 sought to address this problem by a method which became familiar in English schools 130 years later. Schools were to pay for their pupil-teachers out of their block grants.

This had the immediate effect of cutting the numbers and drying up the supply of teachers being fed into the colleges. Some of the men's colleges were forced to close – women's colleges were able to survive because they were cheaper – and the 1860s were a bleak time for teacher training. Then, with the passing of the 1870 Elementary School Act there was suddenly an increased demand for teachers, leading to the restoration of the pupil-teacher/Queen's Scholar system, a new category of Assistant Teacher and the setting up of Day Colleges. Primary education was made compulsory in 1880 and from 1891 these new board-schools were provided free.

Although the state seemed to be taking the initiative, teachers were still being trained in church training colleges, and the religious societies continued to exert their influence on how and what of teaching through the teaching guides they published for teachers. From the 1870s onwards the National Society began to publish a series of 'How to Teach' books, and these small, cheap guides provide an interesting insight into the pedagogy of English teaching in the last quarter of the nineteenth century – and as the case study of D. H. Lawrence reveals, the first part of the twentieth.

The importance of grammar as a central practice in English is revealed in the first book in the second series, *How to Teach Grammar* (National Society 1879a):

> The object of teaching grammar is twofold, viz. (i) to enable children to speak and write correctly i.e. in accordance with the rules of language, and (2) to cultivate their minds through those inductive and deductive exercises which the study of grammar supplied.
>
> National Society 1879a, p. 2

The dialectic with science is indicated by the following prescription: 'Grammar should be studied first as an inductive science' (National Society 1879a, p. 4). A similar desire to be associated with science is expressed in the original 1888 Preface to *The Grammar, History and Derivation of the English Language* by the Rev. Canon Evan Daniel, Formerly Principal of the National Society's Training College at Battersea (Daniel 1898):

> It is commonly assumed that Grammar is a purely verbal science, in which the student is mainly occupied by learning definitions, paradigms and rules of syntax, and that it is, consequently, far inferior an instrument of mental discipline than natural history and experimental science. The mode in which it has been too frequently taught gives colour to this view; but rightly taught, grammar is as much a real study as botany or chemistry . . . The study of [the] laws [of grammar] affords room for just the sort of independent effort as the study of physical science . . . It is

obvious, therefore, that grammar affords room for original observation, for generalisation, for induction and deduction, and that if it were taught in this scientific spirit, its value as a formative study would be very high.

Daniel 1898

The bold rhetoric is not quite matched by the rather plodding Appendices, which consist of: 1. Figures of Speech 2. Hints on Parsing 3. (Grammar) Questions set at Pupil-Teacher Examinations 4. Admission Questions for Training Colleges (Composition and Grammar) 5. Other examinations 6. Hints on answering questions 7. A Table of English Literature.

A similar insight into actual classroom practice is given in *How to Teach Grammar*, which includes specimen lessons 'First Lesson on the Noun', suggesting a concept of teaching that the Secretary of State for Education was to echo in 1998, when he revealed plans to provide teachers with ready-made lesson plans for the literacy hour via the internet, and not one that encouraged the scientific, investigative spirit in quite the way that Daniel recommended.

Other slim volumes in the *How to . . .* series included *How to Teach Reading and Writing* (National Society 1879b), which again offers a description which seems remarkably familiar in the 1990s. Writing defined solely as handwriting may seem a trifle now to modern ears, but the description of reading methods (the 'old-fashioned' alphabet method, the phonic method, and the look and say method) has proved extremely durable. The appeal to the scientific method reappears in *On the Use of Words* (National Society 1879c), while the pedagogic relation and the role of education in the moral formation of the subject is made quite explicit in *On Class Teaching* (National Society 1879d) and *On Discipline* (National Society 1879e). The classroom is the environment in which moral forces must be monitored, and appropriate habits formed:

> The moral forces at work in the class will demand constant care. The moral character is being imperceptibly formed by agencies that are always at work.
>
> National Society 1879d, p. 37

> To teach is to form mental habits: a habit is an unconscious possession.
>
> National Society 1879d, p. 5

The subject of habit formation is given a whole chapter in *On Discipline*, and early on the habits are spelled out in detail:

> Good habits . . . Regularity, punctuality, a love of order, prompt obedience, regard for law, respect for authority, attention to the work in hand, diligence etc are all qualities that will be of life-long value.
>
> National Society 1879e, p. 19

In chapter 6, 'Habits', the handbook further enumerates these habits, which include the familiar Victorian virtues of honesty, candour, benevolence, self-control, the government of temper, the reverence for authority, humility and temperance. Such virtues would be transmitted to pupil teachers as well as pupils, as *How to Teach Pupil-Teachers* (National Society 1880a) shows.

If these general teaching aids seem to move away from the specificity of English, to return more closely to the subject it is worth examining another 1880 volume published in the Advanced Series, *How to Teach English Literature* (National Society 1880b). In contrast to the scientific approach to language, this volume emphasises empathy and appreciation, allied to national pride:

> No other country possesses a literature so rich, so varied, so continuous.
>
> National Society 1880b, p. 4

> The aim of the teacher of English Literature to the scholars of elementary schools should be *to give his pupils a love for literature*.
>
> National Society 1880b, p. 5

The word 'pleasure' makes an early appearance in the discussion of the pedagogy of English Literature:

> It will be plain to the readers of the foregoing observations that nothing in our literature of earlier date than the age of Chaucer . . . can be read with pleasure by anyone who is not an Anglo-Saxon scholar, or with profit by anyone who is not an Anglo-Saxon student.
>
> National Society 1880b, p. 38

But the actual method of teaching reveals a pedagogical practice that is much more mundane than some of the rhetoric may suggest:

> For *practical* purposes the task before the teacher is to secure that his pupil teachers, or, if he 'takes up literature' his scholars of a certain standing – shall be able to repeat accurately and understand a specified portion of poetry or prose, selected by himself but requiring to be approved by HM's Inspector.
>
> National Society 1880b, p. 6

The sections in this book are also revealing of the practices of English Literature teaching at the end of the nineteenth century. Chapter 8 contains a 'Selection of Passages for Committing to Memory', while other sections on the history and growth of English are included as teachers had to be familiar with this body of knowledge. The volume ends with the story of a painfully dull recitation of the first part of the May Queen by a pupil-teacher who is then taken in hand by the daughter of a great tragic actor, and a year later the pupil-teacher delivers the 'New Year' wonderfully, moving the audience to tears. The guide then suggests that the discourse which surrounded claims about the civilising potential of English literature was informing the discourse surrounding the pedagogy of English teaching:

> Of the *fact* there can be no doubt; was it only a marvel of mechanical teaching, or had the girl's whole moral nature been refined in the process?
> National Society 1880b, p. 52

During this period questions began to be asked about the level of education of pupil-teachers, and the advisability of entrusting the teaching of children to immature people. Raising the age of the pupil-teacher to fifteen was one attempt to improve matters, but questions were raised in the 1898 report into Pupil-Teacher System about the quality of Pupil-Teacher Centres. The best of these showed promise and the report recommended that these become secondary schools in which pupil-teachers could work alongside those who had other careers in mind. In 1902 it became possible to pay for certain pupils to attend secondary schools out of the rates and if we return to our case study of Croydon the Education minutes show how education committees responded by drawing up plans for new secondary schools. In the period 1903–1913 Croydon, as the records show, received a series of stinging letters from the Board of Education saying that they would not fund the new secondary school for boys until plans for a secondary school for girls had been drawn up.

Shaping the teacher at the beginning of the twentieth century: the case of the newly qualified teacher in Croydon

D. H. Lawrence taught at a large new elementary school in Davidson Road, and in both his career and his fiction we see a record of educational change. Born in 1885 he won a scholarship to Nottingham High School in 1898, which qualified him for a free place at this secondary school. He left the school in 1901 and in 1902, at the age of seventeen, became a pupil-teacher, first at the British School in Eastwood, and then at a pupil-teacher centre in Ilkeston, where he passed what had now become the King's Scholarship examination, which qualified him for a free place at a teacher training college. He was clearly more ambitious, for during this same period he took and passed his London Matriculation examination, which granted him the right to attend Nottingham University College, though this had to be paid for. He did not have enough money, and so worked for one more year at Eastwood, this time as an Uncertificated Assistant Teacher.

   Some of this experience provided material for *Sons and Lovers* and *The Rainbow*. This is Ursula Brangwen's first week as a teacher at St Philip's School in Ilkeston:

The day passed incredibly slowly. She never knew what to do, there came horrible gaps, when she was merely exposed to the children; and when, relying on some pert little girl for information, she had started a lesson, she did not know how to go on with it properly. The children were her masters . . . The first week passed in a blind confusion. She did not know how to teach, and she felt she never would know.

Lawrence conveys a sense of what an English lesson for a Standard V class involved when he describes the censure of the headmaster who intervenes in Ursula's composition class one morning:

[H]is job was to make the children spell the word 'caution' correctly, and put a capital letter after a full-stop. So at this he hammered with his suppressed hatred, always suppressing himself, till he was beside himself. Ursula suffered bitterly as he stood, short and handsome and powerful, teaching her class. It seemed such a miserable thing for him to be doing. He had a decent, powerful, rude soul. What did he care about the composition on 'The Rabbit'?

The construction of Ursula and the rhetoric of the beliefs which guide her summarise many of the paradoxes we have discussed already. Ursula has a love of beauty, nature and the romantic which is most happy when it engages with art, the countryside or literature, but she must work and she believes in education. Yet she is frustrated when she discovers that the education she believes in cannot be expressed through the aesthetic in which she believes, because external forces prevent her doing what she wants. The struggle she experiences has a resonance for subject specialists in schools throughout the twentieth century, including our own time, perhaps especially our own time, in England:

The quarterly examination was coming and her class was not ready. It irritated her that she must drag herself away from her happy self, exert herself with all her strength to force, to compel this heavy class of children to work hard at arithmetic . . . The school, the sums, the grammar, the quarterly examinations, the registers – it was all a barren nothing! . . . What did it matter if her class did ever so badly in the quarterly examinations. Let it – what did it matter?
  Nevertheless, when the time came, and the report on her class was bad, she was miserable, and the joy of the summer was taken away from her, she was shut up in gloom. She could not really escape from this world of system and work, out into her fields where she was happy. She must have her place in the working world, be a recognised member with full rights there. It was more important to her than fields and sums and poetry, at this time.

We can observe a number of agencies at work here: the assessment system, the construction of the individual teacher as romantic. These are represented as a binary, but during the period when Lawrence was being trained there was a new influence being brought to bear on teachers, the rhetoric of child-centredness and experiential learning.[1] This is from the *Handbook of Suggestions for the Consideration of Teachers and others concerned in the work of Public Elementary Schools* (1905):

> The teacher must know the children and must sympathise with them, for it is of the essence of teaching that the mind of the teacher should touch the mind of the pupil. He will seek at each stage to adjust his mind to theirs, to draw upon their experiences as a supplement to his own, and so take them as it were into partnership for the acquisition of knowledge.
>
> Maclure 1973, p. 160

This may contain a powerful rhetoric, the latter part of which was still very familiar in England at the end of the century, but it remained a rhetoric which a combination of Lawrence's own aristocratic personality and the regular testing system prevented from becoming a reality.

Ursula, like Lawrence, goes on to University College, Nottingham with the intention of getting a BA. This would be a three-year course and would include teacher training, but she would be educated alongside those not intending to go into teaching, and this was the usual experience for a teacher. In fact, Lawrence, failing to acquire the necessary qualification in Latin, did not take a degree but did qualify as a teacher, taking up the appointment in Croydon in 1908 in the boys' department of a newly built elementary school for 1,200 pupils.

The log book and Lawrence's personal file from this period do not reveal a great deal that is specific to English and the training of teachers, but do provide an insight into the welfare of the children that were then as much the subject of inspection as was their intellectual prowess. Two weeks after the school had opened the Headmaster, Philip Smith, recorded the following in the log book:

> November 13th 1907 Inspection of the scholars made in the week specially with regard to clothing. 28 children were discovered to be in want of boots. Many of these scholars were in a deplorable condition.

Sadly, though 100 years on, similar inspections today would probably yield distressingly similar results in some schools.

---

1 This rhetoric always impacts on practice in a modified way, often attenuated way. Child-centredness initially made a real impact on early years' learning, but it took future waves of the so called 'progressive' theory of learning before elementary and secondary school practice changed. But again, the pedagogical relationship may still have remained the same in the case of Subject English.

Inspections were regular, but the reports were very brief. Headteachers were required to copy them into their log books, as in the following instance, an entry recorded seven months before Lawrence 'commenced duties' on 12 October:

> All classes examined during the week. The reading in all classes except Standard 1 was fairly good. Composition was indifferent, and spelling weak. Arithmetic was weak. In Class 1 all subjects were weak.

The HMI report for 7 March 1910, however, records that:

> Written Composition is also well taught. The boys have a sufficiency of ideas which they are able to express copiously. Probably if a little less were written more attention could be devoted to the handwriting.

After a period of regular absence, owing to ill health, the log shows that Lawrence 'left the service of the committee' on 9 March 1912. Ill health and large classes may have made teaching a frustrating activity, but there is evidence that he was a good teacher. In his staff file the headmaster records his 'ability as a teacher' as being 'very good' in 1909, 1910 and 1911 (the 1908 record notes that he has been 'only a few weeks' in employ). Until 1911 there was a separate category 'ability as a disciplinarian and manager of children' and Lawrence achieves a 'good' here. A sceptical Croydon Library archivist described his testimonials as anodyne, but they are glowing, saying that he was an outstanding student in Nottingham. A testimonial from A Henderson, the Professor of Education at University College, Nottingham, dated 18th July 1908, asserts:

He has shown a decided ability in his course of study and especially a taste for, and appreciation of, literature.

It is all the more surprising, therefore, that English is one of the few subjects in which he did not gain a distinction, a fact which somewhat piqued him (Worthen 1991).

A sense of the discourse of the educational culture in which Lawrence worked is provided by the the minutes of the Education Committee. Lawrence entered the service of Croydon as a trained, certificated teacher on a salary of £95.0.0. per annum, but he had been a pupil-teacher as the application form kept in his school file shows. In 1903 the annual salaries for pupil-teachers in Croydon were modest and discriminatory:

	Commencing salary	Annual increase	Maximum
Boys	£17.0.0	£2.10.0	£22.10.0
Girls	£15.0.0	£2.10.0	£20. 0.0

In addition, an allowance of £10.0.0 was paid to pupil-teachers who entered training colleges. Lawrence, too, had started on a salary of £17.00 a year (Lawrence recalled it as 'teaching for 2/6 a week' (Worthen 1991, p. 116) though by his third year this had risen to £24.00 – Nottingham were a little more generous than Croydon).

The minutes show that Croydon were keen to take advantage of the new proposals for day colleges for teacher training, when it was reported that Goldsmith College was planning to provide such training. The concept of day colleges had been willingly seized by universities and university colleges: six teacher training departments had opened in 1890, four more in 1891, four more in 1892. By 1900 there were sixteen, and as the Goldsmith proposals shows, more were to come. Lawrence himself had identified his training as 'two years' training at Nottingham Day College 1906–8'. The ready supply of students for universities was very welcome, and according to Dent the introduction of the Day Colleges not only improved the supply of trained teachers it forced the residential colleges to push up their standards.

The minutes also show the Committee's recommendation that, in response to the Board of Education's regulation that in four years' time all pupil-teachers should be educated in good secondary schools through a system of parental payment or scholarships and that no one under sixteen should teach in an elementary school:

1. From 1904 there should be forty such scholarships (thirty for girls, ten for boys) providing free education at secondary schools
2. Also from 1904 no Probationers or Candidates under 16 shall attend or assist at elementary schools
3. That a school and pupil-teacher centre be opened temporarily at the Central Polytechnic.
4. And that a secondary school be established for co-education of 250 boys and 250 girls and to provide accommodation for 100 pupil-teachers of both sexes.
5. And that finally the training of teachers who did not proceed to college should take place at the Day College at Goldsmith's Institute, New Cross. Lawrence's career would have been governed by very similar developments in the part of Nottinghamshire in which he lived.

The Board of Education was an increasingly powerful force. The Croydon minutes from this period quote the Board's directive that in relation to the recognition of a Higher Elementary School '[a] curriculum will not be approved unless it provides, together with special instruction, a progressive course of study in English Language and Literature'. This 1906 reference coincides exactly with the foundation of the English Association, and is evidence of English's coming of age as a school subject with a literature content. It had made slow progress: over fifty years earlier, in 1853, the Committee of Council, from which Kay-Shuttleworth had resigned as chief executive only four years earlier, had granted £100 allowances for one, two or three years to resident lecturers in training colleges who had above average results in one or two specified subjects, one of which was English Literature (Dent 1975, p. 23). In a practical age, and in a government education department that had been led and was still influenced by an industrious, brilliant bureaucrat, English Literature was being found a central place for practical reasons. Charlotte Brontë, who had met Kay-Shuttleworth when he visited Howarth between 1851 and 1854, the period of his breakdown, gave this verdict in a letter to Mrs Gaskell:

> Nine points out of ten in him are utilitarian – the tenth is artistic. This tithe of his nature seems to me at war with the rest – it is just enough to incline him restlessly towards the artist class, and far too little to make him one of them. The consequent inability to *do* things which he *admires*, embitters him, I think – it makes him doubt perfections and dwell on thoughts.
>
> Smith 1923

To conclude this brief case study of the discourses surrounding one elementary school teacher with a particular interest in English it is worth mentioning the specialist journals available to Lawrence, in particular *The Teacher* and *The Schoolmaster*. We know that Lawrence read the former because he sent the paper a letter: the editors published this letter, including a photograph of an extremely young-looking Lawrence, on 25 March 1905. In it Lawrence heaps praise on the publication, saying that it is the greatest help to any student in the profession. He reveals that for his English teaching he used Evan Daniel, and the English lesson guides provided by *The Teacher* itself.

The Teacher provided much material for the pupil-teacher, serving as a kind of correspondence course. This is an example of the preparation for one of the authors in the English part of the exam:

> George Eliot: *The Mill on the Floss*
> We propose to spend eight weeks in the reading of this novel . . . There will be little to explain. The novel is written in a clear, lucid style, with no complex plot, and is a splendid example of the way a story should be told.
>
> *The Teacher*, 5 January 1907

Questions on English Literature, for second-year students, eventually followed:

> 1. What were the chief traits in the character of Maggie Tulliver? What incidents in her life best illustrated them?
> 2. Tell the story of Maggie Tulliver's escape with the gypsies.
>
> *The Teacher*, 19 January 1907

The same issue carried the latest in a series of articles on schools ('The Secondary Schools X'). In an interview with the Headmaster of the Henry Smith School, Hartlepool, this exchange takes place:

And do you, personally, find time for teaching any particular subjects? Yes; Latin and English – the former principally.

There is much evidence that grammar teaching was the staple diet for older elementary school pupils, with, for example the following advice under the heading 'Notes of a lesson on Relative, Interrogative and Reflexive Pronouns':

Heads	*Examples*	*Method of Treatment*
Function of a relative pronoun	1a This is a beautiful house. My brother lives in it.	Write sentence 1a on the blackboard. Ask how many statements there are. Write
	1b This house in *which* my brother lives is a beautiful house.	sentence 1b on the blackboard. Show how the two statements may be connected etc. . . .

The Teacher, 4 January 1908.

There are advertisements for books with titles such as the *Principles and Practice of Punctuation, How to Read English Literature* and, in the Professor Meiklejohn series, to which Lawrence also refers in his letter, *The Art of Writing English*. In a column entitled 'The Principles of Education: Reading' there is what one might expect – an emphasis on silent reading, composition and the study of the lives of poets. But elsewhere there are hints that education may be moving in another direction. On 29 February 1908 the paper included an article by Jos. A. White with the title 'How to Interest Children in English Literature'. White praises the advances made in the teaching of reading, the fruits, he argues, of thirty years of primary teaching. The mechanical difficulties posed by reading now being largely overcome 'by the poorest class of children at age 12 or 13, and by the child of a better intellect at the age of 10 or 11' attention can now be turned to ways of interesting children in literature. Do not, he warns, make the study of 'The Lady of the Lake', last for a whole year. Instead, introduce twelve books a year, with scenes from *The Merchant of Venice, Robinson Crusoe,* and *Westward Ho!*. In a continuation of the article on 7 March White recommends encouraging interest by including biographical material. So if Coleridge is to be studied, include the date of birth and give facts about the life to provide a context. This is not exactly child-centred learning, but it reflects a shift in that direction.

There is much less evidence of this practical, pedagogical advice in a parallel paper, *The Schoolmaster*, which was then the organ of the NUT. Despite the name there seems much more awareness of women teachers as a group, and in 1907 the paper includes information about suffragette activities, for example. There is a wider political awareness, with columns discussing the developments in Parliament, and many pages devoted to the work of NUT committees. There are many advertisements, for both secondary and elementary posts and for anthologies containing canonical extracts. There is a much greater sense of teaching moving forward as a profession, building on the legacy of thirty years of state education.

Shaping the English specialist 1900–2000

The professionalisation and bureaucratisation of education went hand in hand in the nineteenth century, as Hunter's *Rethinking the School* (Hunter 1994) has shown. At the end of the century, when the Cross Commission discussed the possibility of setting up Day Training Colleges, anxieties were expressed about the moral risks in training teachers outside the 'controlling atmosphere of a residential environment' (Taylor, W. in Thompson (ed.) 1990, p. 230). Nevertheless, the decision to allow universities to do so, enacted in law in 1890, had the effect of giving education academic status to education. As we have seen in the case University College, Nottingham, Education departments – for such they were, rather than teacher-training colleges – could appoint Professors of Education.

The new Day Training Colleges initially trained both elementary and secondary teachers together, but it was not long before a separation occurred which has proved unhelpful to teacher education in England throughout the twentieth century. The Headmaster's Conference of 1897 had agreed on the model for secondary subject specialist teachers: three years leading to a degree, followed by a one-year professional course, a model which has existed until this day. In 1903, one year after the influential Education Act which had set up a Board of Education, the Board issued *Regulations for the Instruction and Teaching of Pupil Teachers and Students in Training Colleges*, which, as we have seen, concentrated the minds of Education Committees throughout the land.

These regulations called for more training and less teaching, and marked the beginning of the end for the pupil-teacher system, though it lingered on in rural areas right up until the start of the Second World War. The need for a qualified profession is indicated by the ratios quoted by Dent: 'In 1900 there was only one Certificated teacher to 75 pupils, only one trained teacher to 128' (Dent 1977, p. 51). In 1906 the King's Scholarship was abolished, and replaced by a bursary scheme which allowed access to teacher training following the successful completion of a two part examination. This had an effect on the poorer working class, who could not do without the income their sons or daughters could have been bringing in between the ages of thirteen and seventeen.

Those who did go on to undertake the two-year training course were expected to commit themselves to a long day. As the timetable for 1910–11 shows, the men at the British and Foreign Society college at Borough Road started sessions at 7.10 in the morning and finished at 9 pm. English featured as a subject on most days, though it was one of several options which also included Maths, German, French or Drawing. Certificate English classes often took place in the evenings, between 6 and 7 or between 8 and 9 pm. In 1880 the equivalent timetable includes Grammar, Reading and Recitation, Composition and Penmanship – but no reference to English as a term.

Women were trained separately at the Stockwell site, and teaching was predominantly a female profession. In London this was as true of secondary as it was of elementary education, for the majority of those training to be secondary teachers were female: 'It is hardly too strong a claim that the idea of a profession of secondary teaching was established by women' (Bryant 1986). The First World War further reduced the numbers of men going into teaching, though it had major impact on the numbers as a whole. Yet the war refocused the mind, and the 1918 Education Act which gave more power to local authorities, followed by the Hadow Report of 1926, which institution-alised the primary-secondary stages, reconceptualised education, so that the 1920s saw a shift in focus from subject-centred to child-centred teaching, and an increasing emphasis on the practical. English benefited from the increasing belief in the 'practical' effect of immersion in a national literature, which the Newbolt Report celebrated in 1921.

The Board of Education generally supported the professionalisation of teaching, and the 1929 proposal to raise the school leaving age from 14 to 15 led to a sudden demand for more teachers which was met, even though the proposal itself was not implemented until after the Second World War. The 1939–45 war once again had a damaging effect on the recruitment of teachers, but once again it took a war to concentrate thinking and to embrace a willingness to accept change. The McNair Report of 1944 addressed a number of reforms which determined the structure of education in England during the subsequent fifty years. These included the raising of the school leaving age, reduction in the size of classes, the need for nursery education, and the grouping of all post-primary education under the umbrella 'Secondary'. Its brief had been to explore 'the present source of supply and the methods of recruitment and training of teachers and youth leaders'. In so doing McNair recognised one category of Qualified Teacher, and proposed a basic salary scale.

McNair, together with the 1944 Education Act itself, caught the mood for reform and the post-1945 years saw a massive expansion in teacher numbers with the Emergency Scheme – a one-year course for men and women who had served in HM forces – running alongside the standard two-year courses offered in existing and many newly created teacher-training colleges. The Emergency Scheme served the need of supplying 35,000 teachers, much needed when the school leaving age was raised to fifteen in 1947, and was so successful in recruiting men that the shortfall was, unexpectedly, in women teachers. The Scheme had a short life, the last Emergency Scheme college closing in 1951, the same year in which GCE O levels were introduced, and the 1911 Pledge to teach for a certain number of years was abolished. In 1960 the two-year training course was raised to three years and the 1960s saw a massive expansion in teacher training, and with the introduction of the four-year Bachelor of Education in 1964 the first move towards a graduate profession.

In 1972 the Government published its response to the James Report which had appeared earlier in that year. The James Report was a *Report of a Committee of Enquiry into Teacher Education and Training* and had an interesting history. It owed its origins to anxieties about the standards of reading in schools (Maclure 1973, p. 354) and the concerns about progressive teaching methods that had been raised by the Black Papers in 1969 and 1970. One outcome of all this concern was the formation of the National Council for Educational Standards.

In a White Paper *Education: a Framework for Expansion* the Government outlined what was to become the future for teacher-training colleges, now more normally known as colleges of education. Basically they were offered one of three options: be absorbed by a nearby university or polytechnic, strive to become specialist higher education centres concentrating on the relationship between the arts and the sciences and their application in teaching and other professions, or close. Some were forced to close, others became Schools of Education in nearby higher education institutions, whilst some took on the new role. Dent ends his study of teacher training (published in 1976) with the ominous remark that thus ended what had been a system of teacher education and training that had endured for two centuries, and that 'it had deliberately been destroyed'.

Yet twelve years later, at the time of the publication of the Kingman Report on English language teaching, *The Times Educational Supplement* could report that '[f]ar ranging recommendations in the Bullock Report of 1975 to reform teacher-training courses have largely been ignored, Sir John Kingman said at the launch of his Committee's report' (*TES*, 6 May 1988). Ten years have passed since then, and it is certainly the case that teacher training now takes place in institutions which have lost their former independence, and that Dent's exaggerated reading of events twenty-five years ago has subsequently been vindicated. The controlling factor is not the university, not the system of assessment, but the system of accreditation laid down by the Teacher Training Agency. In its 10/97 document the Labour Government specified exactly what has to be taught, and there is so much that primary initial teacher education is required to deliver, not least the very large periods students are now required to spend in schools, that many institutions have been forced to reduce the amount of time English specialists spend on their main subject at their own level, whilst some have abolished this altogether. At the beginning of the twenty-first century in England it is the politicians who are shaping the primary and secondary school specialist through a combination of underfunding and government directives. According to Foucault, the control of the subject becomes more discrete and more subtle as societies evolve, and we have argued that it is through English that some of that subject formation has been realised. It is ironical that in England we have moved away from that subtlety to a more direct form of shaping, which appeals not to the individual's need to recruit students to a liberatory vision, but which treats the individual specialist as a police officer, employed to ensure that the law is carried out.

Gender, class and education in the nineteenth and twentieth centuries

It is hard to credit that women at Cambridge were not awarded degrees until 1948. In English, as in other subjects, they followed the same courses as men, they were often taught by the same tutors, and they sat the same exams but at the end their reward was a certificate and not a degree. Sexual discrimination, the nineteenth-century legacy of attitudes to women, meant that in many universities women students were not allowed to join student unions, and women lecturers were not allowed to use the senior common room. The first woman professor outside a teacher-training department was made a Professor of English Language and not Literature.

English teaching in England has developed in an educational environment shaped by attitudes to class and gender. These in turn have determined the construction of the English teacher. We have seen how pupil teachers were recruited from the working class and how the majority were young women. This process has been described (Miller 1992; McDermid 1995) as the feminisation of schooling and education. Jane McDermid makes the distinction between the experience of England and Scotland: in Scotland in the mid nineteenth-century parish schools were run by men as a university education was required. It was the introduction of the pupil-teacher system, imposed on Scotland, that changed the ratio and brought it into line with England. McDermid also points to the different levels of literacy in the two countries: a comparison of English and Scottish marriage registers for 1855 shows that in Scotland 88.6 per cent of the new husbands and 77.2 per cent of the new wives signed their names, while the corresponding figures in England were 70.5 per cent and 58.8 per cent.

So elementary school teachers in England were likely to be working-class women, until the spread of teacher-training colleges began to attract lower-middle-class women. Upper-middle-class women avoided teaching in schools altogether until the early twentieth century.

When women began to enter universities in the second half of the nineteenth century there was an inevitable clash of cultures, because universities had been constructed as largely male environments. Although Oxford and Cambridge tried to exclude women, from the late 1860s women were allowed into the University of London for separate lectures in English Literature. In 1878 London University admitted women to all its degrees on equal terms and the first female graduates received their degrees in 1888 (Sutherland 1990). There was unease about the effect of introducing women into higher education, even in the teacher-training colleges. Chaperoning was required at all higher education institutions in London and at Oxford and Cambridge until the end of the First World War. And attempts at integration met with resistance, sometimes from the women. In 1889 'the newly appointed Principal at Homerton, the Congregation Training College for Teachers, found himself at the head of a dual institution, one for men and one for women' (Sutherland 1990, p. 38). Since the elementary schools they were going into were mixed, the Principal tried to mix the classes, and started a joint literary society. The Literary Society had to be discontinued, however, when the women objected on the grounds that they could not speak freely in front of the men.

As noted earlier, English as a specialist subject attracted women, but no sooner had it won a place in higher education than it transformed itself. The new subject in universities was keen to demonstrate its seriousness, and mindful of its low status compared with established subjects such as theology decided to embrace the texts of modernism and carve out for itself the role of decoder of difficult texts (Kaplan and Simpson 1996). This process parallels the embracing of critical theory in English Departments in universities in the last quarter of the twentieth century, and this raises the question as to whether women who form the majority of undergraduates majoring in English in England are being required to submit to masculine discourses, or whether such a question is itself a product of essentialist rather than performative notions of gender.

The performative argument in relation to the education of girls in the first half of the twentieth century is one which informs Felicity Hunt's study of schooling for girls between 1902 and 1904 (Hunt 1991). Through a study of Board of Education circulars, contemporary books on education and psychology, and official statements about the curriculum shows how perceptions of gender constructed in the nineteenth century continued to ensure that in the twentieth century the aims of education for girls were not the same as they were for boys. In her conclusion Hunt makes clear the vital shaping influence of school expectations as expressed through curricula and examinations:

> The question I raised was whether the aims of education during this period could be assumed to be the same for girls as for boys. The evidence is that they cannot. They have been shown to be different and the differences had a profound effect on how education was promulgated for girls. The girls' perception of their education is of course another matter, not dealt with in this study, but at a fundamental level this is not an issue. It is not an issue because of the crucial role which education plays in shaping children's perceptions of themselves and their capacities and the options open to them.
>
> Hunt 1991, p. 142

It is not a question which has gone away. At the beginning of the twenty-first century, it is asked in a slightly different way, because now the question is not boys outperforming girls because there are higher expectations of boys, but girls outperforming boys in English because boys are often reluctant readers. That has led to an understandable concern with the literacy performance of boys, but it should not obscure the interesting observation of researchers such as Elaine Millard (1997) and commentators such as Dianne Tibbitts, that a new Handmaid's Tale scenario is developing, governed by information technology:

> Boys and communications technology are happy partners. Through these new technologies a new literacy will develop, simply through usage, to become the literacy of the new power brokers. If we continue with our narrow, narrative-based English curriculum through which girls achieve highly and boys are disenfranchised, girls and the women they become will simply be left behind.
>
> Tibbits 1998, p. 46

Quiet work, book work and group work: expectations in the classroom

Pictures illustrating the early nineteenth-century monitorial schoolroom show enormously long benches and seats, and the teacher and the monitors directing children, who appear to be toiling away in silence, all working at the same task. Photographs of early twentieth-century classrooms show children sitting at desks in rows, sometimes working in silence, sometimes responding to the teacher. Effectiveness was often measured by the ability to keep order, and this favoured the more repetitive and teacher-centred activities: the whole class writing the same composition (on 'The Rabbit' for example), reading the same book, and doing the same dictation or spelling test.

In contrast the end-of-century English classroom is likely to be a busy, animated place, with plenty of opportunities given for discussion in groups, for interaction with the teacher, for some whole class and some individual work, for choice and the encouragement of autonomy. The study of the media – newspapers, advertisements, television programmes, films gives the outside world a presence in the classroom, and through the use of information technology students can have seemingly direct contact with that outside world. Textbooks, where they are used, more often than not provide a bank of photocopiable resources. Such books, and the catalogues distributed by NATE, including the English and Media Centre publications, provide a stimulating picture of the diverse range of activities and topics which the English and Media teacher may choose to explore. From *The Soap Pack* to *Picture Power: The CD Rom* the English and Media Centre provide publications which illustrate how English teachers can draw on the knowledge and experience that form the lives of the majority of students in England at the beginning of the twenty-first century. So this will encourage the English graduate to move beyond literature, especially a literature that is likely to be a lot less familiar to the student than it is to the student teacher.

Text books

The way that education publishers present and publicise their books serves as a barometer to the preoccupations and expectations of the period. At the beginning of the 1990s English course books such as *Language Incorporated* (published by Stanley Thornes 1991) for Key Stage 3 and *Do You Read Me?* (published by Blackwell Education in 1990) for GCSE/Key Stage 4 begin with a detailed table showing how each section of the book covered specific elements of the National Curriculum Attainment Targets of Speaking and Listening, Reading and Writing. More recently there has been a shift to acknowledge other requirements. The revised 1998 version of *Touchstones* (published by Hodder and Stoughton) retains a thematic section which links it with the tradition started by *Reflections* in the 1960s, but the promotional material says that one of its key features is 'Full coverage of pre-20th century and contemporary poetry required for Key Stage 3 or GCSE'. The advertising for the 1998 Hodder English 4 Literature Study Books series reproduces the dominant rhetoric and discourse in a more extensive manner. Key features of this series are identified by the publishers as follows:

- In the course book, comparisons of literary and non-literary texts encourage in-depth study of a variety of genres
- Integrated language and literature study ensures pupils develop knowledge, understanding and skills in context
- Rigorous language works is progressive and fully integrated into each area of study
- A wealth of quality literary and non-literary texts include contemporary and pre-twentieth century poetry, fiction, drama and media
- Differentiated activities enable students of all abilities to reach their full potential
- Progression is built into each unity and across the course as a whole so that students develop, revisit and consolidate key skills
- Provides guidance on effective revision and gives opportunities to practise exam techniques

Hodder and Stoughton brochure, 1998

This reveals a subtle and complex awareness of audience and readers: on the one hand, the bullet points are reassuring about the way it is in line with current requirements (it covers literary and non-literary texts, it provides 'rigour', 'quality' 'progression' and 'opportunities to practise exam techniques') while on the other it shows that it is sensitive to the larger, more philosophical beliefs that inform English (the integration of language and literature, the teaching of skills in context, differentiated activities, references to drama and media). It has to be said, however, that this particular text is much more weighted in favour of rigour (in-depth study, develop, revisit and consolidate key skills, effective revision) than it is of the imaginative, a term which does not get a mention at all.

But the beginning teacher is influenced by the culture of the school, and the specific classroom practices that she or he observes (and remembers) perhaps more than anything else. So memories of A level literature lessons, and the wish to get students excited about books, is likely to give poetry, short story and drama lessons a central place, quite apart from the fact that they are a requirement of the curriculum. And the publishers provide plenty of books here, too: the English and Media Centre catalogue for 1998 contained guides to *Gulliver's Travels*, *Six Poems by Tony Harrison*, and class-room materials on *Romeo and Juliet*, *Macbeth* and *Hamlet*.

This takes us back to what is by now a very familiar, fundamental question: why is the study of literature thought to be a valuable practice? When the Bullock Report (DES 1975) addressed this question twenty-five years ago, it summarised both the faith in, and the questioning of, this belief:

> 9.1 This part of the Report would not be complete if it did not end with a discussion of literature, which to many teachers is the most rewarding form of the child's encounter with language. In the main, opinions converge upon the value of literature, if they take separate ways on the treatment it should receive in school. Much has been claimed for it: that it helps to shape the powerful instrument of empathy, a medium through which the child can acquire its values. Writing in 1917, Nowell Smith (Smith 1917) saw its purpose as 'the formation of a personality fitter for a civilised life'. The Newsom Report (HMSO 1963) some fifty years later, said that ' all pupils, including those of very limited attainments, need the civilising experience of contact with great literature, and can respond to its universality'. These are spirited credos, only two of many, and they represent a faith that English teaching needs. They have not, of course, gone unchallenged. In recent years it has been questioned whether literature does make the reader a better and more sensitive human being. What was a matter of self-evident truth in the eighteenth and nineteenth centuries is no longer exempt from question.
>
> DES 1975, p. 124

But even though that questioning was to snowball as the impact of critical theory seemed to make earlier beliefs about the value of literature look ever more quaint and ridiculous, the literature itself has endured in the classroom. Now, however, it is not approached in different ways, it is used for a multiplicity of purposes. Model lessons recommended in PGCE courses, and described in the various supplements of *The Times Educational Supplement*, are another shaping factor in the formation of the specialist. A recent example is an article in NATE News (Bunyan, Catran and Feist, 1998) describing the way in which a poem can be the source of activities exploring a 'whole English' approach. Tony Harrison's poem 'Bookends' is presented unseen and a planning group 'set to work structuring drama approaches to address the narrative, the language and the issues of the poem'. Participants were encouraged to interpret the poem as actions or images, and were arranged into a 'physical manifestation of the "bookend" characters referred to in the poem', while lines of the poem were read. There was mimed action, narration and overheard conversations to be experimented with. Choral reading provided opportunities for reflecting on knowledge about language. There was hot seating and volunteers stepped into role. Another approach favoured pair and group discussion about the title, the dialect and what was happening in the poem.

This model of the changing English classroom is influential in that it offers teachers strategies which encourage an active approach, and the NATE article states clearly that it favours this approach because it is 'anxious about the narrow and functional preoccupations demanded by the political motivation of the National English Curriculum, and, more recently, of the focus upon 'literacy' (Bunyan, Catron and Feist 1998: 6). But the student teacher who then carries these ideas into the classroom, may not be prepared for the extent to which the English classroom and the resources that are made available are driven by the precise nature of the assessment tests and the national curriculum. Assessment at ages 14 and 16 shapes the teacher as much as it does the student. The English Department is a much more rigorous, structured and record-keeping unit than it was in the past, and because these very elements are subject to close scrutiny during any inspections, schools and colleges have appointed Heads of English who are enthusiastic about these developments and who welcome what they identify as a more professional and clear set of groundrules. The system, which had become increasingly concealed, is now visible once more.

What are subject specialists meant to teach? Literacy and literary history

> Like other occupations – medicine,or carpentry, or music-making – education confronts its practitioners with immediate questions (what should be taught, how, and why?)
>
> Selleck 1994

If subject specialists had to listen only to the constituency of politicians and those members of the public who write to or for newspapers, the answer to the questions 'What should I teach?' would be readily and unequivocally answered. The English specialist has always been expected to ensure that his or her students are literate at the most basic and obvious of levels: 'what is English if not literacy?' the world at large has usually asked. Yet, as our earlier outline of history showed, the teaching of reading and writing existed long before any concept of English as a subject, and when that subject emerged in the second half of the nineteenth century it did so in the context of literary study.

That paradox is most obvious in primary schools, where until recently every teacher taught every subject and in the infant school the teacher, whatever her or his specialist subject had been at college, was preoccupied with teaching very young children how to read and write. In an age of specialisms the subject specialist in the primary school has a specialist role, but it is the role of advisor and expert, not of teacher. Unlike certain States in America, the English specialist in English primary schools will not go in to each class to take special reading and writing lessons.

Yet with the institutionalisation of the literacy hour, there will be such lessons, taught by the class teacher, who remains a generalist working supported by the advice offered by the language co-ordinator and the DfEE. There will be whole class sessions and group sessions and each will focus on a specific aspect of literacy. Literature – that is fiction and poetry – may be used as the agency for such lessons, but that is not always the case. Literature no longer sits at the centre in the debates about the best approach to primary language. In that sense there is a victory for the traditionalists, who never abandoned the belief in the teaching of discrete skills, whether these were phonics, spelling tests or handwriting lessons. All now have the official approval of government, and are prescribed. In 1998 the government announced that schools were now free to concentrate on literacy and numeracy as they would not be required to teach all the requirements of the National Curriculum in such subjects as history and geography. The emphasis on the so-called basics is traceable in remarks made by Labour's Education Secretary in 1968, Margaret Thatcher in 1977, Labour Prime Minister Callaghan in his 'back to basics' speech in 1977, the Tory Education Secretary Sir Keith Joseph in 1984, the Tory Education Secretary Kenneth Baker in 1987 and 1988 (even though he was the architect of the National Curriculum that ensured breadth to the point of overload, as far as primary teachers were concerned), the Tory Prime Minister John Major in 1993 and 1996, and the Labour Education Secretary in 1997. The cautious welcome given by teachers' unions and primary school headteachers suggests something amounting to a consensus uniting government, the inspection service and primary schoolteachers. Those arguing for a more complex model of learning seemed to have been marginalised by the weight of the traditional view. Traditionalists had seen off the challenge presented by the child-centred rhetoric that had shaped educational discourse in English, though it had never become the tradition in practice. Primary teachers had always marked spelling and punctuation, paid attention to standard English, and given lessons in formal letter writing even when creative writing was perceived to be a more exciting and liberating activity.

The consequence has been that in the drive to raise literacy standards the

Labour government elected in 1997 set schools ambitious literacy targets, introduced a Year of Reading, and building on advice set in train by the National Literacy Project and the Teacher Training Agency now has a National Literacy Strategy which among other things requires student-teachers to have a knowledge of the terminology and descriptions of basic linguistics, so that they are not only able to recognise the difference between effective and ineffective writing but are able to explain and describe those differences to pupils and teachers. Some research carried out by David Wray (Wray 1993) showed that student teachers had very limited grammatical knowledge, either at the beginning or at the end of the one-year course:

> In terms of beliefs student had moved towards a view that language is a process through which learning takes place rather than a set of skills to be learnt and practised and towards an understanding of the holistic nature of literacy learning. This philosophy of language and literacy learning naturally stress the uses rather than the structure of language.
>
> Wray 1993, p. 72

Having made primary teachers feel that they ought to have knowledge about the structure of language, particularly the grammatical structure, the document 10/97 now requires all teachers to have an awareness of structure and basic linguistic terminology, and for subject specialists to have this awareness at a more sophisticated level. This development is the natural corollary of the abandonment of the Language in the National Curriculum project, which was rejected precisely because it did not endorse the explicit teaching of grammar that politicians have always favoured. If primary student-teachers specialising in English cannot demonstrate that they have undertaken some kind of meta-language study which parallels the content of the National Curriculum for English at Key Stages 1 and 2, they will not achieve qualified teacher status. To say that this amounts to quite heavy pressure is an understatement.

The literacy hour itself, sixty minutes of dedicated time to be used in a very specific and structured way, is recommended to teachers for reasons that have a familiar ring to them:

- The Literacy Hour is intended to bring literacy teaching into focus in every classroom. This has a positive impact on the pace and focus of teaching and brings a constructive sense of urgency to much of the work
- The Literacy Hour creates consistent practices among classes in each school and between schools. This improves continuity and progression and makes for more effective management and monitoring of literacy throughout the school.

- The consistency of the Literacy Hour has already proved beneficial to pupils. The introduction of clear routines and expectations has a positive effect on attitudes and behaviour motivation.

DfEE 1998

The familiarity of the claims about effective monitoring and the 'positive effect on attitudes', claims that were made about literacy assessment and grammar teaching just over 100 years ago is not necessarily a sign that a particular cycle is being repeated, because the lessons of the past hundred years mean that the current Government strategy is far more sophisticated and flexible than that of its nineteenth-century predecessors.

Some still seem to wish it were not so. Melanie Phillips has long argued for a return to the 'systematic grammar teaching' as 'grammar is the code which enables pupils to unlock the mysteries of language and gain control over it' (*The Observer*, 10 May 1998). 'Why is the teaching of grammar still taboo?' she asks, and then supplies the answer: 'Because teachers don't understand it'. Publishers are leaping into this perceived breach, with Pearson publishing, for example, advertising *How English Works* as a 'pack intended to help pupils understand the grammar and punctuation of modern English'. Where governments lead, publishers follow: another Pearson publication is called *Whole Class Teaching*, and the blurb records: 'A recently published OFSTED commissioned report recommends that up to 60% of time should be devoted to whole class teaching. These publications for a comprehensive guide for primary schools'. In secondary schools, colleges, and universities there have been equally powerful challenges to the orthodoxies, and here the position is in complete reverse. The traditional practice established in secondary schools and universities from the beginning of the twentieth century onwards was the teaching of literature. An English teacher in either institution would be a specialist in the art of literary criticism. For this reason secondary specialists are often more reluctant than their primary colleagues to accept the need to move back to grammar. A week after the Melanie Phillips' grammar column, *The Observer* printed this response from a Head of English in a grammar school in West Sussex: 'It is possible to understand Shakespeare, for example, and to write excellent English, without understanding formal grammar. We are not teaching English as a foreign language' (*The Observer*, 17 May 1998). As was suggested earlier, the origins of English as literary criticism relate to the rivalry with science. In the nineteenth century a belief in a simple cause/effect equation that came from scientific positivism led to a belief in scientific objectivity. Although English defined itself in opposition to science, and claimed certain immeasurable transcendent qualities that an immersion in literature could bring forth in the child, at university level it envied the reputation for objectivity that science enjoyed. So it was (Patterson 1995) that literary criticism initially relied on history, which would assist it in the task of interpretation. History would provide facts to justify and control interpretation: we see this in totalising world views such as Saintsbury's *A Short History of English Literature* (1898), or the more specific *Elizabethan World View Picture* of Tillyard (1944). This was the old historicism – the belief that the identification of a unitary and unifying cultural *zeitgeist* would provide the key to unlocking literary meaning.

The reaction to this was predictable: why not seek to make the study of literature as precise and objective as the study of history? If this could be done, then English would cease to be reliant on the support of its older sister History. Russian Formalism, as practised by Roman Jakobson, sought to establish a science of literature, with texts becoming the objects of close study: thus close reading was born. It could be ahistorical because texts contained meanings that were universal and eternal. This remains a powerful belief among many English teachers, as our questionnaire showed. The belief in the humanising properties of literature, properties which made it distinct from other forms of writing, informed both Russian Formalism and the formalism of the American New Criticism. New Criticism, a by-product of the Southern Fugitive movement, combined with the critical practices recommended by Leavis, Empson, and Richards, shaped the way that literary texts were approached in schools and universities in England in the middle third of the twentieth century.

Patterson succinctly identifies the problem which led to the reaction to the reaction:

> [T]he essentialising of literature makes it impossible to understand literary production as itself a form of social practice, to understand it as itself part of both the cultural and material activities of its historical moment.
>
> Patterson 1995, p. 256

And that is precisely what the next generation of scholars decided it was. The demystification of literature was a strand in a wider attempt to demystify and deterritorialise culture itself, so that it is no coincidence that the questioning of the author occurs simultaneously with the questioning of authority in and around 1968, in England and in France. Literary historians became literary anthropologists: 'Far from being divorced from the world, literary production (is seen as) a form of social practice: texts do not merely reflect social reality, but create it' (Patterson 1995, p. 260). This reaction to the belief in the autonomy of the text was to be potentially disastrous for English as a discrete practice. For it involved questioning the idea of 'literature' as a distinct category of writing. For literature to be reabsorbed into contemporary discussions about wider cultural practices then its special status had to be questioned. The most obvious signs of this were the relocation of former English specialists to cultural studies and media studies department. The emphasis on representation entails a shift towards language, and most subject specialists have now encountered the body of critical theory which is more interested in asking the question 'how does this text work and how is it read?' than 'what does it mean?'.

But English has not played the 'Titanic' to the Iceberg of Critical Theory, and it has refused to sink. It began to list, and a number of the passengers and crew transferred to other vessels, but a significant number stayed on board, and the ship is still afloat. It is the iceberg that shows signs of melting. The radical and subversive certainties that accompanied the arrival of critical theory in English universities in the 1970s and 1980s are now themselves questioned: Deleuze and Guattari challenged Lacan, Eagleton questioned post-modernism, and Derrida's scholarship is queried by philosophy professors in the letters page of *The Times Literary Supplement*. The endless fracturing and turning inside out that this entailed has changed the subject for good, however and it will never revert to its former self-contained state. What happened is that old strategies and descriptions are revisited and reformulated, so that we have the New Historicism and the New Rhetoric.

The survival of English should not lead to complacency: it does not prove that those, like Nick Peim, who argued for the abolition of English were wrong. Rather it proves that theoretised appeals for changes in cultural practice are often forced to defer to material practices which serve some larger end. And English continues to serve some larger end. So it survives much as the Pope survived the occupation of Italy during the Second World War: it served the interests of the powers that could have had him removed to allow him his authority of his Church. This is the more bleaker of the Foucauldian conceptions

of discursive formations, which are seen as organised according to structures of dominance and subordination that replicate the structures of society as a whole and so allow for no external purchase that might make possible a reformation or even reversal of power relations. The individual is always already inscribed within a discourse that prescribes its own continuation, and his entrapment.

Patterson 1995, p. 261

But whilst this kind of rhetoric comprehensively extinguishes any claims that English may make to being subversive, there is a danger that it leads to a kind of defeatism and paralysis that is self-confirming. In England commentators as diverse as Charlotte Raven and Terry Eagleton ask us to observe the parallels in the belief in the supremacy of the market in techno-capitalism, and the belief in diversity in critical theory: both appear to privilege a belief in choice above a belief in change, which is why the latter may suit the former.

There is a strong argument that specialists need to revisit history and remind themselves when the concept of literature that informed the birth of Subject English had its roots. Patterson points out that Raymond Williams has shown that the crucial moment in the history of the concept 'literature' is the late eighteenth and early nineteenth centuries. For it was then that the concept, along with its legitimising philosophical parent, the idea of the aesthetic, establish itself as the site where a disinterested concern for formal beauty and emotional authenticity could be protected from the relentless commodifications of consumer capitalism.

Patterson 1995, p. 258

With hindsight specialists may now see this as the Romantic myth, for literature could be commodified as much as anything else. But it would be wrong to underestimate the power of belief, the belief in the power of imaginative writing to provide a bridge to some other world, even if Derrida, Hayden White and Thomas Kuhn have encouraged us to accept that 'all forms of writing [are] as distant from the real world, and as linguistically embedded, as literature had been thought to be' (Patterson 1995, p. 257). For in the discussion so far we have neglected to remind ourselves of the enormous impact that the creative writing movement had, and continues to have, on English lessons in primary and secondary schools in England. Encouraging children to write imaginatively may not enable them to escape their environment, it may not even do much to change that environment, but in tapping into something they know well and validating it on the curriculum, English teachers have believed that they are doing something to ensure that students are treated as stakeholders in that environment.

Such a belief is itself traditionalist, in the sense that the belief in the value of creative writing goes back at least forty years. It is a belief that has been challenged by critical theory, for the reasons outlined above, and by the assessment patterns at GCSE and A Level which have radically reduced the coursework opportunities for creative writing. In universities it survives but often in discrete modules or in part-time masters' courses. Yet, like English itself, it has survived, not simply because English teachers have fought for it, but because there is something about the practice that meets a demand that industry and commerce makes of its citizens. It does seem that for quite materialist reasons we need people – teachers and students alike – who can ask questions and think new thoughts. This, in essence, is the argument against the narrowing of the curriculum and the prescription of the syllabus that has been the trend in England from 1990 onwards. In 1905 it was the official view:

The only uniformity of practice that the Board of Education desires to see in the teaching of Public Elementary Schools is that each teacher shall think for himself, and work out for himself such methods of teaching as may use his powers to the best advantage and be best suited to particular needs and conditions of the school.

Maclure 1973

In England 100 years later there is an apparent consensus that teachers should not enjoy that freedom, and that students should concentrate on a specific range of basic skills. The dissenting view is in a minority, and is most persuasively expressed by those who argue that shifts in technology can result in a corresponding shift in the definitions and perceptions of what we mean by literacy. Here Myron Tuman, Professor of English at the University of Alabama and editor of *Literacy Online* (1992) is discussing the move away from a simple, technical and mechanical model of literacy that took place during the twentieth century:

> What can be readily overlooked in this educational reform is the promul-
> gation of a new model of literacy, one that contained conceptions of
> both reading and writing that, while appearing commonsensical today,
> were truly revolutionary a hundred years ago. In pre-industrial America
> (and in most of the pre-industrial world even today) reading was defined
> largely in terms of the ability to recite socially important (often religious
> or nationalist) texts; and writing, when it was taught at all, was defined in
> terms of the ability to transcribe texts (hence the emphasis on penman-
> ship and spelling). It it only with the great tide of industrialism that
> the now-pervasive definitions of reading and writing as the abilities to
> comprehend and to create new material were established. At the heart of
> this new model is the ability of readers to arrive at – and writer, in turn
> to express – a new understanding based solely on the silent, solitary
> contemplation of written language. Is it any wonder that educators
> motivated by this new model of literacy have long placed such emphasis
> on process? It makes little sense to focus on a fixed product when what is
> valued most is the insight contained in the text that has yet to be read or
> yet to be written.
>
> Tuman 1992, p. 5

To what extent does this assumption that 'process' is the dominant model of literacy agree with the model that informs the Teacher Training Agency inspired document issued in England in 1998?

Towards a national curriculum for teacher education: what subject specialists must know

The National Curriculum for trainee teachers – Circular 4/98 – sets out all the things that primary and secondary education students must cover in their teacher-training courses. The emphasis throughout is on the 'core' subjects of English, Maths and Science and on the requirements that courses and institutions must supply. The Circular requires primary trainees whose main subject is English to have a knowledge of the content of the National Curriculum for English to at least Advanced Level Standard. That may sound straightforward, or laughably simple, but since the National Curriculum for English includes very specific references to the kind of knowledge about language that children are to be taught at sentence, word and text level, the Department for Education has spelt out how all student teachers must have a knowledge of such terms as morphemes and phonemes, then this means that teacher-training institutions are now busy teaching grammar according to a syllabus that would not have been unfamiliar to the Borough Road College of 1880. A small sample of student teachers interviewed at the University of Plymouth in 1998 was convinced that this was in their best interest, saying that grammar was something they had not learned about at school and so it was good that they were learning about it now. So Core English *does* have a content once more: it is not just about method.

As for secondary English, the document contains substantial sections with a linguistics and grammar emphasis, with the requirement that trainees must be taught how to teach spelling, punctuation, grammar, language 'explicitly' and effective strategies for improving skills in the standards of literacy. This is a language and skills-based model, and although there are significant traces of each and every one of the developments in English teaching since 1900 – responding to literature, acknowledgement of the place of drama, media study and information technology in English – the emphasis of the rhetoric is in the direction of Standard English, the idea of a literary tradition, and the development, assessment and monitoring of competencies in pupils. Specialists in Schools of Education appear to have accepted the shift towards the greater self-awareness of writing that the imaginative teaching of grammar can foster, and a PGCE Co-ordinator in the South of England said that there was little in the document that she was not covering already, with the exception of miscue analysis and familiarity with the range of diagnostic tests available on the market. Her criticism was more to do with strategy and effects: the need to do the audit of subject knowledge in such a way that student-teachers were absolutely aware of what they had covered, so that in any inspection they would not say ' we haven't done that' when they had. Everything would have to be geared to inspection: and in that process something is lost.

For two co-ordinators in London, there is a less practical, but equally important omission. Writing of the draft, which was very little altered when it appeared in its final version, Ros Moger and Anne Turvey, note that 'What is absent from this lengthy document is any guiding principle about the nature of teaching and learning and the nature of English at this end of the twentieth century' (Moger and Turvey, 1998). They find the very metaphor of the 'tool box' of skills inadequate to describe process involved in the complex management of the average English lesson. Teaching is not a craft: 'training teachers is not a matter of giving them a good selection of tools and sending them off to get on with their trade'. Their view of the complex processes involved in becoming a teacher is clearly shared by those whose voices we have heard, and the voice we shall hear below.

From probation to induction via the PGCE

The probationary year for teachers was abolished in 1992 by the Conservative Government, but following the victory of the Labour Party in the 1997 General Election the concept was revived, and renamed the 'Induction Year'. Under the draft proposals from September 1999 newly qualified teachers will be entitled to work with the best schools in the area, through either visits or seminars, work with a mentor who will observe and be observed, attend appropriate training courses, join network groups of newly qualified teachers in the area, and work with the special needs co-ordinator and go on visits to special schools.

The proposals envisage duties as well – involving target setting, assessment and monitoring pupil progress and taking responsibility for their own future professional development. A number of these responsibilities relate very specifically to classroom management, with the requirement that good behaviour is secured 'through a regime of rules and discipline' and that a 'sense of social responsibility' is fostered among pupils (DfEE 1998b). Although during the Induction years teachers will only teach 90 per cent of the average contact time of their colleagues, the penalty for failure at the end of the Induction year is the requirement that they will have to train all over again. The Headteacher will ultimately make the decision about whether the new teacher has met the standards and can be recommended for Qualified Teacher Status.

For English specialists in schools the transfer from student status to teacher status is one of the greatest and most rapid transformations in thinking and practice that they will make in their lives. A recent study (Calderhead and Sharrock 1998) attempted to trace the changes in teacher thinking and action through a series of case studies of beginning teachers taking on the mantle of teacher. Not surprisingly, the writers found 'that student learning was frequently content and person specific, so general conclusion could not be drawn' and 'few clear answers to key questions about the education and training of beginning teachers' were provided by the study. (Thornton 1998). Yet the evidence did seem to confirm that students came into teaching with views about equality, social justice and individual needs already in place, and that they were not indoctrinated by their tutors, as is often alleged.

Their anxieties are not necessarily subject specific, but are those shared by the majority of student teachers: classroom control and time management. In a subject which is so person-centred, however, these fears are perhaps magnified in English teachers. This is Sahail Ashraf, reflecting on her PGCE course as it comes to an end:

> Learning to teach is just like riding a bike. A teacher told me this a few weeks before I started a Postgraduate Certificate of Education in September at the Institute of Education in London. I tend to learn quickly, so why should this be any different?

I am learning to teach in a large Essex comprehensive and my specialist subject is secondary English.

It was all rather overwhelming at first and I could not see myself standing up before real children. Control of the class was everyone's concern in those early days. Nearly every BT (Beginning Teacher) I spoke to then admitted this worried them. Would the pupils listen to me?

I knew I could raise my voice above the noise but after a few lessons it dawned on me that this was not the key skill. Once you have the class's attention, you must have something to say that will hold it.

This cured me of the 'Robin Williams Syndrome' (as in the film *Dead Poet's Society*), whereby the sufferer believes a teacher only has to talk and they are instantly charismatic and effective.

Time management is another potential problem which the PGCE department head here at the Institute of Education introduced in the very first lecture.

There are hundreds of books, tapes and articles on it but our leader dismissed all that. He looked at us waiting for divine guidance and said just four words which are all the beginning teacher needs to combat stress and fatigue. Honestly. They were: 'Get plenty of sleep'.

A teacher qualifies on a set of 'competencies' or key skills. Put simply, to become a teacher now you must prove you can 'do' what the DfEE believes a competent teacher is able to do. These areas of competence (which subdivide even further) are: subject knowledge and understanding, planning teaching and class management; monitoring and assessment, plus further professional requirements.

The biggest obstacle I (and a lot of other BTs I talked to) had to overcome was planning lessons. During the first term of practice you are supposed to master this skill.

Thankfully for me it has finally clicked. I can do it but I still spend hours planning lessons, ensuring every minute of a lesson (and it is every minute) is conducive to learning in some way.

Planning is about having clear aims and objectives, the seemingly simple act of matching your activity in class to the requirements of the national curriculum. In other words, it is about having a focus to your lessons. It is a valuable skill of course and one on which I feel we should have spent a lot more time.

The one-year PGCE course is almost like a balancing act of theory and practice. Sometimes the theory side is underweight and we lose out on key skills we need to read and think about rather than fall into clumsily in the classroom. Teaching is hard work, this I have learnt. But what is fascinating is that you make lots of transitions; you find that you wake up one morning, go to school and cope with something you could not last week.

There are times when your pupils pleasantly surprise you. For instance, one of my Year 9 pupils came up to me after a class recently asking if there were any good books that I could recommend him. I found myself smiling uncontrollably, it felt like my enthusiasm for literature had affected a pupil.

Mini-victories make the course worthwhile. This is why I want to be a teacher. I'm nowhere near the level of competence I want to be but I know it will come and eventually it will be just like riding a bike.

Ashraf 1998

As an example of another voice there is much to note here. The emphasis on enthusiasm, the unconcealed delight in seeming to influence a student in a positive way, the rejection of the charismatic model in favour of the competent, thoroughly prepared professional. The goal is not only to manage the class successfully but to match activities to the requirements of the national curriculum and to ensure that learning is taking place all the time. These ambitions are simultaneously law-abiding (the delivery of the national curriculum) and challenging (what are the students learning now?). The metaphor used at the beginning and the end is revealing of the new realism. It is not the rhetoric of subversion, nor of cultural enrichment of students, nor that of taking them into the imagined worlds of writers. It expresses the goal of achieving a level of expertise in which teaching becomes 'just like riding a bike'. In the copies of *The Teacher* that D. H. Lawrence read when he was a beginning teacher there were advertisements for bicycles, aimed at teachers, showing a man in a gown and mortarboard standing next to the bicycle which was presumably his means of getting to work. In current education papers, Apple Computers carry an advertisement for the Apple Education alliance, showing a gowned figure, who could be meant to represent a teacher or a student, or both, riding a bicycle with a computer lodged behind the saddle. The tropes of language, the rhetoric of education and the material world sometimes intersect in interesting and revealing ways.

What is English for?

This was posed as a general question in chapter 1, and in an attempt to round off these three chapters asking questions of English in England it is time to pose it again – but this time in the specific context of formation of the teacher in the 1990s. It is a question beloved of English specialists in higher education: a recent day conference organised jointly by the English Association and the Centre for English Studies at the University of London was called 'What English should we teach?: the undergraduate curriculum and the future'. As a response to the comprehensive CCUE Report 'The English Curriculum: Diversity and Standards' the conference asked whether Subject English should foster interdisciplinarity, and whether it would continue to recruit strongly over the next twenty years. Writing in *The Times Higher Education Supplement*, Judy Simons, the Chair of the Council for College and University English, summarised the findings of the survey, placing particular emphasis on the way that university English did not want to see the subject constrained in the way that it had been in schools:

> [T]he CCUE survey overwhelmingly shows that university teachers of English in the UK are opposed to the idea of a national curriculum, to any external body determining what a university syllabus should contain . . . While academics insist on autonomy and academic freedom, they are also fighting for the fact that an English degree programme cannot be reduced to a series of set books. Rather, the literary syllabus is a stimulus that enables students to explore further, to inculcate a sense of enquiry and imaginative excitement that is uncontainable in any official description of a course module . . . It remains vital that we continue to remind ourselves and our students that the 'value' of literature extends way beyond mere functionalism to release an awareness of the expressive resources of language and the intellectual flexibility that is its natural accompaniment.
>
> Simons 1998

Those who teach or have taught in schools, if they have time to reflect, often endorse the assumptions contained in this paragraph, even though the functionalist model seems to be the one which seems determined to shape their practice. When asked 'What is English for' the responses may reflect a view of English which is governed more by questions of pedagogy than by questions of curriculum, the latter now being more and more prescribed. This is Kathy Smith, articulating a view which reveals the models of teaching that impinge on the contemporary trainee specialists intending to teach in schools:

> In my view, there are at least two strands. One is to do with self-expression and self-development and to do with identity. The relationship between identity and language is incredibly complex, and constantly changing. The second, in terms of schooling, is to do with giving students the tools with which to access life, to access the community, to access culture. So the relationship between the two is not a simple one: we offer the tools to access culture and identity, and also offer selective access to the language and literature of a culture. That's why there are professional English teachers; that's why you shouldn't send someone into a classroom with a checklist of what to teach.

An observer from Australia might be surprised by the passion of these defences of the imagination, of creativity, of self-expression. Are these not the battles that were being fought thirty, forty, fifty years ago, have we not moved on since then? The answer is yes and no. Of course England in the year 2000 is not the England of 1950. Battles have been won, and it is now the marketplace rather than the university that is seen as the main 'driver' in education. But for many the model of teaching, the model of the child, the model of the curriculum to which schools must conform is seen as a return to the 1950s, with a national curriculum for students and student teachers institutionalising some of the practices that were apparently seen off thirty years ago. History never repeats itself, and there are clear reasons why England has not moved in the direction of Australia, and viewed historically it may be that we are simply seeing the growing pains of a national system, with which France has lived comfortably – and successfully – ever since the Napoleonic code. It is an experiment, and every subject specialist and every citizen should earnestly hope that it succeeds.

References

Ashraf, Sahail (1998) 'Almost all the beginning teachers . . . ', *Guardian Education* (London) 26 May

Bauer, Dale M. (1998) 'Indecent proposals: teachers in the movies', in *College English*, Volume 60, No. 3, March

Bunyan, Paul, Catron, John and Feist, Aliston (1998) 'The part that drama plays in whole English', *NATE NEWS*, Spring

Calderhead, James and Shorrock, Susan B. (1998) *Understanding Teacher Education*, London: Falmer Press

Daniel, Evan (1898) *The Grammar, History and Derivation of the English Language*, London: National Society's Depository

Dent, H. C. (1977) *The Training of Teachers in England and Wales*, London: Hodder and Stoughton

DfEE (1998a) *The National Literacy Strategy: The Management of Literacy at School Level – Notes for Conference Delegates*, London: DfEE

DfEE (1998b) *Induction for New Teachers*, London: DfEE

Green, Bill (1993) 'Literacy studies and curriculum theorizing; or the insistence of the letter', in B. Green (ed.) (1993) *The Insistence of the Letter: Literacy Studies and Curriculum Theorizing*, London: The Falmer Press

Goodson, I. and Marsh C. (1996) *Studying School Subjects*, London: The Falmer Press

HMSO (1963) *Half Our Future*, London: HMSO

Hunt, Felicity (1991) *Gender and Policy in English Education: Schooling for Girls 1902–44*, London: Harvester Wheatsheaf

Kaplan, Carola M. and Simpson, Anne B. (1996) *Seeing Double*, London: Macmillan

Maclure, J. Stuart (1973) *Educational Documents England and Wales 1816 to the Present Day*, London: Methuen

McDermid, Jane (1995) 'Women and education', in June Purvis (ed.) (1995) *Women's History: Britain 1850–1945*, London: UCL Press

Millard, Elaine (1997) *Differently Literate: Boys, Girls and the Schooling of Literacy*, Sussex: The Falmer Press

Miller, Jane (1992) *More has Meant Women: The Feminisation of Schooling*, London: Institute of Education/The Tufnell Press

Moger, Ros and Turvey, Anne (1998) 'ITTNC: A National Curriculum for Training Teachers', in *The English and Media Magazine*, Volume 38, Summer

National Society (1879a) *How to Teach Grammar*, Manuals of the Science of Art and Teaching Second Series No. 1, London: National Society's Depository

National Society (1879b) *How to Teach Reading and Writing*, Manuals of the Science of Art and Teaching Second Series No. 5, London: National Society's Depository

National Society (1879c) *On the Use of Words*, Manuals of the Science of Art and Teaching First Series No. 3. London: National Society's Depository

National Society (1879d) *On Class Teaching*, Manuals of the Science of Art and Teaching First Series No. 5, London: National Society's Depository

National Society (1879e) *On Discipline*, Manuals of the Science of Art and Teaching First Series No. 3, London: National Society's Depository

National Society (1880a) *How to Train Pupil Teachers*, Manuals of the Science of Art and Teaching Advanced Series No. 9, London: National Society's Depository

National Society (1880b) *Literature*, Manuals of the Science of Art and Teaching Advanced Series No. 1, London: National Society's Depository

Newman, J. H. (1852) 'Discourse VI "Knowledge Viewed in Relation to Learning"', in *The Idea of a University*, London: Longmans, Green

O'Hanlon, Redmond (1984) *Joseph Conrad and Charles Darwin*, Edinburgh: The Salamander Press

Patterson, Lee (1995) 'Literary history', in F. Lentricchia and T. McLaughlin (eds.) (1995) *Critical Terms for Literary Study*, London: The University of Chicago Press

Sellick R. J. W. (1994) *James Kay-Shuttleworth: Journey of an Outsider*, Ilford, England: Woburn

Simons, Judy (1998) 'Bard news for English', *The Times Higher Education Supplement*, 13 March 1998, p. 18

Smith, Frank (1923) *The Life and Work of Sir James Kay-Shuttleworth*, London: John Murray

Smith, Nowell (1917) *Cambridge Essays on Education*, ed. A. C. Benson, Cambridge: Cambridge University Press

Sutherland, Gillian (1990) ' "The Plainest Principle of Justice": the University of London and the Higher Education of Women', in D. Thompson (1990) *The University of London and the World of Learning*, London: Hambledon Press

Thompson, F. M. L. (ed.) (1990) *The University of London and the World of Learning 1836–1986*, London: The Hambledon Press

Thornton, Mary (1998) 'Becoming a Teacher', in *The Lecturer* (May 1998), London: NATFHE

Tibbits, Dianne (1998) 'New literacies for all: A review of *Differently Literate*', *English in Education*, Volume 32, No. 2, Sheffield: NATE

Tuman, Myron C. (1992) *Literacy Online: The Promise (and Peril) of Reading and Writing with Computers*, London: University of Pittsburgh Press

UCET (1997) *Annual Report*, London: Universities Council for the Education of Teachers

Worthen, John (1991) *D. H. Lawrence: The Early Years 1885–1912*, Cambridge: Cambridge University Press

Wray, David (1993) 'Student Teachers' knowledge and beliefs about language', in Neville Bennett, and Clive Carre, (eds.) (1993) *Learning to Teach*, London: Routledge

Part II

Australia: questions of pedagogy

5 English in Australia: its emergence and transformations

Annette Patterson

In this chapter I attempt to sketch a brief genealogy of the subject, English, in Australian secondary schools. By using the term genealogy I acknowledge a debt to the work of Michel Foucault, a French cultural analyst who called the philosophical-historical investigations he undertook 'genealogies'. He saw his research as opening up 'spaces' for debate rather than dogmatic assertions, describing them as 'philosophical fragments put to work in a historical field of problems'.[1] The preliminary work I describe here focuses initially on curriculum and syllabus statements and on examination documents produced mainly in New South Wales from 1860 onwards. This is followed by a consideration of historical accounts of English published over the past two decades with particular reference to those of Terry Eagleton (1983), John Dixon (1991) and Ian Hunter (1988).

Towards a genealogy of English

Have you ever been struck by the enormity of the claims made for English? For both its responsibilities and its possibilities? English teachers' conferences with titles such as 'Realising the Future' and 'Democracy through Language' and 'Making a Difference' are just one indication of the breadth and scope of the undertaking that is English. The political flavour to these titles may appear to suggest the contemporary social and cultural concerns of the subject. However, there is no reason to think that English teachers' responsibility to – if not change the world – then at least to oversee the transformation

---

1 Foucault, 1981, p. 4 from 'Questions of Method: An Interview with Michel Foucault', *Ideology and Consciousness*, 8, pp. 3–14. (It 1978). Cited in A. McHoul and W. A. Grace (1993) *A Foucault Primer: Discourse, Power and the Subject*, p. 85, Carlton: Melbourne University Press). Foucault has at times characterised his work as an attempt 'to create a history of the different modes by which, in our culture, human beings are made subjects' (from 'The Subject and Power', p. 208, trans. Leslie Sawyer, in H. Dreyfus and P. Rabinow (eds.) *Michel Foucault: Beyond Structuralism and Hermeneutics*, pp. 208–26, 2nd edn., Chicago: University of Chicago Press, 1982).

of their students is a post 1960s phenomenon. Far from it. By the time secondary English emerged at the turn of this century as a school subject in Australia, it already carried those connotations through its links with the subject called English that was taught in primary schools.

It is no straightforward matter, however, to connect secondary English's ambitious claims for the reconstruction of 'the person' to the primary school curriculum or, for that matter, with the existing 'literary studies' in the Classical mould taught in Britain in the ancient universities, public and grammar schools and imported into Australia in the nineteenth century. Even though there are clear statements of intent in early syllabus documents, curriculum statements and teachers' examinations, English was only one area of the curriculum singled out for this special regard. Margaret Mathieson (1975) for example, identifies a nineteenth-century curriculum rivalry between Classics and Science in which representatives of each argued for their subject as the more appropriate 'site' for a liberal, humanising, morally improving and transformative pedagogy to stand at the centre of a sound education. What is clear from early documents is that any subject of a range – that included Classics, Science, Geography, History, Civics and Morals – *could* have been the location of techniques for moral and ethical formation. Already well honed through the educational practices developed in the pastoral Protestant schools of England and Europe, these techniques were seen to be of vital importance in the emerging public systems of compulsory education. But, in the end, it was the newly devised curriculum category, secondary English, that was to draw upon these available techniques for self-formation, self-reflection and self-problematisation – from which, it was envisaged, would emerge the sensitive, empathic and tolerant citizen, capable of self-regulation – with effects and implications that are still apparent.

Many in Education have noted that English is a subject unlike others. Peter Medway, for example, points out that accounts of English do not justify its existence in the same way as other subjects, such as History or Science:

> English teachers do not describe what happens in their lessons as 'learning' or what their pupils end up with as 'knowledge'; or if they do, it is only when referring to subsidiary aspects of the work such as spelling or literary facts, and not to what they regard as the central activities. 'Knowledge' and 'learning' are tied in people's minds to facts and information, and the reason English teachers avoid the terms is that they do not see themselves as dealing with facts. Indeed it is sometimes said that English is 'a subject without a content'.
>
> Medway 1980, p. 13

It is not unusual for English to be discussed in this way: as concerned with more than facts or content; as essentially unaccountable, and even as ultimately mysterious:

Unless English in schools encourages awareness of the Other in the broadest possible religious sense of that concept, then *del futuro fia chiusa la porta*, the door of the future will close. Transcendence over perception is a grave responsibility indeed.

Hansen 1984, p. 56

From its emergence, secondary English was not designed to be about learning literature in the same way as learning science, or learning mathematics. Rather, it was (and is) a subject where students learn to relate to themselves, to others and to the world in particular ways. Literature just happens to have become the 'tool' for that learning. It bears repetition that at the turn of the century Classics, History, Geography, Civics or Morals – all of these subjects – were proposed as possible vehicles for the specific pedagogy we now associate with English. Eventually, however, these subjects were shaped around different kinds of concerns, and by the middle of the twentieth century, it was the subject of English that was the main beneficiary of a much older and widely dispersed set of instructional techniques and educational goals arranged around the cultivation of the personality or the character of the child, and around the construction of 'proper conduct'; that is, conduct befitting the citizen of a modern state.

At this point it is helpful to look in greater detail at possible evidence for these claims, beginning with a brief sketch of the context.

English in Australia

Unlike the United Kingdom, Australia has no nationally centralised system of education. Each of the six states and two territories is responsible for its own arrangement of the education system at primary (elementary) and secondary (high) school levels. This fragmented approach grew out of the British settlement of the country as first one, then separate colonies: English thus emerged as a subject within the formation of secondary education in Australia, colony by colony, state by state. Powerful state-based systems of government installed after Federation in 1901 ensured the survival of this diversity. Each state develops its own curricula, educates its own teachers, and arranges its schools as it sees fit. Students in New South Wales begin high school in Year 7 and complete six years of study while their counterparts just across the border, in Queensland, begin high school in Year 8 and complete five years of secondary education. Each state has a different set of subjects for study at the secondary level, and the Universities in each state have different requirements for entry.

Attempts have been made in recent years to bring some uniformity to the curriculum, at least, but at the time of writing it seems that these efforts have not been successful. It does appear, however, that the Federal Government still retains a goal of unity, and newspaper reports such as the following are not uncommon:

A national system to compare the performance of students and schools in all States is still at least two years away, the Industry Commission report on State and Federal government services has found. The report found it impossible to compare the effectiveness of the States' education systems because their skills tests were different. It said: 'There remains scope to improve the quantity, quality and timeliness of information used to assess the performance of both the whole school sector and government schools across Australian jurisdictions. But it appears unlikely that comprehensive reporting of learning outcomes on a comparable basis across jurisdictions will occur for at least two more years.'

The Sydney Morning Herald, 12 February 1998, p. 7

Such proposals of a unified approach to assessment and accountability is likely to annoy many teachers and other education professionals in Australia. It intersects with 'literacy crisis' rhetoric, which is predictable and prevalent in Australia as elsewhere, while calls 'to compare the effectiveness of the States' education systems' are reminiscent of government accountability measures from a previous era, such as 'payment by results'. The view expressed by one Head of English in a high school in Western Australia encapsulates what I think is a common viewpoint within the English teaching profession:

I don't know what all this outcomes talk is about but one thing I do know after, well, twenty years in the business is that English isn't like any other subject, you know. It's not that I want to plead a special case or anything. I don't want to suggest something like, you know, that every other subject can be measured but not English, but . . . well, you've looked at those outcome statements and you know just how wide they are. I mean, what are we going to measure in English? Is it going to be what we used to measure? How many spelling mistakes to a page and all that rubbish. Is that what we're going back to?

It is not surprising, however, that English is rather ambiguously placed in terms of measurement and accountability. From its emergence, it has represented a curriculum territory that is not solely, or even importantly, linked to a knowledge of content. Instead, it has emphasised the attainment of techniques related to 'person formation' or 'development' – expressed in terms such as 'sensitivity', 'appreciation', 'personal growth' and 'critical consciousness' – implying a high degree of personal autonomy and freedom for the learner. The mix of aesthetics, ethics and to a lesser extent, linguistics, which typifies most English syllabi in Australia, does not readily lend itself to 'testing'.

Furthermore, by discussing 'English in Australia' I run the risk of over-looking not only important inter-state differences, but also *intra-state* diversity in terms of how the current and relatively open syllabus and curriculum statements are interpreted and actualised in the space of the classroom. An English programme is likely to be organised and taught very differently, for instance, in the District High Schools (terminating at Year 10) of more remote regions of Western Australia than it is, say, in the inner-city schools of Perth. Predictably, then, on a number of levels, the issues surrounding 'measurement' and English are extremely complex and the requirement that English students demonstrably fulfil predetermined criteria is a topic of ongoing debate and policy development. The Federal Government has attempted to lay the groundwork for general agreement through the publication of 'A Statement on English for Australian Schools' (1994), and a companion document, 'Profiles – English for Australian Schools' (1994), which provides sets of outcome statements for English students in Years 1 to 10. However, so far, they have provided little more than a starting point for those states that have felt inclined to develop a state-based accountability measure. Tending to mitigate against the national Profiles' usefulness as a diagnostic and reporting mechanism for classroom teachers is the breadth and scope of the outcomes; a perhaps predictable result of their trying to avoid being overly prescriptive.

Current syllabus arrangements, state by state, in fact, allow a remarkable and much appreciated freedom to devise programs suitable for specific groups of students. Until quite recently students were not tested in ways that made their progress in English (or any other subject) comparable at state or national levels in either an individual or a 'group' sense until they reached the final year of post-compulsory high school – Year 12 in most states and territories. In 1997, however, an agreement was reached between the Federal government and the states and territories to 'allow' system-wide testing of literacy and numeracy skills at specified years. This agreement followed several years of negotiation to establish National Goals for numeracy and literacy. The now revised Goal will be met through the development and implementation of 'Benchmarks'. The aims of the benchmarking exercise are to improve student learning in numeracy and literacy, and school performance; and to inform Australian governments and the community about student achievement in literacy and numeracy. Although the agreement is to establish benchmarks at Years 3, 5, 7 and 9 the initial focus is on Years 3 and 5. One of the fears of English teachers is that a state or national testing agenda will begin to drive curriculum and syllabus development, thus jeopardising the freedom of individual teachers to tailor their programmes to the needs of their students. Thus, the agreement on testing is the subject of continuing debate but it is one indicator of a possible 'sea change' for English in Australia.

I will return to the issues of 'testing' and English in the following chapter. What I now want to do is to try to fulfil my promise to look in greater detail at some possible reasons for claiming that the subject of English has been the beneficiary of a widely dispersed set of instructional techniques and educational goals. These goals and techniques appear to have a long history.

More importantly, they are arranged around the cultivation of the person-ality or the character of the child, and around the construction of conduct befitting the citizen of a modern state. To substantiate these claims, I want to frame the emergence of English in Australia within an educational milieu in which it appears that the teaching of linguistic skills became linked to the 'cultivation of ethical inwardness'. By the cultivation of ethical inwardness I mean the teaching of such practices as self-reflection, self-problematisation, empathy, sensitivity, discrimination and critical consciousness that are now so readily associated with the secondary English classroom. I attempt to provide reminders that these techniques, which are now so securely installed within English that they appear natural adjuncts to the study of literature, in fact, have a history, and a rather long one at that.

My intention is to question two common versions of the history of English in both of which the establishment of the subject in secondary schools is described as the result of a fiercely fought battle with the Classics, which were seen as narrow and elitist. In one version the installation of English is represented as a community response to the demands of 'working people' for a curriculum that offered freedom of expression for individuals and the promise of fair and equitable social participation (the 'socialist' argument). The second version sees English similarly beginning in idealism out of class struggle but becoming an imperialist imposition of Arnoldian and Leavisite 'culture' on the masses (the 'ideology' argument). These versions of the history of English, I suggest, have informed the ways in which the *practices* of the subject are conceptualised. That is, they are assumed as a reflection of its history as an emancipatory subject with a moral function of producing people capable of 'realising the future' at both an individual and social level. This way of thinking about the development of English which focuses on the subject's morally elevating and refining critical practices that are said to provide its 'origins' – which have yet to be fully realised or achieved – operates in what has been described as 'the shadow of the model of a single general process' of emergence, struggle and overcoming at whose end lies the 'fully developed' human being or society. The problem with this is that a disparate range of historical events receives a retrospective unity in thinking about what might have contributed to the development of English. As a result, the possibility that these events are amongst those determining what has come to count as English is not taken into account and therefore cannot not be analysed. Once certain 'qualities' and practices become identified with English then history is written backwards to explain not how this identification might have come about, but how these qualities and practices have been blocked and must be emancipated.

English and the teachers' qualifying examinations

I take as my beginning point the late nineteenth century in the colonies of New South Wales and Victoria, these being by far the largest and most representative examples of the extensive school systems available in the colonies at that time. My discussion is also limited to state or publicly funded school systems, even though in each colony (and later, State and Territory) there existed a number of well established private schools including Grammar and church-based schools each offering its own curriculum. By the turn of the twentieth century, these schools, on the whole, tended to focus on a classical education for boys and on an academic and 'accomplishment' education for girls. In some cases a subject called 'English', or 'Literature' did appear on their curriculum prior to 1866, a date I mention here because it marked the successful passage of the New South Wales Public School Act which ushered in the legal recognition of a publicly funded and state managed, school system. It was within this publicly funded system that a subject called English emerged in a coherent and systematic fashion, firstly in the primary school and through the qualifying examinations set for teachers, and later in the secondary schools. After 1866, there was an increasing tendency for the curriculum of the denominational schools and the state schools to coincide due to a combination of state-instigated fiscal coercion and educational enticement arranged around the now familiar term, 'quality'.

Although in the late nineteenth century, secondary education was still some time off in both New South Wales and Victoria, each colony did have a reasonably well established publicly funded primary school system which provided an education right through to matriculation for those few children requiring it. One problem facing the colonial administrators, though, was the provision of adequately qualified teachers. Although technically well prepared for classroom management and organisation, first through the monitorial system and then through the pupil-teacher programme, teachers still lacked academic qualifications. To encourage improvement in this area, the colonial administrators set examinations which teachers had to pass before being allowed to progress to the next salary level.

These examination papers provide interesting detail for the following discussion. In 1885, the examination leading to the Second Class Certificate for teacher qualification in New South Wales included for the first time the term 'English' under the subject heading 'History and English'. Prior to this date the instructions had only included the usual headings 'Reading', 'Poetry' (which was mostly for recitation purposes), 'Writing' and 'Grammar', which for the previous ninety years at least had, along with Arithmetic, comprised the principal subjects of the primary school curriculum. By 1898, the literature aspect of English had been further strengthened by the inclusion of a separate subject heading, 'British Literature' which replaced the previous heading, 'History and English'. This syllabus set down the relevant chapters of Smith's *Smaller History of English Literature* to be studied in each year of the examinations through to 1901.

Five years later, in 1906, these instructions were replaced by the term 'English Language and Literature' and included the following more comprehensive details:

(i) Grammar and Composition (including *précis* writing and the writing of essays).
(ii) The study of the following works:
    For 1908. Shakespeare's *Midsummer Night's Dream, Richard II* and *Coriolanus*; Milton's *Samson Agonistes, Lycidas* and *Sonnets*; Scott's *Lay of the Last Minstrel*, Macauley's *Essays on Warren Hastings and Milton*; Charles Reade's *The Cloister and the Hearth*.

To this list of text books and readings was added the following:

Note: The study of mere verbal minutiae and grammatical form is not required. The works should be read as literature for the sake of their thought and content, and treatment of their subject matter, and their literary characteristics. The candidate should make himself acquainted with some short sketch of the life and literary career of the author.

In this directive on the uses of literature in English we have an early indication of the types of work literature would have to do in the service of a pedagogy which took self-formation as its goal. Although a study of 'literary characteristics' and the life of the author is required, a study of what is dismissed as 'mere verbal minutiae' is not. Nor is 'grammatical form'. This shift away from grammar and rhetoric towards aesthetics and a morally formative use of literature, signalled in the emphasis on reading 'works as literature for the sake of their thought and content, and treatment of their subject matter' is one of the significant features of early twentieth-century forms of the subject.

By 1913 the required subjects for a Second Class Primary Teachers' Certificate in New South Wales included 'English' and this remained the term in use thereafter.

English and secondary education

Peter Board, the first official Director of Education in New South Wales, was appointed in 1905 and retired in 1922. (Arguably, though, it was William Wilkins, Secretary of the Council of Education 1864–1880, who was the first person to occupy the position that came to be known as Director General of Education.) Board's Victorian counterpart was Frank Tate. According to most historical accounts, both were visionary educators and gifted administrators and each, in his own State, constructed, installed and oversaw the foundations of twentieth-century education in Australia. Board was committed to the idea that modern literature had the potential to provide those elements of 'The New Education' that he was determined to install at both the Primary and Secondary levels. Presumably this was not because of his own academic background since he held Honours and Masters degrees in Mathematics. But despite his mathematical background Peter Board is

particularly significant in terms of secondary English since it was his determination to provide space for a literature-based English programme in
secondary schools and to shape the subject around the concerns of 'The New
Education' – moral and ethical formation – that secured for English the
distinctive place it retains to the present in Secondary education in all States
and Territories in Australia. He emphasised his belief in the 'usefulness' of
English and literature study through his syllabus writing and the many notes
he attached to these, and through his reported comments, some of which are
reproduced below.

In writing the first new primary syllabus for the New South Wales system
which appeared in 1904, Board took as his twin guiding principles, curriculum
cohesion and child-centred instruction. As Crane and Walker (1957) note,
Board was particularly impressed with the new emphasis on 'correlation'
which he had observed on his tour of Europe, Scotland and England, but the
point of convergence was to be English.

'The primary school curriculum', he commented, 'should be regarded not
as an aggregation of a number of detailed independent subjects, but as a
concrete and homogeneous body of instruction with one element predominant to give tone and consistency to the whole and with all the elements
intermingled and interdependent, contributing each to the other.' He
suggested that the subjects in the curriculum should be reduced to six main
groups – *English* – *which was to be the hub* – mathematics, nature-knowledge,
civics and morals, manual work, and music. The central study upon which all
school work was to be related had varied in the schemes of different thinkers.
The Germans had used history, de Garmo argued for geography, Dewey in his
laboratory school was using the occupation groups, cooking, sewing, weaving
and shopwork. *Board selected English* (Crane and Walker 1957; emphasis
added).

Peter Board's syllabus for primary schools was adopted and implemented
over the next two decades and remained the foundation of primary education
through to the 1960s. In many respects, however, his syllabus cannot be
described as 'revolutionary' or 'unique', since this type of approach to
curriculum expansion and reform at the primary level took place in each
state or colony at varying times. In South Australia for instance, when John
Hartley renovated the primary school curriculum in the late nineteenth
century, his innovations included the insertion of English literature at every
level of primary schooling and the introduction of music and drawing
as 'new' required areas for study. Similar changes took place in Western
Australia, Tasmania, Victoria and Queensland.

At secondary level, however, it was a more difficult task to change the
curriculum and install English as its centre piece since it was necessary to outmanoeuvre the Classicists. As early as 1905, Peter Board commented that:

the study of the classics has in the past constituted the 'humanities' of
the curriculum, and the swing away from the ancient languages would be

a matter of great regret if there were nothing in the more modern courses to take their place and supply the same cultural elements. [But this is] not the case since English literature, history and geography might be so treated as to bring the student into touch with the human world around him.

Crane and Walker 1957, p. 115

It is statements such as these that could tempt me to see a clear line of development between Classics and twentieth-century secondary English. But this, I suggest, would be a mistake. The fact that Board does not focus on literature alone is one indication that the genealogy of English, as part of what came to be known, and what Board has already named, as the 'cultural' area of the curriculum, is more complex than an assertion of its direct evolution either as heir or opposition to the Classics. History, literature, geography, civics and Scripture were all proposed as providing the proper basis for 'culture' in the curriculum. In addition, as discussed below, an inspection of the various syllabus statements produced through the first four decades of this century indicates a considerable overlap between subjects in the primary curriculum such as Nature Studies, Civics and Morals, English and Literature, suggesting that English in the secondary school owes a great deal more to its primary school antecedents than to the Classics, which, like other subjects, had had to argue for its recognition as the proper place for a liberal, humanising, morally improving and transformative pedagogy to stand at the centre of the curriculum, and, like other subjects, was unsuccessful.

Despite his curriculum innovations and his insistence on the centrality of English and Literature, Board was still concerned in 1909 with what he saw as the neglect of the study of English. Although he had successfully inserted a renovated English subject into education he still felt that the Classics occupied too much of children's study time in comparison with English. Consequently, as Crane and Walker note, 'he did aim at putting Latin in its right place and giving the study of English its proper prominence'. Again, this comment might suggest that English is simply a modern day substitute for Classics. Certainly, Classics did disappear from the state curriculum in large measure by the middle of the century, and English did continue to occupy an increasing amount of time in both the primary and secondary curriculum. On the other hand, if we consider that the set of studies traditionally followed in the primary school – 'Reading', 'Writing', 'Poetry', 'Grammar', and later 'Comprehension' – had always occupied the bulk of the primary curriculum then the amount of time devoted to English in Peter Board's renovated programme of study and his selection of it as 'the hub' is not so surprising. But it also formed 'the hub' for other reasons. English, as Board was at pains to point out, was not a subject area where grammatical constructions and techniques of textual study were to be the main focus: 'The works should be read as literature for the sake of their thought and content, and treatment of their subject matter, and their literary characteristics.' Board, and fellow curriculum writers in other states at the time focused on the potential for English to 'bring the student into touch with the human world around him'. Eventually, it was as a vehicle for a different pedagogy that English would prove its importance. Students of English would learn, as Foucault later termed it, 'techniques of the self' (Foucault 1988), rather than 'mere' rules and procedures for producing and dissecting texts. English as already taught in the primary schools offered a ready-made pastoral pedagogy for a subject entrusted with the task of inculcating techniques for ethical and moral formation, not because it was 'special' but because of contingent and serendipitous circumstances.

At one point, Crane and Walker wonder why Board selected English as the 'hub' of his new curriculum, and on another occasion, Barcan hypothesises that:

> The new emphasis on moral and civic aims in education and the new interest in literature, history and science, widely found in the early years of the 20th century, seems to be associated with the growth of a new middle class with industrial, commercial and professional interests, and with a new morality and a new ideological and cultural approach fostered by this social group.
>
> Barcan 1965, p. 24

But the pedagogy that emerged was one seen as suitable for all classes, and it was located within a subject that was compulsory. The question posed by Crane and Walker, 'Why literature/English?' is probably not the most useful one to ask. It gives far too much credence to the idea that people such as Board were inventing English as a literature-based subject which would carry those elements of the 'New Education' that they most desired: character and citizen formation techniques, and a child centred, experiential approach to teaching. It also supports the idea of 'culture' being driven by the emerging middle class. But we know that the situation was much more complex than this. Firstly, the idea that English could be a subject based on literature, rather than a subject based on language study or philology, for example, had been around for a considerable time before Board and his Victorian counterpart, Tate, arrived on the educational scene. We have already noted that 'English Literature' appeared in primary school curricula during at least the last decade of the nineteenth century in both Victoria and New South Wales, and that it also appeared on the subject list for the teachers' qualifying examination as early as 1885 in New South Wales. And since this examination was equivalent to an educational level not much above current primary school standards we can assume that it was not because the teachers were sitting for university style examinations. Secondly, as already noted above, it was not accepted that Literature/English was the *only* option for including 'culture' in the curriculum. History and geography could work just as well as a means for inculcating good conduct through self-reflective practices, and could provide plenty of scope for teachers to get in touch with students' experiences of the world, or so the architects of state education repeatedly claimed. Nevertheless, the commissioners Knibbs and Turner commenting in 1904 in their *Report on Secondary Education* that '[t]here is an increasing recognition of the cultural value of modern literature' were drawing – like Board in his support of English as 'the hub' of the primary school curriculum – on a broad range of tradition and thinking in curriculum development, in England and Scotland, as well as in Australia.

Principles of conduct

By 1911 the first edition of *Courses of Study for High Schools* had been issued in New South Wales. The preface of this Course noted that

> [i]t is especially in the use of the mother-tongue and the study of literature that the high school will exercise its highest influence upon the general training of pupils . . . Advantage should be taken of the ethical value of school studies. Especially in dealing with literature and history, opportunities will be presented for diverting the pupils to the consideration of principles of conduct, and thereby developing a thoughtful attitude towards moral questions.
>
> NSW 1911

By this time Geography had been dropped from discussions such as this one about the subjects best suited to moral formation, and only History and Literature remained as the most likely subjects to fulfil this role. But English as a subject in the secondary curriculum still remained a collection of the old elements of the primary curriculum (composition, recitation, grammar, spelling, literature study) sitting uneasily in a curriculum framed by the rhetoric of child-centredness, experiential learning and ethics. For instance, from 1911 through to 1929 'English' in the *Course of Studies for Secondary Schools* was divided into two sections under the headings of Language and Literature. Usually listed under Language were Grammar, Spelling and Composition along with reasonably detailed and prescriptive lists of texts and areas to be covered. But in 1929 a rather different course of study for secondary schools appeared in New South Wales. Under the heading 'English' was the statement:

> No work is exclusively prescribed, but the following provisions are made for the guidance of schools:
> i. At least three books (English authors) are to be read in each class;
> ii. It is strongly recommended that one of the books studied be poetry . . .

iii. While teachers are not required to select books from the appended list, they must, if they desire to use others, submit their choice for the approval of the Chief Inspector of Secondary Schools.

NSW 1929, p. 13

The suggested literary titles were arranged under the headings: Poetry, Novels, Mythology and Legends. In each year level a similar format was followed. The apparent freedom offered to teachers in terms of what they selected and how they arranged their programme is not surprising since this had been a stated, if not achievable aim of curriculum and syllabus production since the late nineteenth century in New South Wales at least. What is surprising, though, is the early disappearance of 'Language' as a heading and the total dedication of 'English' to literature study. There remains only one mention of 'language' in the 1929 high school syllabus under the fourth-year programme where the following instruction appears: 'In all schools one hour a week is to be used for the study of language and composition' (NSW 1929, p. 1). English continued to be 'set' in this way until 1941 in New South Wales.

Most accounts of English in Australia assume that the formal study of language did not disappear from the secondary curriculum until the 1960s but the prescribed course of study from 1929 to 1941 in New South Wales gives an early indication of its instability as an element of the English syllabus (if not of actual classroom practice) as well as an early indication of what is commonly considered to be the more modern focus of English on literature. In 1944, however, language reappeared as an explicitly stated element of the English syllabus, with the familiar sub-categories: Grammar, Spelling, Composition and with 'Original and Creative Writing' making an appearance alongside the following comment:

Pupils should be trained and encouraged to give graphic expression to their own thoughts and feeling on topics within the range of their own experience. Such efforts, in the earlier years, should include exercises in narrative, descriptive and imaginative composition. Classes more advanced in the course might be encouraged to attempt essays of a reflective, critical, argumentative and biographical character, with the emphasis on grace and style in addition to lucidity. The study and imitation of suitable models in English prose style are recommended, and exercises in verse composition and the writing of original plays and short stories will be found valuable.

NSW 1944, p. 2

Although the conjunction of 'training' with the expression of 'their own experience', and 'imitation of suitable models' with 'the writing of original plays and short stories', looks rather odd to teachers now well versed in self-expressive and self-reflective genres, there is, nevertheless, a great deal here that is comparable to late twentieth-century English teaching. And there is even more that is recognisable in terms of the design and goals of what was to become known as 'The New English' in Australia in the 1970s that drew initially on the work of English Educators based at the University of London's Institute of Education and elsewhere. The New South Wales 1944 syllabus also suggested that 'pupils should be encouraged to read in the field of Australian literature' (NSW 1944, p. 3). These and other expressions of support for techniques in the secondary school that allowed students to link their 'own experiences' with personal expression and self-reflective writing and reading seem surprisingly 'modern' and yet as noted above they had been making regular appearances in the primary curricula from the 1860s.

Mr Lowry, an Inspector with the Victorian Department of Education in the early part of the twentieth century made the following comments regarding literature:

> But while much can be done by direct teaching, strength of expression comes indirectly. The magic of words and true sense of their use . . . cannot be picked up from dictionaries. They can be learned only from words in fine action that is to say, in the prose and poetry of great writers. The way of it is not by reference, but by infection. It is the felt and remembered word that becomes your own.
>
> Victorian Ministry of Public Instruction, p. 45

As Robin Peel has noted in chapter 2, Newbolt (in Britain), more than a decade later was to make comprehensive and influential pronouncements along such lines. However, I would like to suggest that rather than seeing Newbolt's remarks as inventing and giving 'voice' to personalist English, it is possible to think that Newbolt was reiterating and setting forth the ideas and practices that had been circulating for several decades in England, Australia and the United States.

Some histories of English

I hope that this brief look at syllabus statements, curricula documents, examinations and inspectors' reports provides enough information to unsettle the apparently widely held belief that English emerged as the result of class struggle – only to be misappropriated as a bourgeois ideology – and that its intrinsically political nature drives inherently emancipatory projects. The 'governmental' argument, which is the line I wish to pursue here, takes a different tack.

My use of the term 'governmental' in the discussion that follows draws on the arguments of Michel Foucault in quite specific ways. Rather than using his work to reiterate a well established tradition in Education of ideology critique, I have followed the ideas of pioneers of governmentality studies in Australia and England, who have taken up the later work of Foucault. Their work focuses on the diverse ways in which individuals and populations are formed and governed through conjunctions of power and knowledge. Foucault does not offer a general model of subject or person formation, nor does he unify the forms of subjectivity that individuals may be endowed with in different 'walks of life' and 'departments of existence'. Instead, he argues that capacities, thoughts and desires are inculcated through 'social technologies' that work on the bodies and minds of individuals. These include 'disciplinary technologies' such as the school, where systems of training and surveillance manipulate body and mind directly by means of physically positioning people in particular spaces (classrooms, queues, sporting facilities) and by the teaching of specific physical and mental capacities. There are also 'technologies of the self,' such as religious confession, in which the individual is taught to turn him or herself into a subject by means of guided ethical reflection. In Foucault's argument, these capacities are produced and implanted in 'social apparatuses' that are linked to programmes for the formation and management of 'populations', whereby the individual becomes an individual in relation to a particular class or group. From these arguments it has been suggested that instead of seeing English in terms of emancipatory claims, it might be viewed as a governmental apparatus which uses 'self-problematising' techniques as part of a program for the moral management of a population. The interrogation of values and the improving and elevating 'qualities' so closely associated with English then might be seen as highly normalising, although it is important to add that this is not meant as a criticism.

Governmental arguments rely on a careful mapping of a terrain of practices in terms of the bureaucratic and administrative procedures and techniques invented and installed at various points for the purpose of managing and governing 'populations'. These are often 'new' populations as was the case with the population that became known as state school students, aged between five and fifteen, which emerged around the middle of the nineteenth century as a distinct cohort in need of 'government'. Populations in need of government, Foucault suggests, emerged alongside or as part of the modern state, a sixteenth-century European invention and as he has pointed out, many of the techniques required for the inculcation of 'proper' conduct in specific populations were borrowed and adapted from the self-grooming kits of classical times. Bureaucracies and administrative strategies were required, Foucault argues, to make these techniques more widely available and accessible to vast populations in urgent need of modification if religious wars, oppression through overtly violent means and disenfranchisement were not to continue to dominate the history of human occupation of Europe. Education departments became just one of a number of bureaucracies invented to fill the need for recording, tabulating and disseminating sets of practices designed to 'educate' populations of children in particular ways – ways which were tied to the increasingly important technologies of literacies and person-formation.

I want to now focus on English and the explanations that have been offered for how it came to be arranged in its present form. Terry Eagleton, for example, insists upon the political nature of English and its misappropriation as a bourgeois ideology. He finds in the Romantic aesthetic a de-politicising strategy which, he argues, informs modern English as opposed to English as it should be and might have been. He writes about the study of Literature producing 'an historically peculiar form of human subject who is sensitive, receptive, imaginative and so on . . . *about nothing in particular*' (Eagleton 1986, p. 5). This 'radical depoliticisation' is argued by Eagleton to be always to the advantage of the ruling order in that it works to support dominant power hierarchies with regard to gender, race and class and that this is achieved through the production of particular '*forms of subjectivity* judged appropriate to the society in question' (Eagleton 1985, p. 4).

This mode of theorising is characteristic of many traditional histories of English in that it appears to open up fields for analysis but then *assumes* a 'reality' to be uncovered or revealed. In Eagleton's argument, the reality to be uncovered appears to be what has been known all along: English emerges in possession of the qualities and practices that define it:

> English emerged, then, as a result of a certain class struggle; and it emerged equally because of a conflict of interests between the sexes . . . English began, in short, as the inscription of a certain kind of difference and otherness, in terms of both class and gender, at the very heart of the academic institution – and to say that is to claim that it operated as a kind of deconstruction all in itself.
>
> Eagleton 1991, pp. 5–7

Eagleton then goes on to argue, however, that repression by the academic institution at this moment of birth resulted in the 'erasure of this unnameable difference' and a reconstitution of English as the cultural arm of colonialism. The radical project that Eagleton advocates turns out to be the traditional one: to return to the subject's authentic, originating roots and remain true to their difference and otherness, albeit 'in fresh ways' (Eagleton 1991, p. 7). Thus the future of English lies in its origins which determine its goals. In this amazingly neat and circular history, the opportunity to analyse 'the roots' of English is passed over.

The linking of English with moral universals such as 'difference', 'identity' and 'community', 'experience', 'pleasure', 'democracy' and 'resistance', is in evidence in most accounts of English education, anywhere where English teaching is undertaken, but perhaps it is nowhere more in evidence than in a recent history of English by John Dixon (1991). I cannot hope to do justice to Dixon's argument in such a short space but will attempt to provide a brief synopsis. Dixon offers a variation of Eagleton's history of English in his claim that English grew out of a set of practices arranged around the figure of 'the reader of literature', a figure who developed out of the desire of ordinary people to derive pleasure and self-understanding through literary study. The mechanism for the expression of this desire was the University Extension movement. The strategy for achieving its democratic goals was a new way of reading texts – a way of reading which is familiar to us now but one which, according to Dixon, was generated within the new pedagogical milieu of the Extension courses and out of the peoples' recognition of the authenticity of their experience of literature. This was not a reading practice which 'killed to dissect' as in classical studies or philology but one which embraced and absorbed the text in order to reveal its connections with human experience. Rather than focusing on rhetoric and philology, this new way of reading incorporated a means for relating the experience of the text to the personal and worldly experiences of the reader through practices of self-reflection.

But according to an alternative history of English provided by Ian Hunter, reading practices, in their different forms, owe more to the bureaucratic and pragmatic operations of the pedagogical machinery of which they are a part than they do to a conjunction of events (such as civil unrest, colonialism, or University Extension courses) and desires for democracy, freedom or moral development. Reading practices, even in an aesthetic form, Hunter argues, do not embody the unrestrained expression of the reading experience. In a review of John Dixon's history of English, Hunter points out that the linking of what we now recognise as an expressive or self-reflective reading practice with a specific pedagogical milieu provides an important historical lead which Dixon cannot follow. This lead cannot be followed because Dixon's history like Eagleton's, adopts the strategy of dialectical opposition. That is, whereas Eagleton opposes 'difference' and the 'institutions of the ruling class', Dixon opposes 'pastoral' and 'bureaucratic' aspects of education. That is, he opposes, on the one hand, the potential for freedom offered by a self-reflexive reading practice located in 'true' English teaching, with, on the other hand, the constraints of the educational system within which it is located.

The idea that we have either a potentially liberating reading practice or a constraining administrative imperative enacted through assessment practices and other administrative and accounting practices is a familiar although circular and unhelpful one within critiques and histories of English education. Although 'expressive' or 'self-reflective' reading and writing practices are the centre-piece of secondary English education, they do not simply have a life of their own. They are linked in quite specific ways with particular approaches to teaching. These methods make use of a set of techniques arranged around the figure of the sympathetic teacher and around confessional and self-revelatory strategies for explorations of the self. (I take up these issues in a later chapter.) Rather than posing a threat to the potential 'full' development of the individual or the community, it is possible to see the 'sympathetic teacher' and the 'literary response' or 'the reading' as part of the many techniques for linking personal comportment – self-reflection and other styles of conduct – with literacy events.

The vehicle for this connection between the practices we associate with the

252 'English' in Australia

study of literature and personal conduct is the bureaucratic machinery which goes to make up the ensemble that is English education. Each is a necessary adjunct to the other. In this sense, these techniques are as well embedded within Poststructural and Cultural Studies practices in English as they are within Personal Growth. Approaches to English may come and go, but the actual mechanism for forging the connections between techniques for personal conduct and the acquisition of literacy technologies appears to remain unchanged. For example, the focus on genre now evident in the Queensland syllabus for secondary English in Years 8, 9 and 10 is conducted, I would argue, within the same pedagogical milieu as the previous focus on literary texts and criticism. We can rearrange the deck chairs but we can not alter the course of the ship. Or so it seems. But then why would we want to? A supervisory relationship aligned with pastoral care, concern for ethical conduct, sympathy and nurturance are all excellent techniques for the care and control of populations.

The alarm bells ring, I think for us as English teachers, on the phrase 'care and control'. In English teaching we say 'yes' to 'care' but we say 'no' to 'control'. The two do not appear to go together. They are conceptualised as opposites. It is precisely the point at which the familiar dialectical arguments become activated. Once a space between two terms is opened for inspection it is easy enough to run between them, exposing the potential if not the actual workings of oppression through 'control', 'revealing' the pros and cons of each – and finally reconciling what have been established as opposing 'virtues'. Control is okay, but only if it is deployed in the sense of 'self control' and not in the sense of the imposition of the 'other'. Care is okay as long as it is not controlling. 'Agency', 'inwardness', 'desire', are the tropes by which we as English teachers and theorists reconcile 'control' with 'care' and make it our own. But as Hunter has pointed out, one of the great successes of state education was its ability to bring care and control together, in the interests of governing previously ungovernable populations, through the technique of a newly deployed, but not newly invented, supervisory relationship – that of teacher and students.

References

Barcan, Alan (1965) A Short History of the Education of New South Wales, Sydney: Martindale Press, p. 214
Crane, A. R. and Walker, W. G. (1957) Peter Board: His Contribution to the Development of Education in New South Wales, Melbourne: Australian Council for Educational Research, p. 36
Dixon, J. (1991) A Schooling in 'English': Critical Episodes in the Struggle to Shape Literary and Cultural Studies, Milton Keynes: Open University Press
Eagleton, T. (1983) Literary Theory: An Introduction, Oxford: Blackwell
Eagleton, Terry (1985) 'The Subject of Literature', Annual Conference, National Association of Teachers of English, Nottingham, p. 5
Eagleton, Terry (1991) 'The Enemy Within', NATE News, September, 5–7

English – A Curriculum Profile for Australian Schools (1994) Carlton: Curriculum Corporation

Foucault, Michel (1988) 'The Care of the Self', *The History of Sexuality*, Vol. 3, New York: Vintage Books

Hansen, I. U. (1984) 'English in Secondary Schools', *Meridian*, 3 (1), 54–7

Hunter, I. (1988) *Culture and Government: The Emergence of Literary Education*, London: Macmillan Press

Hunter, Ian (1993) *Rethinking the school*, Sydney: Allen and Unwin

Mathieson, Margaret (1975) *Preachers of Culture: A Study of English and its Teachers*, London: Allen and Unwin

Medway, Peter (1980) *Finding a Language*, London: Writers and readers in association with Chameleon

New South Wales Department of Public Instruction (1911) *Courses of Study for High Schools*. Preface. Sydney: Government Printer.

New South Wales Department of Education (1929). *Course of Study for High Schools, Secondary Schools, and other Schools Following the High School Course*, 11th edn., Sydney: Government Printer, p. 1

New South Wales Department of Education (1944). *Course of Study for High Schools, Secondary Schools, and other Schools Following the High School Course*, Sydney: Government Printer, p. 2

A Statement on English for Australian Schools (1994) Carlton: Curriculum Corporation

The Sydney Morning Herald, 'Why our schools can't be compared', Thursday, 12 February 1998, p. 7

Victorian Ministry of Public Instruction. *Report of the Minister of Public Instruction for the Year 1924–25*, Melbourne: Government Printer

6 Beliefs about English in Australia

Annette Patterson

Education in Australia

Population of Australia: 18.5 million distributed across six States and t Territories. The States, in order of population, are New South Wales (million); Victoria (4.6 million); Queensland (3.4 million); Western Austra (1.7 million) South Australia (1.4 million); Tasmania (0.4 million); Austral Capital Territory (0.3 million); Northern Territory (0.2 million).

Number of schools: 9,609 schools. 7,029 are government schools opera by the State Directors-General of Education (or equivalent) and 2,580 non-government schools. 3.2 million full-time students attend governm and non-government schools.

Stages of compulsory schooling: Primary schooling differs from state state with three states and one territory administering Year 1–Year 7 syste while the remaining three states and one territory administer Year 1–Yea systems. Secondary (Years 7 or 8–Year 10). Non-compulsory school extends to Year 12. All states and territories except Western Australia a Queensland have a pre-year 1. Children generally turn 6 years of age duri Year 1 and 17 years of age during Year 12 although this differs slightly fr state to state. Compulsory schooling extends till the student is sixte years of age. Students generally leave school in order to undertake terti education. This is provided mainly in universities, Tertiary and Furth Education institutions (TAFE) and other Vocational Education and Train institutions (VET) such as theological colleges, private business and co mercial colleges and secretarial colleges. Serious efforts have been made recent years by State governments to retain a higher proportion of studei in High Schools until Year 12. The apparent retention rate is 72% but t varies significantly across States and Territories ranging from 42% in t Northern Territory to 92% in the Australian Capital Territory. The natio retention rate for female students (78%) is higher than the corresponding r for males (66%).

Significant private school system: Approximately 30% of Australian st dents attend non-government schools which comprise 'Anglican', 'Cathol and 'Independent' schools. Non-government schools receive their incor from students' fees, Commonwealth (public) funding and endowments. T percentage of students attending non-government schools increased by 2 between 1996 and 1997 while the percentage of students attending gover ment schools increased by 0.4% during the same period. Approximate 6,000 more boys than girls attend non-government schools.

Number of universities: There are 36 public universities within the Unified National System. In addition there are two private universities, Bond University in Queensland and Notre Dame University in Western Australia.

Curriculum: Each State and Territory designs and implements its own curriculum. Between 1989 and 1993 the Commonwealth, States and Territories collaborated to develop curriculum statements and profiles in English and seven other agreed learning areas. All States and Territories use the statements and profiles in some form for curriculum development while incorporating changes to accommodate local policies and needs.

Standardised assessments in English: Not available at a national level. States and territories administer their own assessment systems and each one is different from the other. Attempts to implement national literacy and numeracy benchmarks at Years 3, 5, 7, and 9 have met with some resistance and at this stage assessment remains state-based.

Publication of results: individual results reported to parents. In some states the overall results of schools in the Year 12 assessments (which differ from state to state) are published in newspapers.

Examinations leading to qualifications: Some states have a completely school-based assessment system, while others combine school-based assessment with external examinations. Each state has its own certification procedures which usually apply at Year 10, Year 11 and Year 12. Each state has its own system for ranking Year 12 students for university places.

Inspection of schools. No. Each state has its own system of reporting from the schools to the Director-Generals or equivalent.

Teaching qualifications: Qualified Primary and Secondary teachers in Australia generally have completed either four or five years of university education. In states or territories where there is no Board of Teacher Registration the prospective teacher must have met particular standards of education. Generally these are either a post-graduate Diploma (a Dip.Ed of one calendar year duration is offered in Western Australia for Primary or Secondary qualifications) or a four year Bachelor of Education degree, or a 2 year Bachelor of Education degree following a Bachelor of Arts or Bachelor of Science degree.

University or school based training. Generally student-teachers undertake university based training with schools playing an important role in professional experience arrangements in all states and territories, and in assessment of professional experience in some cases.

A National Curriculum for Teacher Registration. No. Each state has its own certification arrangements. Some states have a Board of Teacher Registration. The Board monitors the content and delivery of the Education degrees offered by the universities in that state. Most states and territories rely on appropriate university qualifications (Dip.Ed or B.Ed) as the benchmark for employment with the universities in those states setting their own curriculum.

Probationary year: Not generally available although some State Education Departments have an induction or probationary year for beginning teachers in government schools.

All figures are based on Australian Bureau of Statistics data, August 1997. Accessed 17 March, 1999. http://www.statistics.gov.au/websitedbs

Beliefs about English

A number of 'beliefs' about English could be discussed in this chapter. Rather than deciding in advance what they might be, Robin Peel, Jeanne Gerlach and I wanted first to canvass a wide range of opinions about English from students, teachers and other professionals involved in English Education. We used the data that emerged from these discussions, together with that drawn from readings of policy documents, government reports and theoretical and practical accounts of English in the countries in which we work, to identify and consider common beliefs about English. The beliefs discussed in this chapter thus represent the most commonly recurring themes in the Australian responses from a range of students involved in the study of English, and of English teaching, between 1994 and 1997, and in various government reports and policy statements released in Australia during the past two decades.

The following discussion is arranged in two parts. Firstly, I examine the responses of the students involved in English education whose opinions I canvassed. Secondly, by examining selected government reports and policy statements released in Australia since 1980, I provide brief social and historical contexts for the existence of the beliefs about English that were identified in the study.

The Australian study took a slightly different format from that undertaken in the UK by Robin Peel. It involved a mix of student respondents in universities and high schools who, over a period of three years, were inter-viewed or asked to provide written statements. In each case, respondents were asked to respond to two broad questions:

> What functions do you think the secondary school subject called 'English' is meant to fulfil?
> What do you think students in secondary school English classrooms should be doing?

The following is an account of some of the responses to those questions expressed first, by university students studying toward a teaching qualifi-cation, and second, by high school students studying English.

University students talk about English

In each year, 1994, 1995 and 1996, when the new intake of students entered my English curriculum classroom I asked them to write a paragraph or two about what they thought their (future) students should be doing in English classrooms and about what functions they thought the school subject called English was meant to fulfil. Before they began to write, I explained that I was preparing a chapter for a book; that their written responses (which could be written in any format they chose, including note or point form) would not be assessed, but that I would be interested in collecting their responses at the end of the session to use for data purposes. They could decide whether or not to hand in their written comments and whether or not to identify themselves. It is a credit to the students that over the three-year period every one cheerfully volunteered their comments. Some students, however, did choose to withhold their names. Since this was the first class session and, in some cases, I would be their teacher and assessor for this subject, they were understandably wary about giving me an insight into their literacy levels, and perhaps into their level of commitment to teaching generally and to English in particular through an unprepared, un-drafted and rushed piece of writing. However, the fact that no one chose to withhold their comments is testimony to their trust and generosity, for which I am most grateful.

Each class had between twenty and forty participants with a ratio of about five female to each male student. There was a wide range of ages and stages of study represented. In the same class, for instance, students who were studying an undergraduate degree in Education sat alongside students who already had a degree – usually a Bachelor of Arts, with either a major in literature or textual analysis. When the student-teachers, in either the second or third year of their undergraduate degree, or in the first and only year of a post-graduate Diploma, had completed the writing task, they then moved into groups and used their comments as the basis for a discussion about English and English teaching. This served as a useful mechanism for the class members to get to know one another, and for thinking about their future role as English teachers and about the functions of the subject they would teach.

In many ways the students' responses were not surprising. A significant report on English in Australia, 'The Martin Report', released in 1980, had focused on three concerns: first, an understanding from a theoretical point of view that English is arranged around the concept of 'models'; second, a noticeable level of confusion, or lack of consensus among the major stake holders about how English is constituted as a subject; and finally a belief that English is in need of definition. The university students taking part in this study expressed views that coincided with the second and third beliefs discussed in the report. Occasionally, one of the university students would raise the issue of different approaches to textual study, but generally a belief that English was arranged in terms of models was not expressed.

However, in the case of most students it was their first session on English teaching and most, although not all, students were unaware of the ways in which English teaching can be theorised. They had yet to read about the concept of models of English. Some students, however, most particularly those who had an arts/humanities degree from Murdoch University, a 'newer' tertiary institution in Western Australia with a substantial research background in literary theory, were aware that English teaching and learning might be premised on different 'approaches'. They had learnt about the 'theory wars'; they had read post-structuralist writers; they knew about deconstruction and they were able to read these perspectives against what they viewed as the New Critical and Leavisite approaches they were taught in school. But the majority of students were unaware of, or at best only vaguely aware of, these debates. They saw English in 'commonsense terms'; that is, in the terms that they had experienced English in schools, as the study and 'appreciation' of literature, and as the 'effective' use of language.

If English were defined by the university students taking part in this study, it was in terms of broad claims or goals. These included an appreciation of the English language and of its texts and a shared sense of the pleasure to be derived from the study of English (language and texts). In addition, students emphasised the emancipatory potential of English at a personal and at a community level through its focus on self-expression and cultural meaning making. They also agreed that as English teachers, they would have a mission to help their students toward a better understanding of themselves and their society.

But these students also were explicit about the difficulties of defining English, and uncertain about the desirability of attempting such a definition. As Amanda Herbert commented: 'English is more than a language, more than a cultural form, more than an historical period. Can it be defined?' Another student also expressed doubt about ever being able to describe English in definitive terms although, interestingly, she did attempt to do this for herself: 'For me, English has come to mean a critical study of language in all its forms and expression, from the literary text to verbal models of communication' (Anne Partlon). Some students expressed what seemed to be a related concern about the question they had been asked to consider which related to 'function': 'I don't think that English should be thought about in functional terms. The power of English is its ability to critique such discourses' (Anon.). And, 'English provides students with the space to be themselves and that is its "function"' (A. Blair).

In discussing English as the 'study of literature' or, as a few students expressed it, as the study of texts, students' comments focused on concerns about pleasure, enjoyment and the freedom to explore one's 'self'. Most students mentioned their own love of literature, or made explicit references to the pleasure they had derived from English during their school and university study. Most anticipated being able to communicate this pleasure to their students. They hoped to be able to make English study enjoyable and relevant. There was also considerable agreement about English and aesthetics, with English being viewed variously as a 'beautiful language', and its literature as the repository of 'great ideas'. Anne Acton had this to say: 'English, in all its aspects, is the means by which we communicate to each other . . . it is beautiful voices, Hopkins, Burton, books from Chaucer to Asimov, theatre, film, radio and occasionally television. It is the grammar and syntax of a beautifully structured language – or it can be!'

The ambivalence about popular culture apparent here in the phrase, 'occasionally television' and the qualifying exclamation 'or it can be!' is linked with concerns in the undergraduates' responses for teaching students to appreciate the English language and 'selected' texts. On the other hand, the occasional student questioned this approach. English teaching should be about removing notions of high culture associated with 'proper English' and 'validating everyone's experience of the language' (Anon., 1997). Another student wanted 'to show that literature lives beyond Shakespeare and Jane Austen' (Sharon Zehnder).

Almost every person who took part in this study considered English to be central to the experience of school, and vital for literacy development, which was defined broadly in terms of social, cultural and personal development. Margaret James commented that 'English represents the foundation of the English socio-cultural society, through the use of language and an understanding of its texts', and Sharon Zehnder echoed this concern with self and society: 'English is a means for expressing ideas and opinions. It is also a means of empowering students. Mastery of the language means people can participate more effectively in the broader community'.

Students, surprisingly perhaps, rarely mentioned the role of English in the development of a critical perspective although here is one student who was clear about that role: 'I believe that the subject area of English encompasses not only grammatical skills, but also the skills with which students can take a more active part in their society. By not just accepting things as they are, but by looking at why they are, students can use the English classroom to reconstruct all sorts of notions, from gender and class, to age and power' (Anon.).

Not surprisingly, students who had completed a degree with an emphasis on 'cultural studies' were clearer in their thinking about the role of English in developing a critical faculty. Here is Georgina Paterson, a graduate of a course that she describes as 'a cultural studies/semantic one' describing her view of English: 'English encourages new ways of thinking about texts, and our relation to these texts. It involves making, rather than discovering meaning. English provides people with the skills required to create, communicate, comprehend, and assists understanding of the world around texts and our own position in that world, our assumptions, values, beliefs, prejudices. English directs us to a new understanding of that which is often thought to be natural and eternal.' Expressions of this type of view, however, were rare. Self-expression, pleasure and aesthetics were more likely to form the basis of students' understanding of English. However, it might be pointed out that the polarising of views of the subject at one or the other end of the 'personal development'–'cultural studies' continuum is not uncommon among professional English educators and theorists.

The question of 'illiteracy' or 'the literacy crisis' arose on several occasions with some students seeing this as a result of the incursion of popular communications media into the lives of students which had resulted in reduced attention to reading the printed word. One student commented that she was concerned about the apparent rates of adult illiteracy, 'and illiteracy in general and would like to address this problem and hopefully somehow ameliorate it' (Melissa Holmes). Many students, in fact, provided comments that indicated an interest in teaching English in order to ameliorate wrongs, 'change the world', or at least the 'world view' of their students. Margaret James expressed a commonly held belief among the students who took part in this study that they were on a mission to change the lives of their students: 'I consider English to be essential to my very existence. I would like to share the pleasure I derive from not only using my cultivated communication skills, but also from reading, and discussing a variety of novels, poems and plays. Consequently, I believe that as a teacher, I will be able to utilise my knowledge of English by inspiring and encouraging the students I will encounter, to also strive for a similar attainment.' Melissa Holmes again commented along similar lines when she stated: 'I love English and literature and remember fondly my high school English teacher, so if I can perhaps instil a love of books and reading and learning in general into a new generation, then I think English teaching is a worthwhile thing to do.'

High school students talk about English

During 1996 and 1997, twenty-eight high school students, who received grades on their previous report that placed them in one of the two top levels (A or B, or equivalent, where A is the highest grade and E is the lowest), also took part in this study. All participants were in the post-compulsory years of schooling (Years 11 and 12) and all attended co-educational schools. Half the participants attended a state school in Western Australia, although not all participants were from the same class, while the other half attended a private school in Queensland where, again, not all participants were from the same class. Slightly less than half the total number of participants were girls. The groups cannot be viewed as representative of either the states in which they lived, or the schools they attended, however, although separated by geographical distance, by syllabus requirements and possibly by social class, there was a remarkable degree of agreement in the responses of both groups.

The students were asked to respond in writing to the same questions as the university students: that is, 'What functions do you think the secondary school subject called "English" is meant to fulfil?' and 'What do you think students in secondary school English classrooms should be studying?' Interestingly, the high school cohort was much clearer about what students should be doing in secondary English classes than were their university counterparts. Generally, they commented that they should be studying 'texts', and they used the term to refer to a broad range of genres, including newspaper and television texts and literary texts. They thought that in studying texts they should be learning how to interpret different types of texts and how to 'write' or 'make' them for themselves. The following response is typical of the comments made in both states: 'I think English teaches us to appreciate good writing and good films. And [it] teach[es] us to speak properly when we're giving talks. We learn how to write different sorts of texts such as newspaper articles and short stories' (Shannon). Compare that with a university student's understanding of the goals of English: 'Not an easy question to answer! It is certainly not just teaching grammar. I believe that the subject area of English encompasses not only grammatical skills, but also the skills that will enable students to take a more active part in their society. By not just accepting things as they are, students can use the English classroom to deconstruct all sorts of notions, from gender and class to age and power' (Anon.). The university students' views were global in their breadth and range while the high school students, perhaps understandably, focused on the techniques of textual study.

Unlike the university students who used their responses to the questions as a basis for group discussions about the subject and their future careers, the high school students took part in group discussions with me a few days after providing written responses. In these discussions I selected particular themes that I decided had emerged from their written comments and asked them to elaborate. For example, almost all of the high school respondents expressed an interest in English as a subject and most included the word 'enjoy' or variations such as 'like' when referring to their own relation to the subject. Almost invariably the enjoyment or liking was linked with 'creative' opportunities in the English classroom, such as story writing or reading literary texts or talking about the media. However, in the Queensland group, several students had commented that although they enjoyed English they were not sure just what it was that they were doing that allowed them to achieve in the top two grades on assessments.

Myles (Year 11) commented: 'We don't really learn things in English. I don't know what we're supposed to learn. You know it's like you're already supposed to know what it's about before you get to class. They don't teach us . . . it's more like they ask us what we know and then they talk about that. And if we know it then we do okay. I do okay in it.' When asked where else he thought he'd learnt what he was supposed to know in English he elaborated:

I guess at home. You know from mum reading to me and that. And helping me to write. She still helps a bit with assignments and that. And just from general knowledge. We had this assignment to do a couple of weeks back. We had to write a feature article on a topic of our choice. We were given a couple of examples of feature articles from newspapers but I couldn't figure out what we were supposed to do with them. But mum showed me . . . you know from the newspapers and that how it was different from other bits of the paper. So I just like copied the style. But we didn't really learn about that in the class. No . . . we just talked about what interested us and what we might write about.

This view was corroborated by other members of the Queensland group.

Katherine stated that although she 'really enjoyed' taking part in class discussion about issues or about particular texts she was not quite sure what the discussions were meant to achieve:

> It's like I listen to everyone else talking, and I say things too, and it's really interesting listening to ideas and that but in the end . . . in the end I don't know what was right. It's like there's no way of knowing, well . . . is this idea right, or is that idea . . . where we should be going? I guess there's no right or wrong in English. That's it isn't it? We're just learning how to think about things.

When asked if she thought they were learning how to think about things in a critical way Katherine seemed puzzled. 'No, not really critical. But we know both sides [of an argument] and we have to think about our own opinion.' English for this group of students focused in general terms on the relationship between themselves and texts.

The Western Australian group held similar views. Ben (Year 11) commented, 'We just talk in class . . . about things that the teacher asks us about. We don't write much. We do some reading. It's interesting sometimes.' And Ty (Year 12) complained that he had trouble understanding what he was supposed to do in English. 'We get assignments . . . dad helps me figure them out . . . I do okay so I must do what she [the teacher] wants.' Laura (Year 11) confessed to never having read a class novel set for English: 'I just figure them out from the back cover. I skim a bit and ask people who've read it. I write down the names of the characters and learn them. I know the theme . . . and the plot . . . and the setting.' When asked if she thought she would learn a lot more if she read the novels she replied, 'I read a lot of novels but these [class novels] aren't interesting . . . I'm reading Patricia Cornwall now. I've read them all so far.' Still, English for Laura was 'enjoyable'. She commented on the class discussions that were about 'issues' and she felt that she could take part in these and learn from the comments of other students. She found the classroom talk in English 'interesting' and she commented that 'we end up talking about the things in English in recess [that is, during the break].' Overall, these students confirmed the view that English was enjoyable even though they were not quite sure what they were supposed to learn.

Unlike the UK study, students were not asked to comment on different 'models' of English and as the responses and discussion above suggest, the concept of 'models' of English was not part of most Australian students' understandings of how the subject is arranged. It could be argued, however, that the students' comments were orientated towards 'personal growth', indirectly acknowledging an organising rhetoric of English of which they were apparently unaware. In addition, a concept of 'models' is embedded in English policy development and theory, and informs and regulates much curriculum theorising.

Investigating English

The first belief about English to be examined below is that English teaching and learning is arranged through a concept of 'models'. The second belief about English to be examined is that the subject of English is largely 'indefinable' and somehow 'mysterious' or 'elusive'. This belief is held by students in university education courses, who see it as a positive feature of the subject; one that is linked to the subject's alignment with the profound insights into the human condition offered by literature, and to its ability to access individual creativity and to provide avenues for freedom of expression. On the other hand, high school students, who also express the belief that English is 'mysterious', tend to express this belief in negative terms. That is, high school students are more likely to see this as a perverse aspect of English and a frustrating one for them as learners.

But it is not only high school students who consider the 'mysterious' quality of English to be perverse. Also to be examined in this chapter is the apparently contradictory call for a definition of a subject that is at the same time lauded for being unknowable. English, it seems, is in urgent need of 'something' that will provide an agreed upon and workable set of limits while not abandoning the claim of incommensurability. This goal is expressed in different ways by different groups. The need for 'good practice' or workable guidelines by teachers; 'accountability' by bureaucrats; 'definitions' by students. Although this belief appears to contradict the belief that English is indefinable and mysterious, nevertheless, it surfaces through various government reports (often alongside the belief that English is ultimately indefinable) and in discussions with high school and university students studying to become English teachers. The struggle to reconcile these positions – of the need for 'limits' on the one side and for 'freedom' on the other – is part of a long tradition in English education.

In thinking about ways of describing and possibly changing the course of English, theorists and curricula writers often conceptualise the subject as taking different paths at different points in its history. These different paths are variously described as 'models' or 'approaches' to English teaching. Significant reports on English in Australia such as 'The Martin Report' (1980) and 'The Christie Report' (1991) despite being separated by fifteen years, describe English teaching and learning in terms of models, and as Robin Peel has noted in this book, the Cox Report (1989) set out five different models of English.

In 1989 *The English Magazine* carried a useful article by PGCE students discussing Cox's proposed models. The point the PGCE students made was that Cox had left out a vital new turn in English teaching. The 'new' model was 'post-structuralism', or what is sometimes called a 'cultural studies' approach to English. This has become a recognised, if an unevenly used, approach to English education in Australia since the mid 1980s.

The PGCE students also argued that the five models that Cox had identified were not harmonious parts of a whole. They asserted that 'cultural studies' or 'post-structuralist' approaches were distinguished from all previous models by a focus on the politics of language. Certainly, in Australian secondary schools in the 1980s and 1990s, Cultural studies English offered, albeit unevenly, a different kind of critical perspective on texts through an exploration of the themes of power, identity, desire and subjectivity (Gilbert 1989). It would be hard to deny that English became a rather different kind of subject in many schools as state education systems implemented new syllabi that took account of a wider range of text types than 'literary' texts, and shifted assessment requirements away from narrative and essay writing while embracing 'media' studies as a component of the English curriculum. And yet, despite these apparent differences from previous approaches, English has maintained its focus on the twin goals of aesthetics and ethics across all the designated models. It maintains this focus, I argue below, through a particular and unchanging pedagogy. The one attempt to rearrange the terrain of English in Australia by reintroducing a focus on rhetoric by the genre theorists was met generally with hostility in secondary schools.

In making the move from what is described as 'personal growth' English (Dixon 1969) to 'post-structural' (Belsey 1980) or 'cultural studies' English (Corcoran *et al.* 1994) teachers, theorists and curricula writers in Australia often drew on the work of Chalkface Press, an Australian publishing company which pioneered post-structuralist practices in secondary English classrooms through the production of a number of classroom texts calculated not only to teach students different ways of reading and writing but to understand the operation of power through language and meaning. Drawing broadly on the work of early structuralist writers such as Jack Zipes (1993) and Roland Barthes (1957) and on post-structuralist critical theorists such as Catherine Belsey (1985) and Terry Eagleton (1983), the Chalkface publications provided an accessible forum for debate in newspapers, professional journals, organisations and in classrooms. Australian writers such as Wendy Morgan (1994) and Wayne Martino (1994) have extended the range of classroom texts in Australia which addressed English from a 'cultural studies' perspective and writers outside Australia also have been involved in this mission. Hilary Janks (1993) in South Africa, for example, has made a similar commitment to explore the workings of language and power through her classroom texts.

More recently in Australia, however, the work of Tony Bennett (1998), Ian Hunter (1994), Alec McHoul (1996) and Denise Meredyth (Meredyth and Tyler 1993), among others has occasioned a rethinking of the concepts of 'discourse', 'power' and 'subjectivity'. In taking a general lead from this work and by focusing on the uses of texts and on the concept of 'reading occasions' (Hunter 1989) the most recent books from Chalkface Press, *Investigating Texts* (Mellor and Patterson 1996) and *Studying Poetry* (Moon 1998), have provided classroom based texts that challenge the assumption made in previous Chalkface work of a generalised relationship between language, power, society and subjectivity. These ideas have been explored through professional journals in Australia devoted to discussions of a 'post' post-structuralist English (*Interpretations*, Special Issue, beyond Poststructuralism, 1994, 27 (3)).

The presence of different and often competing models, a belief in the transcendental qualities of English combined with a call for definition of the subject and for increased accountability have posed particular problems for policy developers during the past two decades.

Investigating policy

Although as noted previously Australia does not have a 'national' curriculum nevertheless in 1994, following a prolonged period of extensive consultation on curriculum issues, the Australian Education Council (a national council of Ministers of Education) issued two documents which marked the first attempt in Australia to produce a national framework for curriculum: They were a *Statement on English for Australian Schools* (1994) and a companion document, *English – A Curriculum Profile for Australian Schools* (1994). The stated intent was 'to promote a more consistent approach to the development of English curricula throughout Australia and to achieve a better coordinated and integrated system of literacy provision for all children' (1994, p. 1). Since there is no national system of education for children in Australia these documents have had variable effects across the country, with each state and territory making its own decision about the usefulness of the National Statement and Profile for their own system.

The *Statement on English for Australian Schools* begins with the 'Goals of the English Curriculum' and lists these as, among others, 'a knowledge of the ways in which language varies according to context, purpose, audience and content'; 'a sound grasp of the linguistic structures and features of standard Australian English'; 'a capacity to relate literature to aspects of contemporary society and personal experience'; 'the capacity to discuss and analyse texts and language critically and with appreciation'; 'a knowledge of the ways in which textual interpretation and understanding may vary according to cultural, social and personal differences' (1994, p. 3). In this brief and selective run through the objectives for English curricula – outlined at a national level for the first time in Australia – the requirement to be inclusive of a range of models is apparent. This is perhaps as it should be since curricula and syllabi are by necessity practical documents which need to take account of the broad range of existing understandings of the subject among a diverse body of teachers.

One of the problems, however, with a 'models' approach is that it tucks English too neatly into historical periods by suggesting, for instance, that in the 1920s skills dominated English, while in the 1940s, heritage or the cannon dominated, and then in the 1960s and 1970s the New English emerged, followed by cultural studies English in the 1980s and 1990s as the preferred model. Not only does this approach suggest a neat progression of models, it also (and more importantly, I think), overlooks the historical continuity of the subject in terms of its stated preoccupations with more fundamental themes such as aesthetics, ethics and rhetoric.

Ian Hunter (1997) has provided an interesting theoretical lead in suggesting that rather than thinking about English as a subject driven by different ideological perspectives represented by models, the subject we now call English could be thought about as comprising a mix of aesthetics, ethics and rhetoric. Furthermore, he suggests, this has always been so. The differences between different eras of English teaching, thus can be seen in terms of the mix of these elements. In some periods English has maintained a greater emphasis on aesthetics than on ethics, with rhetoric occupying a minor role. At other times, English has focused on ethics rather than aesthetics, again with rhetoric occupying a relatively minor role.

Discussion of models is often accompanied by an assumption that each model carries a different pedagogy. But the point to be considered is that historically, English has maintained a steady focus in terms of pedagogy while appearing to undergo regular – even radical – change in the form of different models. Thus – and consistently so – central to the pedagogical arrangements of English over the past century and a half is the goal of transforming the consciousness of learners through the inculcation of social norms relating to proper conduct. What is deemed to constitute proper conduct differs with each model, but at the core of this conduct is 'transformation' expressed as the ability to 'see things as they really are'. The phrase 'see things as they really are' has an interesting history in English. Mellor and Patterson (1994) have examined the use of this and similar phrases during the past 100 years in the work of Arnold (1903), Leavis (1900), Dixon (1967), and Newbolt (1921). More modern writers also are regular users of this and related phrases. Statements such as 'seeing things as they really are' and 'the very desire to see things as they are' and 'life as it really is' and so on, suggest that English enables us to see beyond the varying obstacles which stand in the way of full recognition of the truth of the text or of the truth of humanity; obstacles which also obstruct the individual's and society's access to complete development (see Mellor and Patterson 1994).

Some of the problems associated with using the concept of models of English teaching as an organising device in theoretical work became obvious during the late 1980s when the 'genre' debate, (referred to above) erupted in Australia. One of the features of this debate was that the pro-genre team went in to bat for rhetoric, while banishing aesthetics to the outfield. A compli-cation, or perhaps misunderstanding, of this debate was that although ethics held a strong place on the genre side it was perceived by the opposition as comprising the 'wrong' sort of ethics; one that affirmed existing power structures by claiming to teach 'disadvantaged' students how to reproduce the genres of power rather than teaching them how to challenge and change those genres. The proponents of genre did not appear to use the traditional rhetoric of English. Expressions such as 'freedom', or the students' ability to 'breakthrough' to knowledge did not feature as ways of talking about English. Opponents to 'genre' often articulated their opposition in terms of the unaccountability or immeasurability of English knowledge which remains a traditional 'defence' of the subject.

'The genre theorists'[1] proposed that the then current practice of deploying a pedagogy based on 'whole language' theory and 'process writing' approaches (Cambourne 1988) was not meeting the literacy needs of diverse groups of children in primary school classrooms. Primary literacy teachers, argued the genre theorists, could not rely on theories of language learning such as 'whole language' because these types of theories deployed a pedagogical mode that required an indirect approach to teaching. Indirect teaching was not assumed to be useful for students who did not have prior access to knowledge about literacy requirements in the school. In a 'whole language' classroom ruled by student choice and teacher facilitation of textual experiences, the genre theorists argued, children 'chose' either well or poorly according to their prior understanding of the importance or otherwise of particular modes of school writing. Instead, the genre theorists proposed, all children needed explicit teaching about how to recognise and use the privileged genres of schooling. The tool for this explicit teaching would be systemic functional linguistics as proposed by the linguist M. A. K. Halliday (Halliday 1985; see also Halliday and Hassan 1985). Although the work of the genre theorists was directed in the main at the primary school, it did have ramifications for secondary education in that some of the ideas found their way into policy documents at that level. The Queensland English syllabus (1994), for instance, is premised on an understanding that secondary English teaching should include a focus on the structure and use of identifiably different types of texts. Although Queensland English teachers are not expected to teach functional linguistics to students, they are expected to have a working knowledge of language in terms of its linguistic functions and uses. In these and other ways related to 'battles' between cultural studies and personal growth approaches to English, the 'genre' debate has had an effect on the shape of school English in Australia.

While theorists and policy makers battled back and forth on the issue of whether or not this or that was the best 'approach' to teaching English, teachers meanwhile went on teaching eclectically in terms of models or approaches, and traditionally in terms of pedagogy. Many teachers informed themselves about the models' debate and then mixed and matched from the

---

1 The term 'the genre theorists' is used generically to refer to groups of academics who were instrumental in producing a 'genre' position. These included among others, Francis Christie, Jim Martin and Joan Rothery. The genre work in schools was informed by the work of the linguist M. A. K. Halliday. For a summary overview of this topic see Baars, Myra (1994) 'Genre theory: What's it all about?' in Barry Stierer and Janet Maybin (eds.) *Language, Literacy and Learning in Educational Practice*, Adelaide: Multilingual Matters and Open University Press.

available approaches, selecting the best of each and combining them in creative and stimulating ways in their classrooms. It is, after all, how teachers usually manage their work in classrooms, through what Mountford (1996) describes as 'informed eclecticism'. This practice, combined with policy shifts and curriculum rewrites, effected a change in classroom teaching over the past two decades. The contribution of theorists to this process of change was arguably marginal, however, it did on occasions assist teachers to articulate their reasons for teaching different kinds of text and language strategies.

Although the era of the genre debates, or 'wars' was a useful phase in discussions about English in Australia because it helped to focus attention on the changing demands for different types of literate practices, nevertheless, it also helped to 'cement' the idea that English is arranged primarily around different models. Apart from being not always helpful in a theoretical sense (for reasons examined below), this move encouraged a polarisation of English professionals as they took up their positions on one side or another as pro or anti genre. While division and dissent may be signs of healthy debate and help to invigorate a profession, nevertheless, the turn towards models as an organising device for English education tended to obscure the more pressing issue of pedagogy and the urgent concerns of an increasingly impatient education bureaucracy. Furthermore, the polarisation of the professional community around models occurred at a time when some state governments were preparing to place English under increased scrutiny in curricula and accountability terms. A professional group side-tracked on an issue as peripheral to the accountability concerns of English as 'models' and defending the ultimate mystery and incommensurability of the subject was not in a strong position to think and act creatively nor communicate effectively about the future of English.

Reporting English: the Martin Report and the Beazley Report

The Martin Report (1980) which preceded the genre debate by several years, also used the concept of models to describe English, except that it did not include 'genre' since that term had not been invented as part of the 'models' or approaches repertoire. Thus, when something which became labelled as 'genre' did appear it tended to be consigned initially to the 'skills' model. However, what is particularly interesting from the perspective of the responses gathered from the study reported above is that the Report provides a set of data about 'beliefs about English' expressed in the late 1970s in Australia. The report was commissioned by the then Director General of Education in Western Australia who provided the following brief to the investigating team: 'to explore and describe the teaching and learning of English in State secondary schools, to identify the most influential factors in that process, and to make recommendations about future directions' (1980, p. iii). Nancy Martin, former Head of the Department of English at London

University Institute of Education, was commissioned to conduct a major survey of English in Western Australia and to write the report.

Two features of the report are of particular interest in terms of the present discussion. Firstly, in the section 'What is English' the writers note that there is a 'lack of consensus about what English is'. This is evident not only in the extensive case studies of particular high schools, but in the statements provided by teachers, students and parents. The responses were selected by the writers of the report as representative of a wide range of views and included the following:

> 'To me English is an art. Nobody can really tell you how to write . . . '
> (Year 12 student);
> 'English is to make us more interesting people' (Year 9 student);
> 'A teacher who can't get kids to weep or laugh over their study of English has missed the point' (School Principal);
> 'Well, it's a subject in their school work, isn't it? Or is it the way they are speaking?' (Parent);
> 'Student's thoughts, feelings, opinions and imaginings are the stuff of English' (Senior English Teacher) (Martin 1980, p. xv).

In these statements, reported in the late 1970s, it is not difficult to recognise some of the recurring themes (in debates about English) also apparent in the statements discussed above made by university students studying to become teachers of high school English in the 1990s.

The second feature of the report that is of interest for this chapter was the conclusion that there was a 'need for a unified conception of English' (1980, p. 64). The call for a more unified conception of English is linked to the previously noted concerns about the inability of professionals, students and teachers alike to provide a definition of English. Given that the state had restructured its English curricula in the years immediately prior to the commissioning of the report, the identification of a need for a unified conception of English seems a little puzzling until we examine the nature of the changes put in place. At the 'post compulsory' end of the secondary school (Years 11 and 12) the subject perhaps aptly titled, 'Leaving English' had been restructured as two separate subjects: 'English' and 'English Literature'. Both subjects were accredited as part of the Tertiary Admission Examination system that was a competitive, state-wide examination-based system for selecting students for places in universities. Students were to be selected only on the basis of their performance in this and other nominated examinations. This meant that the syllabus, content and structure of the English subjects were 'driven' by the requirements of the Tertiary Entrance Examination directed in the main by the University of Western Australia. Setting aside for the moment, questions about the desirability of this level of control, what the examination-based approach to English in the post-compulsory years did provide was a structure or coherence for the subject. Interestingly, when teachers, bureaucrats and university academics working in universities other than the University of Western Australia wanted to challenge the traditions of what they viewed as a 'Leavisite' and New Critical approach to English and literature teaching, the task, perhaps surprisingly, was made easier by the existence of an examination. This was because changes in the syllabi, in both senior secondary subjects 'English' and 'English Literature', were accompanied by changes in the examination. Extensive consultations with teachers regarding changes to assessment, combined with teacher representation on the syllabus committees, encouraged teachers to change their view of English Literature teaching in a sustained and systematic way. Paradoxically, it would seem that in some respects an examination-dominated system can offer more potential for change and renewal of curriculum and syllabi than an apparently freer system, unregulated by specific and openly accountable assessment requirements.

When changes were made to the upper secondary English and Literature syllabi in the late 1980s, teachers, with the support of a well-managed state professional organisation (the English Teachers Association of Western Australia) were able to bridge a gap in professional knowledge through extensive professional development programmes accompanied by stimulating and well-attended state conferences. Although the incentive to develop professionally was provided by a top-down bureaucratic directive in the form of a new syllabus and a new examination, it was met generally with cautious enthusiasm by the majority of teachers, many of whom by this stage were not graduates of the University of Western Australia. Without arguing the merits or otherwise of the new syllabus and examination it is salutary to reflect on the process of change in this instance as an example of one governmental strategy that is available to bureaucratic systems. Generally, members of democratic societies and professionals aligned with a subject such as English that prides itself on its emancipatory ideals, would not be sympathetic to overtly manipulative bureaucratic strategies for change. But in this instance the Secondary Education Authority in Western Australia achieved an unprecedented level of change and rejuvenation of curriculum and teaching practices relatively quickly and painlessly. This is not to claim that the new syllabus and examination were implemented without complaint or resistance but, in the event, the disapproval and anxiety expressed were negotiated through dialogue and compromise on both sides. In addition, the project of syllabus reform was assisted by the implementation in previous years of a new Year 11 English Literature syllabus which, although constituting a discrete subject which was not directly examinable for tertiary selection purposes, did introduce ideas about literary study that were compatible with the new Year 12 syllabus.

At the compulsory end of the secondary school (in some states such as Western Australia and Queensland this is Years 8 to 10, in others it is Years 7 to 10) the scene was a little different. The examination based 'certificates' had given way by the early 1980s to an approach to English that was teacher directed, rather than exam directed, and student centred rather than 'content' centred. It relied on school-based assessments over a period of time, usually a year, and allowed teachers to build a cumulative 'profile' of a student's achievements over the course of their English studies. Teacher assessment was 'moderated' by 'Comparability Tests' which allowed the state education department to monitor student achievements across schools in Western Australia. Yet, despite the limits to English set by 'Comparability Tests', the new approach offered teachers and students a great deal of choice and flexibility in terms of the subject matter taught in classrooms.

In summary, then, English in the junior secondary classroom in Western Australia changed in the 1970s from an examination-focused subject based on a syllabus that was defined to a certain extent by the requirements of the 'certificate' system, to a programme of work that was not based on a syllabus but was designed in local sites by individual teachers or groups of teachers. This more flexible programme was not tied to an official syllabus or to a state-based assessment system, although 'Comparability Tests' were in place. Schools could choose the type of assessment they thought best suited their students and the school-based programme of work. At the post-compulsory end of secondary schooling, Years 11 and 12, one English subject became two subjects. Both were state-syllabus- and state-examination-based.

The two conclusions by the Martin Report that there was a 'lack of consensus about what English is' and further that there was a 'need for a unified conception of English' (1980, p. 64) appeared to be contradicted in part by the recommendations. In recommending, for instance, the abandonment of any external examination process, the Report appeared to suggest that consensus and unification could be achieved by a process of curriculum localisation. Every school was to design and teach its own programme. The Report suggested that 'if any State-wide monitoring is thought desirable, it should be by sampling, and should therefore not appear in any one school more frequently than, say, every three or four years' (1980, p. 259). At the time the Report was released, retention rates beyond Year 10 in Western Australian state schools were around 52 per cent. Students, thus, could conceivably complete their secondary education without ever having their work, or their results, subjected to the gaze of an external moderator, or to any gaze other than that of their classroom teacher. Further, the Report recommended that 'teacher assessment and extended moderation (presumably based on a three- to four-year cycle) should replace that part of the Achievement Certificate now determined by the comparability tests, and should cover the whole examination' (1980, p. 259). Leaving aside the liberatory (from a neo-marxian perspective) potential of this move it is not a suggestion likely to enhance the possibility of providing a more coherent rather than a less coherent view or practice of English. And in a political climate already preparing for more demands for accountability by governments, the call for a less accountable set of practices (in ministerial terms) appears to have been somewhat shortsighted. Nevertheless, within the field of

English education, if not within the field of curriculum policy development it appeared to be in tune with the anti-assessment rhetoric of its time and the belief that English was unmeasurable.

The insistence that English be quarantined from accountability measures and that it eschew transparent and generalisable assessment practices is linked in part to a belief that it cannot be defined, and in part to a tradition of ideology critique within English theorising. A decade later Bill Green provided a neo-marxian critique of the Martin Report in which he commented that 'it worked, in short, with a quintessentially *liberal-bourgeois* vision of educational practice' (emphasis in the original) (Green 1989, p. 21). The weakness of the Martin Report, in Green's view, was in its '*politics* – its inability to move beyond its own ideological limits, so as to draw into its educational project a more explicitly socio-political dimension' (emphasis in the original) (Green 1989, p. 21). To achieve an educational project of this kind it seems that English would need to provide a coherent and critical vision of a school subject which could avoid being equated with such things as comparative system wide 'assessment' and 'credentialling'.

Fast on the heels of the Martin Report in Western Australia came the Beazley Report (1984). Although only four years separated the release of each report they were conceptually at least a decade apart since, as Green noted:

> Although published in 1980, the Martin Report is very clearly a document of the 1970s, not simply because it provided case studies of schools and English classrooms on the basis of research conducted in the late 70s, but also because it articulated a distinctive professional ideology of that period. This is what has been variously known as the 'New English' and 'Growth Model English' – that version of English teaching coming out of the Dartmouth Seminar in 1966 and arguably the major force in English curriculum policy and research in the immediately ensuing period . . .
>
> Green 1989, p. 20

Interestingly, the Martin Report in detailing the case studies of selected schools demonstrated not the successes of the New English but its failure. The causes of the failure were placed in large part with the state-administered assessment practices of the time which continued to 'drive' English teaching in high schools. The idea of a 'blockage' to the 'real' goals and aspirations of English is a familiar and enduring response.

The Beazley Report, however, took an entirely different approach. Unlike the Martin Report that looked only at English, the Beazley Report examined all curriculum areas with a view to recommending curriculum change to the state government. One of the terms of reference for the Committee was: 'the adequacy of present certification arrangements for students proceeding through school and the extent to which tertiary admission requirements should be adjusted to enable the curriculum to be diversified to meet the needs of the widest possible community' (Education Ministry, Western

Australia 1984, p. xiii). On handing down the Beazley Report, it was noted that English had been singled out for special attention: 'The committee decided, because of time limitations, not to investigate the detailed syllabuses of existing "core" subjects (that is, Mathematics, Science, Social Studies, English)'. However, the Committee noted that 'it was obliged by evidence to waive this decision to some extent in regard to the teaching of English. The Committee believed that the relative generality of the English syllabus also provided justification for some closer examination of this subject' (1984, p. 144, 2.139). In view of what the Committee considered to be serious problems associated with the teaching of English in high schools, a discussion paper was circulated during the time of the inquiry and feedback sought from the community. The paper suggested, among other things that: 'There is insufficient relevance in the upper school curriculum to practical situations and contemporary life'; that 'the teaching of English is too closely tied to the teaching of literature'; and that 'too much emphasis is being placed on literary and creative objectives' (1984, p. 145, 2.139).

The Beazley Report recommended on school curricula and credentialling reform in the compulsory years of secondary schooling while the parallel McGaw Report made recommendations relating to compulsory schooling. Together these two reports formed the basis of extensive curricula and credentialling change across all areas in secondary schools and marked the beginning of more, not less, government regulation of English in Western Australia. These reports, however, had more widespread impact and their effects were felt wider afield than in their home state. In many respects they provided a guide to change in other states and territories and were revisited when the states and territories finally sat down at the same table to discuss the possibility of nationally coordinated curricula.

Measuring the unmeasurable

In the intervening years between the release of the Martin Report (1980) and the Beazley Report (1984) and the late 1990s, benchmarking, testing, competency-based training and outcomes-based education have emerged as major issues in planning and policy arenas at a national level in Australia, as they have in the United Kingdom and the United States. The debates in Australia prompted by these movements have effected a shift in thinking among critical commentators on literacy education to the degree that Allan Luke and Christina van Kraayenoord could confidently assert in a recent article that 'few curriculum developers and educational researchers would disagree with the need for interstate curricular coherence, public accountability and systems of assessment'. As long, that is, as this need does not include the development and use of benchmarks linked to testing. 'There is', the writers go on to claim, 'little international evidence that national or State-wide testing systems *per se* will lead to improvements in instructional effectiveness, innovation or student achievement' (Luke and van Kraayenoord 1998, p. 55).

The specific tensions apparent here between the need for 'accountability' on the one hand, and the need for 'improvements in instructional effectiveness' – which presumably are to be brought about without overt regulation on the part of the state – are echoed in literacy debates across Australia. The apparently contradictory position education analysts and commentators now find themselves in – of claiming on the one hand that there is a need for a national system-wide approach to curriculum and assessment and on the other that a national system-wide approach is to be resisted – is not an unfamiliar expression of the problems surrounding testing and English.

Luke and van Kraayenoord draw on the work of Basil Bernstein to make the point that 'it is axiomatic in curriculum theory that what counts as knowledge, practice, skill and competence is driven by assessment systems' (1998, p. 61). The first observation that can be made about this claim is that what counts as knowledge, practice, skill and competence in English is of necessity driven by something. That is, knowledge does not exist in a pure form, un-driven by anything in particular. School knowledge, practice, skill and competence is driven by a range of competing interests and by the necessity for a society to have in place adequate bureaucratic and administrative structures, procedures and processes to ensure the delivery of mass education. To collapse the complexities of curricula implementation in a mass education system into the single category 'assessment' is to understate the case. But, since assessment is clearly one of a number of elements in this complex configuration of curricula, then the challenge might be to ensure that the assessments are indeed assessing what the profession considers to be valuable and what it thinks it is teaching. These assumptions, among others, have driven governments to devise often costly and time-consuming mechanisms for ensuring extensive consultation with teachers in devising and trialling such measures as literacy benchmarks. None the less, an imperfect process for all of that.

Peter Freebody has called upon educators to take the opportunity provided by vigorous debate over benchmarks in Australia to 'examine more specifically and critically the relationship between their assessment practices and the portable outcomes that should be available from their pedagogies' (Freebody 1998, p. 14). But what are these 'portable outcomes'? It seems from the same article, that they include teachers' knowledge about how well 'the literacy practices put on offer enhance our students' abilities to handle the literacy demands in subsequent educational levels' and how well 'they enrich the life of the student outside of school' (Freebody 1998, p. 14). But again, the issue of how anyone knows that 'the portable outcomes' are being achieved, is rather neatly sidestepped by a call to Australian literacy educators to 'draw on a long and productive local tradition of research, theory and debate' to address these issues. Are the portable outcomes so local as to be outside the range of system-wide scrutiny, or so diffuse as to be immeasurable? That was certainly the position taken by the writers of the Martin Report in 1980, and embodied in their recommendation that 'individual schools should, from time to time . . . engage in school-based monitoring' (p. 259).

There remains a high level of suspicion among critical analysts of education in Australia and elsewhere that despite the 'benefits' rhetoric of politicians, education bureaucrats and administrators, testing based on benchmarks will place teachers at risk of further criticism for failing to provide adequate teaching. The possibility that the results of testing based on benchmarks would provide data to support teachers' claims for achieving laudable successes with children in their classrooms in addition to long-term data with which to refute the perennial claims that literacy standards are falling does not appear to have been considered. And perhaps with good reason. The first media coverage of the recent historic benchmarking exercise in Australia was accompanied by outrageous and blatant manipulation of the data by the then Federal Minister for Employment, Education, Training and Youth Affairs. Sections of the popular media in Australia, rarely slow to criticise teachers, moved into top gear. Freebody captured the flavour of the moment with this description of the interview conducted with the Minister on a popular television 'current events' programme:

> The interviewer Ms Liz Hayes, named [the survey results] as 'frightening' and 'terrifying' . . . She inquired tremulously of the Minister whether or not this was a 'scandalous' situation. The Minister could not quell her anxieties: Yes, he vouchsafed, this was a 'scandalous' situation.
>
> Freebody 1998, p. 13

It goes without saying that the 'results' quoted in this interview and in previous publicity for the programme were damagingly inaccurate. In addition, the level of debate was not assisted by a poor grasp of statistical techniques and procedures shown not only by many commentators on the debate but also by professional English educators. Those with the requisite expertise were put in a position of 'correcting' their colleagues' interpretations of the data thereby providing an unwanted impression of a divided and poorly informed group of English professionals.

This problem has been exacerbated by the ways in which the data have been presented and interpreted in reports and articles.[2] In many instances, results from Australia's first national benchmarking exercise were presented in a tabular form that arguably placed teachers at risk of further criticism. It

---

2 For representative examples of interpretations and re-readings of the literacy benchmark data see the following: Alloway. N. and Gilbert, P. (1998) 'Reading literacy test data: Benchmarking success?' *The Australian Journal of Language and Literacy*, 21 (3), 249–261; Freebody, P. (1998); Gill, M. (1998), 'Who set the benchmarks?' *English in Australia*, 121, 9–14; Masters, G. (1997) 'Do we want high literacy standards?' *Australian Language Matters*. 5 (4), 7–8; 'Findings from the literacy scandal: "the same disconcert and tremulousness and meditation"', *English in Australia*, 122, 10–14.

appeared from data tabulated in an accessible but perhaps misleading way, for instance, that 77 per cent of Year 5 children in Australia in the 'Special Indigenous Group' (that is, children identified as being of Aboriginal or Torres Strait Islander descent) failed to meet the reading benchmark, compared with 27 per cent of the total Year 5 cohort who failed to meet the same level (Alloway and Gilbert, 1998, p. 252). 'Blood chilling' is how one colleague described that figure: 'sobering' was the term used by a high-ranking education administrator in the region in which I live. But to interpret that figure fully, it was argued, analysts needed access to the number of students in the 'Special Indigenous Group' cohort, and they required knowledge about whether Indigenous students had been identified accurately as a separate group within the total cohort. This information is not available to observers of the tables represented in articles outside the original full report. Further, the tabulated data suggested that results along socio-economic lines were cause for concern with only 13 per cent of high socio-economic status students failing to meet the benchmark, against 53 per cent of children identified as low socio-economic status (Masters 1997). Leaving aside the problems associated with presenting data in a form that invites comparison across overlapping social categories (ethnicity, socio-economic status, gender) the table provided a too handy weapon with which to take aim at teachers. The impressive achievement by early childhood and elementary school teachers of successfully (by the Government's own standards) educating at least 71 per cent of all children in their classrooms to a nationally agreed-upon reading standard was lost in the dust of the debate over the apparently unacceptable level of 'failure' for the total cohort, despite the best efforts of the teachers' unions and other advocates to focus on the positive aspects of the data and to correct inaccuracies.

Benchmarks in Australia have not reached into the area of secondary education, although they are on the policy agenda of federal and state governments. Students in lower secondary classes in Australia are not required to write external examinations. This has been the case in Western Australia for almost two decades. There have been various moves over this period of time to provide some accountability measures through moderation exercises although these measures have tended to appear and disappear with changes of Government and Ministries.

At the non-compulsory end of schooling in Australia (Years 11 and 12) only the state of Queensland and the territory of the Australian Capital have dispensed entirely with system-wide examinations. All other states and territories either rely extensively on state-wide examinations or, as is more likely the case, on a combination of school-based assessments and state-administered examinations. On the other hand, the compulsory years of secondary schooling in all states and territories employ school-based assessment procedures that are often subject to only superficial scrutiny through state-wide monitoring procedures which involve groups, comprising teachers from across the state, meeting to compare samples of students' work. But perhaps the most systematic attempt to monitor teaching and learning in the compulsory years of schooling came with the introduction of a state-wide sampling technique called Monitoring Student Outcomes in Western Australia. It was linked with the 'outcomes' movement that gained momentum in Australia in the 1990s and comprised a technique for testing an admittedly narrow range of literacy achievements in Years 3 and 7. Although narrow in focus, the items were negotiated with teacher groups and literacy theorists. The monitoring was eventually extended to Year 9 students. The rationale for its introduction by a 'leftist' Labor state government was that it would provide base-line data for teachers beleaguered by accusations of falling literacy standards. This monitoring, claimed the then State Premier, eventually would provide irrefutable, long-term evidence that standards were not declining.

In the event, Monitoring Student Outcomes was introduced without a great deal of negative comment from the teaching community. The tests were based on a set of outcomes already agreed to by teachers, and the various professional bodies representing the interests of teachers took the line that as long as teachers continued to be consulted and involved in the process of outcomes setting, that the tests addressed the outcomes in sensible ways and that they remained as only one indicator among many of the academic progress of students then they would support it. Often governments appear to be slow to understand that extensive community consultation and professional participatory practices, while time-consuming and expensive, are in the long term the shortest paths to change. Whether the effects of those changes are in the best interests of all concerned is rarely something that can be guaranteed in advance. Government, like most social processes, is an imperfect art and science.

Freedom versus regulation?

English is the one area of the curriculum where the important work of teaching through the use of non-coercive strategies, a particular and useful ethical comportment suited to the functioning of a participatory democracy, takes place. As Pam Gilbert (1994) noted, English is

> a potentially powerful educational space in which to reform the curriculum in terms of gender equity . . . English, being one of the central subjects in the curriculum, carries a particular responsibility to deal with and face issues of equity and social justice and it is ideally placed to do so.

Although these observations do not indicate a change in pedagogy, they do locate different 'models' or different 'content' for the subject. The focus of reform in Pam Gilbert's comment is on 'gender equity', but it is clear that any one of a number of targets of reform could be substituted in the above quotation without altering the substance of the claim. English is well placed to assist the necessary transformation (through non-coercive practices) of a particular form of consciousness that is an historically installed requirement of the subject. But it is difficult for English to acknowledge this given its traditional claims for freedom and emancipation – usually understood in terms of escaping the restrictions of the state – and its insistence on non-normative practices.

The beliefs that English is indefinable and therefore untestable, that it lacks consensus, but that consensus can be achieved through individual endeavours in the classroom rather than through systematically negotiated outcomes regulated by systematic assessment, have ensured many lively debates as the Australian states and territories have gradually agreed to more and more regulation at the national level. At the historic meeting in 1989 referred to as the Hobart Agreement, the various State and Territory ministers of Education agreed to a nationally coordinated attempt to produce national curricula guidelines. Subsequently, during the 1990s a great deal of effort has been applied to the task of reaching a consensus in both the national and state arenas about curricula and assessment in what have been identified as eight key learning areas.

Another initiative taken by the Federal Government in the 1990s which addressed the themes of a consensus and a conceptualisation of English was the release of a policy statement titled 'Australia's Language: The Australian Language and Literacy Policy' (1991). As the title suggests the focus was on 'language'. The Martin Report of more than ten years before had noted in its conclusions that 'a lack of consensus means lack of a theoretical base for work in English. It is generally seen as a collection of separate skills. Its central role as a medium and means of learning is not recognised . . . a long-term project is needed from the Education Department to try to alter this situation. The heart of the matter is the concept of learning through language' (emphasis in original, p. 263). This was not an unexpected or particularly prescient observation by the Martin Report writing team since the project team leader (Nancy Martin) was a key member of the group known as 'The London School' which, in the previous decade had pioneered the theme of learning through language. Learning through language in this context meant the use of language for learning about one-self (self-exploration, self-reflection and self-expression) and for learning more about the world and the construction of texts appropriate to their intended audience. Literary texts, however, remained central to the project of learning through language, as the Beazley Report noted.

The focus on language in English policy documents and academic writing about English was combined with an increasing interest in literacy issues and their connection with English. This was more pronounced in the primary school where learning to read and write was of pressing concern to teachers and parents. In the secondary school, where it generally was assumed that students could read and write, literacy issues were slower to take hold. More recent government initiatives to link secondary education to training agendas in Australia have resulted in increased pressure on teachers of high school English (and other subject areas) to pay particular attention to literacy issues. Two reports released this decade indicate these concerns. One is *The Christie Report* (1991) which bears the title 'Teaching English Literacy' and the other is *Teacher Education in English Language and Literacy* (1995).[3] The terms 'English' 'language' and 'literacy' now form a familiar trio in debates about English teaching and learning at the secondary level. Since these two reports focus primarily on the English teacher they will be discussed in the following chapter, 'Shaping the Specialist'.

Conclusion

Beliefs about English expressed by students taking part in this study and expressed through the various reports, policy documents and curriculum statements examined above have focused on the perceived lack of structure of the subject, on its incommensurability, on the need for limits, and on the demand for accountability.

English has not been successful, it seems, in making its goals and assumptions explicit to the students taking part in this study, although the perceived lack of structure was not viewed by all students as a problem. On the contrary, most of the university students studying to become English teachers saw it as a strength of English. In its diffuseness English offered teachers and students alike a space to explore ideas and talk through issues in mutually beneficial ways. The high school students were less convinced that the perceived lack of direct teaching was a bonus but even they were not unduly concerned. They assumed that they were doing well in English because they enjoyed it. They found it interesting because of the opportunities it offered them to take part in discussions about particular issues. On the whole, they enjoyed the variety of texts set for study and the issues that these texts raised. The high school students were not aware of different 'models' or approaches to English and only some of the university students had thought about theoretical points of difference in approaches to text study. The concept of models, however, continues to inform the arena of policy and theory and the belief that English is thus arranged tends to distract attention from the issue of pedagogy. Both are important facets of English and both require attention if English is to be maintained in its current central position. In the preceding chapter I attempted to draw some history lessons for English pedagogy and

---

3 The Christie Report (1991) 'Teaching English literacy: A project of national significance on the preservice preparation of teachers for teaching English literacy', Canberra: Department of Employment, Education and Training; National Board of Employment, Education and Training Australian Language and Literacy Council (1995) 'Teacher education in English language and literacy: preservice and inservice teacher education in both school and adult education contexts, in the fields of English literacy and English as a second language', Canberra : Australian Government Publishing Service.

this theme is taken up again in the chapter Shaping the Specialist on English teacher education.

References

Alloway, Nola and Gilbert, Pam (1998) 'Reading literacy test data: Benchmarking success?' *The Australian Journal of Language and Literacy*, 21 (3), 249–61

Arnold, M. (1903) Equality. *Mixed Essays: The works of Matthew Arnold*, London: Smith, Elder and Company

Australian Education Council (1994) *English – A Curriculum Profile for Australian Schools*. Carlton: Curriculum Corporation

Australian Education Council (1994) *A Statement on English for Australian Schools*, Carlton: Curriculum Corporation

Baars, Myra (1994) 'Genre theory: What's it all about?' in Barry Stierer and Janet Maybin (eds.) *Language, Literacy and Learning in Educational Practice*, Adelaide: Multilintual matters and Open University Press

Barthes, Roland (1957) *Mythologies*, Paris: Editions du Seuil

Belsey, Catherine (1980) *Critical Practice*, London: Methuen

Belsey, Catherine. (1985) *The Subject of Tragedy: Identity and Difference in Renaissance Drama*, London: Methuen

Bennett, Tony (1998) *Culture: A Reformer's Science*, St Leonards: Allen and Unwin

Cambourne, B. (1988) *The Whole Story: Natural Learning and the Acquisition of Literacy in the Classroom* (L. Handy and P. Scown, eds.), Auckland NZ: Ashton Scholastic

Corcoran, Bill, Hayhoe, Mike, Pradl, Gordon M. (eds.) (1994) *Knowledge in the Making: Challenging the Text in the Classroom*, Portsmouth, NH: Heinemann

Cox, Brian (1989). *English for ages 5–16: The Cox Report 1988 and 1989*, London: HMSO

Daly, M., Mathews, S., Middleton, D., Parker, H., Prior, J. and Waters, S. (1989) 'Different views of the subject: A PGCE perspective', *The English Magazine*, 22, Summer

Department of Education, Queensland (1994) *English in Years 1 to 10: Queensland Syllabus Materials: English Syllabus for Years 1 to 10*, Brisbane

Department of Employment, Education and Training (1991) *Teaching English Literacy: A Project of National Significance on the Preservice Preparation of Teachers for Teaching English Literacy* (The Christie Report), Volume 1, Canberra: Department of Employment, Education and Training

Dixon, J. (1967) *Growth through English*, Oxford: Oxford University Press

Dixon, John (1969) *Growth through English: A report based on the Dartmouth Seminar 1966*, Reading: NATE

Eagleton, Terry (1983) *Literary Theory: An Introduction*, Oxford: Blackwell

Education Department, Western Australian (1980) *The Martin Report: Case Studies from Government High Schools in Western Australia*, Perth: Education Department

Education Ministry, Western Australia (1984) *Education in Western Australia*. Report of the Committee of Inquiry appointed by the Minister for Education in Western Australia, under the Chairmanship of Mr K. E. Beazley, AO. Perth (The Beazley Report)

English in Australia, Interpretations, Australian Journal of Language and Literacy, *Times Education Supplement*

English in Australia (1994) September, No. 109; *Interpretations*, Volume 27, No. 3, 1994 Special Edition, Beyond Poststructuralism

Freebody, P. (1998) 'Findings from the literacy scandal: "the same disconcert and tremulousness and meditation" ', *English in Australia*, 122, 10–14

Gilbert, P. (1995) 'Divided by a Common Language? Gender and the English Curriculum'

Gilbert, Pam (1989) *Writing, Schooling, and Deconstruction: From Voice to Text in the Classroom*, London: Routledge

Gill, Margaret (1998) 'Who set the benchmarks?' *English in Australia*, 121, 9–14

Green, Bill (1989) 'Testing times? Literacy assessment and English teaching in Western Australia', *English in Australia*, 89

Halliday, M. A. K. (1985) *An Introduction to Functional Grammar*, London: Edward Arnold

Halliday, M. A. K. and Hassan, R. (1985) *Language, Context and Text: Aspects of Language in a Social-semiotic Perspective*, Waurn Ponds, Vic: Deakin University

Hunter, I. (1989) 'Speculations in the genre market', *Southern Review*, 22 (3)

Hunter, Ian (1994) *Rethinking the School*, St Leonards: Allen and Unwin.

Hunter, Ian (1997) 'After English: toward a less critical literacy', in Sandy Muspratt, Allan Luke and Peter Freebody (eds.) *Constructing Critical Literacies: Teaching and Learning Textual Practice*, Cresskill, NJ: Hampton Press

Interpretations, Special Issue – Beyond Poststructuralism, 1994, 27 (3)

Janks, Hilary (1993) *Language and Position*, Johannesburg: Hodder and Stoughton

Leavis, F. R. (1972) *Nor Shall my Sword: Discourses on Pluralism, Compassion and Social Hope*, London: Chatto and Windus.

Luke, A. and van Kraayenoord, C. (1998) 'Babies, bathwaters and benchmarks: Literacy assessment and curriculum reform', *Curriculum Perspectives*, 18 (3)

McHoul, Alec (1996) *Semiotic Investigations: Towards an Effective Semiotics*, Lincoln: University of Nebraska Press

Martino, Wayne with Mellor, Bronwyn (1994) *Gendered Fictions*, Cottesloe: Chalkface Press.

Masters, Geoff (1997) 'Do we want high literacy standards?' *Australian Language Matters*, 5 (4), 7–8

Mellor, B. and Patterson, A. (1994) 'Producing readings: Freedom versus normativity?' *English in Australia*, 109

Mellor, B. and Patterson, A. (1994) 'The Reading Lesson', *Interpretations*: Special Issue – Beyond Poststructuralism, 27 (3)

Mellor, B. and Patterson, A. (1994) 'Producing readings: Freedom versus normativity?' *English in Australia*, 109

Mellor, Bronwyn and Patterson, Annette (1996) *Investigating Texts*, Cottesloe: Chalkface Press and Urbana: National Council of Teachers of English

Meredyth, Denise and Tyler, Deborah (eds.) (1993) *Child and Citizen: Genealogies of Schooling and Subjectivity*, Griffith University: Institute for Cultural Policy Studies

Moon, Brian (1998) *Studying Poetry*, Cottesloe: Chalkface Press and Urbana: National Council of Teachers of English

Morgan, Wendy (1994) *Ned Kelly Reconstructed*, Melbourne: Cambridge University Press

Mountford, A. (1996) 'Informed eclecticism: Working from context', *Australian Journal of Language and Literacy*, 19 (1)

'The Newbolt Report'. The Board of Education (1921). *The Teaching of English in England*, The Report of Departmental Committee appointed by the President of the Board of Education to enquire into the position of English in the educational system of England. Chaired by Sir H. Newbolt, London: HMSO

Patterson, A. (1995) 'Supervising freedom: The English Profile: English curriculum; English pedagogy', *Australian Journal of Language and Literacy*, 18 (2)

Pride, A. 'Ethics, criticism and creativity', *English in Australia*, No. 109

Zipes, Jack (ed.) (1993) *The Trials and Tribulations of Little Red Riding Hood*, New York: Routledge

7 Shaping the specialist: initial teacher training for English specialists in Australia

Annette Patterson

The question, 'Why teach English' elicited agreement from the respondents on two points: one was the 'desire' to instil in students a love of literature and language and the other was the satisfaction that came from 'connecting' with students, of developing that 'special relationship' that allowed students to grow and develop emotionally, culturally, socially and psychologically. In this chapter I attempt to trace some historical antecedents of these views and to link the 'beliefs about English' explored in previous chapters in the Australian section of the book with sets of practices (bureaucratic, architectural, administrative) designed for inculcating particular ways of conducting the self.

The first teachers in Australia appear to have been two convict women, Isabella Rosson and Mary Johnson. The British Government had not sent an official teacher with the First Fleet although approximately twenty-six children arrived in what is now known as New South Wales with the Fleet in 1788. Ten years later there were almost 1,000 children. The Dame School established at Sydney by Isabella Rosson was taking in children in 1789 and this was followed by a second Dame School at Paramatta established in 1791 by Mary Johnson. Both teachers were supervised by the settlement's first clergyman, the Rev. Richard Johnson who assumed the responsibility for schooling. Little is known about the lives of the two women who taught the first European children in Australia to read except that both were servants (and probably trades women) in England when they were convicted of petty theft and sentenced to transportation. Isabella Rosson's sentence was for seven years, for the theft of goods to the value of 12 shillings. It appears from the sketchy accounts available that, on discovering that she was pregnant, she stole a set of bed curtains from her employer and pawned it in preparation for her expected child.

The teaching services rendered to the settlements by Isabella Rosson and Mary Johnson were soon augmented by the appointment of three male teachers, including Isabella Rosson's new husband and fellow convict, William Richardson, who was put in charge of the first specially constructed school-house in Sydney in 1793. Richardson had been convicted of highway robbery in England and sentenced to death, but this sentence was commuted to transportation. Very little is known about their background, or why they would have been considered suitable people to teach children.

No provision was made in the colony for teacher training, in fact, until the introduction of the monitorial system in the 1820s when children of no less than 13 years of age were 'apprenticed' to a school teacher to learn the 'trade' of teaching. In 1851 The Fort Street Model School which aimed to train teachers apart from the monitorial system was opened under the direction of William Wilkins, himself a graduate of Kay-Shuttleworth's Training School in England, but it was not until 1880 that teachers became public servants with the benefits of employment, permanency and regulated rates of pay. By this time William Wilkins was in charge of education in New South Wales and inventing and adapting the administrative structures necessary for the establishment and maintenance of a state-funded education system designed to meet the needs of all children irrespective of social status, religion, gender, or geographic location. The teachers referred to were infant or elementary teachers. As noted above secondary education, as apart from elite grammar schools in Australia did not commence until more than 100 years later, during the first decade of this century

Nevertheless, references to teachers of English can be found considerably further back than the nineteenth century. In 1587 Francis Clement referred to 'the english teacher' in the preface of his book *The Petie Schole* and from that point on the references to teachers of English or to 'english masters' are commonly in evidence in historical documents (Michael 1985, p. 5). And yet, despite this long history, it is unusual to find accounts of English teaching which date the emergence of the subject, and the English teacher, much earlier than the last decades of the nineteenth century. This may be a result of historians linking specific curricula or subject matter with something called 'English'. The teaching of 'basic' reading in English, for instance, or the teaching of a group of English-like components such as writing, recitation, reading and the study of verse and fables. For Ian Michaels, author of what is probably the best-known historical account of English teaching, the curriculum of a recognisable subject called English consists of 'interpretation, expression and linguistic study' (Michael 1987, ch. 8). All of these components must be present at the same time for the subject to be recognised as 'English'. Still, it is possible to look at accounts of teaching dating from the sixteenth century and claim that these three elements were present in some cases, and yet from the perspective of later centuries historians have not brought themselves to the point of suggesting that what we now call 'English' existed in schools prior to the nineteenth century.

But if I shift the discussion away from curricula components and look instead at pedagogy a slightly different set of issues emerges. Does English designate a particular pedagogical arrangement as well as particular arrangements of curricula components? In the history chapter I suggested that this is the case. In this view it is not so much a question of asking 'what does the English teacher teach?' but of asking 'how does the English teacher teach?'

and to get at that question I need to look at some of the pedagogical antecedents of English and relate these to the goals of current English teacher education. It was clear from the students' responses discussed in the chapter 'Beliefs about English in Australia' that a particular role for the English teacher was assumed. These roles included 'the guide' and 'the facilitator' and it is of interest, I think, to find that these beliefs are a part of the 'folklore' of 'uninitiated' English teachers. ('Uninitiated' in the sense that these students were just beginning their undergraduate preparation for teaching.) On the other hand, perhaps it is not so surprising given the long tradition in primary school and infant education of viewing the teacher in these terms.

Although Robin Peel has examined above the contributions to education of David Stow and James Kay-Shuttleworth I want to revisit this terrain from a slightly different perspective. I want to focus on the emergence of a now familiar figure: that of 'the sympathetic' teacher (Hunter 1988). This figure has appeared in the advice manuals written for 'schoolmasters' and 'mothers' and in historical accounts of teaching dating back to the sixth century (Patterson 1997) nevertheless, its emergence in the nineteenth century within the apparatus of an increasingly secularised education system designed for 'the masses' and destined to be supported by state funding is noteworthy. Its noteworthiness derives from the fact that earlier accounts of the sympathetic teacher were associated with teaching in various sites such as in the home by a private tutor or, increasingly in the eighteenth century, through the mother teaching her children at home. Teaching in the early Sunday Schools and to a more variable extent in the Dame Schools also drew on the ideal of 'the sympathetic teacher'. In each case the partners in the formation of this relationship were children and tutors/teachers located in some households and in the Sunday Schools which were designed for a broader clientele. Interestingly, the provision of a private tutor in the home did not mean that the only children to benefit from this form of education were themselves members of the aristocracy, landed gentry or other monied groups. The children of household servants, both boys and girls, often were included. The reason for spreading the resources of private teaching to most children in the household appears to have been promoted by a desire to have young children kept busy and out of the way of the work of the household rather than through entirely altruistic impulses. Nevertheless, it is in the advice to these tutor/teachers, to mothers, who were urged to educate their own children, and to volunteer Sunday School teachers, that we see the beginnings of a set of techniques for the successful supervision and teaching of children through the establishment of a particular type of relationship: One in which the teacher offers him or herself to the children in an empathetic way, inviting trust and friendship (within certain limits) in order to better regulate and govern through non-coercive means, the behaviour and demeanour of the young charges. Built on a combination of sympathy and surveillance, a friendly demeanour on the part of the teacher joined to a willingness to grant certain freedoms to children in their conduct, this special relationship offered maximum opportunities for observing, regulating and normalising the behaviour of children according to variable norms. Advice to beginning teachers (that is, mothers and tutors) along these lines appears to have been widespread, however, without the support of a 'system' it was destined to remain, as it had for centuries, an 'ideal' of practice with variable and incalculable effects. It was not until this special relationship between teacher and student was formalised within the machinery of a state bureaucracy that it began to have widespread and enduring effects.

The sympathetic teacher, then, was one who could combine surveillance and freedom, who could govern and regulate his or her young charges through a thorough but sympathetic understanding of their dispositions. This remarkable combination of what may appear to modern-day critical analysts of education to be oppositional or mutually exclusive techniques were transported out of the private homes and the Sunday Schools through a range of strategies and techniques developed in the interests of a mass-education system in the nineteenth century and into the early part of the twentieth century. These included architectural innovations such as the playground and the closed classroom (Stow 1834); teacher training programmes (Stow 1850); psychology (Tyler 1993); and a whole array of new systems for observing and reporting, categorising and systematising entire populations that were considered to be in want of regulation (the poor; the sick; the illiterate; the insane). The emergence of the sympathetic teacher within the milieu of a mass education system was a result of a coming together, in quite contingent and piecemeal ways, of an array of strategies and techniques for governing specific populations. The special kind of pedagogical relationship that resulted from the intersection of often disparate and dispersed techniques is familiar to us today in the organ-isation and demeanour of early childhood and elementary schools and teachers, and, I will argue here, of secondary English teachers and secondary English classrooms.

When English politicians and state bureaucrats began to look around for ways of getting state funded schooling established in England in the first part of last century they looked to Scotland, Europe, America and Ireland for suitable models. The person most responsible for eventually inventing and implementing the administrative procedures for state schooling was James Kay-Shuttleworth. But in his extensive reports to parliament, pamphlets, speeches and other writing on education Kay-Shuttleworth focused on the work and the training schools of David Stow in Scotland. Stow had devised a way of teaching children that incorporated some of Wilderspin's ideas on infant teaching with Pestalozzian concepts of child learning. More import-antly for the discussion here, he had defined and described the demeanour and the conduct of the sympathetic teacher, who would appear in a formal and organised way for the first time within secularised mass education.

In the year 1850 David Stow provided a model for the school teacher in terms of how he or she should act and speak to parents and other visitors to his 'training' school. The model was presented through a dialogue in which the teacher had been accused of risking his dignity in playing with the children in the playground. He responded with:

> Well, Madam, respecting playing with the children, you know the first and most important object, in rearing up children 'in the way they should go' is to gain their affections. And we think this important point more easily and more effectually gained by being quite at ease with the little ones, rather than by keeping at a distance, and awakening fear in their tender breasts, instead of love.
>
> Stow 1850, p. 100

It is here that Stow both teaches teachers what and how to respond to questions posed by parents and others about his school system, and, at the same time, provides an instance of a technique for adjusting the behaviour of children borrowed from ancient church-based pedagogies.

At a later point I want to take up some possible lines of connection between this idea that the teacher could adjust the moral and ethical comportment of children by 'gaining their affections' and by 'being quite at ease with the little ones' and the modern-day strategies of English teachers and the arrangements of the English classroom. But at this stage I would like to pursue the question of the significance of the 'playground' as an architectural addition to the school. In the quote above from Stow's dialogue the mention of 'playground' probably passed without notice. But at the time that this dialogue was written, the idea that schools might have playgrounds attached to them and that teachers might take some small part in the activities of children within these playgrounds was both startling and novel.

The playground was a place of both freedom and surveillance. What was novel in this arrangement was the emphasis on the teacher's role in creating the conditions under which the child was 'free' to perform 'naturally' in the playground in order to facilitate the teacher's access to information about the child. In the playground children were free to express themselves under the watchful eye of a friendly or sympathetic teacher. The teacher acted as their moral guide during their demonstrations of their 'true' selves. The architects of state education in England were very clear on this point: the pastoral teacher must guide children by a moral rather than a physical influence. In reality the opposite was generally the case as many personal accounts of children's experience of schooling testify. But this disparity serves to illustrate the distance between the teaching and learning programmes as they were outlined at the time, and their implementation. The techniques for managing populations through 'self discovery' and for adjusting norms of behaviour through allowing children to be 'themselves' were considerably re-worked in the state primary schools of England and Australia during the middle of the nineteenth century. It would take at least another hundred years before we observed the extent of the flowering of the special relationship outlined by the nineteenth-century school reformers.

The 'pastoral' school, then, emerged from a combination of strategies cobbled together from home-based early childhood vernacular teaching and an array of eighteenth- and nineteenth-century educational institutions such as the Dame Schools, Sunday Schools and the Workhouses. Its distinguishing feature was its remarkable capacity for joining teacher surveillance and child-directed activity; obedience and spontaneity; supervision and freedom. I have discussed elsewhere some of the specific features of pastoral schools and their pedagogies with regard to 'reader-response' techniques in the secondary English classroom (Patterson 1993); with regard to English curriculum in Australia (Patterson 1995; Patterson 1997a); with regard to the imperative within English teaching 'to teach and yet not teach' (Mellor and Patterson 1994); with regard to 'critical' literacy and 'personalist' pedagogies (Patterson 1997a) and with regard to early reading instruction (Patterson 1997b). Related work has been undertaken in Australia: Denise Meredyth (1991) in her examination of the emergence of the university tutorial and its relation to person formation and in her later genealogy of schooling (Meredyth and Tyler 1993); and by Ian Hunter on English and schooling (Hunter 1988; 1994). Brian Moon's rethinking of 'resistance' in literary education, and Wayne Martino's work on 'masculinities' and 'English' provides useful guides to the development of an 'ethics approach' to English education and examines possible links between different pedagogies and the formation and deployment of different types of learners, or persons. In focusing on institutional and bureaucratic aspects of education and their relationship to person formation the ethics work differs from other critical analyses of the field, particularly those that focus on a neo-marxist critique of the ideological effects of English or those that focus on identity formation and subjectivity (Eagleton 1983).

Valuable theoretical understandings of English teaching and of 'English' have been produced over the past two decades through accounts of English informed by critical theory. Feminist theories have contributed extensively to this debate as have neo-marxist theories, and an alignment of a range of critical perspectives from 'queer theory' to 'postmodernism' has resulted in a highly productive period of review for all aspects of English from literary criticism through to issues of curriculum and teaching and learning. In their application to English, however, the group of theories that could be described as 'critical' tend to 'work' at the level of ideology critique. At the risk of oversimplifying a complex network of theories, I want to suggest that ideology critiques in the field of English tend to assume a fundamental opposition between 'critical thought' and 'instrumentalism'; between 'creativity' and 'functionalism' and between 'democratic freedom' and 'economic rationalism'. It is of interest that this type of critique is so influential in its application to a subject area such as English where the success of pedagogy relies to a certain extent on combining particular techniques that critical theories tend to separate and place in opposition to one another. A further complication is that aspects of critical theory informed by neo-marxism also have a tendency, as noted previously, to make claims for schooling and English that are both global in scope and transcendent in nature (e.g. Goodson and Medway 1990). On the other hand, Australian work on 'governmentality', taking a lead from Foucault's (1984) notion of 'government' as an historically specific set of techniques for governing populations (rather than as a historically specific vehicle for an eternal and universal will to control), makes less ambitious claims for the range and extent of its analysis. As Ian Hunter has pointed out, two people convinced parliament of the need for state-funded schools: 'an emancipatory radical who held similar views to many modern-day critical theorists (David Stow) and a conservative who held repressive views on education (Kay-Shuttleworth). But, what they held in common was their view of the necessity for a special type of teacher–student relationship. And a key feature of the development of this relationship in the view of both men, was the playground, a novel innovation in school design in the nineteenth century' (Hunter 1994). Stow complained that, 'Schools were not so constructed as to enable the child to be superintended in real life at play' (Stow 1850, p. 5). He set about rectifying this deficiency in school design by detailing the place-ment, layout and dimensions of the playground. 'The playground' claimed Stow, 'allows superintendence and subsequent moral revision' (1850, p. 139). Moral revision was achieved through a process that combined the direct but friendly observations of children by the teacher while the children were engaged in play in the playground. When the class reconvened after the play session, the teacher would draw moral lessons from the activities in the playground, thus 'revising' or shaping the moral development of his or her charges. 'The Play-ground, or the Uncovered School, of sufficient dimensions, is the platform for the development of the real dispositions and habits of the children, and for moral superintendence by the trainer.' Many of the pedagogical strategies and techniques developed around the innovative architectural feature of the playground became integral features of literacy and English classrooms as those subject areas took on the responsibility for 'moral training' through non-coercive techniques.

In insisting on the necessity for the formation of the special relationship between teacher and child and in designing a purpose-built milieu for these new educational practices reformers such as Stow, Wilderspin and Kay-Shuttleworth in England, and William Wilkins and Peter Board in Australia were not so much interested in what we now recognise as a 'child-centred' pedagogy and in the associated liberal or post-Romantic forms of education as in finding a solution to an educational problem: namely, the failure of the monitorial system to achieve the required shift in the ethical and moral demeanour of a new population of children that were believed to be in need of governance. As Stow noted: 'Monitors can only teach facts — they cannot develop or train. A monitor therefore is an imperfect substitute for a master'

(Stow 1850, p. 9). Monitors, in other words, were not capable of developing and sustaining the special relationship described above for reasons ranging from their relative youth and the limits imposed by the architectural spaces in which they were required to work, to their imperfect training.

The shift from a monitorial system to current systems for preparing teachers was relatively rapid and it would be a mistake to underestimate the effect of the techniques and strategies worked out in the primary schools of nineteenth-century England, Ireland, Scotland and Australia on the development of high-school English teaching. Nevertheless, a popular and alternative explanation for the existence of English in its present form in high schools is that it evolved from a concerted attempt by the universities to un-seat classics and replace it with 'English literature'.

Teacher education in Australia

English in the universities

In a country as large as Australia, with an unevenly dispersed population, the various state education systems have had to find their own way of managing and providing education. In this respect, then, we might expect to find clear differences between the various state and territory systems. Interestingly for this study at least is the fact that English, of all the secondary school subject areas, began very early in the history of secondary education in Australia to establish an 'homogeneous' approach in terms of its stated goals and syllabus outlines. This was also true of literature studies in universities in Australia up until the 1960s. Leigh Dale suggests that this congruence of views on literature study at the university level between the 1920s and the 1960s in a country where universities were separated by vast distances was due in the main to the appointment of male graduates of Oxford University to the professorial positions in English literature as they became available through the first 100 years of university teaching in Australia (Dale 1997).

The first university to be established in Australia was the University of Sydney where teaching commenced in 1852. This was followed by the establishment of universities in Melbourne, Adelaide, Hobart, Perth and by 1922, in Brisbane. However, English or literature teaching in most universities was nothing more than an adjunct to classics or philosophy or history until the early 1920s. Dale notes that 'by 1922, specialist positions – chairs of English Language and/or Literature – had been created at the Universities of Melbourne, Western Australia, Sydney, Adelaide and Queensland . . . English was soon to be the centre-piece of the Humanities curriculum, a stunning shift in the status of the discipline' (Dale 1996, p. 47). The homogenised state of English in Australian high schools, however, throughout this century appears to have came about through the congruence of views of the various men who occupied the positions of Director General, or its equivalent, in each state and territory rather than through the imposition from above of a university view of English. University English departments were only getting established during the second decade of this century and were not keen to be involved in the business of secondary schooling. As noted in the previous chapter, Sydney University refused to be involved in setting or marking teachers' qualifying exams until the late 1930s and teachers of English rarely held degrees of any type from a university. Their path into teaching was initially through the completion of a set number of years in high school whilst apprenticed to the principal or Head Teacher, and later through study at the Teachers' Training Colleges. It is more likely then that the congruence of English syllabi between the different states through to the 1970s was a result of the similarity of views held by the men who occupied the positions of Director General of Education in each state. These men formed an elite band of bureaucrats that headed government departments overseeing the establishment and development of Australia's secondary school systems. As noted in the previous chapter, the early Director-Generals did not look to the university for guidance on how to put together an English syllabus. Instead, they looked to the already well-established traditions of education in the extensive primary or elementary school systems.

A different picture emerged in the 1960s, however, with an increasing demand for places in post-compulsory schooling. It is in the development of this type of schooling, senior or 'upper school' studies directly aimed at preparing students to enter universities that university academics had most influence on the development of syllabi and examinations. Their reign extended through the next three decades in most states until the establishment of state government departments in the 1980s with a brief to oversee the future direction of post-compulsory schooling. One reason for establishing these 'departments' or 'boards' in each state was that the cohort of students entering post-compulsory schooling was either no longer university bound or was bound for a number of different universities, all with their own views on what constituted a proper preparation for English studies at their institution. With the possible exception of New South Wales, these departments diluted the contribution of universities and resumed control of the direction of post-compulsory education.

Although arts and humanities faculties around the country are facing serious financial strain and reductions in staffing during the present round of budgetary restraint in universities, English, it seems, is still holding its place. Comments such as the following are a regular feature of newspaper reporting on the current state of universities:

> The president of the Deans of Arts and Social Sciences . . . said that while student numbers into arts had dropped negligibly, arts faculties were extensively reinventing themselves . . . The packaging of BAs with brackets such as BA (Asian Studies), (media), (communication) and (international business) was proving successful in maintaining students numbers . . . At La Trobe [University], the plan is to declare some core

areas – among them English, philosophy and history – as disciplines essential to any arts degree . . .

Healy and Gough 1998, p. 35

Schooling systems in Australia: a demography

Australia is geographically and politically organised in terms of 'states' and 'territories'. There are six states and in order of population size they are New South Wales, Victoria, Queensland, Western Australia, South Australia and Tasmania. The two territories are the Northern Territory and the Australian Capital Territory. The seat of Federal Government is located in Canberra which is in the Australian Capital Territory but each state and the Northern Territory has its own elected government which is responsible, among other things, for the organisation and operation of its own school system. So, although the Federal Government is the only government with the power to levy and collect income tax, and thereby hold the funds for education, the states have statutory control over their own education systems. The Federal Government provides the states with a grant each year for the management and operation of the schools.

The tradition of 'states' rights' in Australia has meant that each state has developed its own education system in its own way and therefore requires and in some cases governs different procedures for gaining teacher certification. There is no national system for registering teachers in Australia and neither is there a great deal of agreement from state to state about what constitute the requirements for teacher certification. In Western Australia, for instance, the holder of Bachelor of Education (of either three or four years' full-time equivalent duration) or a degree (minimum of three years) plus a Diploma of Education (which can be completed in one calendar year) from a Western Australian university (or equivalent) is considered qualified to teach in Western Australia. In Queensland, on the other hand, holding a teaching degree does not equate with teacher qualification. First, a teacher must register with the state governed Board of Teacher Registration before being certified as a person eligible for employment in Queensland schools. Similar differences apply in other states. The new graduate, then, is well advised to teach in his or her own state before seeking positions elsewhere. The variability in qualification hinges on a number of issues not the least of which is the number of days an education undergraduate student has spent in schools taking part in teaching practice during the period of his or her studies. There have been many attempts over recent years to bring the requirements for teacher certification under a single set of regulations, so far without success.

All schools in Australia begin their school year at the end of January or the first week in February and finish sometime in December. The summer vacation is about six weeks in duration from mid-December to the beginning of the new school year. That is about the beginning and the end of similarities between states' systems. The school year is generally divided into four terms ranging between about eight and eleven weeks in length and each is punctu-ated by a 'break' of about two weeks' duration. States rarely entirely coincide their term school holidays, apart from the summer break and even then different states have different beginning and ending dates for their summer break. The division of education into separate systems also has some curious effects as noted in chapter 8. Children moving mid-year during their first year of high school in Victoria, which is 'Year 7', find that they are in primary school in Queensland where high school does not commence until 'Year 8'. In addition children begin school at different ages in the various states and also at different stages in their education, some having been required to attend a 'pre-school' or 'kindergarten' year which is a formal part of the school organisation, while in other states that is an optional path into school.

Each state is in charge of designing and implementing its own curriculum although it is difficult to understand how a country of so few people can continue its present level of curriculum and system diversification. Never-theless, moves toward a 'national curriculum' have begun, and to a certain extent faltered, as noted earlier although the current interventions by the Commonwealth government in the testing of students in literacy and numeracy across the country suggests that a national, unified system of schooling in Australia is not entirely off the policy agenda. One of the effects of having different curricula in each state is that the subjects a student in his or her final year of post-compulsory high school can count towards tertiary entrance differ in each state, and universities have different requirements for entry to their degree programmes. This has the effect of limiting the attendance of 'interstate' students at universities. That is, it is most likely that a student enrolled in an undergraduate degree programme at the University of Western Australia for instance, is actually a resident of that state, and more importantly, has attended secondary school in Western Australia. The geographical isolation of Western Australia perhaps contributes to that like-lihood but similar circumstances apply to most universities in other states. 'Going away' to university is not generally an Australian experience at the undergraduate level at least, unless the students' family lives in the rural regions of the state and even then it is unlikely for reasons outlined above, that the student will attend a university out of his or her state. This means that when students in education take up their first appointment teaching in a school (often in a rural or remote area), it is also quite likely to be their first experience of living away from their parents and of living outside a major metropolitan area.

In land mass terms Australia is only slightly smaller than the United States but it supports a population of less than nineteen million people. The state of Western Australia occupies slightly less than a third of the total land mass of Australia yet it has a population of only 1.4 million with 88 per cent of that population living in Perth and the rest dispersed over a massive land area.

As can be imagined this makes its education system unique in Australia since it still has to find a way to provide teachers and schools in its most remote regions. Naturally, it is most likely that the teachers who staff these remote schools will have lived most of their lives in the relatively large, cosmopolitan city of Perth. High-School teachers of English do not find themselves in the most remote areas of the state since a reasonable population density is required before the state will commit to maintaining a high school.

Disciplinary background of student teachers

In order to qualify for entry to the English curriculum classes at universities in Perth, and at the university in Townsville, each student was required to study a stipulated number of subjects in 'English'. This approach is common in universities across the country although the amount of English required as a pre-requisite for entry to the curriculum classes varies from university to university, and in some cases English or Literature study is rather loosely interpreted as a prerequisite since for convenience or other reasons students were often able to undertake their curriculum studies before they had completed more than one semester of study in English subjects. On the other hand, some students had completed several semesters of English subjects.

In terms of the regulations operating at each university, students had a great deal of freedom about what English-related subjects they would study. In other words, the requirements as described in the university handbooks did not specify which English-related subjects students should study. This resulted in a wide variety of backgrounds. The students who were completing their undergraduate studies at the Perth university in a 'School of Humanities' which specialised in a broad-based approach to studies in 'discourse', language, and textual practices including popular culture and performance areas such as drama and media were more likely to have a 'cultural studies' background. These students had studied subjects with titles such as 'Screen Texts' or 'Culture and Everyday Life' or 'Language and Power' or 'Popular Literature and Culture'. On the other hand, their counterparts at the university in Townsville studied a more traditional range of 'English Literature' subjects which were still offered through an 'English Department'. Subjects with titles such as 'Romantic and Gothic Literature' or 'The Motives for Fiction' or 'Australian Literature' formed the basis of the Townsville students' undergraduate studies in English. In each case, however, the students had a wide variety of subjects from which to choose and they were not required to concentrate on 'literature' subjects, although the Townsville students did focus on this area. Interestingly, the Queensland Department of Education has implemented a syllabus in Queensland which incorporates a functional-linguistics based approach to language and text study for students studying up to the Year 10 level, however, this may not have had time to effect a change in the traditional focus of English on the production and analysis of literary texts. Nevertheless, apart from the appearance of more 'popular culture' texts, and a wider variety of print and non-print texts, the practice of teaching English to students in Years 8, 9 and 10 remains relatively unchanged in both states. This is reflected in the continuing trend for students who are preparing to become teachers of English not to select linguistics or language subjects as part of their undergraduate degree. In Years 11 and 12, students study what is predominantly a literature-based syllabus and in many respects the preparation of students to become teachers of English in high schools remains focused in this area. For instance, only 15 per cent of students studying to be high-school teachers of English and enrolled in the English curriculum subject at Murdoch University in 1995 and 1996 had completed at least one subject associated with linguistics; in Townsville only 2 per cent of students studying to be high-school teachers of English and enrolled in the required English curriculum subject at third year in 1997 had completed a linguistics-based subject. The overwhelming focus on literature- and literature-based subjects is a feature of English teacher education in Australia, and a reflection of the interests of students choosing to become high-school teachers of English.

It would be a mistake, however, to think of secondary school English and literature study as derivative of university study. To go down this path is to miss the opportunity offered by Ian Hunter's (1988) work to understand school English as the repository for a set of teaching and learning techniques aimed at the government of populations, and the inculcation of practices for individual self-management. In the main, as discussed above, these practices derived from the early Sunday Schools and then the infant schools and were installed long before the universities got around to offering English and literature courses and decades in advance of the university extension courses and the working men's groups' provision of 'popular' lectures on literature. In addition, as late as the 1970s very few teachers gained university degrees and even then English was not commonly taught in secondary schools by specialists, that is, by teachers with a university 'major' in English literature (Green 1990). Although it is true that university English departments eventually exerted pressure (more so in some states than in others) on the secondary-school syllabi through their role in the setting and marking of examinations at the various exit points from secondary school, nevertheless, English and literature were established as a necessary and important part of the state secondary-school curriculum in every state well in advance of these 'interferences' through the examination system. In many respects, it is possible to view the pedagogy of English studies in the universities as an extension of the techniques and practices already established in the secondary schools by the beginning of the 1920s, particularly the use of tutorials which became accepted practice during the 1950s but not fully installed until the 1960s and were modelled on school teaching techniques (Meredyth 1991). This and other innovations such as class tests and term examinations were implemented during this period mostly in response to the changes which were taking place within universities and the society: increased student numbers (New South Wales saw a 62 per cent increase in student numbers between 1957 and 1961); increasingly higher failure rates and an increasingly younger student population (in 1951, 53 per cent of students at Sydney University were under 19, but by the late 1950s the figure was closer to 71 per cent) combined with a diverse social background (in 1958 more than half of the students attending Sydney University were receiving financial assistance) (Barcan 1965, p. 288). In the universities as in the schools, new techniques were invented in a piecemeal fashion and in response to contingent events such as changes in the 'student body' and changing expectations of the role and function of educational institutions. We could, for instance, view the invention of the tutorial as a mechanism for oppression of student views, opinions and conduct through the installation of a close supervisory relationship: or we could view it as an institutional response to the fact that the lecture system was not working; or it could be viewed as an institutional response which rather cleverly built on existing teacher–student relationships in secondary and primary schools. In Australian universities in the early 1960s too many students were failing, they were young, there were a lot of them and they came from varied social backgrounds. Populations perceived as being in need of government are a feature of modern states and bureaucracies were invented to manage that process. The great achievement of nineteenth- and twentieth-century educational bureaucracies designed to oversee the introduction of mass schooling was to figure out a way to combine freedom and normativity, care and control, self-expression and discipline. In universities, at least, the tutorial provided just one example of an inventive strategy for achieving some of these goals.

The secondary English syllabi

Given the focus of the upper secondary-school syllabus in each state, and the tradition in each state of teaching a largely literature-based lower secondary-school curriculum, this informal counselling was not misplaced. In both Western Australia and Queensland concerted attempts were made during the last ten years to rewrite the English syllabi at every level of secondary education. This rewriting of syllabi had taken place in Western Australia (mid to late 1980s) before the national initiatives to provide some uniformity in terms of 'outcomes' in designated curriculum areas had begun and although the Queensland rewriting of English syllabi came later, and is still in progress (in 1997) at the upper school level it does not appear to be clearly linked to the national initiatives. Interestingly though, the Queensland lower secondary-school English syllabus (directed at Years 8, 9 and 10) has taken a quite different path from that in Western Australia where despite an attempt to shift the focus to a less literary and more broadly based text study the major part of the Western Australian syllabus suggests study of text areas that would be considered to come under the categories of poetry, prose and drama. Queensland, however, began rewriting its lower secondary-school syllabus much later than Western Australia and had the benefit, although some might claim, 'the disadvantage' of the experience of the genre debates of the late 1980s.[1]

Queensland has devised a syllabus for the lower secondary school that suggests a greater focus on the 'function' of language across a broad range of text types. The 'functional' aspects of language study in this syllabus are loosely derived from the systemic functional linguistic approach to language analysis developed by M. A. K. Halliday. While the state department of education in Queensland was realistic enough not to expect teachers to have a detailed understanding of this approach it was suggested that with adequate support teachers could learn enough about 'functional' linguistics to implement the syllabus. The support for implementation came, in the main, in the form of a set of no less than eight books. The syllabus and support booklets are daunting in their level of detail but they are generally accessible in terms of layout, structure and approach.

Teachers with whom I have talked stress three things about the 'new' syllabus: it constitutes unfamiliar territory in terms of its focus on language rather than literature and on a functional linguistics approach to text analysis; it is far too detailed in terms of the support material supplied, constituting, as one teacher rather wryly put it, 'a crash course in first year [university] linguistics'; and despite extensive initial efforts to provide professional development, there has been little or no on-going support. The professional development that is available was, until the end of 1997, supplied by a limited number of subject 'consultants' within the regional offices but this position was disestablished in the most recent restructure of the regional office of the state department. Readers will have noticed from other sections of this book that this scenario is not restricted to Australia. Robin Peel's comment that 'there are no advisory teacher posts' draws attention to similar problems in England. Some professional development in Australia is provided outside the 'system', usually through university courses or workshops and seminars, and teachers are expected to attend these 'in their own time'. For their part, the administrative systems in each state appear to undergo a 'restructure' on a regular basis, including changes in nomenclature as well as changes in job descriptions and functions. 'Subject consultants', 'curriculum development' officers or whatever the new term is for those people who traditionally helped teachers understand and implement a new syllabus simply come and go as the system cycles through another round of restructuring. Heads of English departments in secondary schools do not have time to establish close links with system staff who could provide the support required to implement a new syllabus and in many cases the support staff position does not appear to exist within the system, or if it does, there is one person to service an entire state, as was the case in Western

1 For a brief discussion of these debates see chapter 8.

Australia in the mid 1990s. In addition to these structural and administrative problems Queensland has variable and somewhat uncertain accountability measures in place for reporting on students 'outcomes' or achievements up to the end of Year 10 so even at a pragmatic level there are few pressing bureaucratic reasons for an already over-stretched teaching corps to adopt new syllabi. These problems are by no means unique to the states of Western Australia and Queensland. Across the country the state-based education systems face similar problems.

In summary then, every state in the country has provided a new English syllabus at the lower secondary end of schooling over the past decade and every state has met the kinds of problems outlined above – problems of acceptance, professional development and implementation. Although syllabi in Australian secondary schools have been rewritten regularly over the recent past the pedagogical practices of English remain much the same, combining as they do personal expression and moral instruction in a formula designed for the expert management of student populations. And, at the risk of repeating myself, I do not wish that sentence to be read as implying that English pedagogy has some hidden agenda for repressing students through the application of techniques for self-scrutiny and self-adjustment arranged in the name of freedom of expression. Discipline and freedom are not mutually exclusive practices, as Foucault went to such lengths to demonstrate. In many cases one is the condition of the other and English provides an interesting example of how this is achieved. It would be a mistake, also, to view the assertion that English pedagogy has remained relatively unchanged over a long period of time as being critical of English in the sense that it might suggest a conservative, or regressive approach to teaching. While English has constantly reinvented itself through the construction of 'new' models the point remains that it has not reinvented itself in terms of its pedagogy. This claim could be viewed as being critical of English for not 'changing'. But that is not the intention of my extensive efforts here to point out the continuities of English pedagogy. Rather, I want to draw attention to its strengths. English pedagogy is purpose built to meet the traditional goals of English for producing personnel skilled in ethics, aesthetics and rhetoric. The production of a particular type of person in the more generalised and non-specialist sense of a population that has undertaken at least ten years of compulsory literacy and English education including the development of a specific set of techniques which constitute the now familiar personal comportment of the expert English graduate are all important attributes of a subject designed, as Peter Board noted, to inculcate techniques for 'proper conduct'.

Why teach English?

What is I think striking about the comments made by school students and student-teachers to the questions: 'What is English for?' and 'What should students be doing in English classrooms' is the overwhelming congruity of their views. In a sense, given the discussion above and that in previous chapters this should not be surprising. English was adapted from existing primary school orientations to the subject and established relatively quickly and with little disagreement at the 'heart' of the secondary school curricula in the second decade of this century. University lecturers in English departments might debate points of theory, but until the 'theory wars' emerged on some campuses (if at all) as an issue for undergraduates as late as the 1980s, 'ways of reading' a text was not a debatable issue. Children read literature for enjoyment, for aesthetic appreciation and for moral reflection. They wrote in the early part of the century for the purpose of honing their skills for clear expression but also increasingly for self-exploratory and self-expressive purposes; they spoke in the early part of the century for the purpose of clear enunciation and increasingly for enjoyment through performance. The reality of classroom practice was no doubt quite different but these, broadly speaking, were the expressed goals and aims of the curricula and syllabus statements produced throughout this century for secondary English in every state in Australia.

The modern English classroom with its emphasis on exploratory talk and writing, and on group work and techniques developed through reader response strategies for surveillance and ethical adjustments towards specific sets of personal and social norms (non-sexist; anti-racist; use of inclusive language and so on) is an extension and adaptation of earlier pastoral pedagogical arrangements. Robert Scholes, in his recent account (1998) of the 'rise and fall of English', suggested connection between the traditions of church teaching/preaching and literature teaching in the universities. What is missing from Scholes' account is an acknowledgment that many of the pedagogical strategies of early Christian teaching were installed in the infant schools of sixteenth-century Germany, England and Scotland. These schools were teaching vernacular reading skills to young children from a broad range of social and economic backgrounds. The emergence of state schooling in the nineteenth century combined many of the existing church based 'pastoral' pedagogical techniques with a range of systematic bureaucratic and administrative interventions at the level of formal government. In giving voice to a desire to instil in students a 'love of literature' and a desire to establish a 'special relationship' with students, the undergraduate English teachers in Australia were reproducing practices that are part of an ensemble of techniques and strategies with a very long history. During the twentieth century English became the curriculum space for the refinement and development of these person-forming technologies and it would be a mistake to underestimate their power and importance for the formation of a self-regulating population. As Denise Meredyth (1994) noted in a thoughtful paper on the relationship between civics education and English: 'English, it seems, is a rare and peculiar means for forming a patchwork range of ethical and literate capacities' (p. 74). Nevertheless, these points appear to be lost in many debates about the future of English in high schools in Australia.

References

Barcan, A. (1965) *A Short History of Education in New South Wales*, Sydney: Martindale Press

Dale, Leigh (1997) *The English Men: Professing Literature in Australian Universities*, Canberra: Association for the Study of Australian Literature

Eagleton, T. (1983) *Literary Theory: An Introduction*, Oxford: Blackwell

Foucault, M. (1984) 'Governmentality', in G. Burchell, C. Gordon and P. Miller (eds.) *The Foucault Effect: Studies in Governmentality*, London: Harvester/Wheatsheaf

Goodson, I. and Medway, P. (eds.) (1990). *Bringing English to Order*, London: The Falmer Press

Green, Bill (1990) Unpublished PhD thesis, Murdoch University

Halliday, M. A. K. (1975). Learning How to Mean, London: E. Arnold

Healy, G. and Gough, K. (1998) 'Staff to go as arts embraces pragmatism', *The Australian* (Higher Education), Wednesday, 18 February 1998, p. 35

Hunter, I. (1988) *Culture and Government: The Emergence of Literary Education*, London: Macmillan Press

Hunter, Ian (1993) 'Culture, Bureaucracy and the History of Popular Education', in Denise Meredyth and Deborah Tyler, *Child and Citizen: Genealogies of Schooling and Subjectivity*, Brisbane: Institute for Cultural Policy Studies, Griffith University

Hunter, I. (1994) *Rethinking the School*, Sydney: Allen and Unwin

Kay-Shuttleworth, J. (1839) *Recent Measures for the Promotion of Education in England*, 13th edn., London: Ridgway, Piccadilly

Mellor, B. and Patterson, A (1994) 'Producing readings: freedom versus normativity?' *English in Australia*, 109

Meredyth, D. (1991) 'Personalities and personnel: rationales for the humanities', in I. Hunter, I. D. Meredyth, B. Smith and G. Stokes, *Accounting for the Humanities*, Brisbane: Griffith University Institute for Cultural Policy Studies

Meredyth, D. (1994) 'English, civics and ethical competence', *Interpretations*, 27 (3)

Michaels, Ian (1987) *The Teaching of English: From the Sixteenth Century to 1870*, Cambridge: Cambridge University Press

Moon, Brian (1994) 'Rethinking resistance: English and critical consciousness', *Interpretations*, 27 (3)

Patterson, A. (1993) ' "Personal response" in English teaching', in Denise Meredyth and Deborah Tyler (eds.) *Child and Citizen: Genealogies of Schooling and Subjectivity*, Griffith University: Institute for Cultural Policy Studies

Patterson, A. (1995) 'Supervising freedom: the English profile: English curriculum; English pedagogy', *Australian Journal of Language and Literacy*, 18 (2)

Patterson, A. (1997) 'A technique for living: some thoughts on beginning reading pedagogy in sixteenth century England', *The UTS Review*, 3 (2)

Patterson, A. (1997a) 'Setting limits to English', in S. Muspratt, A. Luke and P. Freebody (eds.) *Constructing Critical Literacies*, New Jersey: Hampton Press

Reid, Ian (ed.) (1987) *The Place of Genre in Learning: Current Debates*, Geelong, Vic.: Centre for Studies in Literary Education, Deakin University

Scholes, R. (1998) *The Rise and Fall of English*, Yale: University Press

Stow, David (1834) *Moral Training, Infant and Juvenile, As Applicable to the Condition of the Population of Large Towns*, 2nd edn. Glasgow: William Collins

Stow, David (1850) The Training System, the Moral Training School, and the Normal Seminary, 8th edn., London: Longman, Brown, Green, and Longmans

Tyler, D. (1993) 'Making better children', in *Child and Citizen: Genealogies of Schooling and Subjectivity*, Brisbane: Griffith University

Part III

United States: questions of practice and individual expression

8 Teaching English in the United States

Jeanne Gerlach

Historic knowledge can guide us as we change school and college curricula to respond to new conditions. There is no need to reinvent the wheel, if we know the kinds of wheels our professional predecessors rode on.

John Stewig (1983)

What has been said about the diversity of Australia, a vast country characterised by a state based system and a regional specificity of practice, applies equally to the United States. There is also a number of significant differences: the United States has over 200 million citizens, and has been independent of England for over 200 years. Its European settlers often arrived with a determination to build a better world than the one they had left behind, and central to that vision was a non-conformist model of education. Yet as long as the separate settlements remained colonies they were subject to the direct jurisdiction of England, and it was not until the gaining of independence, the confidence that came from the outcome of the 1812 war with Britain, and the growing belief in the possibility of a different American identity that the possibilities of education came to be fully imagined. The period of great moral reform that expressed itself in an enthusiasm for public education and the centrality of the individual had long lasting consequences. The following chapters trace a concise history of Subject English and emphasize the continuing character of the debates over the last 150 years, including the long tradition of student-centred English teaching. In these American chapters the enduring model of individual creativity is most noticeable, and the chapter begins by referring to the diagram which appears overleaf.

Areas of concern in the 1990s and the 1890s

Look carefully at the grid in figure 3. Each box contains an area of concern for today's English teachers in the United States. Of course, there are other topics, but the ones noted in the grid represent some of the major areas of focus in late twentieth-century English teaching. A look at the article titles in the National Council of Teachers of English September, 1998 publication, *The Council Chronicle* gives readers yet another view of today's pressing issues. 'Bilingual Ed Takes Hit in California,' 'Exploring the Teacher as

Learner', 'Reading Excellence Act Dies in Senate', 'Inner City Curriculum "Parched" Kozol Says', 'NCTE Takes Bold Step with Reading Initiative', 'NCTE Web Site Continues To Grow', and 'Flexible, Responsive Classroom Practice: What Writing Teachers Need to Know about Their Fair Use Rights'. Professional conversations around these topics dominate today. They are representative of the sociological, economic, and political forces dominating the era.

Throughout the history of English teaching in the United States, many issues and questions have been addressed and debated. What is English? Why do we teach English? What is good English? What is good literature? What is good writing? What role does language play? How do we teach English? How do we teach teachers to teach English? How does technology fit into the teaching of English? Who decides the answers to these and other questions? Answers have been offered from an historical perspective by many. Some of the most useful include Arthur Applebee's *Tradition and Reform in the Teaching of English* (1974), J. N. Hook's *A Long Way Together* (1980), Jeanne Gerlach and Virginia Monseau's *Missing Chapters: Ten Pioneering Women In NCTE and English Education* (1991), *Consensus and Dissent in Teaching English*, edited by Marjorie Farmer in 1986, and David England and Stephen Judy's *Historical Primer on the Teaching of English*, which appeared as the April 1978 issue of *The English Journal*. Of course there are numerous journal articles and doctoral dissertations which examine these and related issues in an attempt to offer reflections and analyses on a part of the history of English teaching in the United States. Many of the publications give detailed discussions and examinations of particular aspects of English studies as they have occurred throughout our history. Thus, one chapter cannot possibly offer a comprehensive history of professional approaches to teaching English in the United States; therefore, it will provide a sketch of the changes that have happened in English teaching from the colonial days until the present, focusing on twentieth-century contexts. Why the twentieth century? Perhaps England and Judy (1997) offers the best explanation: 'To be sure, our history as a profession has been relatively brief; perhaps we can mark our real beginnings with the Committee of Ten recommendations in the 1890s. In the Report of the Committee of Ten, it was suggested that English be a subject of daily study throughout the high-school years. At that time, this was a revolutionary notion; today, we need to be reminded that ' "English every day in every grade" is largely an idea of the twentieth century' (p. 6).

In its 1894 report, the Committee of Ten, especially through its Conference on English, set two main objectives for English in the schools: communication of ideas and appreciation of literature. While each twentieth-century generation since has reexamined and, at times, redesigned the English curriculum, it has retained its basic character. While the twentieth century will be the era of focus here, the account begins at the beginning and flashes back to colonial times, snapshotting through that period, as well as the eighteenth century. Readers should remember that though the profession of

Response to Literature	Writing Process (Writing Across The Curriculum)	Creative Dramatics
Multicultural Literature Studies	Gender Studies	Action/Teacher Research
Teacher Training Reform	Adolescent Literature	Grammar
Government Involvement	International (Global Perspectives Conversations)	Technology Distance Learning
Reading Literacy	Standards & Assessment	Urban Education
Collaborative Learning	Media Studies	ESL

Figure 3 Areas of concern for English teachers in the United States

teaching English is young, the United States has witnessed a revolutionary war, a civil war, two world wars, the Korean War, several large scale military actions, an economic depression, an unprecedented revolution in communications, and eighteen presidents. The United States has moved from an agrarian nation to an industrialised country and now to an information society. And as England (1979) notes, it has witnessed a generally closed society enfranchise racial minorities, ethnic minorities, women and the physically challenged.

Good Boys at their Books

He who ne'er learns his A, B, C,
Forever will a Blockhead be;
But he who to his Book's inclin'd,
Will foon a golden Treafure find.
From *The New England Primer*

The early history of English teaching in the United States, 1690–1890

The history of English teaching in the United States began over 300 years ago. The text book was *The New England Primer*. The *Primer*, a rather physically small book, two inches by three, included a motivational opening, lists of words up through five syllables, spelling and vocabulary lists, biblical excerpts, the catechism or 'Spiritual Milk for American Babes, Drawn out of the Breasts of both Testaments, for their Souls Nourishment'. For many years children were schooled at home in basic instruction in English, and if they attended the academies or colleges, their instruction focused on Latin and Greek. The early home instruction was often conducted by a community member for his or her own children and the children of the neighbourhood. Instructional emphasis was on ethical and moral lessons, as well as religious dogma.

Soon, as Tchudi and Mitchell (1989) point out, Americans began to feel a need for public education. The Massachusetts Bay Colony 1648 school laws required that any community of more than fifty families provide for public schooling in reading, writing, and arithmetic. They remind us that, 'from the beginning, American education has always grown toward democratisation, extending educational opportunities to more and more people' (p. 3). Literacy has been at the centre of that education, and 'knowing how to read and write is regarded as an unwritten bill of rights for all Americans' (p. 3). Thus, with the establishment of public education, the emphasis of instruction began to shift from a focus on ethical and moral development to one of unity – how to help the United States provide its citizenry with a common tradition of culture and government, a common belief in responsible citizenship, and a common language. While the basic definition of literacy is the ability to read and write, perhaps it was Benjamin Franklin with his secondary academy in Philadelphia that first expanded that definition to include English instruction for young men who were about to enter the commercial arena. They needed to have experiences with language, literature, and composition to be considered successful in their business lives. Tchudi and Mitchell (1989) remind us that English with a tripartite focus made its way into the curriculum in opposition to Latin and Greek.

From the inception of secondary schools, secondary-school teachers in the USA taught grammar in the English classes, and at the beginning of the nineteenth century the grammars of Lindley Murray dominated. These grammars focused on mastery of parts of speech and syntactic analysis. Parsing, a form of sentence analysis was also emphasised. Murray's texts had a strong moral tone that linked language to proper human conduct. Composition was to follow grammar into the curriculum with the emphasis of writing being on narration, description, exposition, argument, persuasion – rhetorical forms and discourse analysis. The emphasis was always on the correctness of the product, and student themes were marked with red pencil or pen. At Harvard College, students who enrolled in composition classes wrote daily papers and corrected them when they were returned for revision. The English faculty at Harvard wanted the secondary-school teachers to follow the same process in composition teaching. Literature was the last component to be added to the English curriculum. While reading had been central to the US curriculum since Colonial times, the study of Literature was on the original Greek and Roman classics. American and British writers were added in the late nineteenth century as a result of the growing literary nationalism. Even then, teachers were more concerned with literary history, biography, and criticism than with the content of the literature.

Literature, like grammar and composition, was taught in the secondary schools primarily so that students could do well on college entrance exams. English teaching, then, was primarily for college preparation. It is necessary to note here that the few students who graduated from high school were usually doing so in order to enroll in college.

American education and the formation of a canon

Colleges developed their own entrance examinations, requiring prospective students to demonstrate their knowledge of grammar, literature, and composition skills. Reading lists were created and passed on to high-school teachers, who in turn included the prescribed works as required reading for their students. Classics of British and American literature were included in the high-school programme, but British literature selections dominated the lists and the teachings. By the late 1880s George Eliot's *Silas Marner* was the most often taught novel in secondary English classrooms. Shakespeare's plays, particularly *Julius Caesar* and *Macbeth*, became the standard fare for high-school literature classes. As a matter of fact, the college reading lists so dominated secondary school teaching that high-school teachers soon called for a single reading list and a unified entrance exam. Groups such as the North Central and Middle States Associations were formed to address these concerns. In 1892, the Committee of Ten, chaired by Charles Eliot, then President of Harvard University, and again in 1894, the members of the National Conference on Entrance Examinations for Colleges chose the literary works to be studied. As a result, all students in all secondary class-rooms were required to read the selections on the common book lists in order to pass the entrance exam which focused on biographical, philological, or analytical aspects of literature. The common reading list or the 'canon' as many would refer to it, consisted almost exclusively of works by British authors, because its compilers thought that familiarity with 'good works' would help students learn to think and express themselves. Many English educators believed that the creation of the common reading list which included mainly works which were not contemporary pieces, and subsequent testing on the common exam destroyed young people's interest in reading literature for pleasure and enjoyment. Consider Oscar McPherson's (1931) comments,

> About twenty-five years ago, or just after the close of the nineteenth century, adolescents in general stopped reading the classics of that century for their own entertainment. I was and am convinced that the demise of those classics, so far as the average boy or girl en route to college was concerned, is traceable directly to the college entrance examination boards. Those boards, then made up largely of members of college faculties, composed their own restricted lists of thus formally decreed classics. The old technique was soon to kill Greek and is now partly responsible for the moribund condition of Latin, and had been and was applied to the English classics. That technique has it as an axiom that language, foreign or native, should be taught philologically. Well, for boys and girls of today Scott and Thackeray and Dickens are no more. True, they would have died even if we teachers hadn't chloroformed them in the classroom, because these books are written in an idiom far different from that of today and because this is a tradition-ignoring age. But we undoubtedly hastened their death.
>
> p. 21

Even though teaching of the classics has survived in many schools, especially for those students who wish to continue their studies in colleges and universities, there are those who still believe as McPherson did, and the debate about how to teach literature still exists.

Readers should remember that long before the twentieth century, a tradition of English teaching was set; the three major components were language, composition, and literature. Language teaching consisted of grammar, focusing on parts of speech, sentence structure, parsing, and diagramming. Students were to memorize the rules and repeat them when summoned to do so. Composition was limited to the study of rhetorical forms, followed by writing themes to be marked by the teacher and then corrected by the student. Again, let the reader remember the focus was always on errors and the correcting of them. Literature teaching which focused on the great works and centred on historical, philological, and analytical perspectives dominated the curriculum; grammar and writing instruction were often integrated into the teaching of literature. Today the integration of reading/literature, writing, and language study has occurred in many classrooms; however, Squire and Applebee (1968) found that a fragmented curriculum still existed in some high schools and again Applebee (1993) found the same to be true: separate courses in grammar, composition, and literature are still being offered, and of the little writing being done, almost none is about literature.

The influence of the colleges and universities continued to shape secondary-school English instruction, but there were those secondary-school English teachers who called for the development of a secondary-school English curriculum which focused on the immediate needs and interests of young people. I must pause here to remind the reader that while the classical English high school opened in Boston in 1821, there were not many high schools until a court case in Kalamazoo, Michigan, in 1874 ruled that it was legal to use taxes to support the schools. As a result of that determination, hundreds of high schools opened their doors to students, many who were children of the working class. These growing middle class students needed schools which provided a different curriculum than the English Classical High School had offered. Many of these students would not qualify for or want to pursue college or university work. They needed preparation for citizenship in a democracy; they needed a diverse curriculum which emphasised choice, a curriculum which accommodated individual needs and individual tastes. Many secondary-school teachers supported this belief; they called for a reorganisation of secondary education and protested against the examinations in English.

The early twentieth century: NCTE and the changing curriculum

Most notable among these teachers were the group of English teachers who formed the National Council of Teachers of English (NCTE) in 1911. Two thirds of the group were teachers or administrators from secondary schools; one third was from colleges or universities. There were no representatives from elementary schools, since their purpose was to deal with high-school/college/university relationships. An Elementary Section was formed in 1912 (Hook, 1979). While the NCTE's main purpose was to protest at college domination of the secondary schools, Hook notes that the other goals included:

Work to 'diminish insularity among teachers of English'
Organise the Council as three departments: elementary, high school, and college
Publicise the excessive load and low pay of teachers of English
Work for improved teacher preparation
Continue work toward improved college entrance requirements
Work to improve the 'chaotic condition of Elementary school English'
Help to articulate elementary and secondary-school studies
Stress 'Culture' and 'Efficiency' as aims of teaching
Develop a 'true pedagogy of English teaching'
Advocate 'power in writing and speaking' as the basis for student promotion
Help teachers to adapt content and methods to individual classes
Stress the humanities
Emphasise composition, not literature, as the centre of the English course
Emphasise oral English
Make quite definite suggestions for an improved high-school course
Help the small schools.

'It is noteworthy, Hook continues, that a majority of these aims still influence the work of the Council' (p. 21).

In 1917, a committee made up of members from the newly organised NCTE and members of the National Education Association (NEA), chaired by James F. Hosic, Secretary-Treasurer of NCTE, declared that English was preparation for life, not college and concluded that the best course of study for all students would also serve to prepare students for college. While the committee was influenced by the progressive philosophy of John Dewey, they missed the mark when they recommended that classic literature was, in effect, a good preparation for life and should appeal to all students because of its greatness. Therefore, many high-school teachers continued to teach 'college prep' literature focusing on 'great books' for all students.

The early years of NCTE (1912–1925) were years of controversies and debates concerning English education in the USA. Through those years English was viewed and discussed by educators as (1) an intellectual discipline and as a means to the acquisition of knowledge, (2) as a socialisation process necessary for individual development, and (3) as a method for character development of democratic citizens. Many believed that English should serve all three purposes, but there were those who felt that English education should serve one purpose more than the other. Those who believed that the curriculum should be organised in such a way that student learning could be predicted and measured adhered to the views of E. L. Thorndike, an American educational psychologist, who stressed the necessity to have accurate measures of educational products. Language, literature, and composition were regarded by Thorndike and his followers as disciplines that would train and strengthen the mind. Students were held accountable for memorisation of facts, facts, facts.

Opposition to these views of English education grew dramatically through the first quarter of the twentieth century. Many educators knew that students needed more than academic skills to survive in society; they agreed that English courses should be structured to meet individual needs, and that students should be encouraged to relate their personal and social experiences to school work. They followed the teachings of G. Stanley Hall who believed that a child's mental and physical growth occurred in developmental stages, and that the onset of the stages varied from child to child; thus, it was ridiculous to teach all children the same thing at the same time. These views helped to pave the way for the development of the progressive movement in education.

James Hosic, the first editor of the *English Journal* was aware of these differing views and promised that the journal would provide a means of expression, would be a general clearing house of experience and opinion for the English teachers of the country and to be a bearer of helpful messages to all who are interested in the teaching of the mother-tongue. Hosic encouraged articles from elementary, secondary, and college teachers, but the first years of the journal contained mostly articles concentrating on secondary-school issues. Articles focused on questions of teaching composition, literature, and grammar. Many of the authors focused on traditional methods of instruction, but there were some who were interested in finding out what the best teaching practices were – which practices resulted in student success. Many of the writers realised that English education needed to be rethought and reorganised. They followed the teachings of John Dewey who said that knowledge was a means of controlling the environment to improve human life. He called for trying out new methods which were related to student interests and connected with contemporary problems and concerns. In other words, English education should include a student's physical and moral well being as well as her intellectual development. Dewey regarded education as incomplete if it ignored these ideas. Soon many educators began to look at English teaching as a socialisation process. They began to teach as though life was the centre of education; therefore, life and language should grow together, composition should be regarded as an attempt to communicate ideas, and literature should be correlated with student interests and life experiences.

One attempt to break with tradition and broaden the curriculum to emphasise students' needs and tastes came with the publication of a book titled *An Experience Curriculum in English* (1935). The report expressed the views of a committee chaired by W. Wilbur Hatfield and presented the idea that both the social value of English and the role of the student's own experience were important in learning. Thus, teachers were encouraged to develop courses that were based on student's prior experiences as well as experiences they needed in order to develop as learners. Additionally, the work called for an emphasis on teaching literature by patterns, themes, and ideas and for teaching useful social skills including letter writing and conver-sation. In sum, it presented educators with an opportunity to broaden English instruction for all students. However, critics thought that the writers were overly concerned with language correctness and the values of the middle class. In addition, according to Squire (1991), by the time it reached the classroom teacher for review and implementation, the world was at war, and attention was focused on practical needs of the country.

Three years later, however, *A Correlated Curriculum in English* was published by NCTE. The work explored ways of correlating elementary, secondary, and college English with work in other content areas. This work is an antecedent of the 1980's movement known as 'language to learn' or 'language across the curriculum'. While English teachers were encouraged to collaborate with their peers in other disciplines and move away from the literary history and syntactic correctness focus, critics believed that *A Correlated Curriculum* might mean the death of English for English's sake. Like An *Experience Curriculum*, *A Correlated Curriculum* gave way to the rally around the World War II effort of promoting patriotism in English classes. Some remnants of both reports remained in the classrooms like the concern for teaching social conversation and telephone skills. Interdisciplinary teaching occurred mostly between English and Social Studies teachers and for the most part, remains so today.

Although the far-reaching potential of the *Experience Curriculum* and the *Correlated Curriculum* was not realised, some success was achieved in estab-lishing a wider variety of acceptable literature for secondary-school English classrooms. Soon to come, however, were the College Entrance Examination Board's emphasis on the Scholastic Aptitude Test (SAT) scores. The focus on these scores continued to remind secondary English teachers that they must prepare their students for success on college entrance exams. As the reader sees, the changing English teaching curriculum seemed to move from one end of the continuum to the other, focusing for a time on the need for basic skills, then for a time on student needs and student experiences.

Subject English in America, 1950 to the present

In the 1950s, the English curriculum reflected the mood of the country, and the mood was a taciturn one. Simmons *et al.* (1990) remind us that the Eisenhower years were years of cooling off from the intensity of World War II and from the war in Korea. 'Don't rock the boat seemed to be the watchword phrase as the decade entered mid-stream' (p. 93). In the English classroom, the chronological-historical approach to literature returned. It was during this time when John Warriner's *Handbook of English* (1951) appeared. Warriner's text like Lindley Murray's before emphasised the basic structure of the English language. It was also during the 1950s that the five paragraph theme emerged as the way to teach composition. Literature instruction which primarily focused on content was offered as a genre course in the tenth grade, an American literature course in the eleventh grade, and a British literature course in the twelfth.

One of the most important events to affect all education in the USA was the 1954 Supreme Court decision on Brown vs. Kansas, a decision which desegregated the nation's schools. Simmons *et al.* (1992) remind us that English classes provided skills which were vital to Blacks' abilities to gain voting privileges and prepare for jobs. Access to a meaningful education became a top priority of civil rights leaders and 'the question of the appropriateness of the English curriculum loomed larger and larger' (p. 93).

Another equally important event was the 1957 Russian launching of Sputnik, the first satellite to orbit the earth. The American government and the public were alarmed and surprised that the Russians possessed such technological skill, fearing that they might use similar technology to launch nuclear warheads at anyone who was considered an enemy. American education was blamed for having a science and maths curriculum that was too soft to produce students who were technologically superior. In 1958, Congress funded the National Defense Education Act (NDEA), which provided funds for curriculum development and professional teacher development in maths and science. There were no funds provided for teachers of English. However, the NCTE published a monograph titled *The National Defense and the Teaching of English* in 1961, arguing for the centrality of literacy in all schools. As a result, Congress provided funds for a series of curriculum study centres in English as a part of NDEA.

The establishment of the centres became known as Project English, and their mission was to examine all aspects of the English curriculum. The results of the study pointed to the failure of traditional methods of teaching; teaching grammar did not help students to become better writers and thinkers; composition with its focus on correctness and the red pen marking of errors had not brought about student writing improvement. Literature teaching which focused on historical study had not created lifetime readers or students who were motivated to read for the sake of enjoying or loving literature.

Thus, English teachers began to look at student-centred approaches to teaching, focusing on students' growth toward development, rather than on the analysis of the content or mastery of form. Tchudi and Mitchell (1989) note that the new way of teaching was supported by several other developments in education.

The romantic critics of education – John Holt, Jonathan Kozol, Herbert Kohl, and George Leonard – wrote indictments of the schools for being oppressive. Learning, they argued, must be natural, positive, and pleasurable. Paperback books became common in the schools along with hardbound textbooks. These books made a wide range of classic and contemporary literature available to English teachers and students at a low cost.

Dartmouth – revolution and retrenchment

An Anglo-American Seminar on the Teaching of English held at Dartmouth College (1966) emphasised the role of language learning in personal growth, stressing the importance of self-expression in writing in response to literature. Electives in English came into vogue, replacing the traditional high-school courses – English I, II, III, IV – with a range from Shakespeare to Supernatural Literature (pp. 23–4). These and other developments such as the establishment of the NCTE Research Foundation brought reform to the English teaching in the 1960s. Almost everyone agreed that the most effective English curriculum would be one that fostered individual growth and development for every student.

Many new curricular projects were developed in the 1960s and 1970s to meet the increased demand for relevance and flexibility. It appeared that a revolution from tradition was under way. The tradition tripartite of literature, language, and composition, with the same course content for all students seemed to have been replaced by student-centred curriculum with a range of course options for everyone.

But as Tchudi and Mitchell (1989) point out, the schools had not entirely discarded tradition. They remind us that much of the revolutionary activity took place at professional conferences and on the pages of professional journals, pointing out that most classroom teachers were too busy with daily concerns to read the journals, and many never attended conventions. Teachers simply could not afford the cost and most school districts did not have dollars to support travel; many districts would not even grant leave time to those who could pay their own way to conferences. Those teachers placed the students' desks in circles, and they spoke of the need for creativity along with correctness. But, the majority kept on teaching their Warriner's.

Furthermore, the 'new English' which gave student choices about which courses they could take had weaknesses that needed to be considered. For example, the 'elective' courses were often found to be traditional courses packaged under a new title – old wine in new bottles. No one seemed to actually know what was actually being covered in elective courses, especially if only one teacher was offering the course. Some believed that the electives tended to cloud the curriculum and result in chance coverage of the basics.

Changes in the early 1970s, then, rather than being inspired by Dartmouth, were fostered by the back to basics movement which produced a series of mastery learning curricula guides that met with both success and criticism throughout the United States. It was apparent that while some teachers had been concerned with language growth and personal development, others had been moving toward assessment and quantification as a means of creating a more effective English curriculum. Many English teachers agreed that the English curriculum should have clear goals and objectives. The new student-centred curriculum would not fit, because it lacked a clear statement of purpose and measurable outcomes. Traditional grammar instruction, on the other hand, could easily be translated into the terminology of the back to basics movement.

Accountability

With the call for 'back to basics' came new rhetoric. The journals were full of articles exploring 'mandated goals', 'behavioural objectives', 'accountability', and 'assessment'. Some educators and citizens believed that measuring the outcomes of these goals and objectives would ensure better teaching and student success. National assessments as well as state and local assessments were developed to rate educational progress. Teachers in all content areas, including English teachers, began writing behavioural objectives and developing assessment programmes for all classroom activities. Perhaps one of the most used books was Robert F. Mager's *Preparing Instructional Objectives* (1962), described as 'a book for teachers and student teachers . . . for anyone interested in transmitting skills and knowledge to others'. English teachers and their colleagues in other disciplines concentrated, for the most part, on minimum essentials in their teaching.

The calls for accountability and assessment increased when, in 1974, the College Entrance Examination Board released the startling news that the scores on the Scholastic Aptitude Test verbal measure had been steadily dropping for over a decade. The media had a field-day with this information. They described the nation's educational system as 'a nation at risk'; parents were outraged and blamed their children for not studying and the teachers for not teaching; teachers blamed the administrators; the assigning of blame continued down the line. But in the end, it was the English teachers who shouldered the most blame, for when such articles as 'Why Johnny Can't Read' (1975) appeared in print, the entire US citizenry knew it was the English teacher's responsibility to teach basic literacy – the ability to read and write. Covers and whole editions of popular news magazines like *Time* and *Newsweek* were devoted to the literacy 'crisis'. Tchudi and Mitchell (1989) cite a 1975 *Newsweek* assertion:

> If your children are attending college, the chances are that when they graduate they will be unable to write ordinary, expository English with any real degree of lucidity. If they are in high school and planning to attend college, the chances are less than even that they will be able to write English at the minimal college level when they get there. If they are not planning to attend college, their skills in writing English may not even qualify them for secretarial or clerical work. And if they are attending elementary school, they are almost certainly not being given the kind of required reading material, much less writing instruction, that might make it possible for them eventually to write comprehensible English. Willy-nilly, the educational system is spawning a generation of semiliterates.
>
> 8 December 1975, p. 58

Tchudi and Mitchell (1989) point out that although this analysis was inaccurate and biased by its outdated views of language correctness and learning, it impacted English teachers enough that many of them returned to teaching basics (some had never left). Elective courses were replaced with courses focusing on grammar and punctuation. Innovative anthologies of the late 1960s were replaced with Warriner's grammar handbook. There were those English teachers who did not return to teaching only the basics; their argument was that the new English was not responsible for the test score decline. Yet, the concern for basic skills continues today; although, there have been many innovative practices which will be mentioned in the remainder of this chapter.

On a personal note, the writer of this chapter began my teaching career in 1974 right in the middle of the basics wars; however, I and many of my colleagues have been active participants in the effort to help students develop as individuals who can think critically and creatively about themselves, their peers, and the world around them. We view teaching as a way of facilitating learning and we believe that learning and knowing occur when one makes information her own through active participation.

As I have noted, many educators, individuals, parents, and groups – all segments of society have expressed concern with the state of student writing since the early 1970s. Criticisms came from parents who blamed the extremely low verbal SAT scores on the schools for neglecting grammar and punctuation. Similarly, content area teachers were alarmed at papers full of misspellings, comma mistakes, and poor organisation. They blamed the English teachers. The English teachers, when they did teach writing, continued to give traditional composition assignments and corrected them with red pencils. When students' writing did not improve, the English teachers cried that over-crowded classrooms and lack of time were the causes of poor writing skills. Despite all these reactions, however, the fact remained that students in American schools did not write very well.

At this point it is necessary to note, that, according to Tchudi (1982), there has never been a time in American educational history when parents, teachers, and society have been satisfied with the way students write. He observes that 'There was no golden age of literacy' (p. 3). Hence, if teachers and parents want students to write better, 'they have to find new ways of teaching writing; they can't go back to the good old days that never were' (p. 3).

The National Writing Project

One of the most promising developments to come out of the literacy crisis was the establishment of the National Writing Project, a model for inservice training in writing for teachers. The project, developed by James Gray and colleagues in 1974, was first known as The Bay Area Writing Project. The Bay Area Writing Project at Berkeley gained foundation support from the

National Endowment for the Humanities and established projects elsewhere to form the National Writing Project. The National Writing Project was based on two major premises about writing:

(1) Writing is a meaning-making activity
(2) Writing is both a process and a product of that process.

Those two premises have had a major impact on the way writing/learning has been discussed in the US since 1974. Let us look first at the writing process.

The reader may remember that many teachers had for years viewed writing as a process of transcription that generates a product on paper. They assigned writing tasks to students, collected the products, marked the surface mistakes with red pencil, and returned the products to the students. The students, in this situation, were passive recipients of rules and advice from the teacher. Rarely were they asked to engage in activities such as brainstorming, free writing, first draft writing, sharing, revising, and editing which researchers agree promote learning. This traditional approach to teaching is, as we have learned, ineffective. As a result of the National Writing Project influence on teaching and an emphasis on writing research, teachers began to realise that writing involved more than concentration on a product; rather, it is a complex developmental process which changes depending on our age and our experiences as writers and the kinds of writing we do. The process may be mostly unconscious and compressed for mature writers working on simple writing tasks. But, as Lindeman (1982) relates, if the writer is inexperienced or if the writer's task is more complex, the process is more complex. Research, too, began to focus on the process of writing itself and less on the finished product (Emig 1971; Britton 1975; Applebee 1981).

Currently the Project has over 100 sites in 44 states, and more than 70,000 teachers are trained at these sites each year. In addition to summer training institutes, the Project provides teachers with a newsletter and various publications dealing with current theory and research in writing.

While attending the summer institute, the selected participants are expected to (1) participate in writing activities, (2) make presentations on some aspect of the teaching of writing, and (3) learn about theory and research in composition by reading and listening to guest speakers (Gere 1984, p. 22). The activities, which are the basis of the writing workshop model, promote instructional change and accommodate the project's emphasis on the teaching and learning of writing. According to Gere (1984), these activities lead to three results: (1) teachers become authors, (2) teachers become expert trainers of other teachers, and (3) teachers become researchers.

Studies (Scriven 1980) of the effects of the National Writing Project on teachers indicate more positive attitudes toward writing. Further, the studies indicate that if teachers participate in writing activities themselves, understand writing research and theory, and develop positive attitudes about writing, they will be better able to foster student writing growth.

Out of the interest and research on the writing process came the national language across the curriculum movement in the 1980s. This movement was based on the view that writing is not only a process and a product of that process, but writing is a meaning making activity. That idea is based heavily on the works of Jean Piaget (1969), Lev Vygotsky (1962), Jerome Bruner (1971), Janet Emig (1971), Arthur Applebee (1981), and James Britton (1971). It assumes that writing for learning is different from writing for informing. The writing/language to learn effort generated cooperation among teachers in many disciplines and stressed the importance of language to learn all school subjects. Furthermore, the movement created an interest among educational researchers. They wanted to know if writing was, indeed, a way of learning, and if so, then what kinds of writing were going on in the schools.

Several studies (Applebee 1981; Goodlad 1984) found that student writing tasks, for the most part, involved answering simple questions and filling in the blanks on quizzes and tests. Concerned with the results of these and other studies, Ernest L. Boyer, president of the Carnegie Foundation for the Advancement of Teaching and author of the book *High School: A Report on Secondary Education in America* (1983), recommended that, 'Writing should be a central objective of education' (p. 91). His report called for the teaching of writing as thinking in every class in American secondary schools. Boyer was voicing what the Committee of Ten on Secondary School Studies had recommended as early as 1983; i.e. that language is the central element of schooling.

As the decade of the eighties progressed and finally drew to a close, there were more reports that called for the need for more quality in education, including *A Nation at Risk, The Need for Quality, Educating Americans for the 21st Century: A Report To the American People, Action for Excellence: A Comprehensive Plan to Improve Our Schools, The Paideia Proposal: An Educational Manifesto and the Paideia Proposal and Possibilities: A Consideration of Questions Raised by the Paideia Proposal*. All these reports reiterated the theme of *A Nation At Risk* – the continuing failure of the schools to teach students to think critically and creatively would have serious consequences in the areas of national strength, defense, technology, and leadership. English teachers found themselves split between teaching the basics and facilitating writing and literature as ways of creating knowledge and making meaning for self. This split led colleagues in the same schools, and the same departments to disagree over what English is and how English should be taught.

As the 1990s approached, educators were having conversations about how schooling had changed so much during the last century and still had remained so much the same.

How can schooling have changed so much over the last century yet still appear pretty much the same as it has always been? . . . Recall that a number of second order reforms established the dominant structures of schooling between the mid-nineteenth and early twentieth centuries, e.g. the self-contained classroom, the graded curriculum, the fifty minute period, frequent testing, the reliance on textbooks and work sheets and the current governance structure of schools were once reforms that have since become institutional bench marks of what constitutes proper schooling . . .

Cuban 1988, p. 343

Dartmouth 2

English teachers, believing that their task for the 1990s would be to chart a course for the future of English teaching in the USA, met at the WYE Woods in Maryland. Under the direction of Phyllis Franklin, Executive Director of the Modern Language Association of America, the group became known as the 1987 English Coalition Conference or Dartmouth Two. The conference, four years in the planning, brought together English teachers from all levels (Kindergarten–University), members of the Modern Language Association and members of the National Council of Teachers of English. The more than participants called for English classrooms where learners would be actively engaged in all areas of the Language Arts – reading, writing, listening, speaking, viewing, thinking, and interpreting. The teachers' tasks would be to facilitate learning, to create situations for student exploration of and practice in the use of language through interaction with their peers. The group concurred that teachers should model good learning through their own writing and various language uses. They called for teachers to encourage students to read widely, emphasising the value of the use of children's and young adult literature over basal readers and anthologies. Equally important, they urged the use of literature that reflects the diversity of American culture. Hydrick (1988), a conference participant believes that students should read literature that challenges their abilities and empowers them. She feels that readings should include:

both traditional literature and literature that reflects the diversity of American culture and that students become familiar with as many different kinds of writing as possible . . . Diversities and pedagogy and curriculum specifics become petty questions compared to the overriding missions of life-long learning, and the empowerment of teachers and students – empowerment which can be derived only from language.

p. 1

Certainly, the Coalition Conference had far-reaching impact on English teaching in the 1990s. English teachers became more aware of the need for multicultural literature and many incorporated it into their teaching. Awareness, however, is not enough. We are not changing at the rate our population is changing. Applebee (1989) points out the continued shortage of works by women and people of colour in the high-school literature curriculum. And some are still fighting the 'canon wars'. Further, while we are realising more and more the need for using language and writing to learn, there are classrooms where teachers still focus on the written product and use the red pencil to mark errors. Even though there has been an emphasis on collaborative learning which emphasizes the social aspects and values of learning, we still find classrooms with students seated one behind the other in straight rows of brown wooden desks often nailed to the floor. The teacher, always in front of the classroom, lectures from a text on specific topics or literature selections. The students, in turn, copy notes from the lecture to be memorised for later recitation or testing. The main emphasis in such a classroom always seems to be on quietness and order, as if learning only occurs when there is silence. The emphasis is on the mastery of facts, facts, facts.

Language arts models in the United States

So it seems that the teaching of English in the USA has moved back and forth from the Mastery Curriculum Model to the Heritage Model to the Process Model. These models have been the existing models for the English curriculum. The Mastery Model emphasises skills and competencies; the Heritage Model stresses the transmission of values and traditions of a culture, and the Process Model emphasises language processes that bring about individual student growth.

The Mastery Model is based on the theories of Carroll (1963) and B. Bloom (1968, 1974, 1981) who agree that students can master both content and skills if they are given appropriate instructional time. Teaching objectives must be clearly stated and course content must be taught in small units hierarchically ordered. The units are introduced at an ever-increasing level of complexity. The model is based on the notion that the teacher has all the facts, knows the information that needs to be taught, teaches it, then tests, and reteaches if necessary. When students have mastered the material taught, they move to the next level.

The Heritage Model finds its roots in 1783 when American educators were concerned with a need to foster a common cultural background for students through the study of English. Webster was one of the first to use the Heritage Model when he stated that one of the goals of the *Blue-Backed Speller* was to foster unity and common culture. Today those who are advocating teaching multicultural literature are criticised for failing to teach a common culture shared by all Americans. Recently there has been a renewed interest in teaching literature that has endured because of its content, style, and moral values and because it constitutes a student's cultural heritage, assuming every student has the same cultural heritage. The National Commission on Excellence in Education recommended in 1983 that the secondary English curriculum should equip graduates to know their literary heritage and provide for them an ethical understanding of the world. Alan Bloom's (1987) *The Closing of the American Mind: How Higher Education has Failed Democracy*, E. D. Hirsch's (1988) *Cultural Literacy: What Every American needs to Know*, and William Bennett's (1987) *James Madison High School; A Curriculum for American Schools* are contemporary best sellers that have the Heritage Model as their bases. Critics of this model assert that it is biased toward a particular culture, and it assumes that all books are good for all students.

The Process-Approach Model is the most student centred of the models. It does not stress mastery of skills or specific authors' works to be read. Instead, it calls for the acknowledgment of differences that exist among students and an environment is created for each student to make meaning from his own experiences from the material studied. The model assumes that although all students might read the same work, their responses are probably different; each student's response should be respected by the teacher. Skills are taught in context with natural language development. This is the model that teachers use when they teach that the process of learning is as important as the product.

The teaching of English in the United States has undergone major changes since the discipline was officially established by the Committee of Ten in (1894). Critics are still wrestling with many questions. How to teach writing? What literature should be taught? When should grammar be taught, if at all? But the situation has also moved on. Take another look at the chart at the beginning of the chapter. Some of the topics in the boxes have been topics for discussions throughout this century; others are new or at least they are being considered from new perspectives. When we look at the boxes, we should ask ourselves how do all these topics fit into teaching and studying English, and as we try to reimagine 'What is English?' we should remember that language is the basis of all content to be studied, including English.

References

Applebee, A. (1974) *Tradition and Reform in the Teaching of English: A History*, Urbana, IL: National Council of Teachers of English
—(1981) *Writing in the Secondary School: English and the Content Areas*, Urbana, IL: National Council of Teachers of English
—(1993) *Literature in the Secondary School: Studies of Curriculum and Instruction in the United States*, Urbana, IL: National Council of Teachers of English
Bennett, W. J. (1987) *James Madison High School: A Curriculum for American Students*, Washington, DC: US Department of Education
Bloom, A. (1987) *The Closing of the American Mind*, New York: Simon & Schuster
Bloom, B. (1968) 'Learning for mastery', *Evaluation Comment*, Volume 1, No. 2
Bloom, B. (1974) 'An introduction to mastery learning theory', in J. H. Block (ed.) (1974) *Schools, Society, and Mastery Learning*, New York: Holt, Rinehart & Winston, pp. 4–14
—(1981) *All Our Children Learning*, New York: McGraw-Hill

Boyer, E. L. (1983) High School: A Report on Secondary Education in America. New York: Harper & Row

Carroll, J. (1900) 'A model for school learning', Teachers College Record, Volume 64, 723–33

Committee of Ten of the NEA (1984) 'Report of the committee of ten on secondary school studies, with the reports of the conferences arranged by the committee', New York: American Book Co. for the NEA

Cuban, L. (1900) A fundamental puzzle of school reform, Phi delta kappan, Volume 69, No, 5, January, pp. 341–8

Emig, J. (1971) The Composing Process of Twelfth Graders, Urbana, IL: National Council of Teachers of English

England, D. and Judy, S. (eds.) (1978) The English Journal: An Historical Primer on the Teaching of English, Urbana, IL: The National Council of Teachers of English

Farmer, M. (ed.) (1986) Consensus and Dissent in Teaching English, Urbana, IL: The National Council of Teachers of English

Gere, A. (1984) 'The most important development in the last five years for high school teachers of composition', English Journal, Volume 73, p. 22

Gerlach, J. and Monseau, V. (eds.) (1991) Missing Chapters: Ten Pioneering Women in NCTE and English Education, Urbana, IL, National Council of Teachers of English

Goodlad, J. (1984) A Place Called School, New York: McGraw-Hill

Hirsch, Jr., E. D. (1988) The Dictionary of Cultural Literacy: What Every American Needs to Know, Boston: Houghton Mifflin Company

Hook, J. N. (1979) A Long Way Together: A Personal View of NCTE's First Sixty-Seven Years, National Council of Teachers of English

Lindemann, E. (1982) A Rhetoric for Writing Teachers, New York: Oxford University Press

McPherson, Oscar (1985) 'Reading hobbies', Library Journal, 15 September 1931. Cited in The English Journal, October

Magar, R. (1962) Preparing Instructional Objectives, Belmont, CA: Fearon-Pittman Publishers, Inc.

Piaget, J. (1967) Six Psychological Studies, New York: Random House

Scrivan, M. (1980) Executive Summary: Overview of the Bay Area Writing Project Evaluation, San Francisco: Evaluation Institute

Simmons, J. et al. (1990) 'The swinging pendulum: Teaching English in the USA, 1945–1987', in J. Britton, R. Shafer and K.Watson (eds.) (1990) Teaching and Learning English Worldwide. Philadelphia: Multilingual Matters Ltd

Squire, J. and Applebee, R. (1968) High School English Instruction Today: The National Study of High School English Programs, New York: Appleton-Century-Crofts

Stewig, J. (1983) Interview in USA Today, p. 14

Tchudi, S. and Mitchell, D. (1989) Explorations in the Teaching of English, New York: Harper and Row Publishers

Tchudi, S. (1982) 'Writing in the content areas'. Unpublished manuscript

The Council Chronicle. (1998) Urbana, IL: The National Council of Teachers of English

Vygotsky, L. S. (1978) Mind in Society, Cambridge, MA: Harvard University Press

9 Beliefs about 'English' in the United States

Jeanne Gerlach

Context: Subject English in the year 2000
Population of USA: 267.6 million
Number of schools: Total number of institutions – 121,855
Elementary and Secondary: 113,318
(public – 87,125)
(private – 26,093)
4 year universities – 2,244
Others (2 year college and non degree institutions – 6,393
Stages of Compulsory Schooling
Elementary (1–6) Junior HS (7–9) Senior HS (10–12)
Elementary (1–8) 4 year HS (9–12)
Elementary (1–4) Middle School (5–8) 4 year HS (9–12)
Significant Private School System? Yes 15.5% of all-level education institutions are private. 12.6% of elementary and secondary institutions are private
Number of universities: 2,244
National or state curriculum: State curriculum
Standardised assessments in English* NAEP† conducts assessment in reading and writing with students in grades 4, 8, 12.
However, federal law specifies that NAEP is voluntary for every pupil, school and state. Some state legislatures mandate state participation in NAEP, while others leave the option to superintend to other education officials.
Publication of Results: Individual results reported to parents. School's results published in newspapers.
Examinations leading to qualifications: None. However, each state has high-school graduation requirements which are generally, 4 years of English, 3 years of mathematics, 3 years of science, and 3 years of social studies as recommended by the National Commission on Excellence in Education (NFCEE)
Inspection of schools. Yes. States differ. *In Texas TEA visits schools and accredits*
Teaching Qualifications: In addition to requirement for formal education (e.g. a Bachelor's degree) teaching certification includes clinical experiences (e.g. student teaching) and often some type of formal testing.
A National Curriculum for Teacher Education: No. *Curriculum for teacher education is general determined by the individual state and individual teacher*

education program. *The US Dept of Education might make recommendations regarding requirements.*
Probationary Year. Differs by state. *Teachers in Texas, who are not certified, are on probation until they meet certification requirements. This varies from state to state.*
Statistical Sources: International Encyclopaedia of Education
NCES: The Condition of Education 1998
http://nces.ed.gov./nationsreport card/guide/ques1.html
US Census Web-page
*TEA – Texas Education Agency
†NAEP – National Assessment of Education Progress

What is English?

It is a difficult task to define English. I will, however, create a listing of words which exemplify what English means to me.

English is . . .

Personal
Emotional
Powerful
Reading/Composition
Liberating
Revealing
Complex
Inviting
Changing
Literature
The Classics/Canon
Relationship between reader/text
Grammar
Freedom
Vocal
Comforting
Passion
Demanding
Challenging
Diverse
Multicultural
Celebration of differences/otherness
Career
My Future

Christina Siriano, September 1996

As a graduate student majoring in English education, Siriano had been asked to respond to the questions: What constitutes the subject of English and what direction should the teaching of English take? Like many of us in the twentieth century, she has trouble putting into prose what exactly English is. She, of course, knows it is more than an integration of literature, grammar, and composition, but she struggles to explain it to a broad audience, so she offered the word list for teachers to ponder and respond to. She elaborates on the word list by explaining that, for her, English is more than classes where students complete workbook activities and prepare for multiple choice, fill in the blank, or true/false tests. She indicates that English teaching may include the classics or the 'canon', but it must go beyond the traditional study of such text and incorporate other entities that will help students use and consume language related activities effectively. She asserts that teachers must provide their students with varied opportunities to use language, to reflect on its use, and to receive feedback. Finally, she notes that teachers must encourage their students to use the Language Arts – reading, writing, speaking, listening, viewing, thinking, to make meaning of the world around them.

So, what is the subject of English Language Arts? What do we believe about English in the United States? As the reader has seen in chapter 8, these questions have been asked, debated, and answered many times in many different ways during the past 100 years. Many agree with Helen Pole (1994), who asserts that 'as a starting point, we must acknowledge that language, both written and oral, is a powerful tool for learning language, and should be used in all classes'. She believes that teachers need to be familiar with the roles language plays so they can teach all students effectively. She sees English teachers as being responsible for an expanded curriculum that includes the 'new' language arts of speaking, listening, and media literacy. She contends that this paradigm shift that overtly includes and elevates the position of oral language is the result of the standards' movement at both the state and national levels. With expanding roles of English teachers, it is clear that, throughout the nation, English teachers should be making changes in the ways they teach.

For many, the quest for identity has become the central mission of English teachers too. Their roles and what they teach have been called into question by their colleagues in other departments, administrators, and the citizenry in general. Dialogue on their purpose revolves around topics including professionalism, theory vs. research, the 'canon', remedial and developmental work, research, culture, intellectualism, and literacy. English faculty members have been asked to reconsider their own roles as they relate to reinventing English teaching. Whatever the outcomes of the reflection may be, teachers know that their conclusions must be internally coherent, rational and comprehensible. Perhaps as they think of what they would answer when asked, 'what it is you do?' Tilly Warnock's (1996) comments may lead to a clearer understanding. She writes: 'English departments teach reading and writing; all members of the department are engaged in literacy work of various kinds, from functional literacy to highly theoretical literacy work. Despite differences in teaching, research, and service, we are all committed to teaching language and literature as strategies for coping and as equipment for living' (p. 148). In sum, she indicates that what teachers do directly affects how students live their lives.

So it goes in the United States. Some would say that English teachers are having an identity crisis about being English teachers and they are unclear about the good we are doing for our students. I, on the other hand, believe, that teachers are not having a crisis, but that by raising these questions, they have opportunities to redefine who they are and what they do before some-one else does it for them. All teachers at all levels need to reflect regularly on their position in regards to their teaching, their mission in life. In this chapter, then, I want to share with you the reflections of my colleagues in English education, and my students (both graduate and undergraduate) as they responded to our research questionnaire: *Developing Views of English*.

Responses to the questionnaire

I distributed over 400 questionnaires (see Appendix A). Of these, 200 went to English education students; 200 went to practising English teachers and English education teachers. Participants were randomly selected; students were selected from students in my own classes and from students who were members of the doctoral student assembly of the National Council of Teachers of English. English teachers and English educators were selected from the National Council of Teachers of English 1995 and 1996 Directories. Of the 400 questionnaires, 280 were returned.

Let me describe their responses in regard to each question on the survey. **Question number one**: 60 per cent of the respondents said the words or phrases they thought of most often when they spoke of 'English' were Language, Literature, and Writing; 10 per cent said they thought of Cultural Studies, while the other 30 per cent indicated they thought of Emotional Responses, Poetry, and Creative Writing. **Question number two**: 80 per cent of the respondents said the Personal Growth Model was most in line with the views they held about teaching English; 12 per cent indicated the Cultural Analysis or Cultural Studies Model reflected their beliefs. The rest were split between the Cross Curricular and the Adult Needs Models. **Question number three**: most of the respondents agreed that between the ages of 11 and 16 a teacher had strong influence on shaping their views of what English is. Many agreed that membership in professional organisations was important. Almost all respondents agreed that many years of experience in teaching had the strongest influence on shaping their views about teaching. **Question number four**: 98 per cent of the respondents agree that their views of teaching English has changed most significantly over the past five years. **Question number five**: almost all the respondents agreed that their percep-tion of English teaching has undergone revision because of societal needs to focus on individual student growth and awareness. **Question number six**: 98 per cent of the respondents strongly agreed that the study of English should include popular mass market fiction, films, television programmes, visual media. Almost that same percentage agreed that it should include cultural studies topics such as propaganda, representations of the 1950s, and Madonna. Five respondents marked, 'Not Madonna'. **Question number seven**: almost all agreed that some literature contains insights and truths which transcend their own time and culture, showing us that human behaviour changes little. Likewise, almost all agreed that texts should be viewed from within the historical and cultural contexts which shaped them, as their meaning will inevitably be governed by these factors. Almost all strongly disagreed that the enjoyment and pleasure which many readers get from texts does not need to be queried. Almost all agreed that readings produce meanings. **Question number eight**: all respondents agreed that English has a role in helping us make decisions about the way we ought to live and the values to which we subscribe, and all agreed that encounters with literature can make us more sensitive human beings. **Question number nine**: all respondents either circled all three options (listening, doing, reading) as their preferred methods of learning or wrote out, 'I use all three methods'. **Question number ten**: all respondents indicated that they frequently learn something new about their subject from their students, and that they were frequently surprised by students' discoveries in the subject.

So, taking each question in turn, what can be concluded from the responses to the questionnaires? Most respondents identified writing, language, and literature as the words that immediately come to mind when they think of English. That response, I think, is consistent with the way English has been taught and thought about for more than 100 years. The 10 per cent who indicated they think of cultural studies and cultural analysis have probably been involved in recent conversations which emphasise the need for helping students understand the world environment as it is shaped by cultures of its inhabitants. While this is a growing view in US schools, it is still not the dominant view held by English teachers and students of English. Others indicated they thought about emotional responses, poetry, and creative writing; three identifiers that indicate a need for respecting the individual's response to life. As we will see later in this chapter, both English teachers and students feel that valuing students' feelings and creative expressions are critically important. However, not all teachers are focusing on this need; rather, they still are more concerned with the 'correct' language, error-free writing products, and the text of literature assignments.

While this may be true, 80 per cent of the respondents indicated a preference for the Personal Growth Model of English which focuses on the child and her use of the experience of English to develop her views and life focus; however, only a few saw a need for a focus on cultural analysis or cultural studies. Likewise, few of the responses indicated a need to focus on skills needed to communicate in adult life. Again, we see some inconsistencies in what teachers feel and what is being done.

It is not surprising to learn that teachers, for the most part, felt that one of the biggest influences shaping their current view of 'English' was a teacher who taught them when they were between the ages of 11 and 16. As we know, this age range is the heart of adolescent development. It is the time in students' lives when they are struggling to 'find themselves', when they need role models the most, when they often establish their life pathways. In addition, it was interesting to note, that teachers believe their years of experience in the profession have been critical in shaping their current views. I am reminded of the cliché, 'Experience is the best teacher'. We know that teaching in all areas at all levels is a developmental process.

Other item responses indicated that teachers' views had changed significantly during the past five years. This answer, I believe, can be attributed to the rapid change in US classrooms, with growth in technology as well as the change in student make-up to include diverse student populations. All respondents indicated a need to include a variety of topics and activities in the classroom to accommodate the different interests of the students. In keeping with this view, most all agreed that English does have a role in helping us make decisions about the way we live and the values to which we subscribe. Finally, all respondents indicated they learn best by listening, writing, speaking, thinking, reading, indicating a need for the integration of all language arts.

In addition to the questionnaires, I want to share some of the email, letters, and short essays that colleagues and students have shared with me regarding their beliefs about English and English teaching. These musings will tell something about the writer, their spirit, their beliefs. Most will indicate a need to make the English classroom a place for students to have the opportunities to use language as a coming to know, as a basis for shaping life. I want to begin with an email message (1998) that I received from my long-time professional friend and colleague Sharon Hamilton. Sharon directs the Campus Writing Program at Indiana University, Purdue University, Indianapolis. In response to my query about her beliefs, she writes,

> Jeanne, that's a good question and, strangely enough, it is not a question I have reflected on throughout my twenty-eight years as a teacher of English.
>
> The first thing that comes to mind is a cliché: I don't teach English; I teach people. And the most important thing about teaching people is helping them to build conceptual bridges between what they already know and what is in the process of being learned. That principle holds true for any subject, not just English. However, it has special meaning for the discipline of English, because our students come to us with many and diverse proficiencies as language users. However, they are not always intellectually aware of their proficiencies. A lot of what we do as English teachers is help our students become aware of the history and structures of what they already do 'automatically' with language. I'm thinking, for example of children's vibrant use of metaphor; of even very young

children's use of complex structures when they are trying to communicate complex situations; of the much researched unthinkingly correct placement of adjectives when several are used to modify one word; and of the tendency to 'make up' words or creatively apply words to fit a new situation.

However, equally important to having our students understand intellectually what they can already do is the work of stretching those capacities in increasingly sophisticated ways: the conscious use of metaphor, for example, to illuminate a concept; the conscious arrangement of supporting details to present a cohesive and persuasive line of argument.

But possibly the most important aspect of our task as teachers of language is to help our students understand that language plays as well as works, the jouissance of language, as Roland Barthes would say.

H. Thomas McCracken, another colleague and English educator at Youngstown State University writes,

Teaching English is establishing a democratic classroom where texts become the means for negotiating language activities. The purpose of those language activities is to explore cultures and subcultures. How one approaches language is as important as what one finds out and creates; therefore, teachers must practice and enable students to practice democracy. I have, in my own teacher preparation classes, attempted to do just that. I believe that language-using is central to English teaching, language-use by students: how they speak and write to each other; how well they listen to each other; how they write about texts; how they write and speak to authority. They should do all of those things in every English class.

Ted Greenlee, a substitute high-school teacher and an English education doctoral student writes: 'Hi Jeanne – I did this on my voice programme, transferred to email and all! Hope it suffices.' (Ted is not only using word processing to send an email message, but he is using a voice actualised software programme to translate his thinking/speaking aloud to text). Here is an example of how the use of technology is changing the writing/thinking process. Eventually, our students will be using this kind of technology in the classroom. How will that influence and shape our teaching? Here are Ted's comments.

English is listening with an inquisitive mind not with bored distraction. English is speaking with informed enthusiasm, not with passive regurgitation. English is reading with anxious anticipation, not with a monotone recitation. And, most of all, English is writing with creative inspiration, not task-oriented monotony. English is taking this glorious language of ours and using it to promote knowledge, understanding, communication, creativity – in short, the whole spectrum of meaningful usage that inspires each generation to succeed and achieve.

Teaching English is a little bit tougher to get a handle on. We all have state and/or county guidelines or outcomes to fulfil, and to some degree teaching to the achievement and competency tests is inevitable. But to me, accomplishing this while limiting the repetitious, boring textbooks/worksheet environment as much as possible is the secret to an energised classroom. Inevitably, I think this means taking the time to get to know the strengths and weaknesses, likes and dislikes of each student in the classroom. This task is not as daunting as it may first appear.

I remember a two-week tour I did at the local junior high when the teacher was out with an extended illness. I was not the first substitute in her classes. That distinction belonged to a retired instructor whose idea of a good class was an obedient class, a quiet class. When I took over, those students acted with such relief that I naturally inquired why. They informed me that for the most part in the former substitute teacher's classes they did worksheets then rested their heads on their arms and slept. As long as they were quiet, he didn't really care. Did they learn anything in this kind of environment? Perhaps the brightest three or four of them. The rest hadn't a clue. I was determined to at least establish a learning environment before their regular classroom teacher returned.

The first step was to walk around the classroom talking with the students, discovering what they liked, what they wished to talk about, what made them tick. I was surprised by how eager they were to share. Of course, these students were actually appreciative of the opportunity to communicate and therefore learn. By the end of the first week, five of the six classes were doing writing assignments, group literature discussions, and oral presentations.

The sixth class presented more of a problem. Despite a non-stratification policy, nine students had been flung together in this English class simply because they were 'non-learners'. Only two of the nine could read above a second grade level, and this was an eighth grade classroom. Obviously, I couldn't undo the neglect of the past seven years in two weeks, but I was determined to at least show them that learning English could be fun. We talked most of the period each day, and I would often interject relevant literature readings from some young adult anthologies such as 'Crossroads', 'Local News', and 'To Break the Silence'.

I stopped on the way to school and bought ten newspapers each morning. We would look over the front page near the end of class and I would ask for volunteers to read a paragraph they would discuss. This worked remarkably well. By the middle of the second week, they were competing to see who could read the paragraph to be discussed.

The writing, of course, was the most difficult. While the other students were writing a page or more about their favourite 'South Park' characters, I felt lucky to get as much as two sentences from these reluctant writers. Most of them told me they had never written a complete sentence in their lives. But through sheer determination, and allowing them the choice of subject matter, I got a good paragraph from all but one by the end of the second week. And yet that one turned out to be my most rewarding student.

Jeremiah was fifteen years old, had been held back twice, and had never written a word on paper in his life. I struggled and struggled with him, much as a first grade teacher might. Lo and behold, because somebody finally cared, he took pencil in hand and slowly crafted words on the page. Through effort, he picked up the capitalisation, although the punctuation eluded him. By the last day, Jeremiah had two sentences he could call his own. My crowning reward for that last two weeks was when Jeremiah came up to me after class that last Friday and handed me a folded up note and walked out. I still carry that tattered note in my jacket pocket to share with fellow educators. It read

> Dear Mr. Greenlee
> I thank you for
> teaching me about
> English I will
> miss you Bye Jeremiah

I feel certain the punctuation will come. Don't you?

Francine Kirk, a former high-school teacher and now a state director for fine arts writes,

> Recently, I worked with ninth grade students on a six week project using performance to teach Shakespeare. In the process, I heard several interesting comments. One student, frustrated with the amount of writing I had assigned, commented, 'I'd rather be doing English'. I assume that he meant grammar since during an interview another student confirmed my suspicion that until the project, the students had studied only grammar in that particular English class. Thus, for these students, English was not the language of their thought, speech, or writing; it was a subject they studied in school – a subject consisting of memorization of prepositions and placing of punctuation.
>
> The same is true for many teachers of English; English is subject matter. That subject matter is made up of rules, and it is the teacher's responsibility to convey those rules to students and then to lord over them as they practice the use of the rules – in isolation, of course. If literature comes into play, it is often because the works are listed in the anthology or the teacher happens to have a classroom set of a novel. Each

novel, poem, short story, play or narrative has a 'correct' interpretation and the students' responsibility is to convey that by parroting back that information on a test. 'Coverage' is the name of the game since the standardised achievement test looms large in the spring.

Granted, not all classrooms follow such a dismal scenario. There are teachers who seek out challenging works of literature and ask their students to read, think, engage, and respond to those works. There are teachers who give meaningful writing assignments related to literature, current events or teenage issues. They give assignments that deal with students' understandings of the rules of the language within their own writing. There are teachers who see English as the language of thought, speech, writing and culture and make classrooms language-rich environments where students can respond to what they read; the students can try out new vocabulary and express and then defend their ideas in speech and writing.

To most people, English is subject matter taught in a forty-five minute block that they never use once they leave high school. In schools, English should be the language of creative expression – the language of argument and debate – the language of meaningful activities which give students the opportunity to explore personal and cultural ideas and information.

When I hear a student say, 'I hate English,' or 'I'm not good at English', it saddens me. How can anyone hate the language that affords them the gift of thought and communication? In truth, what those students 'hate' is the boring forty-five minutes a day they must spend in a class that has been mislabelled English.

I think Francine Kirk, Ted Greenlee, Tom McCracken, and Sharon Hamilton all agree. English teachers should be student centred in their teaching and work to create democratic classrooms rich in language activities that will provide students with opportunities to think, create, and reflect on the content to be studied and, as well, their own views and beliefs. We need to remember that all four of these English educators are seasoned teachers who have had time to develop their own views and ideas about teaching, learning, and knowing English. Let us look now at the comments of several English education graduate students. These students' chronological ages vary, but all have had less than five years in the profession.

Cindy Dawn Moore writes:

English is like a passage into a secret garden. It is discovering and creating. It is so much more than grammar and answering test questions which focus on authors' names and dates. You can create on paper what in reality may never be more than a dream. I feel that, in teaching English, you are presenting others with a gift, something that will always be theirs. It, part of their education, can never be taken away.

Melissa Teets comments:

I love it when people ask me what I do. After trying to explain my occupation to many people, I learned to give this answer. 'I change the world.' The answer usually changes the conversation to another topic if it continues at all. It isn't just that I am being sarcastic – I really believe that is what I do.

I believe that every major discipline is important, but English provides the scaffolding for every other content area (the exception is Trigonometry, for which no scaffolding exists). The knowledge which we develop in English classes makes us human. We learn to laugh, to cry, and to shout at the world. Geometry classes makes mathematicians, science classes create scientists, English classes help us develop our lives – our very ways of being. I do teach English to change the world.

Pam Adams contends:

English is an entity that holds so many diverse meanings. It encompasses so much that if one asked 100 different people 'What is English?', the responses would all be different, unique. When I ask myself this question, I am amazed at the variety of possibilities that enter my mind.

The strongest answer seems to be 'a voice', or a vehicle of expression that allows everyone a means to convey their thoughts. It is a means of self expression and thus, a means of self awareness.

The best way I can describe English is to say that it is a lot of different things to a lot of different people, but it is always a source of knowledge and an avenue for self-awareness.

Barbara Copenhaver Bailey responds:

What I think English is has evolved over most of my life. It began with my experiences in high-school English. They were typical experiences that didn't encourage much creativity for the students involved. So, as I entered my adult life, I thought of English in much the same way as most people do – grammar, literature, composition.

The next time that I began to think much about the purpose of English and English teaching was during my student teaching. I taught social studies on a Navajo Reservation in Arizona. Although I was a history and civics teacher, I found myself teaching English because students' language skills were so poor. This experience coupled with the guidance from several excellent English teachers who I had the good fortune to work with helped me to realise that English is the foundation of all other knowledge. It means speaking, reading, writing, listening, thinking, creating. I believe all subjects are 'sub-subjects' of English. English is part of our life no matter what we are doing. I also think 'English' is not necessarily the best name for the discipline. I'm not sure what word or words would best describe what we do – perhaps Life Studies.'

Joseph Valasko writes:

English is not all literary anthologies and grammar texts; it covers many genres and aspects of human interactions. English is a means to an end. Perhaps it is one of the most unifying factors that speakers of English have. After all, language, as the old saying goes, is what separates man from the animals.

So what do students need to know about English? They need to know that English is the basis of all their other studies. They need to know that English applies to all aspects of their lives. That is why I am so bewildered when a student claims that English is his or her worst subject, when in fact, it is the only subject that they have exposure to throughout their entire lives. I think most students do not realise this. Thus, it is important for teachers to help students understand that English is applicable, necessary, and useful.'

Perhaps Clinton Gaskill's remarks will serve as a summary for the comments for his fellow graduate students.

To learn English is to learn how to learn. It is the grand avenue through which all knowledge is accessible. As a field of study, English excludes nothing. As a necessity for a liberal education, it can be excluded by no one. With an understanding of language and its uses, one can learn anything. Without an understanding of language and its uses, one is destined to isolation in an ever flourishing world.

In addition to opening doors, English, more than any other discipline, is capable of facilitating 'real' learning. 'Real learning', asserts Larry R. Johannessen, 'happens only when students become actively involved and can internalise knowledge or understanding by arriving at the realization themselves' (Elbow, 29). More than any other discipline, English must succeed at facilitating 'real learning'.

English demands that students bring themselves and all their attendant intellectual baggage – values, beliefs, emotions, situations – into the study of a piece of literature or a collection of words. To learn is not to swallow and regurgitate information. It is to engage ideas, reflect upon them, and hopefully, but not necessarily, come to some conclusion. In the process, we must bring our subjectivity to it, agreeing or not, understanding or not, valuing or not. We must bring ourselves to the activity of learning or it does not take place. Reading, listening, reflecting, writing, and speaking are the most valuable ways of facilitating 'real' learning.

The reality is informal education is far from this definition. Indeed, much of what goes on in the English classroom is not English at all – and that's scary.

Clinton F. Gaskill's final comment leads me to comment and conclude that from all the responses to our surveys and the many emails, letters, and essays, most of us agree that English is the most personal of disciplines; it is through language that we come to both our universe and ourselves. Many of the responses draw on the comments made throughout Peter Elbow's book *What Is English?* The statements include:

> English is the subject that everyone happens to take more than any other.
> English is ancillary. It has tended to be a 'handmaiden' to other disciplines in the humble sense of that metaphor – a service discipline.
> English seems to be more divided or disunified across the levels than other disciplines.
> English could also be defined as the one subject that extraneous falls to.
> English is a legacy of the real grammar. It is a tradition where the teacher of grammar taught everything younger children needed to know.
> English is a profession of grammar, literature, and good taste.
> English is freedom that is being able to think what you want.
> English is the field, a big old house that has been around for a long time – lots of wear and tear.
> English is a discipline where the most exciting metatheoretical work is going on.

'English', writes graduate student Caroline Ihlenfeld, 'is everything; and we must accept nothing less than that as the truth.' But to get back to Gaskill's comment, 'much of what goes on in the English classroom is not English at all – and that's scary.' Although, most of the responses to our questions of English indicate that English is all encompassing, others, like Francine Kirk and Ted Greenlee have indicated that some of our classrooms still teach English as a skill to be taught by the teacher, memorised by the students and repeated on teacher-made tests. And that, as Gaskill indicates, is scary. Perhaps there should be a follow-up study to look at what is actually going on in the classrooms in the United States as well as in England and Australia. Certainly, we have many studies that look at elements of what goes on in classrooms, but we do not have a comprehensive study that looks nationwide or worldwide at the teaching of English.

For now, however, let us consider the words of English education graduate student Helena Prachar, a student from Eastern Europe who only recently came to the United States.

What is English?

English is the language belonging the West Germanic branch, spoken by the people of the British Isles and most of the British Commonwealth, and of the United States, its territories and possessions.

English is America.

English is the language of thinking, reading, writing, learning, and speaking.

English is teaching and conversation.

English is terminology, abstract terms, spelling, and imagination.

English is the school of life, it's love to the human being and under-standing of human weaknesses.

English is history, liberty, freedom, and democracy.

English is power and education.

English is reality.

English is growth and development, practical and theoretical knowledge and experience.

English is problems and difficulties, rights and responsibilities.

English is enthusiasm, motivation, and success.

English is love and happiness, friendship and international help; it is the key to understanding each other worldwide.

English is a process of discovery.

English is love of the native country. It is a lot of tears running down the face when the victorious team or a winner is standing on the platform and the American flag is going up.

English is the desire of most Europeans.

English is the most beautiful language in the world.

References

Adams, P. (1997) Personal correspondence

Bailey, B. (1997) Personal correspondence

Elbow, P. (1992) *What is English?* Urbana, IL: National Council of Teachers of English

Gaskill, C. (1997) Personal correspondence

Greenlee, T. (1996) Personal correspondence

Hamilton, S. (1998) Personal correspondence

Ihlenfeld, C. (1997) Personal correspondence

McCracken, H. T. (1998) Personal correspondence

Moore, C. (1997) Personal correspondence

Pool, H. (1900) 'What is English?' *English Journal*, Volume 83, No. 6, pp. 15–16, Urbana, IL: National Council of Teachers of English

Prachar, H. (1997) Personal correspondence

Raymond, J. (ed.) (1996) *English As A Discipline; or Is There A Plot in This Play?* Tuscalosa: University of Alabama Press

Siriana, C. (1997) Personal correspondence

Teets, M. (1997) Personal correspondence

Valasko, J. (1997) Personal correspondence

10 Shaping the specialist: requirements of programmes leading to teacher certification in the United States

Jeanne Gerlach

As demonstrated in chapters 8 and 9, the teaching of English has moved from one end of the continuum to the other. And, as Simmons *et al.* (1990) remind us, that the interim periods of momentary balance were usually disrupted by some socio/political event that reverberated beyond the political arena and into the educational one. Innovation, a movement toward one end of the philosophical continuum or the other, was sure to follow. Another look at the chart at the beginning of chapter 5 recalls the issues and topics with which today's English teachers are grappling – issues including teaching multicultural literature, teacher training reform, international perspectives, technology, standards and assessment. These issues are, indeed, socio/political in nature. For example, regardless of who is in the classroom or what kind of training they have received, students, for the most part, still are not making high scores on state and national exams. Furthermore, many students still do not read on level by third grade. Coupled with all this is the changing face of the US population. Hispanic, African American, and Asian are the fastest growing groups in the country. In some states, such as Texas, the now minority populations are predicted to become the majority populations by 2030. In regard to Texas, the most pressing concern is how to educate the growing minority populations, and that concern is quickly becoming a major issue in other states. In addition to the growth of the minority populations, is the rapid change of our nation from an industrialised to a information society. We can communicate with almost any country in the world at any given time. Students no longer simply think about what the neighbourhood friends are doing after school; rather, many race home to access the internet to communicate with international peers. No longer do students go home after school to work in the fields or tend the livestock; instead, many return to urban neighbourhoods to apartment complexes and concrete play-grounds. Yes, urban centres are experiencing rapid growth, and with that growth comes opportunities to quickly access sports arenas, theatres, museums, and other cultural offerings. However, while there are many positive aspects of urban life, it also brings problems. Students often live in inadequate housing, spend their lives on the streets as members of gangs or prostitution rings, and are exposed to the world of drugs. All this is changing the very fabric of our schools and the nature of what goes on in all class-rooms. And, since English or language is the basis of all we do, the English teacher is often expected to 'fix it' all.

If English teachers at all levels (elementary, secondary, and college) are to play central roles in bringing about positive change in our schools, then they need to have adequate preservice and inservice training. The way teachers have been taught is not a new issue, but questions about what to teach and how to teach have often included the question, how does the teacher get taught? In other words how are future English teachers being prepared for their professional lives? This concern has motivated the National Council of Teachers of English to publish, at ten-year intervals, a set of guidelines for the preparation of preservice English teachers, the latest appearing in 1996. In addition the Holmes Group has compiled a broad agenda for the entire teaching profession in regard to teacher preparation. Further NCATE, a national accrediting association for schools, colleges, and/or departments of teacher education has rigorous guidelines for teacher preparation programmes for those schools who are members of that organisation. Additionally, there are many National Council of Teachers of English groups, committees, and commissions who offer annual programme sessions focusing on English teacher preparation. While all these efforts continue, the fact remains that there has not been much published on the way English teachers are prepared. In short, there is not much literature on the English methods class.

One such study which stands out, however, is Peter Smagorinsky and Melissa E. Whiting's (1995) *How English Teachers Get Taught: Methods of Teaching the Methods Class*. The study is a systematic analysis of the ways in which preservice English teachers learn their craft. Looking across the USA at how professors teach undergraduates in English methods classes, Smagorinsky and Whiting analyse syllabi from eighty-one public universities. The researchers look at the general approaches that structure the experiences of preservice teachers, the number of activities and assessments that students are involved in, and the major theoretical positions which are articulated through the course readings.

Smagorinsky and Whiting consider how each teaching approach is amenable to different activities, assessments, and theoretical positions from the course texts. They began their work by developing a theoretical basis from which to evaluate the effects of different ways of preparing English teachers. The criteria included beliefs that (1) a methods course should be theoretically informed, (2) learning should be situated in a meaningful activity, (3) learning should be transactional, (4) learning should be process-oriented, (5) students should be involved in reflection, (6) learning should be holistic, and (7) students should be involved in good work. They believed that these criteria have the potential for helping to prepare preservice teachers for professional life.

Before discussing the results of the study Smagorinsky and Whiting remind the reader that analysing syllabi has several limitations when one actually tries to predict what happened in the teacher preparation class. For example, syllabi give no knowledge about the quality of instruction, about how the course is situated in the overall teacher education programme, or about how the love of teaching is engendered by the teacher throughout the course of instruction. Further, the researchers remind us that the syllabi do not reflect how the course may change from year to year. In spite of these limitations, they believe that the syllabi reflected fairly accurately how English teachers were prepared.

The findings of the study conclude that (1) the NCTE Teacher Preparation Guidelines have made their way into almost all syllabi and have a positive effect on the development of the methods course, (2) professors focus on the need to have student-centred classrooms, (3) most syllabi stressed the need of a holistic perspective, stressing the connection and continuity of learning, (4) most courses included some sort of situated learning, some being actually based in the field, (5) overall the syllabi reflected that too many requirements were included in the course which might result in fragmentation of the course, (6) models of effective teaching were included, and (7) students were expected to analyse, observe, and practice effective teaching. The study's findings are certainly worthy of consideration and conversation. They may well be, as the authors' hope, the beginning of a discussion that will 'rely less on "lore" and more on formal understandings of how and why we teach as we do' (p. 111).

How English Teachers Get Taught: Methods of Teaching the Methods Class certainly can be looked to as the beginning of a more formal conversation about how English teachers are prepared, but it is necessary to do more and look more closely at how methods classes are actually conducted. It is necessary to know if teachers are actually modelling effective teaching in the classroom. It is necessary to know if teachers are including appropriate field experiences' components as part of the methods course requirements. It is necessary to know if teachers are designing courses which reflect the NCTE *Guidelines for the Preparation of Teachers of English Language Arts*. Answers to these questions will add to the formal conversations and give our profession a clearer look at how English teachers are trained.

Here, I want to comment briefly about the Guidelines. As I noted earlier, the Guidelines have been revised every ten years for the past eighty-five years by the NCTE Standing Committee on Teacher Preparation and Certification; I currently serve as a member of that committee. The Guidelines serve as a guide for developing and assessing teacher preparation programmes in English Language Arts. The document begins with a set of general underlying principles and then examines the attitudes, knowledge, and pedagogical skills that classroom teachers should acquire and be able to demonstrate. The 1996 Guidelines relate the teacher preparation recommendations and require-ments to the NCTE/IRA Standards for the English Language Arts and to other professional organisations' standards. Additionally, the Guidelines discuss how preservice teachers can make effective transitions to classroom teaching. Finally, the work suggests how practising teachers can use inservice training to continue their professional development.

In addition to a move for more formal research on teacher preparation and more consideration and implementation of the Teacher Preparation Guidelines, professional publishers' catalogues include a number of new books calling for new ways of thinking about English teaching and English teacher preparation. Several of the new titles include, *Changing Classroom Practices: Resources for Literary and Cultural Studies, Reshaping High School English*, and *Social Issues in the English Classroom*. These texts call on members of the English teaching profession to be proactive and decide for themselves what our roles are and what we will teach.

Changing Classroom Practices Resources for Literary and Cultural Studies (1994) presents the readers with fourteen essays which consider the socio-political significance of teaching by first acknowledging that teaching is a social and political transaction. All the essays offer suggestions to help students and teachers become more effective in their everyday activities. They suggest that teachers can use literary and cultural studies as they seek to change their own classroom practices and course designs. This book is a part of the Refiguring English Studies series published by the National Council of Teachers of English. The series includes works which concentrate on investigations of the relationships among the discipline of English, the teacher, the students, the institution of learning, and society at large.

Another book focusing on social concerns in the English classroom is *Social Issues in the English Classroom* (1992) edited by C. Mark Hurlbert and Samuel Totten. The authors of the essays included in the work discuss teaching about social concerns like racism, classism, homophobia, sexism, and the ethical and political dimensions of teaching. The editors believe that as teachers of language, literature, and composition, and culture 'have the power to design pedagogies that encourage students and teachers alike to turn the silences forced upon them, and to which they sometimes become resigned, into eloquent and collective calls for change' (p. 6).

In speaking of changing English teaching or rethinking the profession, it is necessary to consider Bruce Pirie's *Reshaping High School English* (1997) which describes an English programme that blends philosophical depth with classroom needs. Pirie explores recent literary and educational theories as they apply to traditionally taught texts including *Macbeth, To Kill a Mockingbird*, and *Lord of the Flies*. Equally important, Pirie calls for teachers to define the heart of our subject before others define it for us.

The need to reinvent or rethink English has been the subject of 1990s books like the ones just discussed. In addition many editorials, journal articles, and convention sessions focus on the topic. It is noteworthy that the upcoming National Council Teachers of English Convention to be held in Denver, Colorado in November, 1999 has as its theme 'Rethinking or Reimagining English'. As demonstrated, however, English teachers in the US generally see themselves as teachers of language, literature, and composition. Although other focus areas have been added over the past 100 years, the main focus is still tied to the two main objectives for English in the schools as identified in 1894 by the Committee of Ten: communication of ideas and appreciation of literature. Even though each generation has reexamined and reshaped, in some part, the English curriculum, it has retained its basic character for over a century. Now, once again, the English teaching profession is in a rethinking mode. Of course, it remains to be seen whether these efforts will lead to continued renewal.

It is apparent that the future of English and English teaching is evolving at many different levels, and I, for one, think that we do need to reinvent what we do. As I have noted earlier, we have a changed society, one that is vastly different from the 1894 society – the audience that the Committee of Ten Report addressed. It is necessary to ask ourselves if our English teaching is producing students who are able to take the reading and writing skills they use in the classrooms into the world at large. It is necessary to question whether teachers are creating readers who will read and enjoy reading for a lifetime? Do courses prepare students who will be able to think critically and creatively about all they do in life? Is society preparing teachers who will focus on student needs as they try to relate course content? In answering these questions it is necessary to think about how we take what is good and needed from what we have already tried and add it to what we know we need today in an effort to reinvent English teaching and English education.

Given this, what should be done? How do we proceed? First, it is necessary to address the needs of students in teacher preparation programmes. It is necessary to have more systematic studies about what should constitute English teacher preparation; research should provide practical descriptions of specific techniques and activities that can be successfully incorporated in the English methods course – descriptions of 'good practice' in the field by both practising teachers and student teachers. Further, we need systematic investigations of the benefits of such activities, in terms of the practising teacher, the student teacher, and the students. In addition to research, English teachers, as practising professionals, need to read voraciously and ask their students to do the same. Learning continues for a lifetime, not when one completes a course or a programme of studies. Thus, it is necessary to seek out professional development opportunities, whether they be local workshops or national and international conventions.

Equally important, English teachers need to ask their students to read and write every single day. Reading about and writing about an issue or a topic are ways of learning the content to be studied. Finally, teachers must read our history. Knowing our history will help us learn from the past, not repeat it. If we know and appreciate our history, we will know what needs to be carried over, what needs to be discarded. In attempting to carry out the preceding suggestions, it is important always to have an open mind; we need to try something before we make a decision about its worth.

Redefining English and the teaching of English can be a wonderful opportunity for all English teachers to build programmes, curricula, and courses
that are for all students, not just a select few. The task can be a process where
teachers strive to develop the equity that is needed for democratic classrooms
where all students have opportunities to learn.

References

Downing, D. (ed.) (1994) *Changing Classroom Practices: Resources for Literacy and Cultural Studies*, Urbana, IL: National Council of Teachers of English
Guidelines for the Preparation of Teachers of English Language Arts (1996) Urbana, IL: National Council of Teachers of English
Hurlbert, C. and Totten, S. (1992) *Social Issues in the English Classroom*, Urbana, IL: National Council of Teachers of English
Pirie, Bruce (1997) *Reshaping High School English*, Urbana, IL: National Council of Teachers of English
Simmons, J. et al. (1990) 'The swinging pendulum: Teaching English in the USA, 1945–1987', in J. Britton et al. (1990) *Teaching and Learning English Worldwide*, Philadelphia: Multilingual Matters Ltd
Smagorinsky, P. and Whiting, M. (1995) *How English Teachers Get Taught: Methods of Teaching The Methods Class*, Urbana, IL: National Council of Teachers of English

Part IV

Shared questions, different answers: different questions, shared answers

11 English for the twenty-first century?

Robin Peel, Annette Patterson, Jeanne Gerlach

'The issues of our time'

In 1962 Sylvia Plath wrote an essay entitled 'Context' which begins 'The issues of our time which preoccupy me at the moment are . . . '. As an American in England Plath was keen to distinguish between those things which were clearly global – in 1962 it was the threat to the environment from atmospheric nuclear bomb tests – and those which were specific to her as an individual poet. The same distinction can be applied to a review of the arguments, views and practices discussed in the previous chapters. There are what might be called global forces which shape developments and debates within Subject English in all three countries. But there are also differences between the countries which are attributable to the specificities of historicism, as the three of us have been made very aware when we have attended conferences and visited schools and universities in one another's countries.

These differences will have been particularly noticeable in the voices we have recorded, including our own. In the unreserved idealism of the statements just reported in the American chapters there is evidence of that direct, personal voice that many would argue is unique to the English teacher. Even where that teacher is more reticent – as with the Tom Hanks character in *Saving Private Ryan* – there is evidence of that powerful engagement with literature and with moral, ethical and aesthetic issues. In its construction this book has attempted in each of its three parts to create a dialectic between the differing kinds of discourse to be found in discussions of Subject English. The overall conceptual pattern involved a move from the discussion about England, where the chapters privilege the rhetorical discourse of academic commentary, towards the discussion about America, where the voice of the classroom practitioner is given a more central place. But each includes a whole range of voices, so that in the end it is a matter of emphasis. To complete the symmetry, in our review of what we have reported we return to the voice of critical commentary.

English in England, Australia, the United States: issues in common

From our discussions it is possible to conclude that we hold some of our experiences of English in common. We feel that we can make the following generalisations in terms of the three countries:

1. The preferred pedagogical relationship is one which emphasises sharing, intimacy, the 'love' of that which is read, spoken and written. The word 'desire' is frequently implicit: the desire to help, inspire, emancipate, empower. Such idealism seems to be part of the contract with the subject: it is also part of the training of the subject. Successful students of English *learn* idealism and arrive at university classrooms equipped with particular understandings about teaching and learning which are reiterated through their undergraduate studies. In the Australia section of the book Annette Patterson examines some historical antecedents for this strand of personal comportment on the part of English professionals.

2. There is a 'church' of English – with its own organisations, its own networks, its own identity. The formal organisational vehicle for the school English community is the professional organisation in each country: National Association of Teachers of English (NATE) in England; Australian Association of Teachers of English (AATE); National Council of Teachers of English (NCTE) in the United States of America. The 'umbrella' organisation is the International Federation of Teachers of English (IFTE). Other countries such as Canada, New Zealand and, more recently, South Africa have their own associations. The debates about English conducted within and between these professional bodies is often fierce and yet English maintains itself as a recognisable community with many shared aspirations, despite an apparent 'fracturing' of the subject through the incursions of cultural studies, media studies, drama, communications studies and literacy practices associated with electronic communications technology. The community is thus made up of disputatious individuals who cherish their individuality in the context of the school, college or university.

3. Despite the current pressures this fiercely protective individuality is translated into the generally positive self-image shared by English specialists. They maintain a high level of self-esteem despite the perceived erosion of teachers' rights and status in each country. Such self-confidence arises in part from a shared interest in and enjoyment of wide reading, and from the generally high level of social competence conferred on English through its focus on reading/viewing, writing, speaking and listening. Successful English students tend to be articulate, well read, and competent writers and users of language generally. In schools, this confidence is sometimes offset by anxieties and insecurity relating to the demand for greater expertise in the field of linguistics, the pressure from testing, and the general demands of classroom management.

4. There is a strong endorsement at national and state government levels of the importance of English as a school subject. However, the current concentration on standardised assessment evident in all three countries looks likely to continue under the banner of 'accountability'. The emergence of 'literacy' as a policy target is apparent in the many reports, statements, funding agencies and so on that focus on something called 'literacy'. Often, 'literacy' is conceived of as being both different from English and a part of English. In Australia, at least, government agencies have focused on installing an understanding of literacy as something that can be specified, taught and measured, hence the move to 'competencies', 'standards' and 'national frameworks' for the adult and post-compulsory school sectors, and 'literacy benchmarks' for primary and secondary students. Generally, there has been a tendency to by-pass 'English' in the government sponsored push for 'literacy'. 'English' has responded in part by adapting its subject offerings in high schools to include 'communications' subjects.

5. In Australia and England the concept of a 'literacy crisis' is generated by politicians and the media linking assumed low literacy rates to broader social and economic factors such as unemployment. For instance, Australia has experienced relatively high levels of unemployment over the past decade and this, according to some political sources, is a result of a decline in literacy standards. The United States of America currently has its lowest unemployment rate in decades. Politicians and the media do not appear to claim, however, that this is a result of high literacy levels. The assumed link between literacy levels and unemployment levels only appear to work in one direction.

6. Ostensibly all the evidence points to a fracturing and future disintegration of the 'Church' of English as groups break away: Cultural Studies, Media Studies, Literacy – all have a specific, separate agenda. English may then be left as a small rump concerned with literary study, which becomes once more an increasingly specialised, and elitist subject. Many of those who identify with the breakaway groups, which favour a more interdisciplinary approach, would welcome such a development. But it is possible that such predictions take insufficient account of the immense appeal of a broad church with its own traditions, identity and practices in schools, colleges and universities. It remains a popular subject in schools. English has survived largely because governments want it to, however.

7. Changes in technology may ensure that the shift from literatures to literacies is the dominant trend at the beginning of the twenty-first century.

8. Finally, despite a sustained critique from prescriptive reading campaigns on the right and from critical and social theory on the left, 'personal growth' approaches to English teaching remain an attractive proposition for teachers in schools in all three countries.

Difference

If these features seem transnational, there is more that is specific to each country. When it comes to the curriculum in general and English in particular the United States is probably more different from England and Australia in its practices than either of those two countries are from one other. For a variety of reasons the United States did not experience in the same hegemonic way the 'progressive' reorientation of rhetoric – and, to a significant extent practice – that characterised the adoption of 'New English' in England and Australia in the late 1960s and the 1970s. The progressive leaders of NCTE in the United States certainly responded very enthusiastically to the Dartmouth Conference, and recommended a new emphasis on creative writing and coursework portfolios, but it is arguable that this was not institutionalised as it was in England and Australia simply because of the enormous population, the diversity within the states, and the fact that American education was not tied culturally to England in the way that Australia was at that time. As Jeanne Gerlach has reported, Dartmouth was quickly overtaken by fresh concerns about literacy standards.

In America NCTE teachers continue to battle for the whole language model, for the teacher as writer as promoted by the National Writing Project, and against a simplistic model of standardised testing. In Universities the curriculum wars still rumble on, but there is evidence of a reassessment of the role of theory in critical practices from its advocates as well as its opponents.

In many senses Australia has offered most hope to those in England and the United States who have felt paralysed by State and Government control. During the 1980s and 1990s schools and universities in Australia took a different path, seeming to construct an English curriculum which drew on a diversity of practices – from whole language, to critical literacy and systemic functional linguistics. Even the spread of standardised assessment is perceived by many as a challenge rather than a defeat: the question has been asked in Australia which is beginning to be asked in England and the United States: if assessment is going to dominate pedagogical practice, how can the assessment models be constructed so as to encourage good practice?

In all three countries there is a mounting call for *evidence* that targets are being met, that policies are in place, that improvements are taking place in numeracy and literacy, and that students are acquiring a set of transferable skills that prepares them for the outside world. The new rhetoric of the vocational, the workplace and the market calls for us all to 'Stick to Evidence, Sir!' to rephrase Mr Gradgrind's opening outburst in *Hard Times*. Dickens makes clear his concerns about trying to measure the unmeasurable by starting the novel with a speech made by a factory owner to a government inspector, a schoolteacher, and a class of children identified by numbers. The book has its own rhetoric of resistance, which appeals to the idealistic tendencies of many English professionals. The carnival world of the circus sounds infinitely preferable to the drudgery of the factory.

Dreaming of the circus

This book started by discussing the position in England, and it is useful to revisit the practices of that country. For tensions between the pedagogical model of teacher autonomy/student self-regulation and external control and regulation continue to be acted out in England in very startling ways, leaving little time to dream of Mr Sleary's circus, and the kind of educational experiment being conducted in England will either become the model for other countries or will be a dreadful warning of how not to regulate a system.

We reported in chapter 1 that the inspiration for this book was a survey carried out by Andrew Goodwyn in 1992. Goodwyn has recently conducted an updated version of this survey (Goodwyn and Findlay 1999), and what is remarkable about it is the extent to which his findings suggest that English teachers from the seventy-nine schools surveyed in 1997 have been alienated by the revised National Curriculum in England:

> [T]he current National Curriculum is now perceived by teachers as diametrically opposite to the preferred models of English. Three-quarters of the 1997 teachers still put Personal Growth as their absolute priority and if the second column is added in this figure approximates 90 per cent whereas the National curriculum is seen as promoting Personal Growth by only 10 per cent. In fact, the National curriculum is seen as prioritising Cultural Heritage by four-fifths of the profession whereas the teachers themselves now place it as their bottom priority, with only 3 per cent placing it first and 50 per cent placing it last.
>
> Goodwyn and Findlay 1999

There are several problems with a survey of this kind, not least (as Annette Patterson has pointed out) the 'model' categories themselves, but it does explain the kind of suppressed rage articulated in some of the responses that the survey elicited: 'Excellent and inspirational teachers of English do not work best in a cage. A love of English is the last thing you need to teach to these orders and syllabuses' (quoted in Goodwyn and Findlay 1999). If that teacher feels caged, this one is simply resentful: 'What I have resented in recent years, more than anything, is the erosion of my professional judgement . . . The level of prescription is now ludicrous . . . When these are wheeled out year after year it becomes more and more difficult to maintain one's freshness and enthusiasm' (quoted in Goodwyn and Findlay 1999).

It would be interesting to see an analysis of these responses by age, to learn if younger teachers are as resentful as older ones: our own work in England suggests this is not the case. But whether it is their third year teaching in a school or their thirtieth, all National Curriculum teachers in England are obliged to work within this tight framework.

Literacy, literacy and literacy

Throughout the election campaign in England that preceded the landslide Labour victory in 1997 Tony Blair said that his government's priority would be 'Education, Education and Education'. As far as Subject English is concerned, this has been translated into 'Literacy, literacy and literacy'.

In the recent pages of English in Education Street (1997) and MacCabe (1998) exchanged contrasting opinions about the new models of literacy. For Street literacy is a set of practices, among which the literacy defined by school is merely one. Home, the street, the workplace – they all have their own literacies, all specific to a culture, all situated. In his response MacCabe argues that this pluralistic model is superficially attractive, but in practice its appears to the public as an example of the disastrous relativism which earns teachers a bad name. We must be explicit about what works in schools, and concentrate our efforts on this.

In Australia the issue of 'free choice' and 'personal expression' in English classrooms was confronted by the 'genre theorists'. This group mapped and documented what they viewed as the effects of 'whole language' approaches on classroom writing practices. These included an emphasis on personal narrative writing and story at the expense of factual and expository prose. The latter, the genre theorists argued, tend to be the 'privileged' and 'powerful' forms of writing necessary for continued success in and out of school. Although this view has been challenged on the grounds that it relies on a simplistic understanding of the relationships among access to education, 'power' and texts, nevertheless, the genre theorists generally have succeeded in broadening syllabi and approaches to the teaching of writing in schools.

In America, too, the movement to reinvent English is being shaped by the rapidly changing population. For example, in many states minority populations are becoming the majority, i.e., California, Texas, and Florida. This change creates new priorities in the English Language/Arts classrooms. English will remain the national language, but teaching it will become more of a challenge and the need for bilingual and English as a second language (ESL) instruction will grow. Equally important, problems of poverty are major concerns. In growing numbers of schools, teachers are teaching children of poverty and thus, need to spend large portions of instructional time on literacy issues, specifically the ability to read and write. Coupled with these concerns is the inability of numerous school districts as well as colleges and universities to recruit nonwhite teachers to serve as role models for the culturally and economically changing student populations. Informed change will be the key to the future successes of teaching English in the US. However, if history is an accurate indicator, American English educators will continue to meet the challenges.

In England, as in Australia, English in post-compulsory or post-16 schooling occupies uncertain terrain. In England the Dearing recommendation that Key Skills should be integrated into all post-16 examinations, including the more academic 'Advanced Level' has implications for English because one of the Key Skills is communication and this is measured according to a series of competencies and this 'goes against the grain of most English teachers' conceptions of the subject' (Reid and Higgins 1997). In the same journal, however, another writer says that 'the content and assessment objectives of the new Cores are broadly acceptable' (Hodgson 1997). This discussion provides one of the more hopeful signposts for the future, particularly for the integration of language, literary and critical awareness.

In Australia each State and Territory manages the two to three years of post-compulsory schooling in its own way. The National Profiles for English end at Year 10. Currently, some states are trialling a 'merging' programme whereby post-compulsory high-school students can gain credit for completing some Tertiary and Further Education courses, including 'workplace literacy' and 'communications' courses which have a vocational emphasis.

The first attempt by the Commonwealth Government in Australia to formulate a cohesive policy on adult literacy and to place adult literacy in relation to other literacy education policies was *Australia's Language and Literacy Policy* document released in 1991. This was followed by the development of 'key competencies'. The competency movement is strong in each country and it is linked to debates about 'standards' and 'accountability'. Since the release of *Australia's Language and Literacy Policy* there have been a number of initiatives to incorporate English language and literacy competencies into industry standards. Two examples of Key Competencies are, collecting, analysing and organising information; communicating ideas and information. The competency movement is part of a wider government-sponsored agenda to define, teach and measure education outcomes. It has resulted in a wide-ranging debate about the nature of literacy, its features and its uses. Work is in progress to integrate common understandings of literacy across most school and education sectors, and industry and there is fierce debate about the role of critical literacy in these processes.

In England the progression from Further Education (FE) to university remains a contentious issue, however: students who apply for English pathways in Higher Education (HE) in the belief that it is going to mean more of the experience that they had at Advanced Level are in for a shock when they encounter as much reading about reading and writing as they do fiction and poetry. But perhaps the biggest change in both FE and HE is the expansion in student numbers, without a parallel increase in funding. This has had two obvious consequences: an increase in the number of lectures, in FE and HE alike (lectures were very rare in FE English, and for a time in the eighties they were on the decline in universities which favoured the seminar and workshop approach). The other development is the pressure to move towards distant and autonomous learning, as a means of encouraging student autonomy and reducing pressures on staff. It also has the effect of saving money.

In England Information Technology provision and use in schools and colleges appears healthy – England has a higher ratio of machines to schools than almost any other country in the world. But there are questions about the age and quality of the machines that schools in England possess, and wider questions 'raised by the Internet to do with access, ownership and the selection of information' (Reid and Higgins 1997) that many argue need to be raised. The changing pattern in communication brought about by the explosion in e-mail and the widespread use of mobile phones will also need to be evaluated and understood.

The relationship in Australia between computer technology and English appears to be somewhat wary. English teachers have been accused of resisting the use of computers in their classrooms[1] and of tending to avoid their use for planning and preparation purposes.[2] In addition Bill Green and Chris Bigum argue that new forms of communications technology are intersecting with current literacy practices and at the same time changing those practices.[3] This is an important issue for English educators and for schools and policy makers generally to track and analyse. Australians traditionally have been quick to embrace new communications technology. From the early days of telegraph to the modern day internet the uses of new ways of communicating have been rapidly adopted and adapted to Australian conditions. This may be due to the sense of isolation from the rest of the world assumed to be felt by non-indigenous Australians, and by the necessity to communicate over vast and sparsely populated distances. Whatever the reason for the desire of many Australians to embrace new communications technology, the use of computers and the take-up of internet access is no exception. The Australian Bureau of Statistics[4] reported that as of November 1998 47 per cent of Australian households had a home computer and 19 per cent of Australians had home internet access. More important, perhaps, for English teaching is the fact that more than 50 per cent of children aged 5–17 years were frequent home computer users. Ownership and access in Australia and elsewhere are inequitably shared with few low income families able to afford either a computer or internet access. This places pressure on teachers and schools to provide access as equitably as possible and to try to redress the disadvantage that will inevitably result for children who are unable to gain access to computer literacies.

1 See Ilana Snyder (1995) 'Reconceptualising literacy and hypertext', *English in Australia* 111, 27–34; Ilana Snyder (1996) 'Integrating computers into the literacy curriculum: More difficult than we first imagined', *The Australian Journal of Language and Literacy*, 19 (4), 231–34.
2 Department of Employment, Education, Training and Youth Affairs (1998) *Digital Rhetorics*.
3 Green, B. and Bigum, C. (1996) 'Hypermedia or media hype? New technologies and the future of literacy education', in Michelle Anstey and Geoff Bull (eds.) *The Literary Lexicon*, Sydney: Prentice Hall.
4 Australian Bureau of Statistics (1998) *1998 Household Use of Information Technology Report* released May 1999.

Towards 2005: shutdown or restart?

If developments in information and communications technology provide one index to the future, the agendas of national conferences for subject specialists act as another kind of barometer. At NATE's last national conference of the millennium two groups of teachers met over four days to outline an English curriculum for 2005 that was not chained to a National Curriculum. Ann Shreeve summarised the outcomes as follows:

The groups concluded that the subject known as English:
–   has elements which are the main objects of study and areas that over-lap with other parts of the curriculum
–   has three main objects of study: languages and varieties of English; literacy, literature and other texts.
The study of English should:
–   involve students in making, creating and responding to texts
–   involve students in making informed and rational choices in order to take control of their own lives
–   include elements of and be determined by local, national and global factors
It was strongly argued that
–   texts should be defined in the broadest sense to include, print, moving images and electronic modes
–   texts should be studied because of their historic, geographic and cultural importance.

Shreeve 1999

This reaffirms the goals that NATE has had for much of the last quarter of the twentieth century, and in seeking to help students 'gain control of their lives' still retains the emphasis on personal growth that in various forms has underpinned English for the whole of the twentieth century.

An emphasis on critical literacy is less obvious in this set of goals, but its presence is being increasingly felt in all three countries. The Expanded Text Consortium at the University of Northumbria in England begins the paper accompanying its Summer 1998 update by stating: 'The discipline of English Studies is changing to encompass perspectives that alter the definition of text and how it is studied' (University of Northumbria at Newcastle: Assessment and the Expanded Text Consortium 1998). This is a process that has been going on for nearly thirty years now, in the form of a long tradition of post-structuralist critique, partly through the influence of English and Media Centre materials and Chalkface books, and partly from the influence of critics such as McCabe, Buckingham and Belsey. Instead of conceptualising reading as a process whose aim is to extract meanings from texts, there is a move towards seeing it as a specific set of practices which can serve specific functions and achieve certain effects. If we want to locate meaning at all, then it can be located in the outcomes, or for the older reader, in an awareness of the rhetoric.

Another way of taking the temperature of a subject is to see the way it discusses itself in its official journals. In the United States the July 1999 edition of NCTE's College English was devoted to 'Symposium: English 1999'. The issues exercising the contributors as they looked across into the next century ranged from the shift towards the contemporary brought about by the move towards Cultural Studies and the challenges presented by the explosion in texts as English Departments embrace Multiculturalism, Post Colonial Studies, and Hypertext. This has implications not just for what we think about and imagine, but the way that we think: 'The structural logic of new media is the logic of the network: expansive, dispersed, decentralised, undisciplined' (Bass, R. 1999). To some, such possibilities offer the vision of new democratic and shared networks.

For the moment there are other, institutional issues with which English, as any subject, must concern itself. Regenia Gagnier (1996) in the paper to which we referred in our Preface, argues that at university level any reconceptualising of reading and thinking must acknowledge another process of reconceptualisation. In her research into the place of English and the Humanities in the market economy, she emphasises that the rhetoric of choice and consumerism dominates all discourses and institutions, and that includes schools and universities.

Primary and Secondary Australian school curricula have generally embraced the idea that texts are culturally, socially and historically situated; that reading, viewing and writing comprise intersecting sets of socio-cultural practices; that 'reading' is not a 'given', but rather that 'readings' are produced in specific sites and under particular conditions. The national Profile includes an understanding of the cultural, social and historical location of texts and most Australian syllabus documents incorporate this idea. The work of M. A. K. Halliday with its focus on meaning production in cultural contexts, among other things, has been influential in informing curriculum development and classroom practice as has the extensive body of work by Allan Luke (1993, 1997) in developing the concept of 'critical literacies', and the research and publications of Pam Gilbert (1989, 1998) (who has extended our understanding of 'language' and 'gender' and whose early critique of 'process writing' stimulated a lively debate in Australia about the cultural and social uses of writing pedagogy). Bill Green's (1997) many publications and extensive work in theorising 'curriculum', 'English' and 'culture' have provided an invaluable guide for policy developers and curriculum writers while contributing significantly to our understanding of *teaching and learning* English. Poststructuralist and critical approaches to reading in secondary English classrooms were pioneered in Australia by Bronwyn Mellor who, for over a decade, has written and published theoretical papers and classroom materials while also directing the work of a team of writers at Chalkface

Press.[5] She and her team have been instrumental in introducing critical reading practices into Australian high-school English classrooms since the publication in 1987 of the first book of this type produced in Australia: *Reading Stories*.[6] The work mentioned above and the contributions of many other academics and classroom teachers has resulted in a shift in understanding in Australia about what constitutes 'reading' and 'writing' in English classrooms. The fact that the term 'text' was used in its broadest possible interpretation and that 'viewing' was an early inclusion in curriculum statements indicates a willingness on the part of English in Australia to embrace a diverse range of textual practices.

A great deal of the discussion that we have encountered focuses on teachers' and theorists' concerns that the space in the curriculum for 'freedom' and 'creativity' that traditionally belongs to English is under threat from such things as testing regimes, standards specifications, syllabus directives, funding restrictions and government led demands for functional literacy. It is clear that the past two decades have been a time of rapid change for English in the three countries reviewed here. Apart from the wide ranging and systematic shifts in policy there have been other factors to contend with not the least of which is the increase in the number of students remaining at school and the increasing cultural and social diversity of students who complete their high-school studies and enter universities, particularly in Australia. English teachers also are expected to respond, perhaps more than teachers of other curriculum areas, to the continuing complaints about literacy levels and unemployment. Industry and education bureaucracy appear to many to have joined forces against the desire of English teachers for 'real' education, hence the refrain in the discussions we have had with English specialists about the stifling and restricting effects of these changes on education.

All of these factors do demand our immediate and consistent attention as part of our efforts to secure the continuation of this important subject area, particularly in secondary schools. However, we suggest in this book that equal attention could be paid first, to the unique methods that English has developed for teaching and learning (sometimes called 'pedagogy') and second, to the important role of English in the formation of professional capacities. Ian Hunter[7] has suggested that English teachers spend too much

5 The team directed by Bronwyn Mellor at Chalkface Press consists of Wayne Martino, Brian Moon, Marnie O'Neill and Annette Patterson. The National Council of Teachers of English plans to re-publish the Chalkface Press series in the United States.
6 Bronwyn Mellor, Marnie O'Neill and Annette Patterson (1987) *Reading Stories*, Cottesloe: Chalkface Press.
7 The discussion here draws on a range of publications by Ian Hunter mentioned in previous chapters. These include his books *Culture and Government: The Emergence of Literary Education* (1988); *Rethinking the School* (1994); and various chapters and articles including 'Culture, bureaucracy and the history of popular education', in D. Meredyth and D. Tyler (eds.) *Child and Citizen: Genealogies of Schooling and Subjectivity*, Brisbane: Institute for Cultural Policy Studies.

time worrying that their activities might be informed by state agendas that are instrumental in nature. English and literacy education do provide a space for ethical formation, where 'ethical' refers to a particular way of conducting the self, or a particular way of relating to one's self and living one's life. Interestingly, in Hunter's genealogy, particular ways of conducting oneself, for example, as a sensitive, empathic person, are taught and acquired in English classrooms which are themselves an effect of state-organised educational institutions. These ethical comportments, in other words, do not emerge as facets of the child's 'true' self. In the English classroom, for instance, literary texts are a device for focusing particular relations such as self-expression and self-correction, inwardness and emulation. English teachers, then, are well equipped with a range of expert capacities for moral and ethical formation of students and, Hunter claims, there is a pressing need for teachers to feel more secure about the worth and integrity of their work. Unfortunately, as the discussions reported in this book indicate, English professionals (and the authors of this book are no exception) tend to distrust the morally normative features of the teaching and learning practices of the English classroom. Hunter urges English specialists to adopt a less idealistic orientation to professional roles and to value and promote the benefits to the community of the routines and strategies of classroom practice. As Denise Meredyth[8] observed, 'English, it seems, is a rare and peculiar means for forming a patchwork range of ethical and literate capacities'. Setting aside our concerns about whether or not we should perform this kind of work is perhaps the first step in rethinking our role as professionals who are able to make a difference for our students and for the communities in which we live.

The analyses offered by Regenia Gagnier and Ian Hunter, building as they do on a long tradition of cultural theory, were attractive to some and anathema to others. Many English specialists bridle at what they see as deflationary implications of an analysis which calls on us to rethink our role, preferring to draw inspiration from descriptions which emphasise creativity, invention and subversion. Yet a fresh appraisal of English does not threaten these qualities: English, it is widely acknowledged, does encourage original thinking and reflection, it does help to question racism and violence, it does encourage team work and analysis, it does have the aim of bringing forth citizens who are able to speak and write persuasively and logically. It may or may not be a subversive subject – our reading of its history suggests that it is a lot less so than was once believed – but let us leave that undecided as one of the possible spin-offs. Given that English wants to be properly funded and valued, it is proving strategically necessary for English to be more modest and specific in the claims it makes for itself as a subject.

8 Denise Meredyth (1994) 'English, civics and ethical competence', *Interpretations*, 27 (3), 70–95.

Conclusion: English in the twenty-first century

The perceptions of English that we have described have not only varied across time, they have varied according to country, and they vary according to the constituency that is being sounded within a country. In England, the Chair of the National Association for the Teaching of English, in her review of the 1998 Conference, described a list of key concerns that had been raised by those who had attended the annual Easter gathering of those who may be regarded as particularly dedicated to their subject. These concerns were:

- the relationship between the English curriculum and its assessment
- the balance between centralised prescription and autonomy
- the difference between 'literacy' and English
- co-operation and competitiveness.

In addressing these concerns Gabrielle Cliff Hodges acknowledges the diversity of responses, even from within such a special group as NATE members-who-attend-conferences. Should structures be regarded as helpful scaffolding or constraining straitjackets? Does the national literacy framework, for example, stifle or empower? 'Is it overly directive or helpfully supportive?' the Chair asks, on behalf of her members. There is no consensus.

Reassessing the practices: literacy is not enough

What can English be said to have achieved during its relatively brief history? What, more recently, has been its post-war record?

- English has achieved post-war identity in secondary schools as a creative practice
- This identity has been challenged in secondary schools by a combination of pressures: the increased emphasis on literacy and reading/writing skills in primary/elementary education, and the critical theory revolution in universities.
- When creativity is squeezed out there is a counter reaction – articulated at the end of the century against the utilitarianism and rhetoric of the marketplace
- Media and drama are drawn into the discussion for this reason – they embody practices that are capable of moving beyond simplistic definitions of literacy.

At all three levels of education – school, college and university – Subject English provides a space for supervised and directed questioning. It is a space in which scepticism is celebrated as a desirable outcome. Literacy is thus not simply a means to an end, but to *ends*. Employment is certainly one such end, but English specialists are particularly vocal when it comes to expressing the need to look beyond the workplace. Despite, however, the widespread belief that it is in the nature of institutions to suppress creativity it is in the interest of governments and industry to foster in its citizens the ability to question but to do so – and here is the important caveat – in a systematic way through the education system. The constant need to shift emphasis is one of the major dynamics driving the political changes in education over the last century in England, the United States and Australia.

In his book *The Rise and Fall of English* Robert Scholes argues that we ought to think of English as a canon of concepts, precepts and practices, rather than a canon of texts (Scholes 1998). In this book we have tried to point out what shapes these practices are, where they have come from, and how they come to assume the status of precepts and beliefs. What we have not done is to offer many concrete examples of these practices – no descriptions of actual lessons, no detailed accounts of the way that Information and Communication Technology is changing the way that we write, read, learn and speak to one another. We have not tried to speculate on the likely consequences of students' increasing access to the internet. There is little about central issues such as multi-culturalism, teaching English as a second language, or the books set for examinations, even though these issues all inform practice. We have deliberately restricted ourselves to the beliefs and issues that seem specific to the practices of Subject English which have evolved over more than the century that English has existed as a school subject. It is a recognition of the enduring nature of these pedagogical practices that may point a clear way forward for English. The alternative is to mask the confusing contradictory tendencies in Subject English by celebrating diversity and difference, a tactic which Alan Brown (Brown 1999) calls less a celebration of pluralities and more an instance of 'managerial spin'.

Whether or not in 2099 English will have survived as a named curriculum subject, the manifest idealism, energy and resolve that is so evident among English teachers is a resource that society will discard at its peril, and the challenge will be to marry it to the discourse about language, learning and the subject itself that has emerged from educationists in Australia, England and the United States, many of whom would not see themselves as English teachers. The critical literacy discussion that has grown out of the work of Paolo Friere (Friere 1972) has its own clearly defined goals and its own visionary political and social agenda. The question is – assuming that both cultures have similar targets and similar pedagogical effects, will they contribute to the survival of 'English as a subject relevant to the needs of students in the twenty-first century?' The answer may be – it depends where you are. In England and the United States it is difficult to see critical literacy issues taking centre stage in the discussion of the school curriculum, but in Australia, in both schools and universities, there is evidence that this is beginning to happen. In seeing the practices, pedagogies and classroom

materials being developed by this network of Australian educators we
believe we have seen a more encouraging model for the future.

References

Alter, Robert (1998) 'A readiness to be surprised', *The Times Literary Supplement*, 23 January 1998, p. 15

ATL *et al.* (1998) *An Evaluation of the 1998 Key Stage 3 Tests in English and Mathematics*, London: ATL

Bass, R. (1999) 'Story and Archive in the Twenty-First Century', *College English*, Volume 61, No. 6, pp. 659–670, Urbana, Illinois: NCTE

Brookes, Winston and Goodwyn, Andy (1998) 'What literacy means: an initial enquiry', *The English and Media Magazine*, Volume 39, Autumn, London: The English and Media Centre

Brown, Alan (1999) 'Practical Criticism Inc', *CCUE News*, Issue 10 Winter

Cliff Hodges, Gabrielle (1998) 'Editorial', *NATE News*, Summer

Freire, P (1972) *Pedagogy of the Oppressed*, Harmondsworth: Penguin

Gagnier, Regenia (1996) 'The Disturbance Overseas': A Comparative Report on the Future of English Studies CCUE Inaugural Conference: English in the Millennium 10 June 1996

Gilbert, P. (1989) *Writing, Schooling and Deconstruction: From Voice to Text in the Classroom*, London: Routledge

Gilbert, P. and Taylor, S. (1991) *Fashioning the Feminine: Girls, Popular Culture and Schooling*, St Leonards, NSW: Allen & Unwin

Goodwyn, A. and Findlay, K. (1999) 'The Cox Models revisited: English teachers' views of their subject and the National Curriculum', *English in Education*, Volume 33, No. 2, Summer, pp. 19–31

Green, B. and Beavis, C. (eds.) (1997) *Teaching the English Subjects*, Deakin, Vic: Deakin University Press

Green, B. and Biggin, C. 'Hypermedia or media hype? New technologies and the future of literacy education', in M. Anstey and G. Bull (eds.) *The Literary Lexicon*, Sydney: Prentice Hall

Higgins, John and Reid, Mark (1997) 'The future of English in further education', *NATE News*, Autumn , Sheffield: NATE

Hodgson, John (1997) The '16+ curriculum', *NATE News*, Autumn, Sheffield: NATE

Luke, A. and Gilbert, P. (1993) *Literacy in Contexts: Australian Perspectives and Issues*, St Leonards, NSW: Allen & Unwin

MacCabe, C. (1998) 'A response to Brian Street', *English in Education*, Volume 32, No. 1, Spring

Moger, Ros and Turvey, Anne (1998) 'ITTNC: A National Curriculum for Training Teachers', *The English and Media Magazine*, Volume 38, Summer

Muspratt, S., Luke, A. and Freebody, P. (eds.) (1997) *Constructing Critical Literacies: Teaching and Learning Textual Practice*, St Leonards, NSW: Allen & Unwin

NATE Working Group (1998) *Position Paper No 3: Literacy*, Sheffield: NATE

NATE Drama Committee (1998) *Position Paper No 4: Drama* Sheffield: NATE

NATE Council (1998) *Position Paper No 5: Coursework and Assessment*, Sheffield: NATE

Scholes, Robert (1998) *The Rise and Fall of English: Reconstructing English as a Discipline*, New Haven: Yale University Press

Shreeve, Ann (1999) ' A Curriculum for 2005', *NATE News*, Issue 3, June, Sheffield: NATE

Street, Brian (1997) 'The implications of the "new literacy studies" for literacy education', *English in Education*, Volume 31, No. 3, Autumn

Appendix A
Research questionnaire: Developing views of 'English'

A survey of students and teachers whose main subject is English. (A Level students should be those planning to continue English in Higher Education.)

Large numbers of people find themselves specialising in the area loosely called 'English'. The aim of this questionnaire is to find out what kind of perceptions we have of 'English', and where and how those perceptions may have been formed. Thank you for giving up some of your time to complete the tick boxes: some insights into the idea of the subject that people carry around in their heads, and the extent to which it changes from 16–60+, is what the results should reveal. An identical survey is taking place in Australia, and whether you are an A Level student, an undergraduate or an English teacher you will have contributed to an international comparison. Thank you again.

Robin Peel
University of Plymouth

Please tick box, as appropriate:

Female		Male	

A Level English Student		BA English Student	
BEd. Main subject English student (primary)		BEd./B.A. (Education) Main subject English student (secondary)	
PGCE or Dip. Ed.		English teacher in First Year	
English teacher (two to five years' experience		English teacher (six to nine years' experience	
English teacher (ten years +)		Head of English	
FE English Lecturer		University lecturer	

Beliefs about 'English'

1. Which of the following words or phrases most immediately come to mind when you think of 'English'? Please number 1, 2 and 3 the three which most readily come to mind.

1	2	3	4
Reading	Writing	Spelling and punctuation	Poetry
5	6	7	
Literary criticism	Creative writing	Discussion	
8	9	10	
Language	Literature	Cultural studies	
11	12	13	14
Difficult language	Authors such as Jane Austen and Shakespeare	Theory	Emotional responses

2. In England the Cox Report of 1989 identified five models of English: indicate, by circling one of the numbers 1–5, the extent to which you agree that the view described coincides with one to which you personally subscribe in a significant way.

(a) **Cultural heritage** (a view which emphasises the role of schools and colleges in leading students to appreciate the books widely regarded as the finest in the language)

1	2	3	4	5
Strongly agree	Agree	Neutral	Disagree	Strongly disagree

(b) **Personal growth** (a view which focuses on the child or student, and uses the experience of English to develop their aesthetic and imaginative lives)

1	2	3	4	5
Strongly agree	Agree	Neutral	Disagree	Strongly disagree

(c) **Adult needs** (a view which emphasises the need to prepare students for the skills they will need to communicate in a fast-changing world in adult life, including the needs of the workplace)

1	2	3	4	5
Strongly agree	Agree	Neutral	Disagree	Strongly disagree

(d) **Cross curricular** (a view which emphasises that apart from being a subject in its own right English is a form of communication which is present in every subject on the timetable, being the medium of instruction)

1	2	3	4	5
Strongly agree	Agree	Neutral	Disagree	Strongly disagree

(e) **Critical literacy/cultural studies** (a view which emphasises the role of English in helping students towards a critical understanding of the way that texts are historically and culturally studied)

1	2	3	4	5
Strongly agree	Agree	Neutral	Disagree	Strongly disagree

3. This question concentrates on the influences that have shaped your current view of what 'English' is. Circle a number in each case.

In reaching my view I have been strongly influenced by:

(a) A teacher who taught me between the ages of 11 and 16

1	2	3	4	5
Strongly agree	Agree	Neutral	Disagree	Strongly disagree

(b) A teacher who taught me between the ages of 16 and 18

1	2	3	4	5
Strongly agree	Agree	Neutral	Disagree	Strongly disagree

(c) The course I did – or am doing – at university (or equivalent)

1	2	3	4	5
Strongly agree	Agree	Neutral	Disagree	Strongly disagree

(d) Membership of AATE, NATE, CCUE or other associations

1	2	3	4	5
Strongly agree	Agree	Neutral	Disagree	Strongly disagree

(e) Books or articles

1	2	3	4	5
Strongly agree	Agree	Neutral	Disagree	Strongly disagree

(f) In-service sessions, including conferences

1	2	3	4	5
Strongly agree	Agree	Neutral	Disagree	Strongly disagree

(g) Someone or something other than the above. Please explain.

4. To what extent has your view of English undergone revision? Respond to each of the following statements by circling an appropriate number.

My view of English has changed significantly

(a) Over the past two years

1	2	3	4	5
Strongly agree	Agree	Neutral	Disagree	Strongly disagree

(b) Over the past five years

1	2	3	4	5
Strongly agree	Agree	Neutral	Disagree	Strongly disagree

(c) Over the past ten years

1	2	3	4	5
Strongly agree	Agree	Neutral	Disagree	Strongly disagree

5. If your perception of English has undergone revision, in what way has it changed?

6. Does 'English', in your experience, presently include the study of (a), (b) and (c) below? Please read the categories and then indicate whether you think that they usually appear as part of the English courses you know.

(a) (i) Popular, mass market fiction such as romance, fantasy novels and horror

1	2	3	4	5
Strongly agree	Agree	Neutral	Disagree	Strongly disagree

(ii) *Should* an English course include the study of popular fiction?

1	2	3	4	5
Strongly agree	Agree	Neutral	Disagree	Strongly disagree

Give reasons, if you wish

(b) (i) Films and television programmes?

1	2	3	4	5
Strongly agree	Agree	Neutral	Disagree	Strongly disagree

(ii) *Should* it include the study of the visual media?

1	2	3	4	5
Strongly agree	Agree	Neutral	Disagree	Strongly disagree

Give reasons, if you wish

(c) (i) Cultural studies such as propaganda, representations of the 1950s, and Madonna

1	2	3	4	5
Strongly agree	Agree	Neutral	Disagree	Strongly disagree

(ii) *Should* it include this kind of study?

1	2	3	4	5
Strongly agree	Agree	Neutral	Disagree	Strongly disagree

Give reasons, if you wish

7. With which of the following views do you agree/disagree?

(a) Some literature contains insights and truths which transcend their own time and culture, showing us that human behaviour is universal and changes little.

1	2	3	4	5
Strongly agree	Agree	Neutral	Disagree	Strongly disagree

(b) Texts should be viewed from within the historical and cultural contexts which shaped them, as their meaning will inevitably be governed by these factors.*

1	2	3	4	5
Strongly agree	Agree	Neutral	Disagree	Strongly disagree

(c) The enjoyment and pleasure which many readers get from texts does not need to be queried.

1	2	3	4	5
Strongly agree	Agree	Neutral	Disagree	Strongly disagree

(d) There is no single, pre-existent 'authorised' meaning of a text and so differing, contradictory readings and responses are to be encouraged.

1	2	3	4	5
Strongly agree	Agree	Neutral	Disagree	Strongly disagree

*Wendy Morgan's words are being used here.

8. Finally, two questions about the impact that 'English' can have on our lives. Indicate the extent to which you believe the following statements to be true

(a) 'English' has a role in helping us make decisions about the way we ought to live and the values to which we subscribe

1	2	3	4	5
Strongly agree	Agree	Neutral	Disagree	Strongly disagree

(b) Encounters with literature can make us more sensitive human beings

1	2	3	4	5
Strongly agree	Agree	Neutral	Disagree	Strongly disagree

9. This is a question about your preferred method of developing your expertise in English.

Circle the number of the statement which you feel is most true

1	2	3
I learn best by listening	I learn best by doing (drama, writing etc.)	I learn best by reading

10. This question, the last, is for English/language arts teachers/lecturers only, and will not apply to you if you are a student.

Read the following statements, and circle the response which most closely matches your own:

(a) I learn something new about my subject from my students

1	2	3
Never	Sometimes, though not often	Frequently

(b) I am surprised by students' discoveries in the subject

1	2	3
Never	Sometimes, though not often	Frequently

Appendix B
English

1. Did you Major in English?
2. What made you choose English?
3. Of the activities traditionally associated with English – reading, writing, talking drama – which do you find most enjoyable?
4. Do you think a particular English teacher influenced you?
5. Would you say that part of the satisfaction of English is the fact that you know that it is a subject that you are good at?
6. Is your own teaching similar in many ways to the teaching you experienced as a student?
7. How do you feel about the inclusion of media education in English – moving beyond literary texts to include all kinds of texts? (clarify that you do not just mean film versions of novels but are talking about the use of television programmes to consider aspects of narrative and point of view, the news for discussion of editing and emphasis, and radio programmes as a focus for collaborative, active work by the class).
8. Has what is generally called post-structuralist, or post-modern theory – had much impact on your classroom practice and what you do with students?
9. Have your views of what 'English' is for, changed much in the past five years? Ten years? Since school?
10. If they have, what has been most influential in bringing about this change (I sometimes list the factors listed on the questionnaire – journals, conferences etc.)?
11. Has IT – computers – had much of an impact on the way you perceive 'English'?
12. How would you summarise what you would hope your students would take away with them after they have completed an English course with you?
13. Do you see yourself as a writer?
14. Are there particular texts that should be studied?
15. Are you able to create the kind of English classroom in which you believe, or are there obstacles which get in the way of implementing your beliefs?

Appendix C
The graduate of the 21st century

The Association of Graduate Recruiters has identified the following skills attributes – career management skills and effective learning skills – wh graduates will need for the new careers of the 21st century.

Self-awareness

Able to clearly identify skills, values, interests and other personal attribut

Able to pinpoint core strengths and 'differentiating factors'.

Equipped with evidence of abilities (e.g. summary statement, record 'portfolio').

Actively willing to seek feedback from others, and able to give construct feedback.

Able to identify areas for personal, academic and professional developme

Self-promotion

Able to define and promote own agenda.

Can identify 'customer needs' (academic/community/employer) and c promote own strengths in a convincing way, both written and orally, sell 'benefits' to the 'customer', not simply 'features'.

Exploring/creating opportunities

Able to identify, create, investigate and seize opportunities.

Has research skills to identify possible sources of information, help a support.

Action planning

Able to plan a course of action which addresses: Where am I now? Where do I want to be? How do I get there?

Able to implement an action plan by: organising time effectively, identifying steps needed to reach the goal. Preparing contingency plans.

Able to monitor and evaluate progress against specific objectives.

Networking

Aware of the need to develop networks of contacts.

Able to define, develop and maintain a support network for advice and information.

Has good telephone skills.

Matching and decision making

Understands personal priorities and constraints (internal and external). This includes the need for a sustainable balance of work and home life.

Able to match opportunities to core skills, knowledge, values, interests etc.

Able to make an informed decision based on the available opportunities.

Negotiation

Negotiating the psychological contract from a position of powerlessness.

Able to reach 'win/win' agreements.

Political awareness

Understands the hidden tensions and power struggles within organisations.

Aware of the location of power and influence within organisations.

Coping with uncertainty

Able to adapt goals in the light of changing circumstances.

Able to take myriads of tiny risks.

Development focus

Committed to lifelong learning.

Understands preferred method and style of learning.

Reflects on learning from experiences, good and bad.

Able to learn from others' mistakes.

Self-confidence

Has an underlying confidence in abilities, based on past successes.

Also has a personal sense of self-worth, not dependent on performance.

Transfer skills

Able to apply skills to new contexts.

This is a higher level in itself. Skills are not automatically transferable.

Source: 'Skills for Graduates in the 21st Century', The Association of Graduate Recruiters 1995.

Index